ASSESSING THE

THE EARLY COLD WAR YEARS

SOVIET THREAT

Woodrow J. Kuhns
Editor

Center for the Study of Intelligence
Central Intelligence Agency
1997

Assessing the Soviet Threat: The Early Cold War Years

Foreword

The documents in this volume were produced by the analytical arm of the Central Intelligence Agency (CIA) and its predecessor, the Central Intelligence Group (CIG), between the latter's founding in 1946 and the end of 1950. During this formative period of the Cold War, President Harry S. Truman struggled to understand the menacing behavior of the Soviet Union and his erstwhile ally, Joseph Stalin. The analysts of CIG/CIA contributed to this process by providing the President with daily, weekly, and monthly summaries and interpretations of the most significant world events. They also provided ad hoc papers that analyzed specific issues of interest to the administration. Because more than 450 National Intelligence Estimates dealing with the Soviet Union and international Communism have been declassified since 1993, this volume features the current intelligence that went to the President in the *Daily* and *Weekly Summaries*. Although some of this material has been available to scholars at the Harry S. Truman Library or has been previously released through the Freedom of Information Act, much of it is being made public for the first time. Taken as a whole, this volume provides the first comprehensive survey of CIA's early analysis of the Soviet threat.

President Truman's directive establishing CIG on 22 January 1946 created the first civilian, centralized, nondepartmental intelligence agency in American history. His purpose was to end the separate cabinet departments' monopoly over intelligence information, a longstanding phenomenon that he believed had contributed to Japan's ability to launch the surprise attack against Pearl Harbor. As he stated in his memoirs, "In those days the military did not know everything the State Department knew, and the diplomats did not have access to all the Army and Navy knew." Truman also was irked because reports came across his desk "on the same subject at different times from the various departments, and these reports often conflicted." He intended that CIA, when it replaced CIG in September 1947, also would address these concerns.

This volume focuses on the difficult yet important task of intelligence analysis. Although less glamorous to observers than either espionage or covert action, it is the process of analysis that provides the key end product to the policymaker: "finished" intelligence that can help the US Government craft effective foreign and security policies. During World War II, American academics and experts in the Office of Strategic Services had virtually invented the discipline of intelligence analysis—one of America's few unique contributions to the craft of intelligence. Although it was not a direct descendent of the Research and Analysis branch of OSS, CIA's Office of Reports and Estimates built upon this legacy in difficult circumstances.

The analysis reaching policymakers in these first years of the Cold War touched on momentous events and trends. Whether the Cold War was the result of a clash of irreconcilable national interests or of a spiraling series of misperceptions, an examination of the current intelligence provided to President Truman during this period—sometimes right, sometimes misleading—opens a fascinating window on what the President was told as he made his decisions.

Equally interesting is the portrait of the analysts, their problems, and the impact on their work of the bureaucratic process, as presented by the editor of this volume, staff historian Woodrow J. Kuhns. Dr. Kuhns makes clear that the lot of the analysts was a difficult one in these early years. Many had been dumped on CIG by other departments that no longer required their services. They were subjected to frequent reshuffling and other forms of bureaucratic turmoil, and they operated under severe time pressure and sometimes with little information at their disposal. CIA's first analysts are not to be envied.

We have ended this study in 1950 because by then the lines on both sides of the Cold War had been firmly drawn. US leaders had reached their conclusions about Soviet intentions; had formed their opinions about Mao Zedong, Ho Chi Minh, and other revolutionaries; and had formulated their policy of containment in NSC 68. In addition, a new Director of Central Intelligence, Walter Bedell Smith, implemented a sweeping reorganization of the Agency's analytical arm in late 1950, breaking the Office of Reports and Estimates into three smaller but more clearly focused offices. The CIA thus entered a new phase of the Cold War with revitalized analytical capabilities in a new Directorate of Intelligence that embodied President Truman's intention to ensure that the US Government was provided with nondepartmental intelligence based on all available sources.

Michael Warner

Acting Chief, CIA History Staff

Assessing the Soviet Threat: The Early Cold War Years

Preface

During World War II, the United States made one of its few original contributions to the craft of intelligence: the invention of multisource, nondepartmental analysis. The Research and Analysis (R&A) Branch of the Office of Strategic Services (OSS) assembled a talented cadre of analysts and experts to comb through publications and intelligence reports for clues to the capabilities and intentions of the Axis powers. R&A's contributions to the war effort impressed even the harshest critics of the soon-to-be dismantled OSS. President Truman paid implicit tribute to R&A in late 1945 when he directed that it be transplanted bodily into the State Department at a time when most of OSS was being demobilized. The transplant failed, however, and the independent analytical capability patiently constructed during the war had all but vanished when Truman moved to reorganize the nation's peacetime intelligence establishment at the beginning of 1946.

"Current" Intelligence Versus "National" Intelligence

The Central Reports Staff, home to the analysts in the Central Intelligence Group (CIG), was born under a cloud of confusion in January 1946.[1] Specifically, no consensus existed on what its mission was to be, although the President's concerns in creating CIG were clear enough. In the uncertain aftermath of the war, he wanted to be sure that all relevant information available to the US Government on any given issue of national security would be correlated and evaluated centrally so that the country would never again have to suffer a devastating surprise attack as it had at Pearl Harbor.[2]

How this was to be accomplished, however, was less clear. The President himself wanted a daily summary that would relieve him of the chore of reading the mounds of cables, reports, and other papers that constantly cascaded onto his desk. Some of these were important, but many were

---

[1] The name of the Central Reports Staff was changed in July 1946 to the Office of Research and Evaluations, and again in October 1946 to the Office of Reports and Estimates (ORE), by which name it was known until it was abolished in November 1950. CIA veterans typically use "ORE" as the shorthand name for the analytical office for the whole period 1946-50.

[2] Truman wrote in his memoirs that he had "often thought that if there had been something like co-ordination of information in the government it would have been more difficult, if not impossible, for the Japanese to succeed in the sneak attack at Pearl Harbor." Harry S. Truman, *Memoirs*, vol. 2, *Years of Trial and Hope* (Garden City, NY: Doubleday, 1956), p. 56.

duplicative and even contradictory.[3] In the jargon of intelligence analysis, Truman wanted CIG to produce a "current intelligence" daily publication that would contain all information of immediate interest to him.[4]

Truman's aides and advisers, however, either did not understand this or disagreed with him, for the presidential directive of 22 January 1946 authorizing the creation of CIG did not mention current intelligence. The directive ordered CIG to "accomplish the correlation and evaluation of intelligence relating to the national security, and the appropriate dissemination within the government of the resulting strategic and national policy intelligence."[5] Moreover, at the first meeting of the National Intelligence Authority (NIA) on 5 February, Secretary of State Byrnes objected to the President's idea of a current intelligence summary from CIG, claiming that it was his responsibility as Secretary of State to furnish the President with information on foreign affairs.[6]

Byrnes apparently then went to Truman and asked him to reconsider. Admiral Sidney Souers, the first Director of Central Intelligence (DCI), told a CIA historian that Byrnes' argument

ran along the line that such information was not intelligence within the jurisdiction of the Central Intelligence Group and the Director [of Central Intelligence]. President Truman conceded that it might not be generally considered intelligence, but it was information which he needed and therefore it was intelligence to him. The result was agreement that the daily summaries should be 'factual statements.' The Department of State prepared its own digest, and so the President had two summaries on his desk.[7]

---

[3] See Arthur B. Darling, *The Central Intelligence Agency: An Instrument of Government to 1950* (University Park: The Pennsylvania State University Press, 1990), p. 81.
[4] Current intelligence was defined in National Security Council Directive No. 3, "Coordination of Intelligence Production," 13 January 1948, as "that spot information or intelligence of all types and forms of immediate interest and value to operating or policy staffs, which is used by them usually without the delays incident to complete evaluation or interpretation." See United States Department of State, *Foreign Relations of the United States 1945-1950, Emergence of the Intelligence Establishment* (Washington, DC: US Government Printing Office, 1996), p. 1,110. Hereafter cited as *Emergence of the Intelligence Establishment.*
[5] "Presidential Directive on Coordination of Foreign Intelligence Activities," United States Department of State, *Emergence of the Intelligence Establishment*, pp. 178, 179. Also reproduced in Michael Warner, ed., *The CIA Under Harry Truman* (Washington, DC: Central Intelligence Agency, 1994), pp. 29-32.
[6] "Minutes of the First Meeting of the National Intelligence Authority," *Emergence of the Intelligence Establishment*, p. 328. The National Intelligence Authority was composed of the Secretaries of State, War, and Navy and a representative of the President, Flt. Adm. William Leahy.
[7] Darling, *The Central Intelligence Agency,* pp. 81, 82.

This uneasy compromise was reflected in the NIA directives that outlined CIG's duties. Directive No. 1, issued on 8 February 1946, ordered CIG to "furnish strategic and national policy intelligence to the President and the State, War, and Navy Departments. . . ."[8] National Intelligence Authority Directive No. 2, issued the same day, ordered the DCI to give "first priority" to the "production of daily summaries containing factual statements of the significant developments in the field of intelligence and operations related to the national security and to foreign events for the use of the President. . . ."[9]

In practice, this approach proved unworkable. Without any commentary to place a report in context, or to make a judgment on its likely veracity, the early *Daily Summaries* probably did little but confuse the President. An alarming report one day on Soviet troop movements in Eastern Europe, for example, would be contradicted the next day by a report from another source. Everyone involved eventually realized the folly of this situation, and analytical commentaries began to appear in the *Daily Summaries* in December 1946—episodically at first, and then regularly during 1947. The *Weekly Summary*, first published in June 1946 on the initiative of the Central Reports Staff itself, was also supposed to avoid interpretative commentary, but its format made such a stricture difficult to enforce. From its inception, the *Weekly Summary* proved to be more analytical than its *Daily Summary* counterpart.

---

[8] National Intelligence Authority Directive No. 1, "Policies and Procedures Governing the Central Intelligence Group," 8 February 1946, *Emergence of the Intelligence Establishment,* pp. 329-331. After CIA was established, National Security Council Intelligence Directive No. 1, "Duties and Responsibilities," issued on 12 December 1947, again ordered the DCI to produce national intelligence, which the Directive stated should be "officially concurred in by the Intelligence Agencies or shall carry an agreed statement of substantial dissent." National Security Council Intelligence Directive No. 3, 13 January 1948, gave CIA the authority to produce current intelligence: "The CIA and the several agencies shall produce and disseminate such current intelligence as may be necessary to meet their own internal requirements or external responsibilities." See *Emergence of the Intelligence Establishment,* pp. 1,119-1,122; 1,109-1,112.
[9] National Intelligence Authority Directive No. 2, "Organization and Functions of the Central Intelligence Group," 8 February 1946, *Emergence of the Intelligence Establishment,* pp. 331-333. Interestingly, Souers, who drafted both NIA Directive 1 and Directive 2, continued to believe that CIG's principal responsibility was the production of strategic and national policy intelligence. In a memorandum to the NIA on 7 June 1946, Souers wrote that the "primary function of C.I.G. in the production of intelligence . . . will be the preparation and dissemination of definitive estimates of the capabilities and intentions of foreign countries as they affect the national security of the United States." "Memorandum From the Director of Central Intelligence to the National Intelligence Authority," 7 June 1946, *Emergence of the Intelligence Establishment,* p. 361.

The Confusion Surrounding "National" Intelligence

Similar disarray surrounded CIG's responsibilities in the production of "strategic and national policy intelligence." The members of the Intelligence Community simply could not agree on the policies and procedures that governed the production of this type of intelligence. Most of those involved seemed to believe that national intelligence should be coordinated among all the members of the Intelligence Community, that it should be based on all available information, that it should try to estimate the intentions and capabilities of other countries toward the United States, and that it should be of value to the highest policymaking bodies.

The devil was in the details. High-ranking members of the intelligence and policy communities debated, without coming to a consensus, most aspects of the estimate production process, including who should write them, how other agencies should participate in the process if at all, and how dissents should be handled. Some of this reflected genuine disagreement over the best way to organize and run the Intelligence Community, but it also involved concerns about bureaucratic power and prerogatives, especially those of the Director of Central Intelligence, the newcomer to the Intelligence Community. Even the definition of "strategic and national intelligence" had implications for the authority of the DCI and thus was carefully argued over by others in the Community.[10]

DCI Vandenberg eventually got the NIA to agree to a definition in February 1947, but it was so general that it did little to solve the problems that abounded at the working level.[11] Ray Cline, a participant in the process of producing the early estimates, wrote in his memoirs that

It cannot honestly be said that it [ORE] coordinated either intelligence activities or intelligence judgments; these were guarded closely by Army, Navy, Air Force, State, and the FBI. When attempts were made to prepare agreed national estimates on the basis of intelligence available to all, the coordination process was interminable, dissents were the rule rather than

---

[10] Emergence of the Intelligence Establishment, p. 367.

[11] The NIA agreed that "strategic and national policy intelligence is that composite intelligence, interdepartmental in character, which is required by the President and other high officers and staffs to assist them in determining policies with respect to national planning and security. . . . It is in that political-economic-military area of concern to more than one agency, must be objective, and must transcend the exclusive competence of any one department." "Minutes of the 9th Meeting of the National Intelligence Authority," 12 February 1947, *Emergence of the Intelligence Establishment*, p. 492. After the establishment of CIA, National Security Council Directive No. 3, 13 January 1948, similarly defined national intelligence as "integrated departmental intelligence that covers the broad aspects of national policy and national security, is of concern to more than one Department . . . and transcends the exclusive competence of a single department. . . ." See *Emergence of the Intelligence Establishment*, p. 1,111.

the exception, and every policymaking official took his own agency's intelligence appreciations along to the White House to argue his case. The prewar chaos was largely recreated with only a little more lip service to central coordination.[12]

In practice, much of the intelligence produced by ORE was not coordinated with the other agencies; nor was it based on all information available to the US Government. The *Daily* and *Weekly Summaries* were not coordinated products, and, like the other publications produced by ORE, they did not contain information derived from communications intelligence.[13] The *Review of the World Situation*, which was distributed each month at meetings of the National Security Council, became a unilateral publication of ORE after the first two issues.[14] The office's ad hoc publications, such as the Special Evaluations and Intelligence Memorandums, were rarely coordinated with the other agencies. By contrast, the "ORE" series of Special Estimates were coordinated, but critics nonetheless condemned many of them for containing trivial subjects that fell outside the realm of "strategic and national policy intelligence."[15]

Whatever CIG's written orders, in practice the President's interest in the *Daily Summaries*, coupled with the limited resources of the Central Reports Staff, meant that the production of current intelligence came to dominate the Staff and its culture. National estimative intelligence was reduced to also-ran status. An internal CIG memo stated frankly that "ORE Special Estimates are produced on specific subjects as the occasion arises and within the limits of ORE capabilities after current intelligence requirements

[12] Ray S. Cline, *Secrets, Spies, and Scholars: Blueprint of the Essential CIA* (Washington, DC: Acropolis Books, 1976), pp. 91, 92. Cline rose to become Deputy Director for Intelligence (DDI) between 1962 and 1966. Another veteran of the period, R. Jack Smith, who edited the *Daily Summary*, made the same point in his memoirs, *The Unknown CIA* (Washington: Pergamon-Brassey's, 1989), p. 42: "We were not fulfilling our primary task of combining Pentagon, State Department, and CIA judgments into national intelligence estimates. . . . To say it succinctly, CIA lacked clout. The military and diplomatic people ignored our statutory authority in these matters, and the CIA leadership lacked the power to compel compliance." Smith also served as DDI, from 1966 to 1971.

[13] Smith, *The Unknown CIA*, pp. 34, 35. ORE began receiving signals intelligence in 1946 and was able to use it as a check against the articles it included in the *Summaries*. Security concerns prevented its broader use. Signals intelligence was sent to the White House by the Army Security Agency (from 1949 on, the Armed Forces Security Agency) during this period. CIA did not begin including communications intelligence in the successor to the *Daily* until 1951.

[14] The delays involved in interagency coordination made it difficult to meet the publication deadline while still including the most recent events in its contents. George S. Jackson, *Office of Reports and Estimates, 1946-1951*, Miscellaneous Studies, HS MS-3, vol. 3 (Washington, DC: Central Intelligence Agency, 1954), pp. 279-287. National Archives and Records Administration, Record Group 263, History Staff Source Collection, NN3-263-95-003.

[15] See the discussion of the Dulles-Jackson-Correa Report on page 10.

are met." It went on to note, "Many significant developments worthy of ORE Special Estimates have not been covered . . . because of priority production of current intelligence, insufficient personnel, or inadequate information."[16] This remained true even after the Central Reports Staff evolved into the Office of Reports and Estimates (ORE) in CIA.[17]

If the analysts in CIG, and then CIA, had only to balance the competing demands of current and national intelligence, their performance might have benefited. As it happened, however, NIA Directive No. 5 soon gave the analysts the additional responsibility of performing "such research and analysis activities" as might "be more efficiently or effectively accomplished centrally."[18] In practice, this meant that the analysts became responsible for performing basic research as well as wide-ranging political and economic analysis. To accommodate this enhanced mission, functional analysis branches for economics, science, transportation, and map intelligence were established alongside the existing regional branches.[19]

A high-ranking ORE officer of the period, Ludwell Montague, wrote that

this was a deliberate, but covert, attempt to transform ORE (or CRS, a staff designed expressly for the production of coordinated national intelligence) into an omnicompetent . . . central research agency. This attempt failed, leaving ORE neither the one thing nor the other. Since then, much ORE production has proceeded, not from any clear concept of mission, but from the mere existence of a nondescript contrivance for the production of nondescript intelligence. All our efforts to secure a clear definition of our mission have been in vain.[20]

[16] Memo from Chief, Projects Division to Assistant Director, R&E, "Proposed Concept for Future CIG Production of Staff Intelligence," 1 July 1947. CIA History Staff Job 67-00059A, Box 2, Confidential. Nevertheless, during its existence ORE did produce over 125 estimates, 97 of which were declassified in 1993 and 1994 and deposited in the National Archives.
[17] This point is made repeatedly throughout George S. Jackson, *Office of Reports and Estimates, 1946-1951*. Jackson himself served in the office during the period of this study.
[18] National Intelligence Authority Directive No. 5, "Functions of the Director of Central Intelligence," 8 July 1946, *Emergence of the Intelligence Establishment*, p. 392.
[19] The Scientific Intelligence Branch of ORE was established in January 1947 and shortly thereafter incorporated the Nuclear Energy Group, which had been in charge of atomic energy intelligence in the Manhattan Project, within its ranks. At the end of 1948, the branch was separated from ORE and elevated to office status, becoming the Office of Scientific Intelligence.
[20] Montague to Babbitt, "Comment on the Dulles-Jackson Report," 11 February 1949. National Archives and Records Administration, Record Group 263, History Staff Source Collection, HS/HC 450, NN3-263-94-010, Box 14. Montague's reference to a "deliberate but covert" attempt to increase the responsibility of ORE refers to the efforts of DCI General Hoyt Vandenberg to boost himself, and CIG as a whole, into a dominant position in the Intelligence Community. Opposition from the other departments largely scuttled his attempts in this direction. See *Emergence of the Intelligence Establishment*, p. 366.

Another veteran of the period, George S. Jackson, agreed with Montague's assessment: "It would not be correct . . . to say that the Office . . . had failed utterly to do what it was designed to do; a more accurate statement would be that it had done not only what was planned for it but much that was not planned and need not have been done. In consequence, the Office had unnecessarily dissipated its energies to the detriment of its main function."[21] He noted that

Requests [for studies] came frequently from many sources, not all of them of equal importance, but there seemed not to be anyone in authority [in ORE] who would probe beneath any of them to make sure that they merited a reply. Nor was there anyone who took it upon himself to decline requests— no matter from what source—when they were clearly for a type of material not called for under the responsibilities of the Office of Reports and Estimates.[22]

A Mixed Reception
NIA Directive No. 5 opened the door to proliferation of various kinds of publications and, consequently, to a dilution of analysts' efforts in the fields of current and national intelligence.[23] Perhaps as a consequence of the confusion over the analytical mission, these products received mixed reviews. The President was happy with his *Daily Summary*, and that fact alone made it sacrosanct. Rear Admiral James H. Foskett, the President's Naval Aide, told ORE in 1947 that, "the President considers that he personally originated the *Daily*, that it is prepared in accordance with his own specifications, that it is well done, and that in its present form it satisfies his requirements."[24] President Truman's views on the *Weekly Summary* were less clear, but lack of criticism was construed as approval by ORE: "It appears that the *Weekly* in its present form is acceptable at the White House and is used to an undetermined extent without exciting comment indicative of a desire for any particular change."[25]

Other policymakers were less impressed with the current intelligence publications. Secretary of State George Marshall stopped reading the *Daily Summary* after two weeks, and thereafter he had his aide flag only the most important items for him to read. The aide did this only two or three times a

[21] Jackson, *Office of Reports and Estimates, 1946-1951,* vol. 1, p. 95.
[22] Ibid., p. 98.
[23] In addition to the publications mentioned above, ORE produced *Situation Reports* (exhaustive studies of individual countries and areas) and a variety of branch-level publications (daily summaries, weekly summaries, monthly summaries, branch "estimates," and reports of various types).
[24] Montague to J. Klahr Huddle, Assistant Director, R&E, "Conversation with Admiral Foskett regarding the C.I.G. *Daily* and *Weekly Summaries*," 26 February 1947, in Warner, ed., *The CIA Under Harry Truman*, p. 123.
[25] Ibid.

week, telling a CIG interviewer that "most of the information in the *Dailies* is taken from State Department sources and is furnished the Secretary through State Department channels."[26] Marshall also stopped reading the *Weekly* after the first issue.[27] The Secretary of the Navy, James Forrestal, considered both *Summaries* "valuable but not . . . indispensable," according to one of his advisers.[28] By contrast, an aide to Secretary of War Robert Patterson reported that the Secretary read both the *Daily* and *Weekly Summaries* "avidly and regularly."[29]

The analytical office's work came in for the most severe criticism in the so-called Dulles-Jackson-Correa Report of January 1949, which assessed both the performance of CIA and its role in the Intelligence Community.[30] This report, commissioned by the National Security Council in early 1948, was prepared by a trio of prominent intelligence veterans who had left government service after the war: Allen Dulles, William Jackson, and Mathias Correa.

Their report candidly admitted that "There is confusion as to the proper role of the Central Intelligence Agency in the preparation of intelligence reports and estimates" and that "The principle of the authoritative national intelligence estimate does not yet have established acceptance in the government."[31] They nevertheless took ORE to task for failing to perform better in the production of national intelligence, noting that, although ORE had been given responsibility for production of national estimates, "It has . . . been concerned with a wide variety of activities and with the production of miscellaneous reports and summaries which by no stretch of the imagination could be considered national estimates."[32]

The trio found unacceptable ORE's practice of drafting the estimates "on the basis of its own research and analysis" and then circulating them among the other intelligence agencies to obtain notes of dissent or concurrence.[33] "Under this procedure, none of the agencies regards itself as a full

[26] Memo from Assistant Director, Office of Collection and Dissemination to Huddle, "Adequacy Survey of the CIG *Daily* and *Weekly Summaries*," 7 May 1947, History Staff Job 67-00059A, Box 2, Secret.
[27] Ibid.
[28] Ibid.
[29] Ibid., p. 5.
[30] Allen W. Dulles, William H. Jackson, and Mathias F. Correa, "The Central Intelligence Agency and National Organization for Intelligence: A Report to the National Security Council," 1 January 1949. The summary of the report is reprinted in *Emergence of the Intelligence Establishment*, pp. 903-911. The entire report is available at the National Archives and Records Administration, RG 59, Records of the Department of State, Records of the Executive Secretariat, NSC Files: Lot 66 D 148, Box 1555.
[31] Ibid., pp. 65, 69.
[32] Ibid., p. 6.
[33] Ibid.

participant contributing to a truly national estimate and accepting a share in the responsibility for it."[34] They recommended that a "small group of specialists" be used "in lieu of the present Office of Reports and Estimates" to "review the intelligence products of other intelligence agencies and of the Central Intelligence Agency" and to "prepare drafts of national intelligence estimates for consideration by the Intelligence Advisory Committee."[35]

The three also were not impressed with ORE's efforts in field of current intelligence: "Approximately ninety per cent [sic] of the contents of the *Daily Summary* is derived from State Department sources. . . . There are occasional comments by the Central Intelligence Agency on portions of the *Summary*, but these, for the most part, appear gratuitous and lend little weight to the material itself."[36] They concluded, "As both *Summaries* consume an inordinate amount of time and effort and appear to be outside of the domain of the Central Intelligence Agency, we believe that the *Daily*, and possibly the *Weekly Summary* should be discontinued in their present form."[37]

The trio concluded disapprovingly that "the Central Intelligence Agency has tended to become just one more intelligence agency producing intelligence in competition with older established agencies of the government departments."[38]

The Analysts
The Dulles-Jackson-Correa Report was extremely, perhaps unfairly, critical of ORE's production record. Intelligence analysis is not an easy job in the best of times—the available information on any given analytical problem is invariably incomplete or contradictory or flawed in some other important way—and these clearly were not the best of times. Signals intelligence, which had proved devastatingly effective against the Axis powers in the war, was less effective against the security-conscious Soviets, and, as noted above, in any event could not yet be cited directly in CIA publications, even in those sent to the President.[39] The sophisticated aircraft and satellites that

---

[34] Ibid.
[35] Ibid., pp. 6, 7.
[36] Ibid., pp. 84, 85.
[37] Ibid., pp. 85, 86.
[38] Ibid., p. 11.
[39] From unsecured Soviet communications, signals intelligence provided reliable information on such things as foreign trade, consumer goods policies, gold production, petroleum shipments, shipbuilding, aircraft production, and civil defense. A weekly all-source publication that did contain COMINT, the *Situation Summary*, was created in July 1950 and sent to the White House. The *Situation Summary's* purpose was to warn, in the wake of the North Korean invasion of South Korea, of other potential acts of aggression by Communist forces. See George S. Jackson and Martin P. Claussen, *Organizational History of the Central Intelligence Agency, 1950-1953*, Chapter VIII, *Current Intelligence and Hostility Indications*, The DCI Historical Series (Washington, DC: The Central Intelligence Agency, 1957), p. 21. National Archives and Records Administration, Record Group 263, History Staff Source Collection, NN3-263-92-004.

would one day open the whole interior of the USSR to surveillance were not yet on the drawing board, and the intelligence collection arm of the new CIA was finding it impossibly difficult to penetrate Stalin's paranoid police state with agents. In the end, the analysts had little to rely on but diplomatic and military attache reporting, media accounts, and their own judgment.

The paucity of hard intelligence about the Soviet Union placed a premium on the recruitment of top-notch analysts. Unfortunately, CIG and CIA had trouble landing the best and the brightest. CIG was in a particularly difficult situation; it had little authority to hire its own staff employees and thus depended on the Departments of State, War, and Navy for both its funding and personnel.[40] Ludwell Montague complained to DCI Vandenberg in September 1946 that these departments were not cooperating: "From the beginning the crucial problem . . . has been the procurement of key personnel qualified by aptitude and experience to anticipate intelligence needs, to exercise critical judgment regarding the material at hand, and to discern emergent trends. Such persons are rare indeed and hard to come by, [and] the recruitment of them is necessarily slow. . . ."[41] Montague was particularly bitter about Army intelligence's (G-2) efforts to fob off on CIG what he termed "low-grade personnel."[42]

The establishment of CIA in September 1947 ended the Office's dependence on other departments for personnel and funds. It permitted the rapid expansion of ORE from 60 employees in June 1946 to 709 staff employees by the end of 1950, 332 of whom were either analysts or managers of analysts.[43] Although this solved the quantity problem, quality remained an issue.

Hanson W. Baldwin of *The New York Times* in 1948 noted that "personnel weaknesses undoubtedly are the clue to the history of frustration and disappointment, of friction and fiasco, which have been, too largely, the story of our intelligence services since the war. Present personnel, including many of those in the office of research and estimates [sic] of the Central Intelligence Agency, suffer from inexperience and inadequacy of background.

---

[40] When the Central Reports Staff began operations, it consisted of 17 people—five assigned to it by State, eight by War, and four by Navy—all of whom immediately became preoccupied with preparing the *Daily Summaries* for President Truman, the first of which they published on 15 February 1946. The Staff published its first piece of national intelligence, ORE 1, "Soviet Foreign and Military Policy," at the end of July. See Document 4.
[41] Montague to Hoyt S. Vandenberg, Director of Central Intelligence, "Procurement of Key Personnel for ORE," 24 September 1946, in Warner, ed., *The CIA Under Harry Truman*, p. 85.
[42] Ibid.
[43] "Table of Organization," 20 December 1950, Job 78-01617A, Box 55, Confidential.

Some of them do not possess the 'global' objective mind needed to evaluate intelligence, coldly, logically, and definitively."[44]

A senior ORE officer, R. Jack Smith, shared Baldwin's view, noting that

We felt obliged to give the White House the best judgment we could command, and we continued to try as the years passed by. Eventually . . . the cumulative experience of this persistent effort, combined with the recruitment of some genuine specialists and scholars, produced a level of expertise that had no counterpart elsewhere in the government. But this was a decade or more away.[45]

Ray Cline agreed with Smith's views. Cline wrote that "the expansion under [DCI] Vandenberg made the Agency a little bigger than before but not much better. It was filled largely with military men who did not want to leave the service at the end of the war but were not in great demand in the military services. The quality was mediocre."[46]

During the critical year of 1948—which saw, among other crises, the Berlin Blockade—38 analysts worked in the Soviet and East European branch: 26 men and 12 women. As a group, their strength was previous exposure to the Soviet Union: nine had lived there, and 12 spoke Russian—both high figures for an era when knowledge about the USSR was limited, even in academia. Their backgrounds, however, were less impressive in other respects. Only one had a Ph.D., while six had no college degree at all. One had a law degree. Of those with college experience, a surprising number majored in fields far removed from their work with CIG/CIA: civil engineering, agriculture, and library science, for example. Far from being stereotypical well-heeled graduates of the Ivy League, many had attended colleges that, at least in that period, were undistinguished. Although military experience was widespread, only one had served in the OSS.[47]

To be fair, the analysts faced a number of impediments that made it difficult for their work to match expectations. The information at their disposal was, for the most part, shared by others in the policy and intelligence communities. Moreover, the pace of the working day was hectic, and the analysts were under constant pressure. The pressure came from outside—from government officials who demanded immediate support—and within, from

[44] Baldwin, "Intelligence—IV, Competent Personnel Held Key to Success—Reforms Suggested," *The New York Times*, July 24, 1948.
[45] Smith, *The Unknown CIA*, p. 36.
[46] Cline, *Secrets, Spies, and Scholars*, p. 92.
[47] Author's survey of CIA personnel files. Another veteran of the period, James Hanrahan, recalls that pockets of greater academic expertise existed in other branches of ORE, such as the West European branch. Interview with James Hanrahan, 16 July 1997.

individuals who realized that career advancement rested on quantity of production. Consequently, analysts had precious little time for reflection. In perhaps the best known example, Ludwell Montague in July 1946 was given only three days in which to research, write, and coordinate with the other agencies ORE-1, "Soviet Foreign and Military Policy," the first estimate produced by CIG.[48]

Nowhere was the pressure greater than in the production of the *Daily Summaries*. Each morning, at nine o'clock, couriers would arrive at CIA headquarters with the previous day's cable traffic from State and the Pentagon. Between nine and 10, an editor would read the cables, write comments on those he thought worthy of using in the *Daily Summary*, and sort them according to ORE's branch organization. The analysts had on average only one hour, between 10 and 11, to draft their articles. Between 11 and noon the articles were edited, and at noon the branch chiefs, editors, and office leadership met to decide which articles should be published. "By one o'clock, the *Daily* was usually dittoed, assembled, enclosed in blue folders, packaged, receipted for, and on its way by couriers to its approximately fifteen official recipients."[49]

Because there were few contacts between the analysts and editors on the one hand and senior policymakers on the other, choosing which stories to include in the *Daily* was a shot in the dark. As R. Jack Smith, then editor of the *Daily* recalled, "The comic backdrop to this daily turmoil was that in actuality *nobody* knew what President Truman wanted to see or not see. . . . How were we supposed to judge, sitting in a rundown temporary building on the edge of the Potomac, what was fit for the President's eyes?" After gaining experience on the job, Smith decided that

Intelligence of immediate value to the president falls essentially into two categories: developments impinging directly on the security of the United States; and developments bearing on major U.S. policy concerns. These cover possible military attacks, fluctuations in relationships among potential adversaries, or anything likely to threaten or enhance the success of major U.S. policy programs worldwide.[50]

The combination of uncertainty over what the President needed to see and the analysts' need to publish as much as possible brought editors, analysts, and branch chiefs into frequent conflict. The analysts and their branch chiefs believed that they, as the substantive experts, should have the final say on the content of the *Summaries*, while the editors felt that the experts were too parochial in outlook to make such decisions.[51] Neither side held

[48] Darling, *The Central Intelligence Agency,* p. 130.
[49] Jackson, *Office of Reports and Estimates, 1946-1951*, vol. 5, p. 583.
[50] Smith, *The Unknown CIA,* p. 34.
[51] Ibid., pp. 31-33.

command authority, so the disputes had to be settled through argument and compromise. The most intractable cases would be bucked up to the office leadership to decide. This situation remained a source of tension within the office throughout ORE's existence.

The Analytical Record

The Threat of War in Europe . . .
From the beginning, the current intelligence sent to the White House contained numerous alarming reports about Soviet behavior from nearly all corners of the globe: the Middle East, Eastern Europe, Western Europe, and Korea in particular. A policymaker reading the *Summaries*, or the original reports on which the *Summaries* were based, could easily have concluded that Soviet military aggression was an imminent possibility.

The most consistent—and perhaps most important—theme of CIG/CIA analysis during this period, however, was that Soviet moves, no matter how menacing they might appear in isolation, were unlikely to lead to an attack against the West. This judgment looks even bolder in light of President Truman's evident intention that ORE was to warn the US Government of another Pearl Harbor—that is, a sudden surprise attack on American forces or Allies. Denied the ability to make comments in the *Summaries* for most of 1946, CIG's first opportunity to put these reports into perspective was ORE-1, "Soviet Foreign and Military Policy," published on 23 July 1946. It noted that, although "the Soviet Government anticipates an inevitable conflict with the capitalist world," Moscow "needs to avoid such a conflict for an indefinite period."[52]

Similarly, a Special Study published a month later and sent to the President noted that "during the past two weeks there has been a series of developments which suggest that some consideration should be given to the possibility of near-term Soviet military action."[53] The authors judged, however, that

The most plausible conclusion would appear to be that, until there is some specific evidence that the Soviets are making the necessary military

---

[52] ORE 1, 23 July 1946, "Soviet Foreign and Military Policy," Document 4.
[53] On 9 February 1946, Stalin had given a harsh speech that convinced many leading Americans, including Secretary of the Navy Forrestal and Supreme Court Justice William O. Douglas, that war with the Soviet Union was becoming increasingly likely. See Walter Millis, ed., *The Forrestal Diaries* (New York: The Viking Press, 1951), pp. 134, 135. Other incidents of this period that caused particular concern were Soviet diplomatic pressure on Turkey over joint Soviet-Turkish control of the straits, Yugoslavia's destruction of two US aircraft, and a vicious Soviet propaganda campaign and internal crackdown (the *Zhdanovshchina*) against Western influences. On the *Zhdanovshchina*, see Vladislav Zubok and Constantine Pleshakov, *Inside the Kremlin's Cold War: From Stalin to Khrushchev* (Cambridge: Harvard University Press, 1996), pp. 123-125.

preparations and dispositions for offensive operations, the recent disturbing developments can be interpreted as constituting no more than an intensive war of nerves. The purpose may be to test US determination to support its objectives at the [Paris] peace conference and to sustain its commitments in European affairs.[54]

Subsequent crises did not shake this assessment. During the March 1948 "war scare," touched off when General Lucius Clay, the US military governor in Germany, sent a message to the Pentagon warning of the likelihood of a sudden Soviet attack, CIA analysts bluntly rejected the notion.[55] During the scare, the State Department reported, in separate cables, that senior members of the Czechoslovak and Turkish Governments also feared the Soviet Union was prepared to risk an imminent attack. In comments on these reports made in the *Daily Summary* on 16 March 1948, analysts said "CIA does not believe that the USSR is presently prepared to risk war in the pursuit of its aims in Europe." On the following day, they added that "CIA does not believe that the USSR plans a military venture in the immediate future in either Europe or the Middle East."[56]

During the Berlin blockade, CIA's position remained the same. "The Soviet action . . . has two possible objectives: either to force the Western powers to negotiate on Soviet terms regarding Germany or, failing that, to force a Western power withdrawal from Berlin. The USSR does not seem ready to force a definite showdown. . . ."[57] The explosion of the Soviet Union's first atomic bomb, on 29 August 1949, similarly failed to change the analysts' judgment: "No immediate change in Soviet policy or tactics is expected" was the verdict in the *Weekly Summary.*[58]

. . . and in the Far East
ORE initially deemed the possibility of aggression by the Soviet client regime in North Korea as more likely.

An armed invasion of South Korea by the North Korean Peoples' Army is not likely until US troops have been withdrawn from the area or before the Communists have attempted to 'unify' Korea by some sort of coup. Eventual

[54] *Special Study No. 3*, 24 August 1946, "Current Soviet Intentions," Document 8.
[55] Clay's message, sent on 5 March 1948, stated that "For many months . . . I have felt and held that war was unlikely for at least 10 years. Within the last few weeks, I have felt a subtle change in Soviet attitude which I cannot define but which now gives me a feeling that it may come with dramatic suddenness." Quoted in Frank Kofsky, *Harry S. Truman and the War Scare of 1948: A Successful Campaign to Deceive the Nation* (New York: St. Martin's Press, 1993), p. 104.
[56] *Daily Summary*, 16 March 1948, Document 64; *Daily Summary*, 17 March 1948, Document 67.
[57] *Weekly Summary*, 2 July 1948, Document 85.
[58] *Weekly Summary*, 30 September 1949, Document 145.

*armed conflict between the North and South Korean Governments appears
probable, however, in the light of such recent events as Soviet withdrawal
from North Korea, intensified improvement of North Korean roads leading
south, Peoples' Army troop movements to areas nearer the 38th parallel
and from Manchuria to North Korea, and combined maneuvers.*[59]

ORE earlier had predicted that Soviet withdrawal from North Korea would
be followed by "renewed pressure for the withdrawal of all occupation
forces. The Soviet aim will be to deprive the US of an opportunity to establish a native security force in South Korea adequate to deal with aggression
from the North Korean People's Army."[60]

Unfortunately for ORE and the policymakers who read its analysis, this line
was revised in early 1950. "The continuing southward movement of the
expanding Korean People's Army toward the 38th parallel probably constitutes a defensive measure to offset the growing strength of the offensively
minded South Korean Army," read the *Weekly Summary* of 13 January.
ORE further stated that "an invasion of South Korea is unlikely unless
North Korean forces can develop a clear-cut superiority over the increasingly efficient South Korean Army."[61] Although this assessment appears
naive in retrospect, it actually fit in well with the views held by senior
American military officers, who believed the South Korean Army was sufficiently strong and no longer required US military aid. South Korean strong-
man Syngman Rhee, moreover, had begun making noises to American
officials about reunifying Korea under his control; the possibility of South
Korean provocation thus was not as remote at the time as it seems now.[62]

The day after the North Korean attack on 25 June 1950, the *Daily Summary*
counseled that "successful aggression in Korea will encourage the USSR to
launch similar ventures elsewhere in the Far East. In sponsoring the aggression in Korea, the Kremlin probably calculated that no firm or effective
countermeasures would be taken by the West. However, the Kremlin is not
willing to undertake a global war at this time. . . ."[63]

---

[59] *Weekly Summary*, 29 October 1948, Document 103.
[60] *Weekly Summary*, 16 July 1948, Document 87. ORE 3-49, "Consequences of US Troop
Withdrawal from Korea in Spring, 1949," published 28 February 1949, similarly predicted
that the withdrawal of US troops from South Korea "would probably in time be followed by
an invasion. . . ." Reprinted in Warner, ed., *The CIA Under Harry Truman*, p. 265.
[61] *Weekly Summary*, 13 January 1950, Document 155.
[62] Melvyn P. Leffler, *A Preponderance of Power: National Security, the Truman
Administration, and the Cold War* (Stanford, California: Stanford University Press, 1992),
p. 365.
[63] *Daily Summary*, 26 June 1950, Document 173.

After initially suggesting that "firm and effective countermeasures by the West would probably lead the Kremlin to permit a settlement to be negotiated between the North and South Koreans," the analysts within days concluded that "It is probable . . . that a concerted attempt will be made to make the US effort in Korea as difficult and costly as possible."[64] A week later, the analysts amplified this theme:

All evidence available leads to the conclusion that the USSR is not ready for war. Nevertheless, the USSR has substantial capabilities, without directly involving Soviet troops, for prolonging the fighting in Korea, as well as for initiating hostilities elsewhere. Thus, although the USSR would prefer to confine the conflict to Korea, a reversal there might impel the USSR to take greater risks of starting a global war either by committing substantial Chinese Communist forces in Korea or by sanctioning aggressive actions by Satellite forces in other areas of the world.[65]

ORE analysts quickly concluded, however, that Chinese intervention was not likely. They reasoned that, although a North Korean defeat would "have obvious disadvantages" for the Soviet Union, "the commitment of Chinese Communist forces would not necessarily prevent such a defeat and a defeat under these circumstances would be far more disastrous, not only because it would be a greater blow to Soviet prestige throughout the world, but because it would seriously threaten Soviet control over the Chinese Communist regime." Moreover, if the Chinese were to emerge victorious, "the presence of Chinese Communist troops in Korea would complicate if not jeopardize Soviet direction of Korean affairs; Chinese Communist prestige, as opposed to that of the USSR, would be enhanced; and Peiping might be tempted as a result of success in Korea to challenge Soviet leadership in Asia." Finally, the analysts believed that Chinese intervention was unlikely because "the use of Chinese Communist forces in Korea would increase the risk of global war, not only because of possible UN or US reaction but because the USSR itself would be under greater compulsion to assure a victory in Korea, possibly by committing Soviet troops."[66]

The *Weekly Summary* of 15 September 1950 briefly described the evidence that suggested Chinese intervention was likely but still concluded that Beijing would not risk war with the United States:

Numerous reports of Chinese Communist troop movements in Manchuria, coupled with Peiping's recent charges of US aggression and violations of

[64] Ibid.; *Weekly Summary*, 30 June 1950, Document 176.
[65] *Weekly Summary*, 7 July 1950, Document 180. Three days after the war began, ORE analysts assured President Truman that "No evidence is available indicating Soviet preparations for military operations in the West European theater. . . ." Nevertheless, the analysts cautioned, "Soviet military capabilities in Europe make it possible for the USSR to take aggressive action with a minimum of preparation or advance notice." *Daily Summary*, 28 June 1950, Document 175.
[66] *Weekly Summary*, 14 July 1950, Document 184.

*Chinese territory, have increased speculation concerning both Chinese
Communist intervention in Korea and disagreement between the USSR and
China on matters of military policy. It is being argued that victory in Korea
can only be achieved by using Chinese Communist (or Soviet) forces, that
the USSR desires to weaken the US by involving it in a protracted struggle
with China, and that the Chinese Communists are blaming the USSR for
initiating the Korean venture and thus postponing the invasion of Taiwan.
Despite the apparent logic of this reasoning, there is no evidence indicating
a Chinese-Soviet disagreement, and cogent political and military
considerations make it unlikely that Chinese Communist forces will be
directly and openly committed in Korea.*[67]

The first Chinese warnings of intervention in the war if UN forces crossed
the 38th parallel were published in the *Daily Summary* on 30 September
without comment, perhaps because they were downplayed by the US
Ambassador to the Soviet Union, to whom others in the Moscow diplomatic
corps had passed the warnings.[68] On 3 October the analysts drew on a similar report from the US Embassy in London to state that "CIA estimates . . .
that the Chinese Communists would not consider it in their interests to
intervene openly in Korea if, as now seems likely, they anticipate that war
with the UN nations [sic] would result." [69] In the same article the analysts
warned, as they had before and would again, that "The Chinese Communists have long had the capability for military intervention in Korea on a
scale sufficient to materially affect the course of events. . . ."[70] Nevertheless,
in eight subsequent *Daily Summaries*, CIA analysts restated their belief that
China would, first, not intervene, and then—as the intervention got under
way—that it would not develop into a large-scale attack. The last *Summary*
containing this judgment came on 17 November, three weeks after the first
Chinese troops, wearing Korean uniforms, entered combat in far northern
Korea.[71]

The Danger of Subversion in Europe

Throughout this period, ORE analysts were far more concerned about
Soviet use of local Communist parties to subvert pro-Western governments

[67] *Weekly Summary*, 15 September 1950, Document 191. For the contemporary research
on this issue, see, for example, John Lewis Gaddis, *We Now Know: Rethinking Cold War
History* (New York: Oxford University Press, 1997), pp. 77-82.
[68] *Daily Summary*, 30 September 1950, Document 193.
[69] *Daily Summary*, 3 October 1950, Document 194.
[70] Ibid.
[71] *Daily Summaries*, 9 October 1950, Document 196; 16 October 1950, Document 200;
20 October 1950, Document 201; 28 October 1950, Document 202; 30 October 1950,
Document 203; 31 October 1950, Document 204; 2 November 1950, Document 205;
17 November 1950, Document 208.

than they were about the possibility of armed aggression by the USSR or one of its Communist allies. As ORE expressed it in September 1947, "The USSR is unlikely to resort to open military aggression in present circumstances. Its policy is to avoid war, to build up its war potential, and to extend its influence and control by political, economic, and psychological methods."[72]

CIG had reached a very similar conclusion about the first serious postwar confrontation with the Soviet Union—its refusal to withdraw its forces from northern Iran and its subsequent support for the breakaway Iranian provinces of Azerbaijan and Kurdistan.[73] After the worst of the Iran crisis had passed, the first *Weekly Summary* warned that the Soviets, having recognized that their policy toward Iran was "heavy-handed and over-hasty" would rely on "gradual penetration." It declared that "the Soviets clearly feel that 'time is on their side' in Iran and that the general economic backwardness of the country and the unpopular labor policy of the British oil companies will forward their cause."[74] "Their cause" was identified as "gaining control over Iranian oil and blocking closer military ties between Iran and the West."[75]

ORE tracked the gradual but inexorable consolidation of Communist power across Eastern Europe, as brought about through a combination of political manipulation by local Communists and pressure from the Soviet occupation forces. The political and economic undermining of the prospects for democracy in Eastern Europe reinforced the analysts' conclusion that this type of subversion was the greatest danger from the Soviet Union. The analysts observed that Moscow's objective in the region was to "establish permanent safeguards for their strategic, political, and economic interests, including . . . stable and subservient, or at least friendly, regime[s]."[76]

The analysts were most troubled by the consolidation of Communist power in Czechoslovakia in February 1948, judging that it would diminish

the possibility of a compromise in Europe between the ideologies of the Kremlin and the principles of Western democracy and individual freedom.

[72] *Review of the World Situation*, 26 September 1947, Document 37.
[73] In December 1945, Iranian rebels under the protection of Soviet forces proclaimed an independent Azerbaijan and an independent Kurdish People's Republic. The Government of Iran protested this Soviet interference in its internal affairs before the UN Security Council in January 1946.
[74] *Weekly Summary*, 14 June 1946, Document 1.
[75] *Weekly Summary*, 18 March 1949, Document 127.
[76] *Weekly Summary*, 5 July 1946, Document 2. The quotation refers specifically to Bulgaria, but the same point was repeated about other East European countries as well. *Weekly Summary*, 19 July 1946, Document 3, for example, contains a piece on Hungary that notes the "Soviet desire to establish the control of the minority Communist Party in anticipation of the peace settlement and the ultimate withdrawal of Soviet troops."

Such a compromise had apparently been achieved in Czechoslovakia. . . .
The coup . . . reflects the refusal of the Communists to settle for anything
less than complete control and their conviction that such dominance could
never have been achieved under a freely operating parliamentary form of
government.[77]

On Germany, ORE anticipated that Stalin would use subversive tactics to try to create a unified German state from the occupied ruins of the Third Reich: "A German administration strongly centralized in Berlin will be much more susceptible than a loose federation to Soviet pressures. . . . Posing thus as the champions of German nationalism and rehabilitation, the Soviets can attempt to discredit the policy of the Western powers and to facilitate the Communist penetration of their zones."[78] The analysts warned that the removal of zonal barriers would place the Soviets in a "position to launch a vigorous campaign to communize the Western zone. . . ."[79]

After the Council of Foreign Ministers (CFM) conference in Moscow in the spring of 1947 failed to reach agreement on Germany's future, ORE analysts advised that the Soviets may be trying to (1) "prolong the unsettled conditions in Europe conducive to Communism; and (2) to encourage the US to expend its patience and energy in a vain quest for agreement until forced by its internal economic and political conditions to curtail its foreign commitments and to leave Europe to the USSR by default."[80]

ORE noted that Soviet efforts to penetrate the western zones of Germany focused on attempts to "extend the SED [Socialist Unity Party, the Communist's stalking horse in the eastern zone] political structure to the west, while, simultaneously, efforts are made to establish Communist front organizations, such as the Freie Deutsche Jugend (FDJ), and to penetrate Western Zone labor unions."[81] ORE warned that if "Soviet efforts at the [November 1947] CFM fail to achieve a united Germany on Soviet terms, the USSR will attempt to blame the Western powers for failure of the conference. At the same time, the Kremlin may announce the recognition of a 'German Republic' east of the Elbe and attempt to secure the removal of the Western Allies from Berlin."[82]

Once the first signs of the Berlin blockade emerged in April 1948, ORE analysts advised that Stalin wanted "a negotiated settlement . . . on terms which would permit ultimate Soviet control of Berlin and Communist

---

[77] *Weekly Summary,* 27 February 1948, Document 62.
[78] *Weekly Summary,* 19 July 1946, Document 3.
[79] *Weekly Summary,* 2 August 1946, Document 5.
[80] *Weekly Summary,* 2 May 1947, Document 23.
[81] *Weekly Summary,* 5 September 1947, Document 34.
[82] Ibid.

penetration of western Germany."[83] After the blockade was lifted in the spring of 1949, CIA assessed that Soviet objectives in Germany remained unchanged: "Soviet agreement to lift the Berlin blockade and enter into four-power discussions on Germany does not represent any change in the Soviet objective to establish a Germany which will eventually fall under Soviet domination."[84]

The analysts also highlighted the Communist threat in France and Italy. Both countries had emerged from the war with widespread devastation and strong Communist parties sharing power in coalition governments. After the French and Italian prime ministers expelled the Communist ministers from their governments in the spring of 1947, ORE predicted that

The Kremlin apparently proposes for countries such as France and Italy: (1) intensive agitation against their present governments and against non-Communist liberals; and (2) the development of highly-disciplined Communist cores which, at the proper moment, could assume control. Such a program is well-adapted to the current situation in France where, [now] relieved of governmental responsibility, the Communists are in a position to threaten (by propaganda, subversion, and trade-union agitation) the stability of the present Government. Where Communism is less powerful, the Kremlin desires to concentrate on gaining control of trade unions and other liberal organizations.[85]

ORE warned in September 1947 that "the sudden overthrow of the De Gasperi government [in Italy] by Communist-sponsored armed force, following [the December 1947] withdrawal of Allied troops," was "within the realm of possibility" because of the Italian Army's weakness. But the analysts thought that outcome was unlikely. They wrote that "the USSR is unwilling to support directly such a step because it might involve war with the US" and because the potential failure of the much anticipated European Recovery Program (better known today as the Marshall Plan) could deliver Italy into the hands of the Communists in the April 1948 elections. ORE worried more that a Communist-inspired general strike could paralyze the important north Italian industrial area; such an event could "defeat the operation of the European recovery program and eventually throw not only Italy into the Soviet orbit, but possibly France as well."[86]

---

[83] *Weekly Summary*, 5 November 1948, Document 105.
[84] *Weekly Summary*, 6 May 1949, Document 134.
[85] *Weekly Summary*, 9 May 1947, Document 24.
[86] *Weekly Summary*, 12 September 1947, Document 35.

A Special Evaluation published on 13 October 1947 concluded that Moscow's establishment of the Communist Information Bureau in September 1947

suggests strongly that the USSR recognizes that it has reached a point of diminishing returns in the attempts of the Communist parties of Western Europe to rise to power through parliamentary means and that, consequently, it intends to revert to subversive activities, such as strikes and sabotage, in an effort to undermine the stability of Western European governments. This move likewise tends to substantiate the contention that the USSR considers international subversive and revolutionary action, rather than military aggression, as the primary instrument for obtaining its worldwide objectives.[87]

ORE concluded that, "In its efforts to sabotage the European recovery program, which is the USSR's immediate and primary target, the Kremlin will be willing even to risk the sacrifice of the French and Italian Communist Parties" by ordering them to use sabotage and violence against the Marshall Plan. "If these Parties are defeated and driven underground, the USSR will have lost no more than it would lose by the success of the European recovery program. CIA believes that the unexpectedly rapid progress of the [proposed] Marshall program has upset the timetable of the Kremlin and forced this desperate action as the last available countermeasures."[88]

The unexpectedly severe defeat of the Italian Communists in the April 1948 national election considerably eased the concerns of ORE's analysts. Noting that the election results had "vastly improved the morale and confidence of the anti-Communists in both Italy and France," the analysts predicted that "for the immediate future, Communist activities in Western Europe are likely to be directed toward rebuilding the popular front rather than an early or determined bid for power." Nevertheless, "the Communists are not expected to relax their efforts to prevent recovery in Europe. . . . Strikes and industrial sabotage . . . therefore can be expected."[89]

The civil war in Greece, which had begun in 1946, received relatively little attention in the current intelligence publications until the British Government announced in early 1947 that it would have to withdraw its forces from the country and significantly reduce its assistance to Greece's

---

[87] *Special Evaluation 21*, 13 October 1947, "Implications of the New Communist Information Bureau," Document 40.

[88] *Daily Summary*, 4 December 1947, Document 48.

[89] *Weekly Summary*, 23 April 1948, Document 72.

non-Communist Government. The *Weekly Summary* of 28 February, published seven days after the British announcement, summarized the dire situation facing Greece:

Alone, Greece cannot save itself. Militarily, the country needs aid in the form of equipment and training. Politically, Greece's diehard politicians need to be convinced of the necessity of a housecleaning, and the prostrate Center . . . requires bolstering. Economically, it needs gifts or loans of commodities, food, foreign exchange, and gold to check inflation. Of these needs, the economic are the most vital. . . . Without immediate economic aid . . . there would appear to be imminent danger that the Soviet-dominated Left will seize control of the country, which would result in the loss of Greece as a democracy. . . .[90]

ORE analysts believed the chain of command for the Communist forces in Greece started in Moscow and ran through Yugoslav leader Josip Broz-Tito to Bulgaria and Albania before reaching the Greek Communists.[91] Nevertheless, they rejected the possibility that armies of those countries would assist the Greek guerrillas, despite numerous rumors to the contrary:

CIG considers direct participation by the Albanian, Yugoslav, and Bulgarian armies unlikely. Such action would obviously have far-reaching international repercussions and might even involve the USSR in a world war for which it is unprepared. The likelihood of direct participation by Soviet troops in Greece or Turkey at this time is so remote that it need not seriously be considered.[92]

In July 1948, ORE advised the President that Tito's rift with Stalin, which appeared in March, would considerably lessen the pressure against Greece.[93] It soon followed with a report of slackening Bulgarian support for the guerrillas, although ORE was unable to specify the cause of the change.[94]

The Threat From Revolution in the Far East
In their coverage of the Chinese civil war in the late 1940s, ORE analysts noted that "the Soviet Union has scrupulously avoided identifying the Chinese Communist Party with Moscow, and it is highly improbable that the Soviet leaders would at this time jeopardize the Chinese Communist Party by acknowledging its connection with the world Communist movement."[95]

[90] *Weekly Summary*, 28 February 1947, Document 19.
[91] *Weekly Summary*, 15 August 1947, Document 31.
[92] *Daily Summary*, 5 September 1947, Document 33.
[93] *Weekly Summary*, 9 July 1948, Document 86.
[94] *Weekly Summary*, 23 July 1948, Document 90.
[95] *Weekly Summary*, 19 December 1947, Document 52.

They later affirmed that the USSR had "given renewed indications that it is not ready to abandon its 'correct' attitude toward the Nanking government in favor of open aid to the Communists in China's civil war."[96] Moreover, "Because of the intensely nationalistic spirit of the Chinese people . . . the [Chinese] Communists are most anxious to protect themselves from the charge of Soviet dominance."[97]

Not until the end of 1948 did ORE analysts begin to worry about what a Communist victory in China might mean for the global balance of power: "A tremendously increased Soviet war potential in the Far East may result eventually from Communist control of Manchuria and north China."[98] At the same time, the analysts began warning that "Recent statements from authoritative Chinese Communist sources emphasize the strong ideological affinity existing between the USSR and the Chinese Communist party . . . and indicate that Soviet leadership, especially in foreign affairs, will probably be faithfully followed by any Communist-dominated government in China."[99]

After the Communists' final victory over Chiang Kai-shek's Nationalist regime in the autumn of 1949, the analysts doubted that Mao's protracted stay in Moscow, which began in December 1949 and lasted for nine weeks, was a sign of potential trouble in the alliance: "Although the length of Mao's visit may be the result of difficulties in reaching agreement on a revised Sino-Soviet treaty . . . it is unlikely that Mao is proving dangerously intractable. Mao is a genuine and orthodox Stalinist, [and] is in firm control of the Chinese Communist Party."[100] The analysts believed that "The USSR can be expected to gradually strengthen its grip on the Chinese Communist Party apparatus, on the armed forces, on the secret police, and on communications and informational media."[101]

ORE initially devoted little attention to the French struggle in Indochina against the Viet Minh independence movement led by Ho Chi Minh—in fact, the office devoted much more coverage to the problems the Dutch were having in their colony in Indonesia. Although most of ORE's information came from French officials, the analysts were skeptical that Paris would be able to put down the rebellion.[102] They concluded that "Any Vietnam government which does not include Ho Chi Minh or his more moderate

[96] *Weekly Summary*, 9 January 1948, Document 55.
[97] *Weekly Summary*, 27 February 1948, Document 62.
[98] *Weekly Summary*, 12 November 1948, Document 106.
[99] *Weekly Summary*, 3 December 1948, Document 111.
[100] *Weekly Summary*, 13 January 1950, Document 155.
[101] *Weekly Summary*, 17 February 1950, Document 160.
[102] *Weekly Summary*, 10 January 1947, Document 17.

followers will . . . be limited in scope of authority by the perimeters of French military control and will be open to widespread popular opposition and sabotage."[103]

Ho was not at first portrayed by ORE as either a Communist or a Soviet ally. The analysts referred to him as "President Ho."[104] The first mention of a tie to Moscow, made in May 1948, was a grudging one: "Ho Chi Minh . . . is supported by 80 percent of the population and . . . is allegedly loyal to Soviet foreign policy. . . ."[105] As late as September 1949, analysts wrote that "Ho's relationship with the Kremlin and the Chinese Communists remains obscure. . . . Ho has stated his willingness to accept military equipment from the Chinese Communists. On the other hand, Ho still maintains that neutrality between the US and the USSR is both possible and desirable. . . ."[106]

Moscow's recognition of Ho's government on 31 January 1950 prompted the analysts to change their stance dramatically, however.[107] They saw the likelihood of a series of regional governments falling in turn under Soviet influence:

If France is driven from Indochina, the resulting emergence of an indigenous Communist-dominated regime in Vietnam, together with pressures exerted by Peiping and Moscow, would probably bring about the orientation of adjacent Thailand and Burma toward the Communist orbit. Under these circumstances, other Asian states—Malaya and Indonesia, particularly—would become highly vulnerable to the extension of Communist influence. . . . Meanwhile, by recognizing the Ho regime, the USSR has revealed its determination to force France completely out of Indochina and to install a Communist government. Alone, France is incapable of preventing such a development.[108]

The analysts concluded that, although only the United States could help France avoid defeat, the "Asian nations . . . would tend to interpret such US action as support of continued Western colonialism."[109]

Soviet Aims in Israel
Like many in the State Department and elsewhere in the US Government, ORE, worried by reports that the Soviets were funneling arms and money to

---

[103] *Weekly Summary,* 14 March 1947, Document 21.
[104] *Weekly Summary,* 24 October 1947, Document 41.
[105] *Weekly Summary,* 14 May 1948, Document 77.
[106] *Weekly Summary,* 9 September 1949, Document 143.
[107] Communist China had recognized Ho's government on 18 January 1950.
[108] *Daily Summary,* 1 February 1950, Document 156.
[109] Ibid.

Zionist guerrillas, suggested that the creation of Israel could give the USSR a client state in the Middle East.[110]

Formation of a Jewish state in Palestine will enable the USSR to intensify its efforts to expand Soviet influence in the Near East and to perpetuate a chaotic condition there. . . . In any event, the flow of men and munitions to Palestine from the Soviet Bloc can be expected to increase substantially. The USSR will undoubtedly take advantage of the removal of immigration restrictions to increase the influx of trained Soviet agents from eastern and central Europe into Palestine where they have already had considerable success penetrating the Stern Gang, Irgun, and, to a lesser extent, Haganah.[111]

Not until November 1948, six months after Israel declared its independence and defeated a coalition of Arab opponents, did ORE suggest that events might turn out otherwise: "There is some evidence that Soviet . . . enthusiasm for the support of Israel is diminishing."[112] ORE later suggested that the change in attitude stemmed from a Soviet estimate "that the establishment of Israel as a disruptive force in the Arab world has now been accomplished and that further military aid to a country of basically pro-Western sympathies would ultimately prove prejudicial to Soviet interests in the Near East."[113]

Conclusion

ORE met its end shortly after Lt. Gen. Walter Bedell Smith and William H. Jackson, of the Dulles-Jackson-Correa survey team, arrived in late 1950 as Director of Central Intelligence and Deputy Director, respectively. They abolished ORE that November and replaced it with three new units: the Office of National Estimates, the Office of Research and Reports, and the Office of Current Intelligence. These steps finally ended the confusion over the analytical mission, primarily by splitting the competing functions of national, current, and basic intelligence into three offices.

Much maligned by insiders and outsiders alike, ORE's record is perhaps not as bad as its reputation. Its analysis holds up well when compared to both the views held by other agencies at the time and our current understanding of events in that period. Of course, ORE, like all intelligence organizations in all eras, had its failures. Dramatic, sweeping events, such as wars and revolutions, are far too complex to predict or analyze perfectly. Even with the benefit of unprecedented access to Russian and Chinese sources, for

[110] *Daily Summary*, 25 June 1948, Document 82.
[111] *Weekly Summary*, 14 May 1948, Document 77.
[112] *Weekly Summary*, 12 November 1948, Document 106.
[113] *Weekly Summary*, 17 December 1948, Document 112.

example, contemporary historians are unable to conclusively pinpoint when and why Mao decided to intervene in the Korean war.[114]

Gaps also exist in our knowledge about what intelligence President Truman saw, understood, believed, and used. Judging the impact of intelligence on policy is difficult always, and especially so from a distance of 50 years. On many issues, such as the Communist threat to Italy, ORE's work tended to reinforce what many policymakers in the administration and officials in the field already believed.

It does seem fair to conclude, however, that ORE's repeated, correct assurances that a Soviet attack in Europe was unlikely must have had a steadying influence when tensions were high and some feared a Soviet onslaught. In this, the analysts of ORE served President Truman well, and their accurate assessment ultimately must be considered ORE's most important contribution in those early, fearful years of the Cold War.

[114] The two sets of sources appear to be at least partially contradictory. See the discussion in Zubok and Pleshakov, *Inside the Kremlin's Cold War*, pp. 65-69, and in John Lewis Gaddis, *We Now Know*, pp. 77-80.

Chronology

1945

March

02 Soviet pressure on King Michael of Romania forces him to appoint a Communist-controlled, pro-Soviet government under Petru Groza.

19 The Soviet Union denounces the Turco-Soviet nonaggression treaty of 1925. Moscow begins to place diplomatic pressure on Turkey over control of the Dardanelles.

April

12 President Roosevelt dies; Harry S. Truman becomes President of the United States.

May

08 Germany surrenders and is divided into four zones of occupation, as is its capital, Berlin. These are administered by the United States, the Soviet Union, Great Britain, and France.

June

28 A Polish Government of national unity is formed under Socialist Premier Eduard Osobka-Morawski. Although recognized by the West, it displays a marked pro-Soviet orientation.

July

03 James F. Byrnes becomes Secretary of State.

17 President Truman begins meetings with Prime Minister Attlee and Soviet leader Stalin at Potsdam.

August

06	The United States drops an atomic bomb on Hiroshima.
08	The Soviet Union declares war on Japan.
09	The United States drops an atomic bomb on Nagasaki.
14	Japan surrenders, ending World War II.
17	The United States and the Soviet Union agree to divide their occupation zones in Korea at the 38th parallel.

September

02	Ho Chi Minh declares Vietnamese independence from France.
20	Executive Order 9621 dissolves the OSS effective 1 October. The Research and Analysis Branch is transferred to the Department of State, while the espionage and counterintelligence branches are moved to the War Department, where they are renamed the Strategic Services Unit.
27	Robert P. Patterson becomes Secretary of War.

November

03	Hungarians vote the anti-Communist Smallholders' Party into power.
10	The Communist leader Enver Hoxha becomes Premier of Albania.
18	An election with limited choice returns a Communist-controlled government in Bulgaria.
27	General George Marshall begins his efforts to mediate a solution to the Chinese civil war.

December

16	Rebels in Iranian Azerbaijan, acting under Soviet protection, declare independence.
19	Rebel Kurds in western Iranian Azerbaijan, also acting under Soviet protection, declare independence.

1946

January

06	The Government of Poland begins nationalization of industry.
22	President Truman creates the Central Intelligence Group (CIG), appointing Rear Admiral Sidney Souers the first Director of Central Intelligence.
31	Yugoslavia adopts a Soviet-style Constitution.

February

09	Stalin raises fears in the West with a speech in which he declares that Communism and capitalism cannot coexist.
15	The first *Daily Summary* is published for the President by the Central Reports Staff of CIG.
22	US diplomat George F. Kennan sends his influential "Long Telegram" from Moscow analyzing the sources of Soviet conduct.

March

05	Winston Churchill delivers his "Iron Curtain" speech in Fulton, MO.
25	Moscow announces the withdrawal of its forces from northern Iran.

April

22	The merger of the Communist and Socialist Parties in the Soviet zone of occupation in Germany creates the Socialist Unity Party.

May

26	Communists emerge as strong political force in Czechoslovakia after an election to a constituent assembly. Communist Klement Gottwald forms a coalition government with non-Communists.
May	The Greek civil war begins, with Yugoslavia, Bulgaria, and Albania channeling support to Communist guerrillas who aim to overthrow the Greek Government.

June

10   Lt. General Hoyt S. Vandenberg, US Army Air Forces, succeeds Admiral Souers as Director of Central Intelligence.

July

19   The Central Reports Staff is renamed Office of Research and Evaluations to reflect the broader responsibilities given it by National Intelligence Authority Directive No. 5.

23   CIG produces its first piece of "strategic and national policy" intelligence, ORE-1, which analyzes Soviet foreign and military policy.

October

20   Strategic Services Unit field personnel are transferred to CIG's new Office of Special Operations.

27   Elections for a constituent assembly in Bulgaria that are manipulated by the Communist-dominated government result in a Communist majority. The veteran Communist George Dimitrov returns from Moscow to head the government.

29   The name of the Office of Research and Evaluations is changed to Office of Reports and Estimates out of deference to the Department of State, which claims that research and evaluation are State responsibilities.

November

19   Voters in Romania return to power a Communist-dominated government after a campaign of violence and intimidation against the opposition.

December

19   The French war against the Vietminh begins in Indochina.

1947

January

01   The US ar   ish zones of Germany are merged.

08	General Marshall ends his efforts to mediate a solution to the Chinese civil war.
19	Manipulated elections in Poland return a huge Communist majority. The United States and Britain protest.
21	George C. Marshall becomes Secretary of State.

February

21	The British announce that they will cease providing aid to Greece and Turkey.
25	Bela Kovacs, a leader of the Hungary's Smallholders' Party, is arrested, beginning a purge of anti-Communists from that party.

March

12	President Truman, in a message to Congress, articulates the Truman Doctrine of providing aid to countries threatened by Communism.

May

01	Rear Admiral Roscoe H. Hillenkoetter is sworn in as the third Director of Central Intelligence.
05	Communist ministers in the French and Italian cabinets are dismissed by their premiers.
31	Hungarian Premier Nagy is accused of treason by the Communists and resigns. The disorder in the Smallholders' Party permits the Communists to win a general election on 31 August.

June

05	Secretary of State George Marshall calls for a European Recovery Program, soon dubbed the Marshall Plan.
06	The leader of Bulgaria's anti-Communist Agrarian Party, Nikola Petkov, is arrested and later executed. His party is dissolved in August.

July

02   Moscow rejects participation in the Marshall Plan. The other East European Communist Parties soon follow suit.

15   The leader of Romania's anti-Communist National Peasant Party is arrested and sentenced to life in prison. His party is dissolved later that same month.

26   President Truman signs the National Security Act of 1947, which provides for a National Security Council (NSC), Secretary of Defense, and a Central Intelligence Agency.

September

17   Secretary of the Navy James V. Forrestal becomes Secretary of Defense.

18   The Central Intelligence Group becomes the Central Intelligence Agency under the provision of the National Security Act of 1947.

27   The Communist Information Bureau is established, signaling the start of the Stalinization of the East European Communist parties.

October

24   The anti-Communist leader of the Polish Peasant Party, Stanislaw Mikolajczyk, is forced to flee the country, and his followers are purged from the party.

1948

January

13   The Dulles-Jackson-Correa Survey Team is formed to assess the performance of CIA and its place in the Intelligence Community.

February

25   A Communist coup in Czechoslovakia ends democracy in that country.

March

17   Alarmed by events in Czechoslovakia, five West European countries sign the treaty of Brussels, establishing the West European Union.

18   The Soviet Union recalls its military and technical advisers from Yugoslavia and expels Belgrade from the Cominform on 28 June.

April

01	The Soviets impose restrictions on road and rail traffic into West Berlin.
18	Italy's Christian Democrats beat a Communist-Socialist bloc by a surprisingly large margin in the country's first national election under its republican constitution.

May

14	Israel becomes an independent state.

June

18	The Western powers introduce currency reform in their occupation zones in Germany.
19	Congress reinstates the draft.
24	The blockade of Berlin begins in earnest; Soviet authorities cut electricity and halt all land and water traffic into West Berlin.

August

15	The Republic of Korea [South Korea] is proclaimed.

September

09	The People's Democratic Republic is officially inaugurated in North Korea under the leadership of Kim Il Sung, who had been placed in power by Moscow in 1946.

November

02	President Truman wins reelection by defeating Governor Thomas Dewey of New York.

December

25	Soviet forces complete their withdrawal from North Korea.

1949

January

01	The Dulles-Jackson-Correa Report is submitted to the NSC; it criticizes the performance of the Office of Reports and Estimates.
21	Dean Acheson becomes Secretary of State.
22	Beijing falls to the Communist forces of Mao Zedong.
25	Moscow announces the formation of the Council of Mutual Economic Assistance to counter the Marshall Plan.
28	The UN Security Council orders the Netherlands to end its war against Indonesian rebels and grant independence to the country.

March

04	V. M. Molotov is replaced as Soviet Foreign Minister by Andrey Vyshinsky.
28	Louis Johnson becomes Secretary of Defense

April

04	Twelve Western countries sign the North Atlantic Treaty.

May

12	The Soviet Union lifts the Berlin blockade.
23	The Federal Republic of Germany is established out of the US, British, and French occupation zones.

June

05	The Emperor Bao Dai is restored to power by France in a ploy to win legitimacy away from the Vietminh rebel forces seeking to oust the French from Indochina.
29	US occupation forces complete their withdrawal from South Korea.

August

05   The United States halts aid to China's rapidly crumbling Nationalist government.

September

23   President Truman announces that the Soviet Union has successfully tested an atomic bomb.

October

01   The People's Republic of China is proclaimed in Beijing.

7   The German Democratic Republic is established in the Soviet occupation zone.

December

08   The Chinese Nationalist Government is established on Taiwan.

16   Mao Zedong begins a nine-week visit to the USSR for his first meeting with Stalin.

1950

January

10   The Soviet delegate to the UN Security Council begins boycotting meetings as a protest over the continued seating of Nationalist China in the UN.

12   Secretary of State Acheson, in a well-publicized speech, leaves South Korea outside the US "defense perimeter" in Asia.

31   The Soviet Union recognizes Ho Chi Minh's Democratic Republic of Vietnam.

February

09   Senator Joseph McCarthy attacks the State Department for harboring Communists.

April

25   NSC 68 adopted by the NSC; President Truman approves it on 30 September.

June

25   North Korea invades South Korea.

27   President Truman sends US naval and air forces to assist South Korea and orders the Seventh Fleet to "neutralize" the Formosa Strait in order to prevent hostilities between the two Chinas.

30   President Truman commits US ground forces to Korea.

August

05   US forces in South Korea are penned within the Pusan perimeter.

September

15   General MacArthur lands behind North Korean lines at Inchon, beginning the rapid disintegration of the North Korean Army.

October

07   Lt. Gen. Walter B. Smith becomes the fourth Director of Central Intelligence. William H. Jackson becomes Deputy Director.

26   Wearing Korean uniforms, small numbers of Chinese troops begin fighting in northern Korea.

November

13   The Office of Reports and Estimates is dissolved and replaced by three new offices: the Office of Research and Reports, the Office Current Intelligence, and the Office National Estimates.

20   UN forces reach the Yalu River border between North Korea and China.

26   Chinese forces attack in strength in North Korea.

Contents

41

1. Weekly Summary Excerpt, 14 June 1946, The Azerbaijan Settlement

The Azerbaijan Settlement

Premier Qavam's success in reaching an agreement with Azerbaijani leaders on the terms which he originally proposed is qualified by the established presence of Soviet elements in Azerbaijan and the concessions which he has been compelled to make to the Soviet-supported Tudeh Party in the rest of Iran. The settlement, which, according to Azerbaijani leaders, was finally concluded on Soviet orders, represents a modification of the previous stand of the Soviet-supported "Democrats." The Azerbaijani "Army" is to be incorporated into the Central Iranian Army, land distribution and internal reform are to be carried out according to Qavam's proposals, the Azerbaijani have officially given up their bid for "autonomy," and Qavam is free to carry out his professed ambition to restore them to full allegiance to Tehran.

Qavam, however, will be hindered in his efforts to develop a unified and genuinely independent Iran by the presence of Soviet officers and men in key positions in the Azerbaijani "Army" and police, and by the growing power of the leftist Tudeh Party in the rest of Iran. In order to better his position in negotiations with the USSR, Qavam recently has played up to the Tudeh Party and has carried out severely repressive measures against conservative elements.

In the last analysis, however, Qavam's future success in maintaining Iran's independence will depend upon great-power policy. The Soviets appear to have recognized that their recent Iranian policy, while accomplishing its immediate military and economic objectives, was heavy-handed and over-hasty. Qavam's skill in mobilizing Iranian resistance and in exploiting world opinion through the UN apparently helped to convince the Soviets that gradual penetration (employed so effectively in Sinkiang) would succeed better. Accordingly, with their oil and military objectives assured, the Soviets could afford to withdraw full support from the Azerbaijani "Democrats." Moreover, the Soviets clearly feel that "time is on their side" in Iran and that the general economic backwardness of the country and the unpopular labor policy of the British oil companies will forward their cause.

- 4 -

TOP SECRET

Political Tension in Bulgaria

The political situation in Bulgaria has grown more critical as intensified efforts by the Communist-dominated coalition Government to consolidate its control over the country have met with increasing resistance from the opposition. A Government campaign of intimidation and unprecedented violence is now under way, and the opposition is reported even to be preparing for possible armed resistance. Both groups have been impelled by the same factors: the anticipated general elections this fall, prospects of the withdrawal of Soviet troops when a peace treaty has been concluded, and the moral support given the opposition by the Western Powers.

Before the Soviets withdraw their troops, they must establish permanent safeguards for their own strategic, political, and economic interests, including a stable and subservient, or at least friendly, regime. Soviet interests, however, also dictate that these aims be achieved without provoking civil war.

As a new step in that direction, therefore, the Soviets have set about to neutralize the Bulgarian Army which under its present leadership has exercised a major restraining influence on Communist policy. By giving political commissars authority over troops equal to that of operational commanders, effective control of the Army is being transferred from the Conservative Minister of War to Communists in the Government and a thorough purge of all non-Communists in the ranks is imminent. This purge probably will be successful because the presence of Soviet occupation troops would forestall any effective resistance. In addition, the Soviets are reportedly preparing to assign technicians to the Army who would be competent to take over Bulgarian military establishments in the event of internal unrest after Soviet troop withdrawal, and are infiltrating into the country large numbers of Soviet citizens both as administrators of Soviet-acquired German property and as civilian members of the NKVD.

These measures may give the Communists sufficient security to permit them to relax the rule of terror and, as a bid for recognition by the Western Powers, they may offer the opposition more favorable terms for participation in the Government.

- 3 -

TOP SECRET

3. Weekly Summary Excerpt, 19 July 1946, Implications of Soviet Policy Towards Germany; Soviet Demands on Hungary

Implications of Soviet Policy Towards Germany

By rejecting both the US federalization and the French dismemberment proposals Molotov has given a clear indication that the Kremlin has, at least for the time being, decided that the bulwark of Communism in the west is to be Germany and not France. A German administration strongly centralized in Berlin will be much more susceptible than a loose federation to Soviet pressures, particularly in a Germany economically debilitated by such exorbitant reparation payments as the Soviets are currently demanding. Posing thus as the champions of German nationalism and rehabilitation, the Soviets can attempt to discredit the policy of the western powers and to facilitate Communist penetration of their zones.

At the same time Molotov has left the door open for a subsequent change of tactics. By blocking Secretary Byrnes' proposal for the immediate designation of deputies to begin consideration of future Allied policy toward Germany he has left the way clear for a different Soviet approach when the Council of Foreign Ministers next discusses the German question. At that time the Kremlin will be better able to judge the progress of its penetration in the western zone.

The Soviet pronouncement on Germany has caused consternation in the ranks of the French Communists. Having been among the most vigorous proponents of the political separation from Germany of the Ruhr and Rhineland, they have been forced quickly to resort to the familiar Communist stratagem of befogging the issue, explaining the Soviet position as in the Leninist tradition of "protecting the German proletariat by opposing British imperialism." As a result the Communist party in France can hardly fail to suffer some loss of prestige.

- 1 -

3. *(Continued)*

Soviet Demands on Hungary

The Hungarian Government last week acceded to Soviet demands for a number of strong measures against allegedly anti-Soviet and "fascist" organizations and Government officials. The Soviet action was directed against the chief centers of resistance to leftist domination of Hungary: the conservative Smallholders' Party and the Catholic Church. It undoubtedly reflects the Soviet desire to establish the control of the minority Communist Party in anticipation of the peace settlement and the ultimate withdrawal of Soviet troops.

In the free Hungarian elections of last November the Smallholders' Party won a majority of seats in the Assembly. Since then the Hungarian Communists have led a campaign to nullify, or at least to modify, the election results. Following a demand by the Moscow radio for the "crushing of Hungarian reaction," the campaign developed into a powerful drive against the right wing of the Smallholders' Party. Early in March, following open leftist threats of violence, twenty of the more conservative Smallholders' Deputies to the Assembly were expelled from the Party. In return, the leftists promised certain concessions, including larger Smallholders' representation in provincial and local government, but these have not yet been put into effect.

- 2 -

3. *(Continued)*

TOP SECRET

6.

In June the leftists resumed their attacks on the Smallholders with demands for a further purge of "reactionaries." This time the Smallholders and their leader, Premier Nagy, presented considerably stiffer resistance. Nagy indicated in private his determination to refuse further demands, even at the cost of a cabinet crisis and a complete breakdown of coalition government.

On 28 June the Soviet Chairman ACC Hungary, without consulting the US or UK representatives in the ACC, accused the Government of violating the anti-fascist provisions of the armistice agreement and demanded the dismissal of several Government officials, abolition of organizations found to be aiding "fascist" elements, dissolution of Catholic and other youth organizations, and prevention of anti-Soviet propaganda by the Catholic clergy. The demands for anti-Catholic measures are attributable in part to the fact that the Catholic Church in Hungary, and particularly its leader, Cardinal Mindszenty, have recently formed a rallying point for many extreme anti-Soviet forces.

Premier Nagy, now confronted with an international rather than inter-party issue, conceded the majority of the Soviet demands. However, it is not certain that these concessions will either satisfy Hungarian leftists, or be accepted by the Smallholders without considerable defection among Nagy's supporters. The Hungarian Communist Party is apparently being pushed by its own left-wing leaders toward an open break with the Smallholders. Leaders of the Smallholders believe that the country is being "driven into two irreconcilable camps," and fear that a breakdown of coalition government might result in civil war and the retention of Soviet troops in Hungary.

The US representative ACC has protested the presentation of the Soviet demands without consultation of the US representative, and has requested that the Soviet demands be suspended pending three-power agreement in the ACC.

- 3 -

TOP SECRET

4. ORE 1, 23 July 1946, Soviet Foreign and Military Policy

ORE 1

23 July 1946

~~TOP SECRET~~

COPY NO. _____

CENTRAL INTELLIGENCE GROUP

SOVIET FOREIGN AND MILITARY POLICY

SUMMARY

1. The Soviet Government anticipates an inevitable conflict with the capitalist world. It therefore seeks to increase its relative power by building up its own strength and undermining that of its assumed antagonists.

2. At the same time the Soviet Union needs to avoid such a conflict for an indefinite period. It must therefore avoid provoking a strong reaction by a combination of major powers.

3. In any matter deemed essential to its security, Soviet policy will prove adamant. In other matters it will prove grasping and opportunistic, but flexible in proportion to the degree and nature of the resistance encountered.

4. The Soviet Union will insist on exclusive domination of Europe east of the general line Stettin-Trieste.

5. The Soviet Union will endeavor to extend its predominant influence to include all of Germany and Austria.

6. In the remainder of Europe the Soviet Union will seek to prevent the formation of regional blocs from which it is excluded and to influence national policy through the political activities of local Communists.

7. The Soviet Union desires to include Greece, Turkey, and Iran in its security zone through the establishment of "friendly" governments in those countries. Local factors are favorable toward its designs, but the danger of provoking Great Britain and the United States in combination is a deterrent to overt action.

8. The basic Soviet objective in the Far East is to prevent the use of China, Korea, or Japan as bases of attack on the Soviet Far East by gaining in each of those countries an influence at least equal to that of the United States.

9. The basic Soviet military policy is to maintain armed forces capable of assuring its security and supporting its foreign policy against any possible hostile combination. On the completion of planned demobilization these forces will still number 4,500,000 men.

10. For the time being the Soviets will continue to rely primarily on large masses of ground troops. They have been impressed by Anglo-American strategic air power, however, and will seek to develop fighter defense and long range bomber forces.

~~TOP SECRET~~

4. *(Continued)*

TOP SECRET

11. The Soviets will make a maximum effort to develop as quickly as possible such special weapons as guided missiles and the atomic bomb.

12. Further discussion of Soviet foreign policy is contained in Enclosure "A"; of Soviet military policy, in Enclosure "B".

TOP SECRET

4. *(Continued)*

TOP SECRET

ENCLOSURE "A"

SOVIET FOREIGN POLICY

THE BASIS OF SOVIET FOREIGN POLICY

1. Soviet foreign policy is determined, not by the interests or aspirations of the Russian people, but by the prejudices and calculations of the inner directorate of the Communist Party in the Soviet Union. While the shrewdness, tactical cunning, and long-range forethought of this controlling group should not be minimized, its isolation within the Kremlin, ignorance of the outside world, and Marxist dogmatism have significant influence on its approach to problems in foreign relations.

2. The ultimate objective of Soviet policy may be world domination. Such a condition is contemplated as inevitable in Communist doctrine, albeit as a result of the self-destructive tendencies of capitalism, which Communist effort can only accelerate. In view, however, of such actual circumstances as the marked indisposition of democratic nations to adopt the Communist faith and the greatly inferior war potential of the Soviet Union in relation to them, that goal must be regarded by the most sanguine Communist as one remote and largely theoretical. While acknowledging no limit to the eventual power and expansion of the Soviet Union, the Soviet leadership is more practically concerned with the position of the U.S.S.R. in the actual circumstances.

3. For the present and the indefinite future the fundamental thesis of Soviet foreign policy is the related proposition that the peaceful coexistence of Communist and capitalist states is in the long run impossible. Consequently the U.S.S.R. must be considered imperiled so long as it remains within an antagonistic "capitalist encirclement."* This concept, absurd in relation to so vast a country with such wealth of human and material resources and no powerful or aggressive neighbors, is not subject to rational disproof precisely because it is not the result of objective analysis. It is, deeply rooted in a haunting sense of internal and external insecurity inherited from the Russian past, is required by compelling internal necessity as a justification for the burdensome character of the Soviet police state and derives its authority from the doctrine of Marx and Lenin.

4. On the basis of this concept of ultimate inevitable conflict, it is the fundamental policy of the Soviet Union;

   a. To build up the power of the Soviet state; to assure its internal stability through the isolation of its citizens from foreign influences and through the maintenance of strict police controls; to maintain armed forces stronger than those of any potential combination of foreign powers; and to develop as rapidly as possible a powerful and self-sufficient economy.

   b. To seize every opportunity to expand the area of direct or indirect Soviet control in order to provide additional protection for the vital areas of the Soviet Union.

---

* In this context socialism (as distinguished from communism) is considered as antagonistic as capitalism.

TOP SECRET

4. *(Continued)*

TOP SECR

c. To prevent any combination of foreign powers potentially inimical to the Soviet Union by insistence upon Soviet participation, with veto power, in any international section affecting Soviet interests, by discouraging through intimidation the formation of regional blocs exclusive of the U.S.S.R., and by exploiting every opportunity to foment diversionar antagonisms among foreign powers.

d. To undermine the unity and strength of particular foreign states by discrediting their leadership, fomenting domestic discord, promoting domestic agitations conducive to a reduction of their military and economi strength and to the adoption of foreign policies favorable to Soviet purposes, and inciting colonial unrest.

5. Although these general policies are premised upon a conviction of late and inevitable conflict between the U.S.S.R. and the capitalist world, they als assume a postponement of overt conflict for an indefinite period. The doctrine of Marx and Lenin does not forbid, but rather encourages, expedient compromise or collaboration with infidels for the accomplishment of ultimate Communist pur poses. The Soviet Union has followed such a course in the past and has need tc do so still, for time is required both to build up its own strength and to weak and divide its assumed antagonists. In such postponement, time is calculably c the side of the Soviet Union, since natural population growth and projected ecc nomic development should result in a gradual increase in its relative strength. It is manifestly in the Soviet interest to avoid an overt test of strength at least until, by this process, the Soviet Union has become more powerful than ar possible combination of opponents. No date can be set for the fulfillment of that condition. The Soviet Union must therefore seek to avoid a major open con flict for an indefinite period.

6. The basis of Soviet foreign policy is consequently a synthesis betweer anticipation of and preparation for an ultimate inevitable conflict on the one hand and need for the indefinite postponement of such a conflict on the other. In any matter conceived to be essential to the present security of the Soviet Union, including the Soviet veto power in international councils, Soviet policy will prove adamant. In other matters Soviet policy will prove grasping, but opportunistic and flexible in proportion to the degree and nature of the resistance encountered, it being conceived more important to avoid provoking a hostile combination of major powers than to score an immediate, but limited, gain. But in any case in which the Soviet Union is forced to yield on this account, as in Iran, it may be expected to persist in pursuit of the same end by subtler means.

SOVIET POLICY WITH RESPECT TO EASTERN EUROPE

7. It is apparent that the Soviet Union regards effective control of Europe east of the Baltic and Adriatic Seas and of the general line Stettin-Trieste as essential to its present security. Consequently it will tolerate no rival influence in that region and will insist on the maintenance there of "friendly" governments – that is, governments realistically disposed to accept the fact of exclusive Soviet domination. That condition being met, the U.S.S.F does not insist upon a uniform pattern of political and economic organization,

TOP SECR

4. *(Continued)*

TOP SECRET

but adjusts its policy in accordance with the local situation. The immediate Soviet objective is effective control, although the ultimate objective may well be universal sovietization.

8. In some cases no Soviet coercion is required to accomplish the desired end. In Yugoslavia and Albania the Soviet Union finds genuinely sympathetic governments themselves well able to cope with the local opposition. In Czechoslovakia also, although the government is democratic rather than authoritarian in pattern, no interference is required, since the Communists and related parties constitute a majority and the non-Communist leaders are "friendly." Even in Finland the Soviet Union has been able to display moderation, Finnish leaders having become convinced that a "friendly" attitude is essential to the survival of the nation. In these countries the Soviet Union seeks to insure its continued predominance by the creation of strong bonds of economic and military collaboration, but does not have to resort to coercion other than that implicit in the circumstances.

9. In Poland, Rumania, and Bulgaria, however, the Soviet Union encounters stubborn and widespread opposition. The "friendly" governments installed in thos countries are notoriously unrepresentative, but the Soviet Union is nevertheless determined to maintain them, since no truly representative government could be considered reliable from the Soviet point of view. In deference to Western objections, elections may eventually be held and some changes in the composition of these governments may be permitted, but only after violent intimidation, thoroughgoing purges, electoral chicanery, and similar measures have insured the "friendly" character of the resulting regime. Continued political control of the countries in question will be reinforced by measures insuring effective Soviet control of their armed forces and their economies.

10. The elected government of Hungary was both representative and willing to be "friendly," but the Soviet Union has apparently remained unconvinced of its reliability in view of the attitude of the Hungarian people. Accordingly coercion has been applied to render it unrepresentatively subject to Communist control in the same degree and manner as are the governments of Poland, Rumania, and Bulgaria. The end is the same as that of the policy pursued in those countries — the secure establishment of a reliably "friendly" regime, however unrepresentative, coupled with Soviet control of the economic life of the country.

SOVIET POLICY IN AUSTRIA AND GERMANY

11. Soviet policy in Austria is similar to that in Hungary, subject to the limitations of quadripartite occupation. Having accepted an elected Austrian government and unable to reconstruct it at will, the Soviet Union is seeking, by unilateral deportations and sequestrations in its own zone and by demands for similar action in others, to gain, at least, economic domination of the country as a whole and to create, at most, a situation favorable toward a predominant Soviet political influence as well, on the withdrawal of Allied control. The Soviet Union will prevent a final settlement, however, until it is ready to withdraw its troops from Hungary and Rumania as well as Austria.

TOP SECRET

4. *(Continued)*

~~TOP SECRET~~

12. The Soviet Union hitherto has been content to proceed with the consolidation of its position in eastern Germany free of quadripartite interference. Now, rejecting both federalization and the separation of the Ruhr and Rhineland, it appears as the champion of German unification in opposition to the "imperalistic" schemes of the Western powers. A German administration strongly centralized in Berlin would be more susceptible than any other to Soviet pressure, and the most convenient means of extending Soviet influence to the western frontiers of Germany. The initial Soviet objective is presumably such a centralized "anti-Fascist" republic with a coalition government of the eastern European type, but actually under strong Communist influence and bound to the Soviet Union by ties of political and economic dependency.

SOVIET POLICY IN WESTERN EUROPE

13. For a time it appeared that the Communist Party in France might prove able to gain control of that country by democratic political processes and Soviet policy was shaped to support that endeavor. The Communists recent electoral reverses, however, appear to have led the Soviet Union to sacrifice a fading hope of winning France to a livelier prospect of gaining Germany. The French Communists remain a strong political factor nevertheless, and exercise disproportionate influence through their control of organized labor. That influence will be used to shape French policy as may be most suitable for Soviet purposes, and to prepare for an eventual renewal of the attempt to gain control of France by political means. A resort to force is unlikely in view of the danger of provoking a major international conflict.

14. In Italy also the Communist Party is seeking major influence, if not control, by political means, with a resort to force unlikely in present circumstances. The Party and the Soviet Union have played their cards well to divert Italian resentment at the proposed peace terms from themselves toward the Western Powers.

15. The Soviet Union misses no opportunity to raise the Spanish issue as a means of embarrassing and dividing the Western Powers. Any change in Spain might afford it an opportunity for penetration. Even its goading of the Western Powers into expressions of distaste for Franco appear to have afforded it an opportunity to approach him.

16. For the rest, the Soviet Union is concerned to prevent the formation of a Western Bloc, including France and the Low Countries, or a Scandinavian Bloc, in accordance with its general policy. As opportunity offers, it will seek to facilitate the growth of Communist influence in Scandinavia and the Low Countries, but not at the sacrifice of more important interests or at the risk of provoking a strong reaction.

SOVIET POLICY IN THE MIDDLE EAST

17. The Middle East offers a tempting field for Soviet expansion because of its proximity to the Soviet Union and remoteness from other major powers, the weakness and instability of indigenous governments (except Turkey, and the

~~TOP SECR~~

4. *(Continued)*

TOP SECRET

many local antagonisms and minority discontents. It is, moreover, an area of Soviet strategic interest even greater than that of eastern Europe, in view of the general shift of Soviet industry away from the European Frontier, but still within range of air attack from the south, and of the vital importance of Baku oil in the Soviet economy. It is in the Middle East, however, that Soviet interest comes into collision with the established interest of Great Britain and that there is consequently the greatest danger of precipitating a major conflict. Soviet policy in the area must therefore be pursued with due caution and flexibility.

18. Given the opportunity, the Soviet Union might be expected to seek the following objectives:

<u>a</u>. At least the withdrawal of British troops from Greece, and at most the incorporation of that country in the Soviet sphere through the establishment of a "friendly" government.

<u>b</u>. At least the political and military isolation of Turkey and the imposition of a new regime of the Straits more favorable to Soviet interests; at most the incorporation of that country in the Soviet sphere through the establishment there of a "friendly" government.

<u>c</u>. At least implementation of the recent settlement with Iran, which assures the Soviet a continued indirect control in Azerbaijan and an opportunity to develop any oil resources in northern Iran; at most, incorporation of that country in the Soviet sphere through the establishment there of a "friendly" government.

Soviet policy in pursuit of these objectives will be opportunistic, not only in relation to the local situation, but more particularly in relation to the probable reactions of the major powers.

19. Soviet interest in the Arab states is still directed rather toward exploiting them as a means of undermining the British position in the Middle East than as objectives in themselves. Their principal asset, the oil of Iraq and Saudi Arabia, would be economically inaccessible, although its denial to Britain and the United States in the event of war would be of important consequence. But, by fomenting local demands for the withdrawal of British troops, the Soviet Union can hope to deny effective British support to Turkey and Iran. To this end the Soviet Union will exploit anti-British sentiment among the Arabs, and particularly the vexing Palestine issue.

20. The Soviet Union has shown no disposition to intrude into the involved Indian situation, possibly finding it as yet impossible to determine the most advantageous course in that regard. It also shows no present aggressive intentions toward Afghanistan, although the establishment of a "friendly" government there would seem a logical, albeit low priority, objective.

SOVIET POLICY IN THE FAR EAST

21. The basic Soviet objective in China, Korea, and Japan is to prevent their becoming potential bases of attack on the Soviet Far East. This requires

TOP SECRET

4. *(Continued)*

that the U.S.S.R. exert with respect to each an influence at least equal to (and preferably greater than) that of any other power. Since in this region Soviet policy encounters that of the United States, it must be pursued with due circumspection.

22. Although the Soviet Union cannot hope to establish a predominant influence over the whole of China, at least for a long time to come, it could accomplish its basic objective through either the formation of a coalition government, with the Chinese Communist Party* as a major participant, or a division of the country, with the Chinese Communist Party in exclusive control of those areas adjacent to the Soviet Union. The U.S.S.R. should logically prefer the former solution as at once involving less danger of a collision with the United States and greater opportunity for the subsequent expansion of Sovie influence throughout China through political penetration by the Communist Part and the course of its relations with the Chinese Government would seem to confirm that preference. The U.S.S.R., however, would not be willing to sacrific the actual political and military independence of the Chinese Communists unles: assured of their effective participation in the proposed coalition. If, there fore, efforts to establish such a coalition were to fail and unrestricted civi: war were to ensue, the Soviet Union would probably support the Chinese Commun ists in their efforts to consolidate their effective control over Manchuria and North China.

23. In Korea the Soviets have shown that they will consent to the unification of the country only if assured of a "friendly" government. In default of unification on such terms, they are content to consolidate their control in the north and to bide their time, trusting that an eventual American withdrawal will permit them to extend their predominant influence over the whole country.

24. The Soviets have been extremely critical of American administration i Japan, which has afforded them no opportunity to establish the degree of influence they desire. Regardless of the prevailing influence, they probably desir to see Japan politically and militarily impotent. The greater Japan's politic: disorganization, the greater would be their opportunity to establish an equal and eventually predominant influence there.

SOVIET POLICY ELSEWHERE

25. Soviet policy in other areas will follow the general lines set forth in paragraph 3, seeking to undermine the unity and strength of national states to foment colonial unrest, to stir up diversionary antagonisms between states,

---

* Despite a widespread impression to the contrary, the Chinese Communists are genuine Communists, differing from other foreign Communist Parties only in a certain local self-sufficiency derived from territorial control and the possession of an army, in consequence of which they exhibit unusual initiative and independence. In all essentials they are an unusually effective instrument of Soviet foreign policy.

4. *(Continued)*

TOP SECR

and to disrupt any system of international cooperation from which the U.S.S.R. is excluded. Activity along these lines is constant, though often inconspicuous. Its importance to the Soviet Union derives not from any prospect of dire gain, but from its effect in enhancing the relative power of the U.S.S.R. by diminishing that of potential antagonists.

26. Because of their position in world affairs, the United States and Great Britain will be the primary targets of such Soviet activities. In addition to domestic agitations, the effort will be made to distract and weaken th by attacks upon their interests in areas of special concern to them. In Latin America, in particular, Soviet and Communist influence will be exerted to the utmost to destroy the influence of the United States and to create antagonisms disruptive to the Pan American system.

TOP SECT

4. *(Continued)*

TOP SECR

ENCLOSURE "B"

SOVIET MILITARY POLICY

1. Soviet military policy derives from that preoccupation with security which is the basis of Soviet foreign policy. (See Enclosure "A", paragraphs : and 4a.) On the premise that the peaceful coexistence of Communist and capitalist states is in the long run impossible, and that the U.S.S.R. is in constant peril so long as it remains within a "capitalist encirclement," it is th policy of the Soviet Union to maintain armed forces capable of assuring its security and supporting its foreign policy against any possible combination of foreign powers. The result is an army by far the largest in the world (except the Chinese).

2. Even the populous Soviet Union, however, cannot afford an unlimited diversion of manpower from productive civil pursuits, especially in view of manpower requirements for reconstruction and for the new Five Year Plan. Consequently it has had to adopt a demobilization program which is a compromise between the supposed requirements of security and those of the economy. By September the strength of the armed forces will have been reduced from 12,500, to 4,500,000 men."* Further reduction is unlikely.

3. The probable geographical distribution of the total strength indicate will be 1,100,000 in occupied Europe, 650,000 in the Far East, and 2,750,000 i the remainder of the U.S.S.R. The composition will be 3,200,000 (71%) in the ground forces and rear services, 500,000 (11%) in the air forces, 300,000 (7% in the naval forces, and 500,000 (11%) in the MVD (political security forces). The post-war reorganization includes unification of command in a single Minist of the Armed Forces having jurisdiction over all forces except the MVD troops, which remain under the Ministry of Internal Affairs.

4. In addition to its own forces, the Soviet Union is assisting and participating in the reconstitution of the armed forces of its satellites in such manner as to insure its effective control of them. While in this its object i primarily political, such forces supplement its own as locally useful auxilli ies.

5. Soviet experience during the war was limited almost exclusively to th employment of large masses of ground troops spearheaded by mobile tank-artill infantry teams. Air power was employed chiefly for close ground support. Nav operations were insignificant. The Soviets had only limited experience in amphibious operations, almost none in airborne operations, and none with carrie based air operations.

6. It appears that for the time being the Soviet Union will continue to rely primarily on large masses of ground troops, but with emphasis on increase mechanization and further development of the tank-artillery-mobile infantry spearhead. The ground support capabilities of the air forces will be maintai

* As compared with 562,000 in 1933 and 1,000,000 in 1935.

TOP SECT

4. *(Continued)*

At the same time, the Soviets may be expected to give increased attention to the strategic employment of air power, in view of demonstrated Anglo-America capabilities in that regard, and to develop both fighter defense and long range bomber forces.

7. Although there have been indications that the eventual development of a high seas fleet (or fleets) is a Soviet intention, its early accomplish ment is prohibited by inexperience, lack of shipbuilding capacity, and the higher priority of other undertakings. Even were these hindrances overcome, geography handicaps the Soviet Union as a naval power, since naval forces on its several coasts would be incapable of mutual support. It is, however, within the capabilities of the Soviet Union to develop considerable submarin light surface, and short-range amphibious forces.

8. The industrial development, which competes with the armed forces fo manpower, is, of course, intended to enhance the overall Soviet war potentia Beyond that, intensive effort will be devoted to the development of special weapons, with particular reference to guided missiles and the atomic bomb. Some reports suggest that the Soviets may already have an atomic bomb of sor or at least the capability to produce a large atomic explosion. In any case a maximum effort will be made to produce a practical bomb in quantity at the earliest possible date.

TOP SECRET

Soviet Propaganda Increases Attacks on US

During the past two months Soviet propaganda against the United States has increased in volume and intensity, while attacks on Great Britain, the chief Soviet propaganda target during the early part of the year, have diminished. The Soviet press, which last March extolled the tradition of "unvarying political friendship" between the US and USSR, now sees US "atomic diplomacy" and its alleged attempt to impose a "pax Americana" on the world as the principal threats to international peace.

The shift of propaganda emphasis from the UK to the US appears to have several aims. One is to influence US policy by arousing anxiety among US groups who fear the consequences of a firm US attitude toward the USSR at the Paris Peace Conference and in other fields of conflicting interests. Another is to prepare the Soviet people for a possible deterioration of relations with their former US allies. A third objective, which the Soviets appear to feel was not achieved by their attacks on the British, is to split the "Anglo-American bloc." In support of this aim the Soviet press has played up clashes between British and US economic interests in Yemen, the oilfields of the Middle East, and Anglo-American competition for the markets of India and the Far East.

In the current shift of emphasis from the UK to the US, however, the basic aim of post-war Soviet propaganda remains the same: to prevent the formation of any bloc of countries outside the Soviet sphere, and to maintain the unity of the Soviet people behind the Government by emphasizing the menace of "capitalist" powers seeking to "encircle" the USSR.

Soviet Aims in Supporting German Unity

The recent Soviet proposals in support of the unification of Germany must be viewed in the light of developments in the Soviet Zone to appraise their true significance.

Within the Soviet Zone, the USSR dominates almost completely the political and economic life of the people. Political control has been

- 1 -

TOP SECRET

5. *(Continued)*

assured by the Soviet-created SED Party, which was formed by forcibly merging the Socialist and Communist Parties. The effectiveness of Soviet control is evidenced by the recent affirmative vote on the nationalization of property in Saxony, and it appears certain that the SED Party will dominate the coming elections. Although complete nationalization has not been enforced throughout the entire Soviet Zone, private commercial and industrial property in the US sense of the term can be said to be non-existent. It is particularly noteworthy that these developments in the Soviet Zone have taken place in large measure while the Allied Control Authorities have been considering uniform property treatment to be applied throughout Germany.

In view of the need to consolidate the gains already made, it is unlikely that the social revolution in the Soviet Zone will proceed much further during the next year or two. However, the USSR's proposals looking toward the removal of zonal barriers suggest that the Soviets consider that their control over Eastern Germany is now secure and that they are in a position to launch a vigorous campaign to communize the Western Zone as soon as the zonal barriers are removed.

Hungary's Coalition Under Increasing Tension

The Hungarian Government's acquiescence in Soviet demands for a purge of "fascist" organizations and Government officials has produced increasing tension between Hungarian leftists and conservative groups, and a near-revolt within Premier Nagy's Smallholders' Party. Members of the Smallholders' Party in the Assembly have demanded the resignation of the Communist Interior Minister responsible for carrying out the Soviet demands. The Minister subsequently agreed to reinstate Government officials who had been purged, and a final decision on the dissolution of Church organizations has not yet been reached. Nevertheless, Cardinal Mindszenty, a leading anti-Communist, reportedly plans to order the resignation from the Government of influential clerics who have endeavored to avoid an open break with the leftists. Such a step would remove an important moderating force from conservative Government circles and widen the split between leftists and the Church.

- 2 -

5. *(Continued)*

Meanwhile Nagy has had great difficulty in avoiding an open split within his own Smallholders' Party, a large part of which opposes his concessions to leftist and Soviet demands, and insists upon the expulsion of left-wing members as "fellow-travelers." Nagy appears exhausted and despondent and would eagerly give up his official responsibilities were it not for his conviction that he and Mikolaczyk in Poland are the principal barriers to the Communist sweep in Eastern Europe.

Nagy's continuance in office will depend on the Soviets, who, for the present, appear determined to preserve at least the form of coalition government in Hungary. It seems likely, however, that Hungary's condition may soon come to resemble that of Poland, Rumania, and Bulgaria, with an entirely pro-Soviet regime prepared to tolerate only a paralyzed and ineffectual opposition. Political developments in Hungary after the peace treaty is signed will depend largely upon the size of the Soviet force left in the country to guard Soviet lines of communication.

- 3 -

6. **Weekly Summary Excerpt, 16 August 1946, Soviet Proposal for Revision of Straits Convention; Bulgarian Government Prepares for Elections**

Soviet Proposal for Revision of Straits Convention

The Soviet note to Turkey proposing revision of the Montreux Convention is in part similar to last November's US and UK proposals. The Soviet note differs from those of the US and UK in urging restriction of responsibility for the Straits to "Black Sea powers" and joint Soviet-Turkish organization of Straits defense. The Turks appear certain to reject these Soviet proposals, which they regard as aimed at establishing Soviet bases in the Straits. In their rejection they can presumably rely upon US and UK support, and are in fact citing their 1939 treaty with the UK as the basis of their Straits policy.

The Soviet proposals have not surprised the Turks, who had late in July expressed fear of a surprise attack in case Soviet diplomatic methods proved unsuccessful, and had been reported fortifying the Straits (under a British plan) for a last-ditch stand. The Turks recently have conducted their first national election in many years and appear to have maintained national unity despite the vigorous showing of the opposition Democrat Party and the subsequent formation of a new "tough" Cabinet to deal with opposition elements. All Turkish factions, including the Democrats, have united in assailing the Soviet proposals and are expected to manifest their traditional stubbornness in the face of a threat from the North. The Turkish Premier has indicated that he will discuss the "reasonable" elements in the Soviet note but will refuse to consider those items which threaten Turkish sovereignty.

Soviet policy toward Turkey, as expressed in the revision note, aims at virtual control over the Black Sea Straits; the fundamental Soviet objective is the establishment of a "friendly" government in Turkey as well as in the other countries of the Middle East. These aims spring from a combination of strategic and political factors. Soviet security requirements from the Baltic to the Black Sea are at least temporarily fulfilled except for extension of control over Turkey. The Kremlin may, however, regard the Caucasus oil fields and the newly-developed industrial centers east of the Urals as vulnerable from the South. Moscow has long coveted the warm-water ports and rich oil deposits of the Black Sea-Persian Gulf area. The Soviet Union hopes for positions which could threaten the British "life line" and

- 1 -

6. *(Continued)*

British strategic oil fields. Soviet dominance of Turkey would establish the USSR on the threshold of Arab territories which offer a fertile field for political and economic intrigue.

It appears unlikely that the Kremlin will follow up its note to Turkey with a resort to armed force, although such a possibility cannot be ignored in view of Zhukov's presence in Odessa and rumors of military and naval activity in that area. There seems to be no evidence to support rumors of a possible Soviet-supported offensive from Bulgaria, since Red Army strength in that country is estimated to have been cut from 155,000 in May to 80,000 in July. The Soviet Union already is extended in Eastern Europe and may decide to forego further expansion until its control over the satellite states can be more thoroughly consolidated. An attack now not only would destroy the UN (which still can be useful to the Kremlin), but would reveal too clearly the true responsibility for such destruction. The USSR probably has once again presented extreme demands in the hope of attaining a somewhat more limited objective.

- 2 -

71

6. *(Continued)*

Bulgarian Government Prepares for Elections

The Communist-controlled Government of Bulgaria is rapidly completing its preparations for the national referendum on 8 September and the election of a constituent Grand National Assembly on 27 October. Since no important political group in the Government or opposition favors retention of the Monarchy, the referendum will result in the choice of a republic and will represent a true expression of the national will.

Despite assurances to the US that the elections will be free, it is clear that actually they will reflect the wishes of only a small minority of the population. The opposition parties will be unable to offer any serious threat to the Government. Prominent opposition leaders are now scheduled for trial as "traitors" and "Fascists," while lesser leaders and the opposition rank and file have been subjected to increasing terrorism. The recent compulsory labor law, authorizing the mobilization of all persons not engaged in "useful social activity," is directed against all opponents of the regime, particularly the well-to-do, who are characterized as "agents of the foreign powers." The purge of the Bulgarian Army, formerly regarded as the chief obstacle to complete Communist domination of the country, has culminated in extended "sick leave" for War

- 4 -

6. *(Continued)*

Minister Veltchev and the dismissal of about half of the officer corps. Many of the latter are scheduled for political trials. The officer corps thus has been reduced to a "hard core" of Government and Communist supporters and the regime has been relieved of the danger of a military coup.

Despite its effective suppression of the opposition, the Government during the coming weeks will probably make a major effort to dissuade its opponents from boycotting the elections. The Government apparently feels that opposition participation in the voting will make it difficult for the US or UK to question the legality of the results. The opposition's only remaining weapon thus appears to be its ability to prevent such a fraudulent appearance of national unity.

- 5 -

TOP SECRET

SOVIET MILITARY POLICY IN EASTERN EUROPE

The Soviet Union is engaged in a systematic effort to consolidate its military influence in Eastern Europe before the European peace treaties are signed. This effort is an integral part of the larger policy of assuring the permanent political, economic and military orientation of that area toward the USSR. In particular it is designed to prevent any Eastern European country from becoming an accomplice to a future attack on the USSR, or providing an avenue of approach for a hostile army. Soviet authorities hope to achieve this end by organizing the armed forces of the Eastern European nations so that they can be swiftly integrated at any time into overall Soviet strategic plans -- defensive or offensive.

The eight nations in this Soviet sphere of influence (Yugoslavia, Albania, Bulgaria, Rumania, Hungary, Czechoslovakia, Poland and Finland) have a combined population of approximately 86,500,000. Their armies at present total slightly more than 1,000,000 men, a very large proportion of whom have had experience in wartime campaigns or partisan operations. However, with the exception of Czechoslovakia, which has extensive armament industries, they suffer from lack of modern equipment and have from the Soviet view-point serious shortcomings in organization, leadership and political reliability.

In their efforts to improve this situation the Soviets have distinguished between the nations which supported the United Nations and those which fought with the Axis. To the former (Yugoslavia, Albania, Czechoslovakia and Poland) the USSR is giving extensive military aid in the form of equipment, training, improvement of communications and general supervision of organization. In the latter (Bulgaria, Rumania, Hungary and Finland), Soviet policy is chiefly concerned with eliminating potential anti-Soviet elements and developing a well-organized cadre of thoroughly indoctrinated Communist personnel.

The present Yugoslav Army numbers about 300,000 men. It probably will not be expanded in the near future, but a steady improvement in organization and equipment is expected to continue under Soviet auspices. Last June the USSR concluded a military pact to furnish the Yugoslavs with undisclosed quantities of arms and equipment. Since

-1-

TOP SECRET

7. *(Continued)*

early this year a Soviet military mission, with representatives in all parts of Yugoslavia and in all tactical units, has assisted in the training and reorganization of the Yugoslav Army. Meanwhile several hundred Yugoslav officers and specialists are being trained in the USSR. Road, rail and bridge construction for military purposes is being carried out in strategic areas by Soviet engineers or under their direction.

The Albanian Army, estimated at 100,000 men, is closely affiliated with that of Yugoslavia. An estimated 1,500 Soviet troops are supervising the construction of roads and coastal fortifications in Albania, and key Albanian Army officers are studying in the USSR.

The Czechoslovak Army of about 140,000 men apparently is being enlarged. After the conclusion of hostilities in Europe Soviet authorities undertook to equip some nine Czechoslovak divisions. In the military accord recently reached in Moscow they agreed to furnish on long-term credits additional equipment, possibly for as many as ten additional divisions. These agreements will serve the double purpose of standardizing Czechoslovak military equipment on Soviet lines and allowing part of Czechoslovakia's large armaments industry to be diverted to civilian production. Czechoslovak officers are receiving advanced training in Soviet military schools, and the Czechoslovak internal security force is controlled by Soviet officers. On the other hand, the trend toward Communist domination of the Czechoslovak Army has been slow.

The Polish Army is presently estimated at 215,000 and Polish authorities have indicated their intention of enlarging it with Soviet aid to 500,000 in the near future. Although the Army is headed nominally by a Polish Marshal, all important decisions are made by a Soviet General. Many key posts are held by Soviet officers, and the supply and transportation system is in Soviet hands. Virtually all weapons and equipment are Soviet-supplied, and new equipment is to be furnished by the USSR on a long-term credit basis.

The Bulgarian Army, now approximately 65,000, will probably be reduced under the peace terms to a maximum of 55,000. Relatively little material has been given the Bulgarian Army, although a small

- ii -

7. *(Continued)*

TOP SECRET

number of Bulgarian officers are being trained in the USSR. In anticipation of the withdrawal of Soviet troops 90 days after the Bulgarian peace treaty becomes effective, the Soviet authorities have instigated a drastic purge of all Bulgarian officers not in sympathy with Communist ideology. The primary Soviet aim appears to be the establishment of a Communist cadre which will bolster the pro-Soviet Bulgarian regime after the withdrawal of Soviet forces.

The Rumanian Army of 140,000 men will probably be reduced by the peace treaty to 120,000. Soviet military aid has consisted chiefly in the training and equipping of two complete divisions which constitute the bulk of the Army's tactical striking forces. In the remainder of the Army there has been less progress than in Bulgaria toward the establishment of a Communist-indoctrinated cadre.

While Hungarian authorities have offered strong resistance to Soviet penetration and control, a Communist has been installed as Chief of the General Staff and other important posts are held by Communist sympathizers. The draft peace treaty allows Hungary an army of 65,000, but her military strength will be determined by the degree of future Communist pressure, which aims to keep the Army small and the leftist-dominated internal police force large.

Soviet policy has been to keep the Finnish Army small and impotent. Repeated purges under Soviet pressure have curtailed its efficiency, and under the draft peace treaty the Army is to be limited to 41,500 men. However, Communist attempts to penetrate the Army have met with determined Finnish resistance.

Despite varying degrees of unrest and resistance to Soviet domination among the Eastern European countries, it is expected that when the present draft peace treaties are concluded, the entire western border of the USSR will be effectively flanked by a Soviet-controlled military bloc.

- iii -

TOP SECRET

8. Special Study No. 3, 24 August 1946, Current Soviet Intentions

TOP SECRET

CURRENT SOVIET INTENTIONS

24 August 1946

I. During the past two weeks there has been a series of developments which suggest that some consideration should be given to the possibility of near-term Soviet military action.

A. Soviet propaganda against the US and UK has reached the highest pitch of violence since Stalin's February speech and follows a line which might be interpreted as preparing the Russian people for Soviet military action.

1. It states that "reactionary monopolistic cliques" and "military adventurers" are now directing US policy toward "world domination" through "atomic" diplomacy. The US has abandoned the Rooseveltian policy which gave hope of collaboration with the USSR and the other "freedom-loving people" of the world.

2. It attacks the Anglo-American "bloc" as "dividing the field" throughout the world and gives a detailed account of Anglo-American "imperialistic" actions, including British troop movements to Basra and Palestine and US military operations in China and attempts to secure outlying air bases.

3. Embassy Moscow interprets the attacks outlined in 1 above as notice to the Communist Party in the USSR that there is no longer any hope of friendly relations between the USSR and the Western Powers.

4. Tito, in his speech of 21 August on the international situation, raised the issue to a world-wide ideological plane when he stated categorically that there is no question today of two fronts: Western and Eastern. The question today is one of true democracy versus reactionaries throughout the world. In Soviet terminology this obviously means communism versus non-communism.

- 1 -

TOP SECRET

8. *(Continued)*

B. The Soviets have re-opened the Straits issue with a note to Turkey demanding exclusive control by the Black Sea Powers and joint Soviet-Turkish defense of the Straits.

C. Yugoslavia, after sending the US a note protesting the violation of her sovereignty by daily flights over her territory of US transport and military aircraft, has shot down two US aircraft, and defended such action as justified.

1. US Military Attache Belgrade in commenting upon these incidents stated that while he had not previously believed that Russia and Yugoslavia were ready to fight, he regarded these incidents as indicating that they were willing to risk a "prompt start."

D. Molotov in his speech on the Italian treaty indicated clearly that the Soviets intended to exclude the Western Powers from Danubian trade and stated that if Italy respected the most-favored-nation principle she would lose her freedom to the monopolistic capitalism of the Western Powers.

II. As opposed to the above indications which suggest the possibility of aggressive Soviet intentions, it may be noted that:

A. We have as yet no information of any change in the Soviet demobilization program. In fact, the latest indications are that it has been slightly accelerated.

B. We have as yet no indications of any unusual troop concentrations, troop movements, or supply build-ups which would normally precede offensive military action.

C. We have had no indications of any warning to Soviet shipping throughout the world.

D. There appears to be no reason, from the purely economic point of view, to alter our previous estimate that because of the ravages of war, the Soviets have vital need for a long period of peace before embarking upon a major war.

- 2 -

8. *(Continued)*

TOP SECRET

E. There are no indications that the Soviets have an operational atom bomb.

III. In spite of the factors outlined immediately above, the Soviets might conceivably undertake a concerted offensive through Europe and Northern Asia on one or a combination of the following assumptions:

A. That a foreign war was necessary to maintain the present leadership in power, in the face of serious internal discontent.

1. There have been indications of discontent in the Ukraine and in the Murmansk and other areas. There have been a number of purges. The Soviet press, in appeals to the people for improvement, has revealed internal difficulties in many fields. The recent inauguration of a wide program of Marxist reindoctrination suggests a breakdown in discipline. However, we have no real basis for evaluating the extent and seriousness of such discontent or its potentialities for effective resistance to the present regime.

2. Although the people of the USSR are tired of war and industrial production is down, the Party is probably still sufficiently powerful to secure, through propaganda, acceptance of further war.

B. That in view of the strength of the Soviet forces in Northern Asia and in Europe (as opposed to Allied forces) a sudden offensive might secure these areas without much difficulty, and place the USSR in an impregnable economic and political position.

C. That the US was war-weary and would not hold out against a *fait accompli* in B above.

D. That a combination of militaristic marshals and ideologists might establish ascendancy over Stalin and the Politburo and decide upon a war of conquest.

1. Evidence to date, however, indicates that the Party dominates the military.

- 3 -

TOP SECRET

8. *(Continued)*

IV. In weighing the various elements in this complex situation the most plausible conclusion would appear to be that, until there is some specific evidence that the Soviets are making the necessary military preparations and dispositions for offensive operations, the recent disturbing developments can be interpreted as constituting no more than an intensive war of nerves. The purpose may be to test US determination to support its objectives at the peace conference and to sustain its commitments in European affairs. It may also be designed equally for internal consumption: to hold together a cracking economic and ideological structure by building up an atmosphere of international crisis. However, with the Soviet diplomatic offensive showing signs of bogging down, the possibility of direct Soviet military action or irresponsible action by Soviet satellites can not be disregarded.

- 4 -

TOP SECRET

Soviet Internal Problems

Available information on current conditions inside the USSR, though meager and inconclusive, leaves little doubt that there is discontent among the people and confusion in the state economic machinery. The USSR faces its tremendous task of post-war reconstruction handicapped by disturbing internal stresses.

The few foreign observers who have had a chance to talk with Soviet citizens report frequent complaints over the hardships of every-day life and disappointment that the long-promised fruits of victory have not been forthcoming. While the general attitude seems to be one of characteristic Russian fatalism rather than resentment, there have been occasional reports of overt resistance to state authority, especially in the Ukraine. The situation is no doubt aggravated by returning mili-tary personnel, who bring back stories of relative luxury in other coun-tries and who find civilian living standards below those enjoyed by the Red Army. The Kremlin's sensitivity to these developments is probably increased by its awareness of the substantial number of cases of deser-tion and collaboration with the enemy during the war. Another cause for alarm, according to Party organs, is the recurrence of private property conceptions among the rural population, especially in areas previously under German occupation.

Disaffection in higher circles also is evident. Persistent reports of shake-ups in the Army high command tend to substantiate rumors that the Marshals are not satisfied with their peace-time status, while "social-ist justice" seems to be overtaking a number of prominent Party, govern-mental and literary figures. Explanations are varied, but it is likely that the militant domestic and foreign policies now being laid down necessitate weeding out those suspected of pro-Western leanings. The dismissal of Litvinov and the transfer of Zhukov, both closely identified with Soviet-American collaboration, are particularly significant.

Economic difficulties, which in most cases are officially attributed to inefficient local management and corrupt minor officials, are probably due also in part to war-worn factories and sagging worker morale. There is evidence that personal profiteering and the falsification of production figures, which are now receiving so much attention in the Soviet press,

- 1 -

TOP SECRET

~~TOP SECRET~~

were relatively common practices throughout the war and often were carried on with the knowledge of the highest authorities. The sudden and violent campaign against them may result from the Kremlin's desire to disown what has become a widely-known scandal.

While the evidence outlined above indicates that Soviet internal difficulties are serious, there is no reason to suppose that they are critical. The Kremlin may be counted on to take all possible steps to correct them, and one such step is to point to the threat of foreign aggression. The resulting atmosphere of crisis can serve to stimulate effort and distract attention from the hardships of everyday life.

Should Soviet internal conditions, in the eyes of the Kremlin, reach an alarming state of deterioration and the Soviet diplomatic offensive fail in its current objectives, Soviet leaders might conceivably seek a "short and easy" war in order to strengthen internal cohesion, regain domestic control, and exploit their present military superiority in critical areas.

- 2 -

~~TOP SECRET~~

10. Weekly Summary Excerpt, 20 September 1946, Effect of Demobilization on Soviet Military Potential; Effects of Soviet Propaganda

Effect of Demobilization on Soviet Military Potential

The third stage of the Soviet demobilization program was approximately completed on 1 September. Seven classes (1922-1928, inclusive) remain under arms. Current reports support previous estimates that no further substantial demobilization is presently intended.

The strength of the Soviet armed forces is now estimated at 4,500,000 men, well below the wartime peak of 12,500,000, but well above the pre-war norm of 562,000 in 1933. Even with the release of 8,000,000 men to civilian tasks of reconstruction and development, the Soviet armed forces remain most formidable in both absolute and relative terms.

There are now 1,600,000 Soviet troops in Europe outside the USSR, and even where forces in Europe have been reduced, heavy equipment has been left behind so that it can be manned on short notice. The Soviets also have shown a marked interest in equipping and training satellite armies along Soviet lines. The Yugoslav Army, for example, plans to reach a strength of 1,000,000 men by 1948, and for all practical purposes should be included in considering the Soviet potential.

The massive Red Army of the past, designed primarily to defend the vast Eastern European front, was deficient in transport, equipment and organization and proved unwieldy in many operations. Almost all of its offensive successes were achieved through the skillful use of mobile striking forces. As a result of these lessons, mobility is the prime concern of present Soviet military planning. In achieving it, the release of masses of "peasant" infantry troops and the retention in service of smaller numbers of highly-trained and well-equipped specialists is a logical step.

The Soviet demobilization to date has resulted in no reduction of Soviet military strength in critical areas. Discontinuance of demobilization at this point indicates an intention to retain overwhelming superiority in immediately available military power for an indefinite period.

- 1 -

10. *(Continued)*

TOP SECRET

Effects of Soviet Propaganda

The continuing Soviet propaganda barrage against the "reaction-ary" and "war-fomenting" activities of the US and UK appears designed, first, to keep alive in the US and the UK active opposition to any firm policy toward the USSR; and second, to spur the Soviet masses to greater effort by raising the specter of imminent patriotic war.

In its first objective, the undertaking has met with considerable success. Many moderate and liberal groups have been so divided over the issue of policy toward the USSR that their potentialities for opposing Soviet tactics have been at least neutralized.

The effects of the campaign within the USSR are more difficult to appraise. While there is little doubt that it has seriously alarmed the Soviet people, scattered reports indicate that it has depressed rather than inspired them. The average citizen of the USSR seems to be anxious and distressed over the prospect of another war, and bewildered as to why the US and Britain should "want" it. The Soviet masses are suffering from severe emotional and physical exhaustion, and in many cases are bitterly disappointed that the long-promised increases in free-dom and comfort have not followed the defeat of the Axis. Ideological purges and alarmist propaganda have not checked this condition, and the majority of the Soviet people appear eager for any straw of reassurance as to Anglo-American intentions.

- 2 -

TOP SECRET

Significance of Personnel Changes in Soviet Hierarchy

The announcement that V. S. Abakumov has been appointed Minister of State Security and that G. M. Malenkov has been relieved of his duties as member of the Presidium of the Supreme Soviet and designated Deputy Chairman of the Council of Ministers, may have some connection with reports that Stalin is in poor health and is absent from Moscow. If Stalin really is ill, any present jockeying for position among members of the Kremlin's ruling clique may foreshadow a serious rivalry among possible successors.

Little is known of Abakumov's background except that he was reportedly chief of the Soviet Army's counter-intelligence service during the war, and has since been Deputy Commissar of the NKVD (now MVD) in charge of counter-espionage. The first hint of his elevation to ministerial rank was the prominent position given him at Stalin's dinner for the Czechoslovak Premier on 25 July. His role as chief of the Ministry of State Security (MGB) is one of great responsibility, since that organization has assumed most of the secret police functions formerly carried out by the NKVD.

Abakumov's appointment confirms rumors which have been circulating for some time to the effect that the former MGB chief, V. N. Merkulov, had been dismissed from his post. Some of these rumors have suggested that Merkulov had fallen into disfavor, but it is equally possible that he has been shifted to some other responsible work. He was formerly considered the right-hand man of Marshal Beria, ex-chief of NKVD, who is now believed to be supervising the Soviet atomic project. Merkulov may have joined Beria in this undertaking.

Malenkov's reassignment is of particular interest in view of his apparent preeminent position in the Kremlin's inner circle. He has often been mentioned as the candidate most favored to succeed Stalin. He has for some time held the positions of Secretary and Director of Personnel of the Central Executive Committee of the Communist Party—positions comparable to those which Stalin held at Lenin's death. While there is no evidence that Malenkov has been removed from these key positions, a report from a usually reliable source indicates that he has fallen into

- 1 -

TOP SECRET

disfavor. Such a possibility takes on added weight from the fact that in the current clean-up in intellectual and agricultural circles, Zhdanov, another contender for supreme power, appears to have been selected to serve as Party "hatchet man."

Communist Setback in Hungary

Premier Nagy's majority Smallholders Party appears to have won its latest behind-the-scenes struggle for political power with the leftist parties and to have averted temporarily any further Soviet domination of Hungary.

Since the formation of the present coalition Government, Nagy, despite his Party's 60% majority, has compromised both with the right wing in his Party, which resents Communist participation in the Government, and with the Communists. The latter have relied on the presence of the Soviets to extend their influence in the Government far beyond that justified by their popular vote (16% of the total) in the last elections. Although Nagy's middle-of-the-road policy has resulted in numerous political crises, Hungary has been far more successful than other satellite states in maintaining a degree of independence from Soviet control. The Soviets have deeply penetrated Hungary's economy through the formation of joint Soviet-Hungarian corporations, but the country still enjoys substantial freedom of press, religion and political activity.

The latest crisis grew out of Nagy's determination to capitalize on popular discontent with Soviet failure to support Hungary at Paris. Accordingly he increased his resistance to Soviet influence and encouraged political and economic orientation to the West. It was expected that the Communists would retaliate with demands for sweeping concessions from the Smallholders, including expulsion from the Party and the Assembly of extreme rightist Smallholders, and for sweeping electoral "reforms." However, the reluctance of the USSR to intervene in behalf of the Communists and of the leftist Social Democrats to support the extreme Communist position forced the Communists to modify their demands to a point where they can be acceptable to the Smallholders.

- 2 -

12. ORE 3/1, 31 October 1946, Soviet Capabilities for the Development and Production of Certain Types of Weapons and Equipment

ORE 3/1

31 October 1946

~~TOP SECRET~~

Copy No._____

CENTRAL INTELLIGENCE GROUP

SOVIET CAPABILITIES FOR THE DEVELOPMENT AND PRODUCTION
OF CERTAIN TYPES OF WEAPONS AND EQUIPMENT

1. Herein is presented an estimate of Soviet capabilities in the development and production, during the next ten years, of certain weapons and equipment, as follows:

The atomic bomb	Fighters
Guided missiles	Radar
Heavy bombers	Submarines

2. Any report of this nature is at best educated guesswork. An estimate of capabilities ten years hence obviously cannot be based on evidence, but only on a projection from known facts in the light of past experience and reasonable conjecture. The estimates herein are derived from the current estimate of existing Soviet scientific and industrial capabilities, taking into account the past performance of Soviet and of Soviet-controlled German scientists and technicians, our own past experience, and estimates of our own capabilities for future development and production.

3. In view of the Soviet Union's relatively low industrial potential, of the evident necessity to devote much of her effort to restoring and developing her transportation system and heavy industry in general, and of her limited technological advancement, particularly with respect to precision instruments and electronic controls, it seems reasonable to assume that during the next ten years she could not carry out advanced development and quantity production simultaneously in all of the fields under consideration. The selection of those fields in which a maximum effort was to be made would be governed by political or politico-military considerations. The common assumption, supported by many indications, is that every other Soviet program has been subordinated to the development of an atomic bomb. It is not clear that the Soviet authorities have yet made a firm determination of other priorities. In any case, it must be understood that the estimates which follow assume a maximum effort in each case, that such an effort is not possible in every case, and that in some cases actual development will fall short of the maximum capability indicated, in accordance with the priorities assigned.

4. *The atomic bomb.* Our real information relating to this subject is meager. It is probable that the capability of the U.S.S.R. to develop weapons based on atomic energy will be limited to the possible development of an atomic bomb to the stage of production at some time between 1950 and 1953. On this assumption, a quantity of such bombs could be produced and stockpiled by 1956.

5. *Guided Missiles.*

   a. *Ground to ground.* The U.S.S.R. is not believed to be capable of carrying out advanced development and quantity production of radically new weapons of this type within the next ten years. However, by making full use of German facilities under Soviet control, the U.S.S.R. is capable of attaining by 1950 quantity production of V-1 and V-2 missiles with increased ranges and some improvement in accuracy. The possibility that the German A-9, A-10, and associated missiles may be developed to an effective range of 3000 miles within the next ten years is considered remote.*

  b. *Surface to air.* The U.S.S.R. is considered capable of putting into production by 1950 anti-aircraft missiles of the German Wasserfall or Smetterling type.

  c. *Air to surface.* The U.S.S.R. is considered capable of developing to the production stage by 1950 a missile of similar type to the German HS-293, possibly equipped with a proximity or influence fuse.** Fighter or bomber borne missiles with rocket assisted impact power can be expected in quantity within the next ten years.

  6. *Heavy bombers.* The U.S.S.R. is capable of developing and producing by 1948 a bomber with the approximate characteristics of the B-29, and of achieving a production rate of 150 per month by 1950. By 1951 the Soviets will be capable of maintaining 2000 operational aircraft of such type supported by a stored reserve of equal strength. The development of new types of destructive agents may reduce the importance of bomb carrying capacity and make range and speed the primary factors in design.

  7. *Fighter aircraft.* Within the next five years the U.S.S.R. is capable of developing and producing an effective defense force of jet interceptors of subsonic speed. Fighter aircraft will be almost entirely jet propelled, but it is considered improbable that supersonic speeds will be developed in this period.

  8. *Radar.* Within ten years the Soviets will have the construction and operational capabilities in the radar field which existed in the United States in 1945. They will exploit the use of radar in establishing integrated systems of warning networks.

  9. *Submarines.* It is believed that the U.S.S.R. will concentrate on building the German type XXI boat, since in feasibility of both construction and further development this type offers the prospect of most immediate returns. Using German facilities, the U.S.S.R. should be capable of constructing up to 300 of these craft by 1950. Thereafter production would be virtually unlimited except by priorities. The U.S.S.R. is capable of developing by 1956 a guided missile launching device for use on these submarines.

---

  * AC/AS-2 holds that it is "entirely possible that quantities of 3000-mile rocket propelled missiles . . . will be available to the Russians in 1955."

  ** AC/AS-2 would emphasize the view that by 1950 the U.S.S.R. will also have stockpiled "quantities of missiles similar to the German 'Bomben Torpedo,' equipped with a proximity or influence fuse, which will have lethal capabilities against sea-borne forces."

13. Weekly Summary Excerpt, 8 November 1946, Communist Pre-Electoral Tactics in Rumania

Communist Pre-Electoral Tactics in Rumania

The Communist electoral pattern, so successfully delineated in Yugoslavia and Bulgaria, will be repeated with only minor variations on 17 November when the Rumanian people vote in their first post-war election. The Groza Government, although faced with an opposition conservatively estimated at 75 per cent of the electorate, is determined to win an 85 per cent victory. It has accordingly conducted a campaign of violence and terrorism that will make it impossible for the Opposition to register its full strength at the polls. The Rumanian election, therefore, will probably reflect the will of the people even less truthfully than did the elections in Bulgaria and Yugoslavia, where opposition to Communism was neither as well organized nor as determined.

The Government's extreme measures against the Opposition indicate the Communist Party's estimate of what was necessary to insure a vote that would justify complete Communization of the country. Under the guise of the Communist-sponsored and administered electoral law, large numbers of potential Opposition voters have been unable to register, many do not yet know whether they are registered or not and those protesting non-registration must present 16 separate documents, many of which are unobtainable. Communist control of printers' unions, the radio, newsprint

- 2 -

13. *(Continued)*

TOP SECRET

distribution, and censorship has successfully prevented the Opposition from publicizing its campaign. The Government has attempted to discredit Opposition leaders by accusing them of subversive activity and subjecting their homes to frequent search. Many are in jail without formal charge. Violent physical attacks on Opposition leaders are an almost daily occurrence. Communist strong-arm squads, with the tacit approval of the police, have successfully disrupted the majority of the Opposition's political meetings.

The Communists have further strengthened their position by the now familiar tactics of dividing the Opposition parties and of currying or forcing the support of minority groups. Both historical parties (National Peasants and Liberals) have dissident groups represented in the Groza Government. The Jewish Groups, fearful of the growing anti-Semitism in Rumania, have promised their 200,000 votes to the Government Bloc in return for substantial concessions. The Communists, in their desperate search for support, have even allowed several former fascist Iron Guard leaders to retain prominent Government positions. For the first time in Rumania's history, the Army, now "revitalized," will vote (with obvious results, despite reliable reports that the individual Rumanian soldier has not accepted Communist ideology).

Election day will probably be quiet. Opposition leaders admit their impotence to combat a reign of terror which on that day will be backed by the Army, the secret police, the militia and an estimated 10,000 armed Communist reservists specially called up for the occasion.

- 3 -

TOP SECRET

TOP SECRET

COMMUNIST MANEUVERS IN HUNGARY

Summary: The Hungarian Communist Party and the Soviets are making a persistent effort to split the Smallholders' Party in order to strengthen their control over Hungary prior to the withdrawal of Soviet troops and the signing of a peace treaty. There is disagreement within the majority Smallholders' Party as to concessions which it must make to the Communists to avoid Soviet retaliation. If Premier Nagy can resolve these differences within his Party, he may be obliged to acquiesce only to a mutual assistance treaty with the USSR.

Renewed efforts by the Soviets and the Hungarian Communists to dominate Hungary prior to the withdrawal of Soviet troops have precipitated another serious crisis for Premier Nagy's coalition Government. The Soviets, despite their effective control of the country's major industries through joint Soviet-Hungarian monopolies, recognize that Communist strength is not sufficient to insure a Government "friendly" to the USSR. The Communist Party is therefore making a persistent effort to split the majority Smallholders' Party, which controls 60% of the National Assembly and is therefore an effective brake on Communist encroachment.

Although all parties, including the Communists, agree on the need to maintain a coalition Government, the Communists are working to increase the number of parties in the coalition in order to improve their relative position and increase their influence. They have therefore encouraged the formation of the new Freedom Party, which is composed of rightist elements purged from the Smallholders' Party. The Communists have also made numerous demands upon the Smallholders primarily aimed at causing dissension between the right and left wings of the Party. These demands include: (1) expulsion of additional right wing members; (2) postponement of local county and municipal elections; (3) changes in the electoral law which would disenfranchise many "reactionary" Smallholder supporters; (4) curtailment of the political activity of the Catholic Church, and particularly its control of the educational system; and (5) abandonment of the Smallholders' plan to establish "Grange" organizations which would be independent of the Communist-dominated Trades Union Council. In addition to these political maneuvers, evidence

- i -

TOP SECRET

exists that the Communists and the Soviets are deliberately obstructing the country's economic rehabilitation in order to capitalize on the resulting unrest.

The Communist plan to divide and rule has partially succeeded. President Tildy and Premier Nagy, both Smallholder leaders, reportedly disagree as to what concessions they must make to the Communists to avoid Soviet retaliation. Tildy apparently believes that the Soviets will insist on full compliance with Communist demands as the price for preservation of the Smallholders' majority position in the Government. Nagy, on the other hand, believes that further submission to Communist pressure would be as detrimental to the Smallholders' Party as any possible Soviet retaliation. Nagy also believes that the Communists may be bluffing, since (1) they would probably not risk a fair test of strength at the polls; (2) they are as anxious as the Smallholders to maintain the coalition Government; and (3) there are indications that the leftist National Peasants and Social Democrats may themselves revolt against Communist domination of the Leftist Bloc.

The future of the Smallholders' Party appears to depend largely on Nagy's ability to maintain a united front within the Party to resist the Communists' demands and on the present Government's ability to survive a winter of inevitable economic hardship. In the last analysis, however, the Kremlin's attitude will be the deciding factor. Although the Soviets will not relax their efforts to strengthen the Communist Party in Hungary before signing a peace treaty or withdrawing their troops, there are indications that they may be unwilling to take extreme measures if the Smallholders' Party refuses to meet the Communists' demands. They may then be forced to settle temporarily for a mutual assistance pact with the present regime in the hope that it would cooperate sufficiently to protect immediate Soviet military and economic interests.

- ii -

15. Weekly Summary Excerpt, 20 December 1946, The Soviet Outlook in Iran; Soviets Reverse Their Tactics in Austria

The Soviet Outlook in Iran

Within a week following their entrance into Azerbaijan on 9 December, Central Government troops had virtually completed their conquest of the province. The Tabriz Government had collapsed, and national troops had occupied key points on the Azerbaijan-Soviet frontier. Furthermore, Qazi Mohammed (the rebel who had established a Kurdish "Republic" in Western Azerbaijan) and other Kurdish leaders had submitted to the Central Government and declared their loyalty to Qavam.

The Soviets are confronted not only with the Azerbaijan debacle but also with the greatly reduced effectiveness of the Tudeh Party (their chief Iranian tool) and the increased strength of all anti-Soviet elements. Accordingly, the USSR may now be expected to abandon direct action in Iran in favor of intensified infiltration and clandestine activity. The Soviets doubtless will also use the projected oil concession as an important means of penetration.

The USSR is likewise in a position to exert considerable economic pressure on Iran through the dependence of the Northern provinces upon the Soviet economy and the existence of large British concessions in the South. It is to be expected that Qavam will attempt to maintain friendly relations with the USSR and, if necessary, will support economic concessions which do not infringe upon Iranian sovereignty.

The Soviets, however, have suffered a serious set-back in Iran and to some extent have lost face in the Near East. Iranian independence appears to have been re-established unless the USSR is prepared to resort again to overt action and to risk UN intervention.

Soviets Reverse Their Tactics in Austria

The USSR's tactics in Austria have undergone drastic revision. After indicating that its forces would be withdrawn from the country by the third quarter of 1947, the Soviet Command concurred in two important US-supported resolutions which it had hitherto strongly opposed in the Allied Council. It agreed (1) to place both indigenous and imported food resources at the disposal of the Government for distribution throughout Austria; and (2) to settle the denazification issue along lines acceptable

- 1 -

15. *(Continued)*

to the US. This latter concession is of special significance because the Soviets previously indicated that they were dissatisfied with the results achieved by the Austrian Government and that they would remain in occupation until they considered the program completed. They will now be unable to use the denazification issue in order to block consideration of an Austrian treaty.

The Austrian Government is planning, in January, to enter into bilateral negotiations with the USSR on the very difficult subject of German assets in eastern Austria, provided the US, UK and the three parties to the Austrian coalition Government concur. The Soviets have consistently refused to discuss the assets question in the Allied Commission and are in disagreement with the Austrians as to what constitutes legitimate German assets under the Potsdam agreement. The Austrians, however, are now proposing bilateral negotiations, in the belief that the Soviets are now in a frame of mind to make substantial concessions for the sake of a quick settlement.

The USSR now apparently is on the defensive in Austria and desires to secure its economic position by reaching an agreement with the Figl Government before discussion of Austrian peace terms this coming spring. Moreover, it has weakened its bargaining position by having given advance notice of its intention to withdraw by the third quarter of 1947.

- 2 -

16. Weekly Summary Excerpt, 3 January 1947, The Polish Election; Possible Reopening of the Straits Question

The Polish Election

Preparations by Poland's Communist-dominated Government for the country's first post-war election on 19 January differ little from those which swept Leftist blocs to victory in Bulgaria and Rumania. The Polish Government has flagrantly disregarded the Potsdam agreement regarding free elections and has intensified its ruthless suppression of all potential opponents. The election results, therefore, are predetermined. Vice-Premier Mikolajczyk's Peasant Party, which is backed by approximately 70% of the population, will probably be allowed no more than 25% of the vote.

Mikolajczyk has waged a determined but futile struggle against the now-familiar Communist electoral tactics. These include mass arrests of Opposition leaders and candidates, restriction of public speech and assembly, intimidation by secret police and armed forces, and manipulation of the electoral machinery. The Government has exploited the existence of an active underground as a pretext for its oppressive control of the country by secret police. It has also handicapped Mikolajczyk by linking him with the underground.

The certain defeat of the anti-Government forces on 19 January, coupled with scarcities of food and clothing, and exorbitant taxes, will produce an explosive situation which will challenge the law-enforcing powers of the new Government. Outright civil war, however, is unlikely. The underground, although well-organized, is not capable of effective action against the Polish Army and Security Police, both of which are firmly under Communist control and backed by Soviet occupation forces. More important, however, is Soviet unwillingness to allow widespread disorders at this time. Although armed conflict would give the Soviets an opportunity to annihilate the Opposition, it would also endanger Soviet communication lines to Germany and would give the lie to Soviet claims that the present Government has the support of the masses.

16. *(Continued)*

TOP SECRET

The Polish Government has flatly denied US and UK charges of failure to fulfil the Yalta and Potsdam agreements. Communist leaders, furthermore, probably consider the loss of Western economic assistance and good will less important than the immediate risk of endangering their control of the Government by adherence to Western principles of democracy. The Communists' post-election plans, however, may include an offer of surface concessions to the Opposition in an attempt to avoid widespread internal disturbances and to obtain some economic aid from the US and UK. Mikolajczyk presumably would reject such concessions because their basic purpose would be to weaken the Opposition's ability to resist further Communist control of the country.

Possible Reopening of the Straits Question

The principle signatories of the Montreux Agreement on the Straits (1936) have recognized that some of its terms are out of date. No conference for revision has yet been called, however, because of Soviet insistence that the Black Sea states alone should control and defend the waterways; and Turkey, with US and British support, has refused to enter into discussions on this basis.

The recent conciliatory trend of Soviet foreign policy, particularly the USSR's non-intervention in the Azerbaijan affair and its failure to veto the Security Council's decision to investigate alleged border violations in Greece, have apparently suggested to the Turks the possibility of reaching an acceptable agreement at this time on the Straits issue. The Secretary General of the Turkish Ministry for Foreign Affairs recently told US Ambassador Wilson that he was considering the possibility of proposing a "regional agreement" for the war-time defense of the Straits to be undertaken by the US, USSR, UK and Turkey.

Such a proposal would provide a further test of the Soviet desire for genuine international collaboration. An abandonment of the Soviet insistence that the riparian states alone control the Straits would open the way for a general settlement of this issue. If, on the other hand, the USSR maintains its previous position, the Turks will have lost nothing by exploring the possibilities; the current deadlock will merely continue.

- 3 -

TOP SECRET

17. Weekly Summary Excerpt, 10 January 1947, Prospects in Indochina

Prospects in Indochina

Since French Overseas Minister Marius Moutet's visit to Indochina, French policy in regard to Vietnam has been committed to the "restoration of order" before negotiating with Vietnam. To restore order by force in northern Indochina would require military operations by large French forces for a period which the French estimate at six months to a year, but which would probably extend to two years or more. The French have attributed the fanatical Vietnam opposition they have so far encountered to the presence of many Japanese in the Vietnam ranks. In reality, few Japanese have been found either dead or alive in the fighting in Vietnam and French military difficulties may more accurately be ascribed to the tenacity and courage of the Vietnam defense as well as to the French lack of infantry and experience in handling armored units. (Approximately 2,500 former German prisoners of war are now unwillingly serving in French forces in Indochina.)

French authorities in Indochina now believe that extremist elements within the Viet Minh League (the political party of Vietnam) were responsible for the attack on Hanoi on 19 December which they feel destroyed all chances of compromise by its premeditated violence. Ho Chi Minh is believed to have come under the control of these extremists, though perhaps not wholeheartedly, and he is still held responsible by the French for Vietnam actions in the present hostilities. French colonial administrators in Indochina have expressed the naive belief that the people of Annam and Tonkin resent the "terrorism" of the Viet Minh League and would choose a more moderate and pro-French government if allowed to make a choice.

When order is restored, the French hope to establish a government in Vietnam which will permit French control of Indochinese foreign

- 5 -

17. *(Continued)*

relations and which would consent to a separate state in Cochin-China. Such a government would be powerless to enforce its authority in Northern Indochina in the face of extremist resistance and popular contempt for its puppet status. The continued instability of Northern Indochina under such circumstances would spread to Southern Indochina and would threaten French control in Laos and Cambodia.

Leaders of Free Laos and Free Cambodian groups in conjunction with Vietnam representatives in Bangkok have issued a memorandum calling for UN intervention in the present situation in Indochina. The Vietnam radio has appealed for the support of Free Laos and Free Cambodian movements, and there are indications that these broadcasts have received a favorable response. Important Free Laos leaders have recently left Bangkok for the border territories and may take advantage of French involvement in Vietnam to oust the pro-French administration in Laos. Such an expansion of hostilities together with successful Vietnam resistance to the French would surely encourage extremist leaders in Burma, Malaya, and the Netherlands East Indies to stiffen their opposition to Western colonial powers.

- 6 -

18. Weekly Summary Excerpt, 17 January 1947, Communist-Instigated Purge in Hungary

Communist-Instigated Purge in Hungary

The Hungarian Communist Party, in an attempt to extend its control of the country before the withdrawal of Soviet troops, has renewed its attack on the Smallholders' Party by arresting many of its leaders on charges of plotting to overthrow the Government. Neither the extent of the arrests, nor the truth of the Communist charges, nor even the degree of Soviet complicity can yet be definitely ascertained from the welter of conflicting rumors and counter-charges circulating in Budapest. This much is certain: the Communist-dominated Ministry of Interior and the political section of the Ministry of Defense are arresting all persons suspected of anti-Government activity, the majority of whom are rightist Smallholders who were active in the anti-German resistance movement. The Communists have accused them of belonging to an alleged subversive organization (The Hungarian Unity Movement), of plotting the overthrow of the Government, and of planning to return Admiral Horthy to power. There is little doubt that the Hungarian Unity Movement exists, but its members probably do not desire the return of Horthy or the overthrow of the present Government. More likely the Movement comprises a group engaged in long-range planning to prevent a possible Communist coup after withdrawal of Communist troops.

Premier Nagy's position is admittedly difficult. Although the Communists, as a means of achieving their political aims, have undoubtedly magnified the plot far beyond its actual importance, they have collected enough evidence implicating important Smallholder leaders to prevent Nagy from taking steps to quash the investigation and to make it difficult for him even to deny Communist charges that his Smallholders' Party is implicated with the accused. There is no evidence of direct Soviet complicity in initiating the arrests, but knowledge that the Communists have Soviet backing will also soften Nagy's resistance to Communist machinations.

- 6 -

18. *(Continued)*

Regardless of the outcome of the trials of the accused, the Communists have already attained certain primary objectives. Premier Nagy's control over the present coalition Government and his ability to resist further Communist demands (see Weekly Summary of 13 December 1946) have now been weakened. The Communist practice of representing, on the basis of fragmentary evidence, normal political differences of opinion as subversive tendencies will also frighten all potential anti-Communist groups into a policy of extreme caution. This latest Communist maneuver may, therefore, cause the downfall of the present Government. Neither the Rightists nor the Leftists, however, have the strength to rule alone, and the Communists probably do not yet consider their police control of the country strong enough to risk another election in the immediate future. Some sort of uneasy coalition will probably continue, with Communist participation and influence considerably increased.

19. Weekly Summary Excerpt, 28 February 1947, The Greek Crisis

The Greek Crisis

The fate of Greece may be decided within the next few months, if not weeks. Militarily, a demoralized, under-equipped army is losing ground to guerrilla forces backed by the Soviets and their satellites. Politically, a compromise government of Rightists, through inefficiency and political narrowness, is losing what little popular confidence it once possessed. Economically, a country unreconstructed from the devastations of war, is losing its fight against starvation, inflation, and internal and external debt.

Since the liberation, two factors have saved Greece from relentless attempts by the USSR, through its satellites and local Communist elements, to dominate the country: (1) The presence of British troops; and (2) loans, including UNRRA aid, from the US and the UK. Now, in the face of an all-out Soviet effort to capitalize on the current crisis, British troops (except for a small token force) are being withdrawn, and the US and the UK are finding it increasingly difficult to obtain money to bolster Greece's economy. Because of the UK's own financial straits, economic aid from that source may cease completely.

Alone, Greece cannot save itself. Militarily, the country needs aid in the form of equipment and training. Politically, Greece's diehard politicians need to be convinced of the necessity of a housecleaning, and the prostrate Center, which traditionally includes the majority of the population, requires bolstering. Economically, it needs gifts or loans of commodities, food, foreign exchange, and gold to check inflation. Of these needs, the economic are the most vital.

If Greece withstands Soviet pressure during the next few months, and can contain the guerrillas, the Center, which is ineffectual at the moment, may become sufficiently aroused by the increasing atrocities

- 5 -

TOP SECRET

of the Leftists and the continued bungling of the Rightists to reorganize itself and to take control of the Government, excluding both the Right and the Left. Such a move might be led by the moderate Sophoulis or the old republican Plastiras.

Without immediate economic aid, however, there would appear to be imminent danger that the Soviet-dominated Left will seize control of the country, which would result in the loss of Greece as a democracy of the Western type.

- 6 -

TOP SECRET

20. Weekly Summary Excerpt, 7 March 1947, Significant Personnel Changes in Soviet Government; Anti-Communist Trends in Czechoslovakia

EASTERN EUROPE

Significant Personnel Changes in Soviet Government

Recent changes in Soviet political personnel indicate a desire on the part of the Kremlin to clarify and strengthen administrative responsibility among Politburo members and to facilitate the solution of the pressing problems created by growing nationalism and agricultural breakdowns in the Ukraine.

The appointment of Lazar M. Kaganovich as First Secretary of the Ukrainian Communist Party surpasses in importance that of General Bulganin as Stalin's successor in the post of Minister of the Armed Forces (a change believed to have been an administrative fact for some time). Kaganovich, one of the most energetic and forceful of Soviet administrators, is expected to campaign vigorously against Ukrainian nationalism -- a matter of grave concern to the Kremlin -- and for improved agricultural production in the Ukraine. Andrei Zhdanov's resignation as Chairman of the Council of the Union is expected to leave him free for his more important duties as a member of the Politburo, the Orgburo, and the Central Committee Secretariat of the Communist Party.

Anti-Communist Trend in Czechoslovakia

The Communist Party in Czechoslovakia is gradually losing ground despite its overwhelming victory in the May 1946 elections. Barring direct Soviet interference, Czechoslovakia, because of the intense nationalism and individualism of its people, will probably emerge as a modified Socialist state friendly to but not patterned on the USSR. Particularly in the economic field, Czechoslovakia's orientation toward the West should gradually increase.

Following the country's liberation, the Czechoslovak Communist Party attained substantial popular support by avoiding an extremist position. Subsequent Communist efforts to by-pass Parliament, to widen the scope of the nationalization program, and to control the police, the army, and the press have, however, alienated many former supporters. Successful resistance by the Moderates to Communist efforts to dominate the country is demonstrated by (1) the refusal of Parliament to delegate

- 4 -

20. *(Continued)*

authority to the Cabinet; (2) the reduction of Communist control over the Secret Police; (3) the removal of Communists from many local governing bodies; and (4) the maintenance of cordial relations with the West.

The Social Democrats, upon whom the Communist Party depends for the small leftist majority in Parliament, have voted recently against the Communists on all major issues and have won decisive victories in several labor union elections. A recent split within the Czech Communist Party over the extension of State ownership of industry beyond the limits of the two-year plan indicates basic Czechoslovak opposition to Soviet regimentation.

The integration of Czechoslovakia's economy with that of the USSR and its satellites has also become increasingly difficult. The nation's two-year plan presupposed substantial imports of raw materials from the East, which, in actuality, are not being received in sufficient quantity and quality. Czechoslovakia must, therefore, make up this deficit by imports from the West which, in turn, can only be paid for by exports to free exchange countries. Barter trade with the East must, therefore, be reduced. Because the Communists bear the major responsibility for the execution of the two-year plan, they may be forced to divert trade from the East to the West rather than to jeopardize the entire nationalization program.

The Soviet attitude will, in the final analysis, determine the success of the Moderates in preventing Communist domination of Czechoslovakia. The Kremlin is aware that strong-arm methods would meet with stubborn resistance and substantially reduce the value of its most important Eastern European source of supply. The USSR, therefore, probably will avoid direct interference in Czechoslovakia's internal affairs as long as Czechoslovakia has a "friendly" Government and continues to supply the USSR with vitally needed industrial products.

- 5 -

21. Weekly Summary Excerpt, 14 March 1947, Prospects for Vietnam Settlement

FAR EAST

Prospects for Vietnam Settlement

The difficulties of solving the Vietnam problem by force have resulted in several French attempts to establish a puppet regime in order to circumvent the necessity of negotiating with the present Vietnam government of Ho Chi Minh. These attempts began shortly after the commencement of hostilities in December when the French insisted that no conversations were possible with Ho Chi Minh or members of his government. Contact was made in Hong Kong with the former Emperor of Annam and Japanese puppet, Bao Dai, as a figure around whom a new government, amenable to French influence, might be created. At the same time an alternative plan was conceived, which provided for the enthronement of Bao Dai's young son, Bao Long, with a French-dominated Regency exercising actual power. Both possibilities are still being pursued by the French, and Bao Dai's former Prime Minister is now in Saigon negotiating with the French.

In recent weeks, the protracted resistance by Vietnam forces and the unwavering native support of the Viet Minh Communist-front party have forced the French to recognize that Ho Chi Minh continues to be popular and powerful. The increasingly critical French military manpower situation and the unfavorable international reaction to French policy will force the French to seek an early end to hostilities. Consequently, French authorities are maintaining contact with Ho Chi Minh through his representative in Saigon and also through Socialist Deputy Eugene Thomas, who recently arrived in Indochina ostensibly to inspect local communications.

Any imperial regime under Bao Dai or his son would lack popular support and meet with opposition from the Chinese. The latter prefer a government which would include Annamite Nationalists as a counterbalance to the Communists. Such an arrangement however, could not prove satisfactory from the French standpoint because the Nationalists are potentially as inimical to French objectives in Vietnam as the Communists.

Any Vietnam government which does not include Ho Chi Minh or his more moderate followers will, like the present Provisional Government of Cochin China, be limited in scope of authority by the perimeters of French military control and will be open to widespread

- 5 -

21. *(Continued)*

popular opposition and sabotage. France's experience with its regime in Cochin China should discourage a similar attempt in Vietnam and may lead to the eventual formation of a government which would include Ho and moderate Viet Minh elements, several pro-French Annamite Catholics, and perhaps Bao Dai as a private citizen. The French presumably would find it possible to negotiate with such a government and might be willing to concede to it a greater measure of independence.

- 6 -

GENERAL

Reaction to President Truman's Speech

Reaction to President Truman's speech on Greece and Turkey has, in general, been as expected: conservative and middle of the road elements have welcomed the statement of a "new US foreign policy," and Communists have attacked US "imperialism" and "dollar diplomacy."

Some commentaries, while generally applauding the speech, contain a significant note of warning. In England, France, Switzerland, and the Scandinavian countries, for instance, there is a feeling of uneasiness over the future of US-Soviet relations. Some observers fear that these countries, caught between two powerful blocs, must review their own foreign policy and perhaps eventually choose between them. On the other hand, in France, at least, the speech appears to have had a tangible effect in encouraging the center elements to take a stronger stand against the Communists.

The Soviet Government has so far made no official statement. PRAVDA and IZVESTIA have attacked the speech, but with no more than their customary virulence. The USSR probably has not yet decided just what tactics to pursue in attempting to counter the effects of the President's statements. The Soviet satellite countries have followed the line laid down by the Moscow press. There is clear evidence, however, that opposition elements within these countries have been greatly encouraged by the President's forthright words. Indeed, they have possibly exaggerated the significance of the speech to themselves, thinking that it implies aid for all anti-Communists in the satellites.

The speech was gratefully received in Turkey and Greece. The Turks feel that credits will help them to rehabilitate their economy and expand their industry, thus increasing the national security. The immediate reactions in Greece have been a new tendency toward political unity, a general upswing in morale (except among Communists and the Communist armed bands, where morale has deteriorated), a new stability in the currency, and a general improvement in business confidence.

- 1 -

22. *(Continued)*

NEAR EAST-AFRICA

Turkey Weighs its Defense Requirements

Turkey's stubborn refusal to accede to Soviet demands for a dominant position in the control and defense of the Turkish Straits (and for the annexation by the USSR of strategic areas in northwest Turkey) has been a major obstacle to the extension of Soviet influence in the Near and Middle East.

- 5 -

22. *(Continued)*

TOP SECRET

The ability of the Turks to withstand continued Soviet pressure will not depend upon the strength of Turkey's armed forces, because, irrespective of the volume of foreign aid, Turkey can never create an army strong enough to defend the country against an all-out Soviet attack. In the final analysis, Turkey's ability to resist Soviet demands will depend upon the maintenance of a healthy economy as an antidote to Communist infiltration, and upon the support of its political integrity by the Western Powers or by an effective United Nations.

The Turkish Government appears to take cognizance of these fundamental factors in Turkey's position in suggesting that, before any new credits are allocated, a study be made of the relative importance of military and of economic expenditures to the national defense. The Turks see clearly that modernization of transportation and communications, and increased agricultural and coal production, would strengthen both the military potential and the economic stability of the country and, at the same time, improve the prospects for the repayment of the loans and the maintenance of the Government's financial integrity.

- 6 -

TOP SECRET

Soviet Strategy in the CFM

The Soviet Delegation at the recent CFM meeting obviously was intent upon delaying or preventing the solution of most of the vital issues under discussion.

A major consideration underlying the Soviet strategy was probably the dilemma in which the Kremlin was placed by the announcement of the Truman Doctrine. The USSR could not immediately adopt a more conciliatory policy without offering confirmation that the President's program was effective in checking aggression. The USSR likewise could not harden its policy without encouraging increased support in the US for the Truman Doctrine. Furthermore, the encouragement which the President's statement gave to European anti-Communists may have increased the Kremlin's concern over its eastern European position and its determination to block an Austrian Treaty in order to maintain Soviet forces in that country and communication troops in Hungary and Rumania.

The USSR, therefore, may have considered it even more imperative: (1) to prolong the unsettled conditions in Europe conducive to Communism; and (2) to encourage the US to expend its patience and energy in a vain quest for agreement until forced by its internal economic and political conditions to curtail its foreign commitments and to leave Europe to the USSR by default.

The Kremlin now appears concerned over the reaction which its obstructionism has produced among the Western Powers. Through diplomacy and propaganda, the USSR seems to be seeking to reassure the West by insisting that the achievements of the Conference should not be minimized and that "time and patience" eventually will solve most of the remaining problems. For the present, therefore, the Kremlin appears to be pursuing a dual policy of preventing a European settlement while trying to keep alive western hopes that such a settlement eventually may be possible.

- 2 -

TOP SECRET

24. Weekly Summary Excerpt, 9 May 1947, Indications of Changed Emphasis in Communist Strategy

EASTERN EUROPE

Indications of Changed Emphasis in Communist Strategy

The Kremlin's concern over the present position of the Communist program abroad -- particularly in central and western Europe -- is reflected in a recent PRAVDA article commemorating the 30th anniversary of Lenin's "April Theses." The article appears designed as a guide to foreign Communist Parties in combatting the US program of aid to countries threatened by Communism and the competition of non-Communist liberals for working-class support -- considerations which the Kremlin apparently believes are sapping the revolutionary strength of the proletariat.

The PRAVDA article compares the current world situation with conditions in Russia in April 1917, when the Revolution threatened to terminate in a parliamentary democracy. Lenin, recognizing the numerical weakness of the Bolsheviks, urged that open rupture with the Provisional Government be avoided until the Bolsheviks achieved sufficient power to overthrow the Government and replace it with the Bolshevik-dominated Soviets (local councils). Instead Lenin urged (1) a revitalization and consolidation of the Party; (2) an intensified propaganda campaign against the Provisional Government and those leftist elements which showed a tendency toward compromise; and (3) increased efforts to gain control of the Soviets through legitimate and conspiratorial means. (Until that time, the Soviets were loosely-organized leftist groups with mass support but without centralized leadership.)

The current applicability of this strategy to central Europe -- where the Communists are delicately balanced between success and failure -- is obvious. In accordance with Lenin's program and experience during the Russian Revolution, the Kremlin apparently proposes for countries such as France and Italy: (1) intensive agitation against their present governments and against non-Communist liberals; and (2) the development of highly-disciplined Communist cores which, at the proper moment, could assume control. Such a program is well-adapted to the current situation in France where, relieved of governmental responsibility, the Communists are in a position to threaten (by propaganda, subversion, and trade-union agitation) the stability of the present Government. Where Communism is less powerful, the Kremlin

- 3 -

24. *(Continued)*

desires to concentrate on gaining control of trade unions and other liberal organizations. Current Soviet propaganda evidently envisages the World Federation of Trade Unions as a primary vehicle of Soviet ideological expansion.

The Politburo apparently has decided that the time has come for an all-out offensive, aimed at capturing the leadership of the working class, neutralizing the influence of non-Communist liberals, and discrediting "capitalist attraction and deception of the masses."

- 4 -

25. Weekly Summary Excerpt, 20 June 1947, Apparent Soviet Plans in Eastern Europe; Further Communist Moves in Hungary

EASTERN EUROPE

Apparent Soviet Plans in Eastern Europe

The USSR apparently has accelerated its program for the cultural, economic, and military coordination of its satellites. Although the Truman Doctrine may have stepped up the USSR's timetable, events of the past few weeks are all essential components of the basic plan which the USSR had probably intended to consummate before the withdrawal of its occupation troops.

As part of this accelerated program, however, the USSR may have modified what is believed to have been the first phase of its plan for Eastern Europe. The plan was thought to have envisaged the formation of a South Slav or Balkan Federation, including Yugoslavia, Bulgaria, Albania, and probably Greek Macedonia. The next step would then have been a Danubian Federation, comprising Hungary, Rumania, and possibly Czechoslovakia. It now appears that the USSR may have abandoned this concept in favor of a less formal system of control through Communist Party channels and a network of interlocking cultural, economic, and military agreements and alliances. Poland, Czechoslovakia, and Yugoslavia are already linked to each other and the USSR by such an arrangement. The recent Rumanian-Yugoslav accord and the apparently imminent Rumanian-Bulgarian agreement will enlarge the circle. With Hungary now more effectively under Soviet control, that country may also be expected to become an integral part of the network.

To the USSR such a network of alliances would have several advantages over a formal federation. A South Slav Federation would be separated from the USSR by non-Slav Hungary and Rumania. Inclusion of the latter countries on such a basis would create a larger coordinated area which would be of obvious economic advantage to the participants and to the USSR. As long as the USSR considers membership in the UN profitable, it will avoid any formal federation in Eastern Europe that would bar UN membership to the participating states. Moreover, as a formal federation would intensify strong nationalist opposition, the USSR probably prefers a less formal arrangement during the present transitional stage preceding outright incorporation of these countries into the USSR.

The recent discussions in Belgrade among Balkan representatives, therefore, were probably merely another step toward implementation of

- 2 -

113

25. *(Continued)*

the master plan for the Eastern European satellites. The talks appear to have been held: (1) to draft a Yugoslav-Rumanian accord; (2) to resolve Yugoslav-Bulgarian politico-military problems; and (3) possibly to formulate more detailed plans for intensified military activity in support of the Greek guerrillas. The presence in Belgrade of such a large number of Eastern European leaders may also have been welcomed as an opportunity to conduct a war of nerves directed at Greece and to exploit for propaganda purposes the theme of Communist and Slav solidarity under the aegis of the USSR.

Further Communist Moves in Hungary

Since its assumption of power in Hungary, the Communist Party has moved swiftly and forcefully to weaken opposition by the Smallholder Party and to ensure political and economic domination of the country. The appearance of normal constitutionality has been maintained in order to preclude interference from the UK and the US or action by the UN, and the semblance of a balance of power among the political parties in the coalition government has been preserved.

Prior to the coup the Communists tried unsuccessfully to nationalize the four leading Hungarian banks. On 1 June, however, the Council of Ministers, by decree, placed thirteen principal banks under state control and assigned to each a ministerial commissioner to control its activities and to preserve its capital, thereby ensuring complete Communist domination of 75-80% of Hungarian industry. The extension to 30 Septembe 1947 of emergency powers by the National Assembly permits the Cabinet Council to continue to govern by decree; the present Communist-controlled Cabinet will thus be unopposed in its administration of Hungarian affairs. Initial steps have also been taken to avoid a repetition of the Communist defeat in the free elections of November 1945. In preparation for the control of future elections, Party members have been sent to study electoral methods employed in Poland, Bulgaria, and Rumania, and a new electoral law is being drafted which will further exclude opposition elements from the polls.

26. Daily Summary Excerpt, 30 June 1947, USSR: Soviet Plans for Exploiting US Aid Program

~~CONFIDENTIAL~~
38
~~TOP SECRET~~

3 0 JUN 1947

419

EUROPE

4. **USSR:** Soviet plans for exploiting US aid program--Commanding General US Forces Austria has learned from a Soviet Major, formerly a trusted Communist Party member, that certain Communists among the Soviet Forces in Austria recently have been directed by the Party Central Committee in Moscow to make a study of "US aid, its effects, and how it can be made to serve Soviet aims." The Moscow directive reportedly suggest that the US aid program should be encouraged for the purposes of "exploiting and/or eliminating vital materials in America" and of creating inflation in the US. The achievement of either objective would, according to the

- 1 -

~~TOP SECRET~~

~~CONFIDENTIAL~~

Document No. _077_
NO CHANGE in Class. ☐
☐ DECLASSIFIED
Class. CHANGED TO: TS S
DDA Memo, 4 Apr '77
Auth: DDA REG. 77/1763
Date: 3/4/78 By: 004

115

26. *(Continued)*

directive, "be in line with the necessity to destroy our greatest enemy -- the US economy and its capabilities."

(CIG Comment: In view of the initial enthusiasm with which the Marshall proposals have been greeted throughout Europe, the USSR may well conclude that implementation of the proposals is inevitable and that open opposition would be futile. The Kremlin may therefore seek a substantial share of US assistance for the Soviet satellites, and perhaps even for the USSR itself; and it may encourage increased US assistance in the hope of depleting US resources and inflating the US economy.)

SOVIET OPPOSITION TO THE RECOVERY PROGRAM

Soviet opposition to a European reconstruction program will be
demonstrated at the Paris Conference of 12 July by the absence of delegates from the USSR and its Satellites, including Czechoslovakia. Less
direct indications of Soviet opposition will be seen in the future in
Communist interference within the participant countries and in vigorous
propaganda emanating from Moscow. British support of the program, on
the other hand, will continue to be strong. French support, now that the
Soviet position is fully clear, will probably continue strong despite the
expected domestic Communist opposition.

The basis for British interest in a successful implementation of
the US proposals is fully apparent. The UK will benefit immediately by
the provisions of the program and ultimately by general European recovery
More particularly, in the face of a new economic crisis, the proposals provide an escape for the UK from having to choose between increased domestic austerity and the application for another US loan. Both choices are
politically unpalatable, if not impossible. The UK has therefore seized
upon the proposals and has been the driving force in constructive action
to implement them. The clear-cut Soviet refusal to join in the program
has solidified British support through its effect in uniting the Labor Party
on foreign policy, particularly vis-a-vis the USSR.

French interest in the success of a European recovery program
is as strong as British, but French ability to participate hinged upon the
strength with which Foreign Minister Bidault resisted pressure from the
USSR and from French Communists. In order to side with the UK against
the USSR Bidault had to abandon the postwar French policy of preventing
an East-West division of Europe. In holding to his courageous decision
to support the recovery program despite Soviet opposition, Bidault was
considerably strengthened by the efforts of Bevin to put the French in a
position of apparent leadership at the Big Three meeting. Bidault also
strengthened his own hand in future dealings with the French Communists
by offering a last minute "compromise," which did not actually compromise on fundamentals. This move, in anticipation of final Soviet refusal,
was designed to disarm the French Communists and to align French public
opinion behind the present government.

- 9 -

27. *(Continued)*

Soviet opposition to joint action on the basis of the Marshall proposals was based upon more than the familiar concept that Communism flourishes upon economic distress. On this occasion the USSR was caught in a real dilemma. If the USSR chose to participate in the recovery program, it would have been obliged to sacrifice the exclusive economic controls established in Eastern Europe since the war and to permit a western reorientation of Satellite economies into the broader European economy envisaged by the program. Such a course, which would jeopardize Soviet hegemony in Eastern Europe, was absolutely unacceptable. On the other hand, by refusing to participate the USSR would violate a cardinal principle of Soviet policy: to permit no combination of powers without Soviet participation with power of veto. The ultimate decision to follow this latter course, despite its potential dangers to Soviet interests, was probably made in the confident expectation that France would not dare to enter the program after Soviet refusal. This decision to gamble upon a French withdrawal gained further support from Soviet conviction that the US will suffer an economic collapse before the recovery program can become effective, and that such collapse can be hastened by Soviet non-participation.

The strength of the Soviet opposition to the European reconstruction program can best be measured by the last-minute refusals by the Satellite nations to participate. Until the final word was received from those countries, there was every evidence of their strong desire to participate. Such evidence of overpowering Soviet opposition gives warning that the USSR will utilize every opportunity to defeat the ends of the recovery program.

In the immediate future the USSR can only resort to a propaganda onslaught upon the program, because more overt action (such as a wave of Communist-led strikes in France) might weaken the Soviet position in Western Europe still further. Two premises will probably be guiding concepts in the Soviet propaganda campaign: (1) that the European states, because of their rivalries and conflicting interests, are incapable of developing an effective program; therefore, the projected program will only disappoint the exuberant hopes of the participants and thus promote further antagonism among them; and (2) that the US within a year will undergo an economic collapse that will make impossible the fulfillment

- 10 -

27. *(Continued)*

of its proposals and may finally lead to the collapse of capitalism generally. Soviet propaganda will thus: (1) seek to increase suspicion and division among the participating states; (2) capitalize upon every snag and failure in the development of the program; (3) continue to cast suspicion upon US motives; and (4) predict the collapse of the US economy before the program can be fully effective.

In view of the certainty of vigorous Soviet counteraction, both Bevin and Bidault have shown anxiety regarding any delay in the effective implementation of the prospective program. Bevin is particularly apprehensive lest the USSR should succeed in persuading the participant European states that it is vain to hope that timely US aid will actually be forthcoming. He has predicted that, if effective US support is deferred until the late fall or winter, Europe, including France, will be "lost."

- 11 -

27. *(Continued)*

EFFECTS OF NON-PARTICIPATION ON THE SATELLITES

Non-participation by the Eastern European countries in the forth-coming Paris Conference on the Marshall proposals will seriously complicate the discussions and will create numerous problems for the Communist-dominated governments.

Poland, Hungary, Yugoslavia, and Rumania are in desperate need of western economic aid to reconstruct their war-ravaged economies. The economies of Czechoslovakia and Finland, while less dependent on western aid, are so inextricably tied with those of participating nations that the USSR's decision has presented them with the gravest problems. The Marshall proposal, therefore, has dramatically highlighted the basic conflict in these countries between national self-interest and subservience to the Kremlin. Non-participation will inevitably increase popular resentment and magnify the difficulties already facing the Communists in maintaining their police control over these countries.

Participation in the plan by the nations of Eastern Europe, however, could have benefited the entire European economy only if the USSR had also agreed to cooperate and to relax its economic demands upon the Satellites--particularly for Polish coal, Rumanian and Hungarian oil and food, and Yugoslav raw materials. Given continued Soviet obstructionism, therefore, western aid to the Satellites would materially increase their economic potential without producing corresponding benefits to Western Europe.

The political nature of the Soviet decision is underlined by the inescapable conclusion that the USSR had more to gain economically from participation by its Satellites than Western Europe. Increased Polish coal production, without which full recovery and greater industrialization of the Polish economy is impossible, is dependent upon the import of western machinery. Moreover, Poland's decision will seriously impair its chances to obtain a World Bank loan of $100,000,000. The USSR, therefore, appears willing to lose an opportunity to make Poland economically strong in order to deprive Western Europe of increased quantities of Polish coal. The USSR would have similarly benefited by Rumania's participation in the plan. Increased production of Rumanian oil and food resulting from the import of western machinery, agricultural equipment, seeds, etc., is essential if Rumania is to recover economic stability; and the USSR probably would have demanded the greater share of any such increases in the form of reparations.

- 12 -

27. *(Continued)*

TOP SECRET

One of the major problems facing the conferees at Paris will be the extent to which the countries of Western Europe can count upon the continued fulfillment by the Satellites of existing trade agreements. Czechoslovakia's trade with the West is far greater than with the USSR and its Satellites. Approximately 7,000,000 tons of Polish coal is committed to participating nations during the next year. Yugoslavia, Hungary, and Bulgaria also have fairly extensive trade relations with many of the western nations. A logical extension of the USSR's decision--now that the lines are so definitely drawn--might well be gradually to sever all economic ties between Eastern and Western Europe. Such a move would be a tremendous short-range detriment to the economy of Eastern Europe, and at the same time it would be a serious threat to the success of the Marshall proposals. Moreover, it would free the US to make a substantially larger contribution in return for economic stability in only half of Europe.

- 13 -

TOP SECRET

28. Daily Summary Excerpt, 18 July 1947, USSR: Soviet Reaction to Marshall Proposals

38
~~CONFIDENTIAL~~
~~TOP SECRET~~

18 JUL 1947

434

EUROPE

3. **USSR:** <u>Soviet reaction to Marshall proposals</u>--US Ambassador Steinhardt in Prague has been informed by a reliable source that the Czechoslovak delegation to Moscow was severely reprimanded by Stalin personally. Communist Prime Minister Gottwald reported that he had never seen the Soviet leader so angry. Stalin categorically told the delegation that Czechoslovakia must withdraw "immediately" from the Paris conference and that failure to do so would constitute a "hostile act" toward the USSR and a

Document No. _015_

NO CHANGE in Class. ☐

☐ DECLASSIFIED

Class. CHANGED TO: TS   S

DDA Memo, 4 Apr 77

Auth: DDA REG. 77/1763

Date: 10 APR 1978 By: _009_

- 1 -

~~TOP SECRET~~

~~CONFIDENTIAL~~

28. *(Continued)*

violation of the Czechoslovak-Soviet alliance of 1943. Stalin seemed unconcerned over the adverse effect of such a withdrawal on western opinion and minimized the importance of Czechoslovak trade with the west. Stalin seemed especially angered by the fact that prompt Czecho-slovak acceptance of the invitation to attend the Paris conference may have contributed to persuading wavering Swiss and Scandinavians to participate. Source believes that the USSR will tighten its control over Czechoslovakia and that Gottwald, in an attempt to recover his prestige with the Kremlin, will willingly cooperate in such an undertaking.

(CIG Comment: This report is accepted as a more accurate account of the meeting than that in Daily Summary of 16 July, item 3, in which Stalin is represented as speaking with restrained reasonableness. Stalin's anger was probably genuine and a reflection of exasperation and discomfi-ture in the Kremlin. It is to be expected that the USSR will act to prevent any similar show of independence by any Satellite, Czechoslovakia especial-ly, and that Gottwald will outdo himself in order to redeem his blunder.)

Czechs report Stalin in excellent health --Source also told Ambas-sador Steinhardt that the Czechoslovak delegation reported Stalin in ex-cellent health and apparently more vigorous and self-confident than in 1945.

~~TOP SECRET~~

STRATEGY OF SOVIET DELAY IN TREATY RATIFICATION

Six months after the signing of the Italian and Satellite peace treaties, it appears likely that the USSR will postpone ratification at least until September and perhaps indefinitely. By delaying ratification of these treaties (all have been ratified by the US, UK, and France) the USSR hopes to facilitate consolidation of its control over Eastern Europe and to prolong unrest and uncertainty throughout the continent.

The Truman Doctrine and the Marshall proposals have forced the USSR to reconsider its position in regard to Hungary, Rumania, and Bulgaria. In the face of a passive Western policy, the Soviet Union might have considered its control in these countries sufficiently strong to permit early ratification of the treaties without jeopardizing its ultimate domination. The effect of US aid to Greece and Turkey, however, coupled with the Satellites' desire to share in the US program for Europe, has intensified Soviet determination to maintain its extraordinary powers of control over these countries, now exercised through domination of the Allied Control Commissions and the presence of occupation forces.

Although the Dimitrov regime in Bulgaria is sufficiently well-entrenched to stand on its own after the withdrawal of Soviet troops, the USSR has compelling reasons for not ratifying the Bulgarian treaty. Direct supervision of the stepped-up campaign in support of the Greek guerrillas would be more difficult after the withdrawal of Soviet troops which both aid in the war of nerves against Greece and Turkey and contribute logistic support to the guerrilla bands. The recent arrest of Petkov and the terrorist campaign against other Agrarian Party leaders indicate the advantages to the USSR of consolidating its control prior to ratification. Had these actions been taken after ratification, the Soviet Union and the Bulgarian Government would have had to answer to the UN for violations of the peace treaty provisions. In order to avoid foreign intervention, therefore, the USSR will probably delay ratification until all vestiges of opposition in Bulgaria are eliminated.

Conditions in Rumania also favor postponement of treaty ratification by the USSR. Despite nearly complete control over the Rumanian economy, the Soviet position in Rumania would be insecure after ratification so long as King Michael and Maniu, leader of the opposition National Peasant Party, remain as symbols of popular opposition to the Communist Government. The treaty will probably not be ratified,

- 1 -

~~TOP SECRET~~

therefore, until Maniu and the National Peasant Party are eliminated from Rumanian politics, and until some means has been found to dispose of King Michael. The absence of any popular demonstration against the recent arrest of Maniu and many of his supporters may encourage the Communists to hasten their decision on Michael.

In Hungary, the USSR was confronted with a government distinctly pro-Western. The "coup" which resulted in Premier Nagy's resignation in June was the first step in a series of necessary preparations for ratification of the peace treaty. New "rigged" elections are expected by September. Even the holding of these elections does not, however, presage early ratification because post-election house cleaning will still be necessary in Hungary as it has been in Bulgaria and Rumania.

In addition to these political considerations, the USSR needs more time to consolidate its economic and military control over the Satellites. Partially in response to the European recovery program, the need has become more pressing to strengthen economic ties among the Satellites and the USSR. Imposition by the Soviet Union of the economic controls necessary to achieve this goal in the ex-enemy states is far more practicable under existing conditions than it would be after ratification. Through the Allied Control Commissions and with the help of occupation troops, the USSR maintains an effective stranglehold on the internal economy of these countries and, by controlling their foreign trade, can block Western economic penetration. Meanwhile, the USSR is using its dominant position in the area to implement a network of military alliances through which Satellite armed forces will become no more than auxiliaries of the Soviet Army.

Although ratification of the Italian peace treaty would benefit the USSR by forcing the withdrawal of US-UK troops, thus giving Italian Communists a freer hand, other considerations militate against early ratification. By depriving Italy of independent status, the USSR prolongs the existing unrest and uncertainty in Italy and retards political and economic stability. (Italian Communists capitalize upon the unpopularity of the Italian treaty by pointing to the "quick" ratification by the US and UK as contrasted with Soviet "reluctance" to ratify.) Moreover, the USSR will continue to delay because it is not yet ready to implement the peace treaty provisions for the Free Territory of

- 2 -

Trieste. There is little likelihood that a pro-Soviet governor will be appointed for Trieste. The USSR therefore prefers to retain the status quo in order to maintain conditions favorable to infiltration and eventual control by the Yugoslav Communists.

- 3 -

30. Daily Summary Excerpt, 2 August 1947, Germany: Creation of a German Government in the Soviet Zone

EUROPE

4. GERMANY: <u>Creation of a German Government for the Soviet Zone</u>--
CIG sources report that the Soviet Military Authority (SMA) has renewed discussions with German political leaders concerning the
creation of a government for the Soviet Zone, including the Soviet
sector of Berlin. (see Daily Summary of 1 July, item 2). The USSR
reportedly desires that the formation of such a government be completed by 14 August.

(CIG Comment: The USSR has denounced the union of the US
and British Zones in Germany as political rather than economic.
Having already matched the US-UK bizonal economic administration
with a central economic administration for the Soviet Zone, the SMA
would regard the creation of a zonal Government as a logical development. Manifestly such a Government could readily be converted
into a Soviet satellite state in Germany, its nominal independence
exerting considerable attraction upon Germans in the Western Zones.
That further step, however, would compromise the USSR's present
effective pose as the champion of German unity in opposition to
separation and partition. It is not likely to be taken unless and until
the CFM meeting in November proves unification on Soviet terms
to be impossible and partition an accomplished fact perversely
attributable to Western "imperialism.")

- 3 -

31. Weekly Summary Excerpt, 15 August 1947, The Military and Political Chain of Command in Communist Greece

THE MILITARY AND POLITICAL CHAIN OF COMMAND IN COMMUNIST GREECE

The military and political chain of command from the USSR to the Greek Communists is shown in the accompanying chart. Although the chart is partly conjectural, as certain information can not be confirmed and some omissions may have been made, it is essentially an accurate picture of the Communist organization for Greece. The chart is largely self-explanatory, but several of the boxes may require comment.

Balkan Confederation. No formal organization is known to exist. It is probable, however, that a close working agreement between Yugoslavia and Bulgaria has been established to implement designs on Greek Macedonia and Thrace. A "Balkan Council" (including Greek members) has been reported as meeting at Skoplje.

Bitolj. The actual location of General Dapchevich's headquarters is not certain. Bitolj is, however, a transportation and communication center for military movements. General Dapchevich is not a formally trained soldier, but by virtue of partisan experience in Spain and occupied Yugoslavia has become an expert in guerrilla warfare. He was in command of the Yugoslav 4th Army when it entered Trieste.

NOF. These units, active during the war, have been de-emphasized by Tito because of lingering NOF sentiment for an autonomous Macedonia which would be independent of Yugoslavia. Recently, at Skoplje, Macedonian autonomists have been tried and condemned as traitors.

Para-legal Central Committee. This is composed of at least one Yugoslav, two Bulgarians, and two Albanians. The KKE (Greek Communist Party) Central Committee is still legal in Greece.

Special Anti-US Aid Deuxieme Bureau. Composed mostly of non-Greeks, its sole object is to render ineffective the American aid program by propaganda and sabotage.

Committee for the Liberation of Cyprus. This committee was organized to harass the British and to divert attention from the promises of territorial concessions in northern Greece which have been made by Greek Communists to the Satellites.

KOSSA. This unit exploits disaffection in the Greek National Army. The government has been forced to segregate in labor batallions many soldiers of doubtful loyalty.

ERGAS. This Greek Communist labor organization works in close liaison with French labor leaders.

EAM Front. In addition to the five parties of the EAM Front, the two leading socialist parties of Greece are under the domination of KKE.

- 5 -

128

31. *(Continued)*

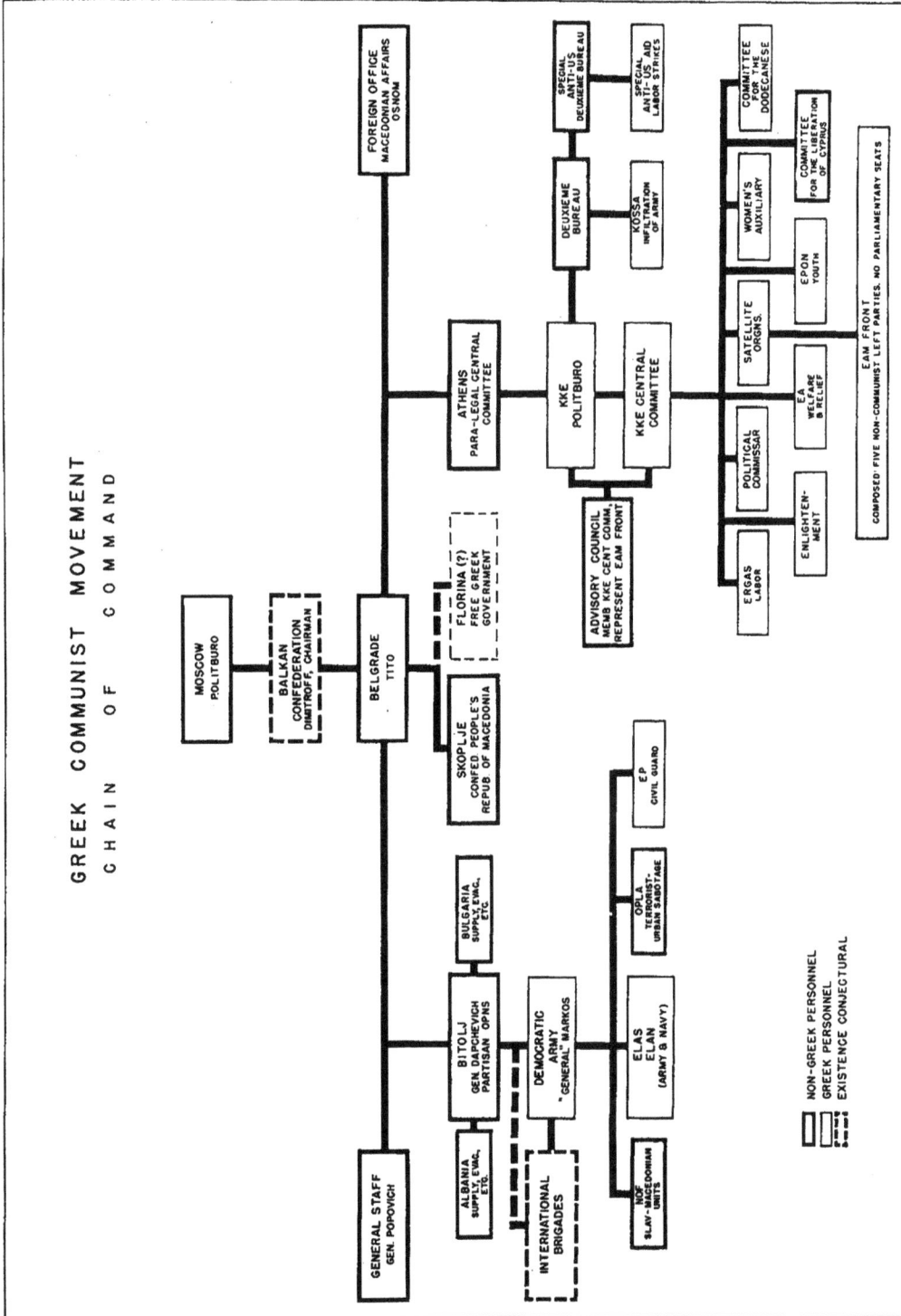

GREEK COMMUNIST MOVEMENT
CHAIN OF COMMAND

129

SOVIET INTENTIONS IN AUSTRIA

The US economic program in Austria is unlikely to bring about any major changes in Soviet policy. The USSR will continue to promote political and economic unrest both as a means of immediately increasing its influence and of ultimately forcing Austria into the Soviet orbit. Meanwhile, the USSR, in attempting to counteract the benefits to Austria of Western assistance, may be expected to: (1) continue to delay the Austrian treaty and thus weaken the national economy by prolonging the four-power occupation; (2) tighten control over the industries and resources of eastern Austria, linking them with the economy of the Soviet Satellites; and (3) place greater restrictions on both inter-zonal trade and trade between Austria and the Soviet Satellites. The USSR apparently acts on the assumption that the Austrian Government will eventually be willing to acquiesce to these Soviet demands, if only to rid the country of the occupation troops.

In addition to this economic and political pressure, the USSR will attempt to draw Austria into an eastward orientation by improving the position of the small Austrian Communist Party. With Soviet backing the Austrian Communists will probably be able to break the Socialist hold on organized labor in plants controlled by the USSR. Furthermore, there may be an increase in Communist-directed strikes, sabotage, and unrest throughout Austria.

Should the Kremlin decide that these measures are inadequate, the USSR may further tighten its controls over eastern Austria and thereby force a partition of the country. From the Soviet point of view, such a move might appear advantageous, particularly because the Austrian peace treaty might be less advantageous to the USSR and because the Austrian Communists appear incapable of gaining control of the Government without vigorous Soviet help.

The USSR probably does not, however, desire partition at the present time. The Soviet Union now enjoys most of the economic advantages and at least some of the political advantages which could be achieved by partition. The USSR already has possession of a large number of industrial assets, including Austria's valuable oil resources, and cannot be deprived of these properties except by its

- 4 -

32. *(Continued)*

own agreement. Furthermore, from the Soviet point of view there are several objections to complete partition: (1) eastern Austria is dependent in part on Western Europe for coal and machinery and on the US for relief; (2) partition would probably damage Soviet chances of absorbing all of Austria because it would forfeit western Austria to the US, UK, and France; and (3) partition would unnecessarily provoke the US as further indication of Soviet expansionism.

For the present, therefore, the USSR will probably continue the present policy of exploiting its zone of occupation to the detriment of the Austrian economy. Meanwhile, Communist propaganda against the US aid program will doubtless continue to emphasize the following themes: (1) Austria's sovereignty is violated by the control provisions of the program; (2) in extending aid, the US wishes to exploit Austria's economic weakness by subjecting the country to capitalist control; (3) Austria's dependence on the West for aid is preventing Austria from enjoying the benefits of normal trade with the "democracies" of Eastern Europe; and (4) the aid program is ineffective in rehabilitating Austria's economy.

If the USSR decides to admit US aid into eastern Austria under the US-Austrian Relief Agreement, Soviet propaganda will then claim that Austrian independence has been protected by the concessions which the USSR has wrung from the US. Meanwhile, failure by the US to meet the relatively small relief requirements of eastern Austria on an interim basis would almost certainly provide the USSR with a convenient excuse to divide Austria economically by banning the shipment of foodstuffs from the Soviet eastern zone to western Austria.

- 5 -

33. Daily Summary Excerpt, 5 September 1947, Greece: Rumor of All-Out Attack From North Discounted

EUROPE

2. **GREECE:** <u>Rumor of all-out attack from north discounted</u>--[

   ]ed "preparations for a bulky and blitz attack" along the entire Greek northern frontier prior to 16 September. Source reports that the attack will be launched by guerrillas, assisted by the armies of northern neighbors, and that Soviet troops will participate only in the event of foreign interference in defending Greece. Source also believes that eastern Turkey is to be attacked. The MA comments that an attack on Greece is unlikely at this time, and that the report may be a "plant" in the current war of nerves.

   (CIG Comment: No tangible evidence which substantiates this rumor has been received to date. While an increase in guerrilla activity this fall is highly probable (see Daily Summary of 2 September, item 6), CIG considers direct participation by the Albanian, Yugoslav, and Bulgarian armies unlikely. Such action would obviously have far-reaching international repercussions and might even involve the USSR in a world war for which it is unprepared. The likelihood of direct participation by Soviet troops in Greece or Turkey at this time is so remote that it need not seriously be considered.)

- 2 -

34. Weekly Summary Excerpt, 5 September 1947, Soviet Efforts to Strengthen Position in Germany

SOVIET EFFORTS TO STRENGTHEN POSITION IN GERMANY

In the weeks remaining before the Council of Foreign Ministers (CFM) meets in November, the USSR will endeavor to strengthen its position in Germany in order to gain a strong bargaining position, vis-a-vis the Western Powers. Such maneuvers will also enable the USSR to take advantage of the almost certain failure of the conference. The USSR has undertaken a ruthless exploitation of the Soviet Zone for essential goods, capital equipment, and dollar exchange credits. The allocation for Soviet use or sale on foreign markets of 90% of current industrial production, renewed reparations dismantlings, and a higher export quota of lignite coal(for which the Zone receives $1.25 per ton in marks and which is resold on the foreign market for $15.00 per ton in dollars) are some of the current means to this end.

In the political field, the USSR has expanded the influence of the Communist front organizations (Antifa) and further restricted non-Communist parties of the Zone. It has also organized through the Socialist Unity Party (SED) an information service (ID) closely connected with the Soviet secret police and very similar to the old Nazi Sicherheitsdienst. Thus the Soviet-controlled SED will have command of the Soviet Zone, regardless of CFM decisions.

In addition to these efforts in the Soviet Zone, the USSR is penetrating western Germany. The main line of attack is to extend the SED political structure to the west, while, simultaneously, efforts are made to establish Communist front organizations, such as the Freie Deutsche Jugend (FDJ), and to penetrate Western Zone labor unions. Soviet efforts to gain control of established unions may be aided by the desire of Catholics in the Rhineland to withdraw from these unions and set up separate Catholic unions. Finally, in order to facilitate terrorism in the Western Zones, a branch of the ID has been organized, and western Germans who oppose Communism will be subjected to underground intimidation.

If Soviet efforts at the CFM fail to achieve a united Germany on Soviet terms, the USSR will attempt to blame the Western Powers for failure of the conference. At the same time, the Kremlin may announce the recognition of a "German Republic" east of the Elbe and attempt to secure the removal of the western allies from Berlin.

- 4 -

<u>TOP SECRET</u>

ITALIAN COMMUNIST INTENTIONS

The imminent withdrawal of Allied troops from Italy has increased the possibility of direct Communist action to seize power and has rendered more effective other Communist methods for taking control of the country. Although Communist Leader Togliatti this week has, in effect, issued a call to arms against the De Gasperi Government, other Communist tactics appear more likely under present conditions.

In carrying out their offensive, the Italian Communists have open to them two main courses of action: (1) sudden over-throw of the De Gasperi Government by Communist-sponsored armed force, following withdrawal of Allied troops; and (2) Communist-inspired general strikes to paralyze the important north Italian industrial area, and thus seriously interfere with future implementation of the program for European recovery.

By the employment of tactics similar to those used in Greece, the first course is within the realm of possibility. Although the Italian Army and Carabinieri have some 200,000 troops to oppose approximately 50,000 Communist guerrillas, the addition of partially-armed and trained Italian and Yugoslav Communists and fellow-travellers could appreciably increase the strength of the revolutionists. Furthermore, redeployment of Italian armed forces to protect the Yugoslav frontier following the withdrawal of Allied forces would remove certain troop units from important Communist-dominated centers in north Italy.

Recent developments within the Communist Party in Italy may increase the likelihood of direct military action. There has long been a division within the Italian Communist Party between the Togliatti faction, which has favored peaceful political infiltration, and the pro-revolutionary group headed by Luigi Longo (member of the International Brigade during the Spanish civil war and Partisan-leader in Italy during World War II). The recent departure of eight members of the "direct action" group for Moscow may indicate closer coordination between this element and the USSR and consequent intensification of Communist paramilitary activity. Togliatti's last speech may mean that he will go along with the revolutionary faction.

- 2 -

<u>TOP SECRET</u>

35. *(Continued)*

Two factors, however, militate against Communist revolution in Italy. The USSR is unwilling to support directly such a step because it might involve war with the US. An even more potent reason against it is that the failure of the European recovery program, or even failure of the US to provide Italy with emergency wheat and dollars during this critical interim period, might deliver Italy into the hands of the Communists by popular vote at the next national elections. It would therefore seem more logical for the Italian Communists to await the outcome of the elections, scheduled for April 1948, before using revolutionary tactics.

The continuation of threats and intimidation is, of course, a permanent policy, and any Communist statements regarding the necessity for violence can be considered to be made partly for propaganda purposes. It will be remembered that Togliatti made a speech threatening "direct action" prior to the Sicilian elections in April, and it is certain that the leftist majority in that former stronghold of conservatism was created in part by the Sicilians' terror of Communist reprisals.

Of the two courses of action, the second seems most likely, and there is evidence that it has already been embarked upon. Paralysis of the north Italian industrial section, which is perhaps second only to the Ruhr in its importance to the European economy, through "spontaneous" general strikes could defeat the operation of the European recovery program and eventually throw not only Italy into the Soviet orbit, but possibly France as well. The strike of 600,000 agricultural workers in the Po Valley, which began on 9 September, indicates that the Communists are now making every effort to bring production to a standstill.

Communist-sponsored strikes are causing a further deterioration of the critical economic situation, which has already compelled the Premier to appeal for emergency wheat from the US in order to restore Italy's essential pasta ration. The De Gasperi Government must cope in some way with the desperate economic crisis before the 23 September meeting of the Constituent Assembly, when a vote of no confidence proposed by Left Wing Socialist Nenni will be discussed.

35. *(Continued)*

Whichever course the Communists follow, their chances of success are excellent unless the De Gasperi Government can ameliorate the economic crisis by procuring sufficient wheat or through successful operation of the European Economic Recovery program.

- 4 -

136

46

~~TOP SECRET~~

DO SEP 1947

THE C.I.A. HAS NO OBJECTION
TO THE DECLASSIFICATION OF
THIS DOCUMENT.

488

GENERAL

No. _009_

· EUROPE

3. FRANCE: <u>Communists plan mass action</u>--US Embassy Paris has
received "reliable" reports that Moscow has instructed the French
Communist Party to prepare for large-scale strikes and other mass
demonstrations. Moreover, according to a trustworthy source,
Thorez has warned the Political Bureau that the Party must be
ready for action "especially in the event that the Soviet Union is
obliged to depart from the UN."

(CIA Comment: Such acceleration of mass action, presumably
designed to embarrass the present French Government and force the
re-entry of the Communists in the Cabinet, would parallel the recent
wave of strikes in Italy and the country-wide protest against the non-
Communist Government scheduled for 20 September.)

Document No. _069_
NO CHANGE in Class. ☐
☐ DECLASSIFIED
Class. CHANGED TO: TS   S
      DDA Memo, 4 Apr 77
Auth: DDA REG. 77/1763
Date: 1 0 APR 1978 By: _009_

- 1 -

~~TOP SECRET~~

CONFIDENTIAL

SECRET

REVIEW OF THE WORLD SITUATION AS IT RELATES TO THE SECURITY OF THE UNITED STATES

26 September 1947

SUMMARY

1. Among foreign powers, only the U.S.S.R. is capable of threatening the security of the United States.

2. The U.S.S.R. is presently incapable of military aggression outside of Europe and Asia, but is capable of overrunning most of continental Europe, the Near East, northern China, and Korea.

3. The U.S.S.R. is unlikely to resort to open military aggression in present circumstances. Its policy is to avoid war, to build up its war potential, and to extend its influence and control by political, economic, and psychological methods. In this it is deliberately conducting political, economic, and psychological warfare against the United States.

4. The greatest danger to the security of the United States is the possibility of economic collapse in Western Europe and the consequent accession to power of Communist elements.

5. Stabilization and recovery in Europe and Asia would tend to redress the balance of power and thereby to restrain the U.S.S.R.

6. From the point of view of containing the U.S.S.R. and eventually redressing the balance of power the order of priority among the major regions of Europe and Asia is:

    a. Western Europe.

    b. The Near and Middle East (but within the region the situation in Greece is of great importance and the utmost urgency, while the situation with respect to Palestine is extremely dangerous).

    c. The Far East (but within the region Japan is important as the only area capable of relatively early development as a power center counterbalancing the Soviet Far East).

SECRET

38. Daily Summary Excerpt, 3 October 1947, Iran: Soviet Troop Concentrations Reported on Border

NEAR EAST-AFRICA

2. IRAN: <u>Soviet troop concentrations reported on border</u> -

the USSR recently moved several infantry regiments, 200 medium tanks, and more than 10 artillery battalions to points near the Iranian frontier west of the Caspian.

orders have been issued to Iranian commanders to open fire, if Soviet troops enter Iranian territory.

US Ambassador Allen reports Prime Minister Qavam's opinion that the USSR will not attack Iran so long as the oil proposal is not definitely rejected but will immediately send irregular bands into Iran to create disturbances, and will send troops as soon as the disturbances are sufficiently serious to provide a pretext for intervention.

(CIA Comment: CIA believes that: (a) the USSR is not planning an invasion of Iran at this time; (b) Soviet troop concentrations are designed to intimidate Iran, as a whole, and to give encouragement to pro-Soviet elements of the population; and (c) the USSR will inspire disorders in Iran when the Soviet oil proposal is rejected.)

- 2 -

EASTERN EUROPE

Soviet officials in Berlin and their adherents in the
Socialist Unity Party (SED) apparently are planning to merge the
Soviet sector of Berlin with the Soviet Zone following the Council
of Foreign Ministers' session in London. This decision seems to
be predicated upon the Soviet conviction that the Council will fail
to reach agreement on Germany. The Soviet Zone headquarters
probably will be transferred to a city less accessible to the Western Powers. Although the USSR does not intend, initially, to risk
compelling the other powers to evacuate Berlin, quadripartite
government will become even less of a reality than it is now. In
addition, the USSR plans to strengthen the central government of
the Soviet Zone at the expense of the governments of the component
states and will maintain the eastern boundary of Germany at the
Oder-Neisse line.

- ii -

40. Special Evaluation No. 21, 13 October 1947, Implications of the New Communist Information Bureau

IMPLICATIONS OF THE NEW COMMUNIST INFORMATION BUREAU

13 October 1947

The significance of the establishment of the Communist Information Bureau, representing the Communist parties of nine European countries, may be evaluated in terms of the answers to the following questions:

    a. What are its immediate and long-range objectives?

    b. Why was its establishment accompanied by such extensive publicity?

    c. What will be its immediate effect on Western Europe?

    d. What light does it throw on Soviet tactics?

    e. What is the background of its members?

The Bureau was probably established at this time with the immediate objectives of:

    a. strengthening Communist control and improving the integration of Communist policy in the Satellite areas;

    b. coordinating more effectively the operations of the Communist parties in the Satellite countries with those of the Communist parties of Western Europe, in order to prevent European economic recovery under US leadership. The Communist parties in the Satellite countries have made tactical mistakes and errors in timing which the USSR must regard as militating against the effectiveness of its opposition to the US-sponsored program for European economic rehabilitation. These errors in timing and tactics include the execution of Petkov while the Italian Communist leader, Togliatti, was defending before the Italians the rights of man, and the failure of the Czechoslovak Communists to prevent the initial Czechoslovak acceptance of the invitation to participate in the European economic recovery program;

- 1 -

SECRET

    c. serving notice on the Communist parties in France and Italy, as well as those in other Western European countries, that they are not their own masters and that they must adhere to the policies and plans of the Kremlin.

The Bureau's long-range objectives are:

    a. to expand the organization to cover the European continent and eventually to set up similar organizations in other areas;

    b. by expelling the non-cooperating Socialists and misguided fellow-travellers from the "Democratic" ranks, to prepare a hard nucleus of ideologically sound Communists, capable of direct action and of reversion to underground methods if such procedure becomes necessary.

The formation of the information Bureau and the accompanying manifesto of intentions were widely publicized in order to impress the fence-sitters, the waverers, and the opportunists of Western Europe with the solidarity and vitality of the Communist organization, as opposed to the disunity and inherent weaknesses of the US-supported capitalist-socialist world. It was also designed as a declaration of war against the US-sponsored European recovery program and may have been launched with the hope that it would induce pacifists in the US and the UK to revive their activities. This publicity is entirely consistent with the Soviet practice of supporting any important project, once undertaken, with the maximum strength and volume of propaganda.

The immediate effect upon Western Europe, however, will be to reduce the voting strength of the Communist parties, particularly in the approaching elections in France and Italy. The Nationalist pose of these parties has now been dropped, and the leaders stand forth clearly as the obedient servants of the Kremlin. If it were not for the threat of an economic crisis, it could be safely predicted that the position of the moderate non-Communist parties in the governments of Western Europe would be substantially strengthened by the formation of the Bureau.

- 2 -

SECRET

40. *(Continued)*

The establishment of the Information Bureau, therefore, throws considerable light on Soviet tactics. It suggests strongly that the USSR recognizes that it has reached a point of diminishing returns in the attempts of the Communist parties of Western Europe to rise to power through parliamentary means and that, consequently, it intends to revert to subversive activities, such as strikes and sabotage, in an effort to undermine the stability of Western European governments. This move likewise tends to substantiate the contention that the USSR considers international subversive and revolutionary action, rather than military aggression, as the primary instrument for obtaining its worldwide objectives. Furthermore, the fact that the USSR has taken this step, so obviously injurious to the electoral prospects of the Communist parties, prior to important elections in France and Italy, gives further confirmation to the belief that the USSR is convinced of a pending economic collapse, first in Europe and subsequently in the US, which will provide the Communist parties with an opportunity to achieve their objectives through subversive and revolutionary action.

The delegates who met in Warsaw to form the Bureau of Information were hardbitten Communists of long-standing. The leading figure unquestionably was Zhdanov, member of the Soviet Politburo, former key figure in the Comintern and probably second in importance only to Stalin in directing the strategy of world Communism. Ex-Comintern officials were well represented, among them Djilas, Pauker, and Duclos. In addition, at least two delegates took active and important parts in the International Brigade during the Spanish Civil War. The leadership of the new Information Bureau, therefore, has the required stature to carry forward, under the direction of the Kremlin, the Communist program of world revolution. It was probably to create the illusion of freedom from Kremlin control that headquarters were set up outside the Soviet Union. Under the circumstances, Yugoslavia was a logical choice because of the success and stability of the Communist regime in that country, the character and experience of its ruling clique, and its proximity to high priority Communist targets such as Greece and Italy.

The formation of the Information Bureau is the first open avowal of the creation of blocs to supplement, and eventually to assume, the functions of the Comintern as the Kremlin's instrument

- 3 -

40. *(Continued)*

for attaining world domination. In taking this step, the Kremlin appears to have abandoned any program of parliamentary cooperation with non-Communist parties and has reverted to the original program of expansion by control and support of international revolutionary Communism. It has taken this step likewise in full knowledge that it will alienate those Western fellow-travellers and democratic elements which have thus far clung to hopes of political cooperation with national Communist parties and of a compromise between the East and West.

- 4 -

SECRET

41. Weekly Summary Excerpt, 24 October 1947, Prospects for French Success in Indochinese Campaign

PROSPECTS FOR FRENCH SUCCESS IN INDOCHINESE CAMPAIGN

Even though the current French offensive in northern Indochina appears to have achieved certain limited objectives, the campaign will probably not be successful in forcing the Vietnam Republic to negotiate for peace on French terms. Moreover, a consequent decline in French prestige may weaken the control over native peoples in other parts of the French Empire.

Although French military authorities are holding all publicity on Indochina to a minimum and are claiming that the campaign is no more than a minor operation (probably in order to avoid the possibility of UN intervention), larger French forces are engaged in these actions than have been committed ever before against the Vietnam Republic. The purposes of the French drive are: (1) to cut overland arms-import routes between Vietnam and China by establishing French control along the northern Indochinese border; (2) to weaken the resistance of the Vietnam Republic by killing or capturing its leaders, by increasing combat attrition of its ammunition and equipment resources, and by disrupting its communication and propaganda facilities; and (3) to compel the Vietnam Republic, as a result, to negotiate for peace on French terms.

Prospects for significant French success in the fall offensive are meager largely because the guerrilla tactics adopted by Vietnam forces will conserve their ammunition and materiel while drawing French forces into mountainous and difficult terrain. The disruption of Vietnam communication facilities will probably not seriously hamper Vietnam administration and forces because they have demonstrated during the past year their ability to operate on a decentralized basis and to coordinate effectively the military activities of northern and southern Vietnam groups. The French expectation that the Vietnam Government would be willing to negotiate on French terms ignores the intensity of the hatred and contempt felt for the French by most of the population of northern Indochina. These feelings are not associated solely with the Vietnam Republic but would continue even if the Vietnam Republic should suffer grave defeat. None of the political figures advanced by the French or by native groups in French-held areas as alternatives to President Ho and the Vietnam Republic can command enough popular support to weaken the Vietnam Republic by inspiring important defections from it.

- 8 -

French military authorities have committed their forces to the fall offensive, despite these factors opposing their success, probably because: (1) they underestimate Vietnam determination to resist; and (2) no French political party can support a move to conciliate the Vietnam because such a precedent might lead in a direction dangerous to the French Empire.

If the French fail to weaken the Vietnam Republic by their fall operations, the coming of the spring rainy season will place the French in the awkward position of maintaining extended lines of supply while defending themselves against the mobile operations of the Vietnam guerrilla forces. If the French forces are forced to withdraw in the face of such circumstances, they will have expended much military equipment and manpower for small returns. The consequent decline of French prestige will easily lead to wide defections among the native elements in French-held areas who have previously been cooperative.

- 9 -

42. Daily Summary Excerpt, 29 October 1947, Reported Soviet-Inspired Military Operations in Greece

3. <u>Reported Soviet-inspired military operations in Greece</u>--US Charge
        in Sofia reports that, according to a reliable informant, the
    Soviet "master plan" at present anticipates the initiation of military
    operations against Greece by its northern neighbors on or about
    15 December. According to source,

                                                    Dimitrov
    had written from Czechoslovakia describing Soviet intentions. She.

42. *(Continued)*

stated that the Soviet internal situation is so "restive" that the Soviet people must be distracted by a military offensive.

(CIA Comment: Although there have been numerous unconfirmed reports of increased movements of troops and arms in Yugoslavia and Bulgaria, such reports probably suggest intensified covert military aid rather than overt operations by the Satellites. CIA discounts the above report for the following reasons: (a) it is improbable that Dimitrov would write concerning plans of this nature in a letter or that any precise information would be transmitted to the secretary's wife; (b) the reason given by source for such Soviet action is untenable; (c) the USSR is committed by the peace treaty to withdraw its troops from Bulgaria by 15 December and will probably not sanction overt military operations at a time when world attention will be focused on Soviet compliance with this treaty provision; and (d) it is still believed that the USSR is not ready to risk precipitating a war with the West.)

- 3 -

43. Weekly Summary Excerpt, 7 November 1947, Soviet Preparations to Gain Control in Greece

SOVIET PREPARATIONS TO GAIN CONTROL IN GREECE

Reports of recent military activity in Yugoslavia and Bulgaria indicate that the USSR, temporarily blocked in Western Europe, may have begun a more intensive campaign to gain control of Greece. Besides making preparations for increased Yugoslav and Bulgarian assistance to the guerrillas in Greece, the USSR appears to be building those two countries as the dominant military powers in Southeastern Europe. Full development of the Soviet plans is not expected, however, until after the London meeting of the CFM.

Increased Soviet military aid to Yugoslavia and Bulgaria is indicated by reports that: (1) Soviet arms and munitions are being sent to Yugoslavia and Bulgaria, both overland from Austria and by water through Black Sea ports; (2) the USSR has transferred several naval vessels to the Bulgarian Navy; and (3) extensive stockpiles of war supplies are being built up along the Greek and Turkish borders.

In addition to preparations for greater aid to the Satellites, Communist plans to increase direct military assistance to the Greek guerrillas are revealed by recently available reports of secret military clauses agreed upon at the Bled conference last August. According to these reports, a General Staff of the Central Balkan Council has been established under the chairmanship of Admiral Rodionov, former Soviet Ambassador to Greece. His staff will reportedly include Yugoslav, Bulgarian, Albanian, Rumanian, Hungarian, Czechoslovak and Greek-guerrilla officers who will assist in the operation of an International Brigade, or a "Balkan Army," consisting primarily of Greek, Yugoslav, Albanian, and Bulgarian personnel. Moreover, recent indications point to the imminent formation of a civil government in northern Greece. Such a development would permit more overt utilization of the military forces being organized in Yugoslavia and Bulgaria.

Despite these intensive military preparations and the failure of the USSR to begin withdrawal of its troops from Bulgaria (scheduled under the peace treaty to be completed by 15 December), the USSR probably does not intend at present to participate in overt military operations in Greece. Instead, the USSR is preparing to meet any

- 4 -

43. *(Continued)*

TOP SECRET

developments arising from the London meeting of the CFM. Meanwhile, these activities not only increase the Satellite potential for clandestine military aid to the Greek guerrillas, but also constitute an effective weapon in the war of nerves against the Greek Government. Finally, these actions serve to strengthen Yugoslavia and Bulgaria as effective defensive buffers against any "imperialist" aggression from the south.

- 5 -

TOP SECRET

44. Daily Summary Excerpt, 19 November 1947, Germany: Soviet State in Eastern Zone Reported Fully Prepared

4. GERMANY: <u>Soviet state in eastern Zone reported fully prepared</u>--
US Consul General ⎯⎯⎯⎯ in Bremen has been "reliably informed"
that the Social Democratic Party of the western Zones of Germany
has "incontestable evidence" that a Soviet state in the eastern Zone
of Germany is already "fully prepared."

(CIA Comment: Although the Soviet Union may have drawn
up such plans, CIA doubts that it intends to put them into effect at
this time. CIA believes that the Soviet Union will hold them in
abeyance for possible subsequent application as "retaliatory
measures.")

- 3 -

THE LONDON CFM CONFERENCE

Since the adjournment of the Moscow Conference of Foreign Ministers on 24 April 1947, subsequent international meetings have given no evidence of any change of position by the USSR on the issues concerning Germany and Austria which will be discussed at the forthcoming London Conference of the CFM. Neither the protracted meetings of the Austrian Treaty Commission in Vienna nor the present largely fruitless efforts of the deputies at London to reach agreement even on minor matters have indicated the slightest adjustment of Soviet aims and objectives. Meanwhile, the US, the UK, and France have reached closer agreement on Germany and Austria.

The US and British positions on the German and Austrian problems are practically parallel. France has been drawn into closer accord since the Moscow Conference by participation in the European recovery program and by the elimination of the Communists from the French Government. Even though deep-rooted concern over security makes the French position on Germany different from that of the US and the UK, and although the French are not completely reconciled to the Anglo-American program for raising the level of German industry, France will undoubtedly modify its position in the interest of Western unity if the USSR remains inflexible at the London Conference. If there is such an outcome, the French can be expected to merge their zone with the US-UK zones and to accept a higher level of industry for Germany in return for adequate security guarantees (such as an international control program for the Ruhr and Rhineland) and for assurances of sufficient coal and coke.

Fundamental Soviet objectives at the London meeting of the CFM will undoubtedly be basically the same as those the USSR pursued at the Moscow Conference. At Moscow, it became evident that the USSR seeks to communize Germany as an essential step in a plan to extend Communist control over all Europe. To carry out this objective, the USSR demanded a share in the control of the Ruhr, a centralized government of the Weimar type which could easily be scuttled, the payment of reparations from current production (which would have forced the US and the UK to bear much

- 1 -

of the financial burden), and freedom for trade unions and "demo-cratic" parties to organize in all zones. When the USSR was unable to obtain these demands, the Kremlin directed its efforts toward keeping the Soviet Zone in Germany economically sealed off from Western Europe. Such a policy was designed to reduce western Germany to a social and economic morass and was supported by the conviction that the US would inevitably have a severe depres-sion which would force the abandonment of European commitments.

Since the Moscow Conference, however, major developments have occurred which will hinder the USSR in the attainment of its objectives. Chief of these developments has been the inception and drawing up of the European recovery program. Nearly as signifi-cant, however, has been the stiffening in attitude toward the USSR of the western participants in the CFM. Because of these develop-ments, the USSR now is confronted with the imminent prospect of the unification of the three western zones in Germany and a con-sequent improvement in their economy. Moreover, the predicted US depression has not materialized.

In recognition of this change in the situation since the Mos-cow Conference, the USSR may make certain offers at London which will appear, on the surface, to be new and sweeping concessions. Such concessions might take several forms: (1) some scaling down of claims to German reparations; (2) the proposed establishment of a central economic administration which will apparently promote German economic unity but would also further Soviet political ob-jectives; (3) the offered withdrawal of all occupation troops from Germany, which would secure the removal of US forces from Europe while merely requiring Soviet units to fall back to nearby Poland. Because Austria has been placed at the bottom of the proposed Soviet agenda, probably no Austrian concessions will be offered prior to acceptance of the German concessions. For these reasons, it is likely that any concessions offered by the USSR will be made more with an eye to their propaganda value than with any serious expectation of acceptance. The offers would be carefully drawn so as to prepare the way for placing the onus of failure to reach agree-ment on the US and the UK.

If these offers are made and are rejected by the Western Powers, the USSR will doubtless continue to maintain the present division of Germany, thereby denying to western Germany the possibility of exchanging its manufactures for the raw materials of eastern Germany and Eastern Europe. The USSR will thus be forced to continue a policy which was originally laid down on the hypothesis that the US would be crippled by a depression before it could make Western Europe a solvent and productive economic area.

- 3 -

46. Daily Summary Excerpt, 1 December 1947, Reported Communist Drive to Seize Power in France and Italy

GENERAL

1. <u>Reported Communist drive to seize power in France and Italy</u>--US Ambassador Dunn in Rome has received [   ] a document, which the [   ] evaluates "authoritative," relating to a recent special Cominform conference in Poland. According to [   ], the document indicates that: (a) the Soviet Politburo is directing a coordinated all-out Communist campaign to take over the French and Italian Governments by violence rather than constitutional methods; (b) although the initial emphasis is apparently on the use of general strikes timed to block the operation of the European recovery program, the Communists will not be restricted to this method; (c) the campaign is personally directed from Moscow by Zhdanov, secretary-general of the Soviet Communist Party, through his "personal representative," Foreign Minister Ana Pauker of Rumania; (d) Mrs. Pauker is a member of a new special committee in Belgrade--composed of representatives of the Soviet, Yugoslav, French, and Italian Communist Parties--which operates independently of the Cominform and will regulate and synchronize Communist action in France and Italy; and (e) the committee has been assured unlimited means--apparently including financing, food, and military stores--in order to carry out its campaign effectively.

   (CIA Comment: CIA suggests, preliminary to the receipt of the reported document, that the document is: (a) an Italian Government plant for the purpose of expediting interim aid by impressing on the US Congress the urgent need for countermeasures against Soviet plans; (b) a Cominform device to stimulate activity on the part of the Italian and French Communists and does not reflect any real intention to take the course indicated; or (c) an authentic and accurate indication of Soviet plans, which have as their maximum objective Communist seizure of the French and Italian Governments and as their minimum objective the creation of such economic and political chaos in France and Italy as will preclude the successful implementation of the European recovery program.

   (CIA does not believe that the French or Italian Communists are capable of seizing control of their respective Governments without material outside support. The supplying of such support, however, would involve the risk of a major conflict for which the USSR is presently unprepared.)

- 2 -

RESULTS OF COMMUNIST STRIKES IN FRANCE

The defeat of the crippling Communist-led strikes in France is the result of vigorous and effective action by the Schuman Government and the growing split in French labor between Communists and non-Communists. The Government has gained in prestige through its victory over the Communists. Communist prestige and support have been correspondingly reduced and the Communists have suffered a setback in their aim to wreck the French economy. However, they have caused a serious loss in production of coal and other industrial products which will adversely affect the European recovery program.

Although the French Communists have been defeated in their first effort to employ against the Government the full economic power inherent in their control of labor, they can be expected to continue to wield economic power for political gains. Their objectives remain unchanged: to wreck the French economy, to render US aid ineffective, and eventually to assume control in France. The Communists probably will not launch widespread strikes again in the near future, but they will continue to exercise their capability to dislocate the French economy by sabotage and violence. Under direction from the Kremlin, they may even engage in such direct action as to cause their Party to be outlawed in France but, even in that event, they will be capable of disruptive clandestine action.

In any case, the newly-strengthened Schuman Government will face difficult tasks in the months to come. While trying to prevent further work stoppages, the Government must: (1) seek to overcome the serious economic setback resulting from the recent strikes; (2) resolve anticipated disagreements between Socialists and Radical Socialists in the coalition regarding methods for economic recovery; and (3) weather the adverse effects of a hard winter and the unpopular measures which it must take to combat inflation. If the Government can succeed in all these respects, it may be able both to defeat the Communists and to remove the possibility of De Gaulle's return to power. If Schuman fails, a Gaullist solution will become probable, and Schuman's vigorous action against the Communists will have prevented them from forcing De Gaulle to power prematurely.

- 1 -

48. **Daily Summary Excerpt, 4 December 1947, France: Communists Increasing Violent Action**

EUROPE

4. FRANCE: Communists increasing violent action-- [   ] has expressed to US Embassy Paris his concern over the increasing tendency of Communist shock troops to attempt sabotage and to provoke the police to militant action. [   ] said that such actions might eventually cause the Government to outlaw the Communist Party. [   ] was puzzled by the apparent readiness of the USSR to risk driving underground "one of the best-organized Communist parties in Europe" unless this reflected "Soviet willingness to face general war in the near future." US Embassy and US Military Attache Paris are skeptical of this conclusion. They consider that [   ] perhaps exaggerates the present importance to the Kremlin of the French Communist Party.

(CIA Comment: In its efforts to sabotage the European recovery program, which is the USSR's immediate and primary target, the Kremlin will be willing even to risk the sacrifice of the French and Italian Communist Parties. If these Parties are defeated and driven underground, the USSR will have lost no more than it would lose by the success of the European recovery program. CIA believes that the unexpectedly rapid progress of the Marshall program has upset the timetable of the Kremlin and forced this desperate action as the last available countermeasure.)

)

- 2 -

49. Weekly Summary Excerpt, 5 December 1947, A Revival of Soviet Designs on Iranian Azerbaijan

A revival of Soviet designs on Iranian Azerbaijan is indicated in the USSR's stepped-up propaganda campaign against Iran, following the sharp exchange of notes on the oil question at the end of November. Soviet agents are increasingly active in Azerbaijan; the official Soviet press and radio are again promoting "independence" for Azerbaijan; and the clandestine radio, in its appeals to Kurds and Azerbaijanians, states that the struggle for the province will "now" begin. Moreover, the unconfirmed report of a planned invasion of northern Iran by Soviet-organized Iranian minority elements specifies that the drive will begin on 13 December, the first anniversary of the recapture of Azerbaijan from the autonomous, pro-Soviet rebels. Meanwhile, the Iranian Cabinet has resigned because of disagreement with Prime Minister Qavam over domestic policies, and it appears that Qavam himself will soon be forced out of office.

FAR EAST

8. KOREA: <u>Future Soviet tactics in Korea</u>--   has been told by a usually reliable source that at a conference of high ranking North Korean and Soviet military and governmental officials, held on 19 November in Pyongyang, the following tactics were discussed: (a) a decrease of electric-power supply to South Korea in order to cause unemployment and widespread unrest; (b) the organization of a strong fifth column in important South Korean cities; (c) the withdrawal of Soviet forces following the establishment of an independent North Korean government "according to the desires" of the North Korean people, despite UN action; (d) the maintenance of the People's Army in a state of readiness to occupy South Korea with the aid of the fifth column.

(CIA Comment: The North Korean Peoples Council is now preparing a "provisional Korean constitution" which would provide a "legal" basis for formal Soviet recognition of the North Korean regime. CIA believes that the USSR will initiate a series of moves similar to those indicated in this report in an effort to force the withdrawal of US forces and to frustrate implementation of the UN resolution on Korea.)

- 3 -

51. Daily Summary Excerpt, 13 December 1947, De Gasperi Fears Communist Insurrectionary Action

49

~~CONFIDENTIAL~~

13 DEC 1947

558

GENERAL

1. De Gasperi fears Communist insurrectionary action--According to US Ambassador Caffery in Paris, Premier De Gasperi has informed the French Foreign Office through the Italian Ambassador at Paris that the situation in Italy is very serious and that De Gasperi fears the Italian Communists may resort about 20 December to some form of insurrectionary action particularly in North Italy. De Gasperi believes that his Government can eventually put down a revolt but that, if the Italian Communists receive substantial help from the French Communists, the Italian Government's ability to deal with the Italian Communists would be seriously impaired. De Gasperi therefore proposed that immediate contact be made between French and Italian military and civil intelligence with a view to thwarting the Communists in both countries.

Caffery has been reliably informed that the French have agreed to the proposal and contact has already been established as suggested.

(CIA Comment: In view of the existing inadequacies in arms and equipment of the Italian Army and security troops, CIA believes that the Italian Communists at present have the capability of obtaining temporary control of Northern Italy. If the Italian Communists receive material assistance from the French and/or the Yugoslav Communists, the Italian Government would probably not be able to regain control of North Italy unaided.)

- 1 -

~~CONFIDENTIAL~~

160

PROSPECTS FOR ADDITIONAL COMINFORMS

Despite persistent rumors of the imminent creation in the Far East and in Latin America of companion organizations to the Belgrade Cominform, it is extremely doubtful that the Soviet Union intends to set up such overt regional organizations at this time.

The inclusion in the Belgrade organization of only major European Communist parties indicates that the Kremlin regards considerable local Communist party strength as a prerequisite to membership in a Cominform. A Cominform is neither a loose federation of Communist parties nor an organization devoted to building local party strength; rather, it is the center for the direction of militant activity in areas where Communist strength is already substantial. Although the creation of additional regional Communist groupings, particularly in Latin America, is a possibility, there would be little advantage at present to formation by the Soviet Union of additional Cominforms. Furthermore, it is difficult to believe that, from the Soviet point of view, the advantages of Cominforms in Latin America and the Far East would sufficiently compensate for the repressive measures which might result from the open acknowledgment by local parties of their subservience to Moscow.

Establishment of a Far Eastern Cominform (already rumored to exist at Harbin) presupposes a radical change in Soviet Far Eastern policy. In the past, the Soviet Union has scrupulously avoided identifying the Chinese Communist Party with Moscow, and it is highly improbable that the Soviet leaders would, at this time, jeopardize the Chinese Communist Party by acknowledging its connection with the world Communist movement.

The considerable current liaison between Latin American and European (especially French) Communist leaders, is believed to represent nothing more than normal co-ordination of Party policy. The USSR for the time being at least cannot hope to offset the US position of leadership in Latin America, and the role of Communist parties in that area must necessarily be negative in the event of an early East-West war. It is, therefore, most unlikely that the USSR will sponsor a Cominform in the Western Hemisphere.

- 1 -

53. Daily Summary Excerpt, 23 December 1947, Czechoslovakia: Communist Drive Expected in January

4. CZECHOSLOVAKIA: <u>Communist drive expected in January</u>--US Charge [   ] in Prague reports current indications that beginning in January 1948 the Communists will make every effort to achieve their objectives in Czechoslovakia by constitutional rather than extralegal means. He cites three reasons which militate against extralegal Communist action: (a) because of their non-revolutionary character, the Czechoslovak people would probably react unfavorably to un-constitutional methods; (b) as Czechoslovakia is the only peripheral country with a highly developed industry, unorthodox Communist election methods would impair the country's ability to obtain necessary raw materials from the West and thereby jeopardize the export of

- 2 -

53. *(Continued)*

Czechoslovak products vital to the USSR; and (c) President Benes, who is extremely popular and highly respected, would strongly resist extralegal measures.

- 3 -

PROSPECTS FOR COMMUNIST ACTION IN ITALY

The Italian Communists are expected to instigate in the near future a new wave of strikes throughout the country. These strikes ostensibly will be aimed to win benefits for the workers similar to those recently granted in Rome and Sicily. If the De Gasperi Government demonstrates weakness in dealing with widespread disorders, the Kremlin may direct insurrectionary action before the national elections in March or April.

The potentialities for effective Communist employment of force to further Soviet objectives in Italy remain undiminished, despite De Gasperi's recent success in putting down the general strike in Rome. Communist capabilities for overt armed action are particularly strong in North Italy, where the Party has a large membership, controls many city councils and labor organizations, and commands a partisan following estimated at 50,000 well-armed and 50,000 partially-armed fighters. The Communists apparently also possess adequate truck transportation in that region. Against this force, the Italian Army and security troops can place only limited strength, inadequate in arms and equipment. Rightist semi-military forces are believed to number only 20,000 at the most, and these are very poorly equipped for combat. Such Rightist forces would be more likely to impede rather than to increase the effectiveness of the Government troops.

If the Italian Communists, with assistance from the Communists of France and/or of Yugoslavia, should seize control of North Italy (as is within their capabilities), the De Gasperi Government would probably require outside aid to regain possession of the area. However, two factors at present apparently militate against an imminent Communist coup: (1) the Communists have not yet succeeded in creating a truly "revolutionary situation"; and (2) they do not appear to have given up hope of winning the next elections. Neither the decision nor the order for insurrectionary action, however, is likely to originate in Italy itself. Such authority obviously rests in the Kremlin which will presumably direct such action as it considers necessary to defeat the European recovery program.

- 1 -

54. *(Continued)*

Meanwhile, in order to weaken De Gasperi's support the Communists can be expected to exploit the dissatisfaction of the South Tyrol People's Party with the Government's draft legislative provisions for Italy's German-speaking population. Although De Gasperi has not yet been directly charged with bad faith in implementing the Austro-Italian agreement of September 1946 (for the local autonomy of the South Tyrol), the issue is one which the Government must handle carefully lest it increase the Communist following in an area where Communist political and military strength already presents a substantial threat. Dissident elements among the South Tyrolese could impede the Government's efforts to regain control of North Italy, in the event of a Communist insurrection.

55. Weekly Summary Excerpt, 9 January 1948, Growing Soviet Interest in China

Evidence in the Moscow press of growing Soviet interest in China may foreshadow a more active Soviet role in Chinese affairs. The USSR, however, is not likely at this to establish a closer relationship with the Chinese Communists. It has given renewed indications that it is not ready to abandon its "correct" attitude toward the Nanking Government in favor of open aid to the Communists in China's civil war. Increased Soviet activity could, however, be directed toward obtaining concessions from the Chinese, including Chinese cooperation with the USSR on Japanese peace treaty issues, or the extension of Soviet influence in China's border regions.

56. Daily Summary Excerpt, 14 January 1948, France: Alleged Communist Plan for Military Activities

5. FRANCE: Alleged Communist plan for military activities—
US Ambassador Caffery in Paris has obtained from French
Communist sources a report that the principal task of the
recent Italian Party Congress at Milan was to "coordinate
military activities of French, Italian, Swiss, and Spanish Communist parties." These sources say that the strategic plan,
which is to be placed in operation in case the Kremlin decides
that the international situation demands extreme action, would
place the southern littoral of France under Communist control
from the Spanish frontier to Switzerland, and inland centers,
such as St. Etienne, would become "Soviet bases" connected
with northern Italy. The informants add that the French and
Italian Communists admit that they were recently obliged to
make a "strategic retreat" and intend to reorganize in accordance with lessons learned in the recent "dress rehearsal" in
France and Italy.

(CIA Comment: Although such a plan may have been
considered, it is extremely unlikely that this plan would be implemented under present conditions. CIA considers that such
a program will not be attempted unless: (a) Communist strategists estimate that the French Government is too weak to resist; (b) the Communists have gained control of northern Italy,
from which area the operations in France can be directly
supported; and (c) it appears reasonably certain to the Communist strategists that such a move would not provoke US
intervention.

- 2 -

SOVIET POLICY IN EASTERN EUROPE

The USSR has recently intensified its efforts to obtain direct military, economic, and political control over the Eastern European Satellites. This intensification is revealed in the rapid conclusion of a series of mutual assistance pacts now linking nearly all the Satellites, the signing of long-range trade agreements by the USSR with Poland and Czechoslovakia, and the increasing emphasis on the Cominform as the principal organ for the implementation of Communist policy in the area. The USSR will continue to strengthen its controls over the Satellites but will take no action which will either: (1) weaken the direct ties binding each individual Satellite to the Kremlin; or (2) run counter to the Kremlin's plan for ultimate absorption of the Satellites in the USSR.

The immediate objective of the USSR is the organization of a unified military force in Eastern Europe for defensive purposes as well as for possible overt support of the Markos regime in Greece. The Rumano-Hungarian mutual assistance pact nearly completes such a system of intertwining alliances between the Satellites. The recent pacts have differed from those concluded prior to 1947 by the USSR with Poland, Czechoslovakia, and Yugoslavia, in that they are directed against any attacker rather than against Germany alone. Moreover, the USSR is not directly involved. The Soviet Union, therefore, has forged a military weapon which will insure united Satellite action in Greece should the occasion warrant but will simultaneously minimize the risk of direct conflict between the US and the USSR.

Although these pacts provide for sweeping economic co-ordination between the participating nations, they do not presage political or economic union in the near future. Rather, they represent a transitory stage in the development of the Satellites as members of the USSR. In addition to providing the machinery for the integration of the Satellite armed forces with the Soviet Army, these pacts can serve the USSR as basis for propaganda designed gradually to minimize the traditional rivalries which formerly divided the Eastern European nations.

- 4 -

57. *(Continued)*

TOP SECRET

The USSR is exercising its actual political and economic control over the Satellites through Communist Party channels. Although the Kremlin may originally have planned for an eventual Balkan federation, recent evidence indicates that this plan may now be abandoned or its implementation postponed for some time. The PRAVDA editorial of 28 January, which disavowed Bulgarian Premier Dimitrov's prediction of a Balkan-Danubian customs union and eventual federation, may have been prompted by the Kremlin's realization that the many practical difficulties obstructing consummation of such a plan made Dimitrov's speech premature. Moreover, the Kremlin may have feared that announcement of a Balkan federation would hasten acceptance of Bevin's proposal for western European union. More important, however, the USSR probably does not consider conditions in the Satellite states sufficiently secure to permit any loosening of the ties binding the Kremlin directly with each country. As long as the Kremlin exercises through the Cominform direct operational control over each Communist Party, unified Satellite action can be achieved more effectively than by delegating this authority to a federation head.

In obtaining economic control over the Satellites, the USSR can gain greater advantage by promoting direct Soviet-Satellite trade than it can by encouraging inter-Satellite trade through a formal federation. The recent long-term trade agreements signed by the USSR with Czechoslovakia and Poland indicate that the USSR does intend to integrate each Satellite economy directly with the USSR. Similarly, Soviet economic exploitation of Hungary and Rumania is indicative of the desire of the USSR to extract the maximum economic benefits from each country and thereby retard the growth of trade between the Satellites themselves. Such a policy, by insuring that each country's economy is meshed directly with that of the USSR, will facilitate eventual absorption of the Satellites into the Soviet Union.

- 5 -

TOP SECRET

46

13 FEB 1948

609

~~CONFIDENTIAL~~

GENERAL

1. <u>Possible Soviet plans for Poland</u>--US Ambassador Smith in Moscow believes that the provisions in the new Polish-Soviet economic agreement for the investment of capital equipment by the USSR in Poland and in Polish-administered Germany reflect a long-range Kremlin decision "never to let go of eastern Germany" and to develop Poland as the first Satellite to be incorporated into the USSR. Smith adds that "if the east-west cleavage continues and deepens, the absorption of Poland might well take place in the not too remote future."

(CIA Comment: CIA concurs in the belief that the USSR intends to hold eastern Germany and eventually to incorporate the Satellites into the USSR. However, because absorption of Poland would increase anti-Communist opposition and add to the security problem of the USSR, the Kremlin will probably not order such a step until all latent opposition to such a plan has been eliminated.)

This publication contains current intelligence exclusively and therefore has not been coordinated with the intelligence organizations of the Departments of State, Army, Navy, and Air Force.

Document No. ___637___

NO CHANGE in Class. ☐

☐ DECLASSIFIED

Class. CHANGED TO: TS S Ⓒ

- 1 -

~~TOP SECRET~~ Auth: DDA Memo, 4 Apr 77

~~CONFIDENTIAL~~ DDA REG. 77/1763

Date: _____ By: _____

59. Daily Summary Excerpt, 19 February 1948, Czechoslovakia: Communists May Precipitate Crisis

EUROPE

4. CZECHOSLOVAKIA: Communists may precipitate crisis--
US Charge [   ] in Prague, in commenting on the current
political crisis in Czechoslovakia over the question of Communist control of the police, expresses the view that if the
Communists regard a breakdown of the National Front coalition government as unavoidable, they will precipitate it at
once. [   ] believes that the Communists would want to
utilize trade union meetings already scheduled for 22 February as a basis for public demonstrations.

(CIA Comment: CIA concurs in this estimate. The refusal
of the Communists to comply with the recent demand of the Moderates for changes in the police organization reveals that the Communists believe continued control of the police to be essential to
their victory in the May elections.)

- 2 -

SOVIET EXPANSIONISM IN KOREA

The intention of the USSR to establish an independent regime in North Korea and eventually to dominate all Korea has been further revealed by the following recent events: (1) the announcement by the North Korean radio of the completion of the "draft provisional constitution of Korea"; (2) the staging of a Communist-instigated strike in South Korea as a protest against the UN Commission's "illegal interference" with Korean independence; and (3) the review at Pyongyang in North Korea of the "Korean People's Army" and the subsequent propaganda announcements that this army would be the future liberator of the "oppressed" South Koreans.

Although the USSR has scrupulously avoided direct implication in these events, there is no doubt that the Kremlin has been engineering their development for many months. Since the beginning of the occupation, the USSR has been organizing a North Korean army, clandestinely trained by Soviet advisers and equipped with Soviet weapons. The "draft provisional constitution," which envisages a regime remarkably similar to that of the USSR, anticipates eventual incorporation of all Korea into the "People's Republic of Korea" and goes so far as to specify Seoul, capital of the present US zone, as the future capital of a united Korea.

The "draft constitution" probably will be acclaimed by "people's representatives" of both North and South Korea at a mass demonstration at Pyongyang on 1 March (a Korean patriotic holiday) and will be adopted by a special assembly of the North Korean People's Council in mid-March. The questions of whether to hold a plebiscite in order to secure "popular approval" prior to the adoption of the constitution and whether subsequently to extend formal recognition to the regime will probably be decided by the Kremlin in accord with political expediency.

Despite the relative complexity of these day-to-day tactical maneuvers, the underlying trend in Korea remains clear. Soviet intransigence and expansionism are driving

- 7 -

61. Daily Summary Excerpt, 24 February 1948, Czechoslovakia: Estimate of Political Crisis

EUROPE

4. CZECHOSLOVAKIA: Estimate of political crisis--US Ambassador Steinhardt reports that events have moved so rapidly in Czechoslovakia recently that the sole restraining influence upon the Communists appears to be President Benes' constitutional authority and his personal popularity.

    (CIA Comment: CIA believes that the Communists will make every effort to preserve a semblance of legality in their drive to gain control of the government. However, the Communists are already so committed by their public pronouncements and actions that it would be political suicide for them to accept a compromise which did not enable them to retain sufficient power, including control of the police, to insure a Communist victory in the May election.)

- 2 -

62. Weekly Summary Excerpt, 27 February 1948, Communist Coup in Czechoslovakia; Communist Military and Political Outlook in Manchuria

COMMUNIST COUP IN CZECHOSLOVAKIA

The establishment of a Communist police state in Czechoslovakia has further diminished the possibility of a compromise in Europe between the ideologies of the Kremlin and the principles of western democracy and individual freedom. Such a compromise had apparently been achieved in Czechoslovakia where Communists and non-Communists had nearly equal power in the coalition Government, where the majority of the people approved of many Communist economic policies, and all parties were willing to follow the lead of the USSR in matters of foreign policy. The compromise was shattered, however, by the refusal of the non-Communists to permit continued Communist control of the police and by the Communist realization that an electoral victory was impossible without this control. The coup, therefore, reflects the refusal of the Communists to settle for anything less than complete control and their conviction that such dominance could never have been achieved under a freely operating parliamentary form of government.

The ease with which the Communists effected the coup reveals the extent to which they had been paying only lip service to the freely-elected coalition Government which has been in power since 1945. Having won the key cabinet posts in the May 1946 elections (Premiership, Interior, Information and Finance), the Communists have since steadily extended their control of the positions necessary for seizure of the government. By gaining direction of the Ministry of National Defense through the appointment of General Svoboda, a willing Communist tool, the Communists were able to neutralize the army. Communist command of labor was effectively implemented through the National Trade Union Organization. Despite these basic prerequisites for a coup, the seizure of power by the Communists would have been more difficult if they had not already gained a majority position in provincial, city, and village local governing bodies and had not organized "action committees" composed of trusted Communist Party members. Through these organizations, the Communists were able to seize physical control of all national and local government offices,

- 1 -

62. *(Continued)*

factories, newspapers, radio stations, and virtually every important public or private institution in the country. The acceptance by President Benes of the new Communist cabinet, therefore, represented little more than a formal acknowledgment of a fait accompli.

The Communist Party can now stifle any remaining opposition in the country. The five representatives of the Moderate parties included in the new cabinet have been assigned minor positions and will act as willing Communist supporters. The Communists will liquidate all effective opposition through a series of "treason" trials and will rapidly complete the communization of the nation's economy.

Assumption of power by the Communists will have a disrupting effect, at least temporarily, on the nation's economy. For political reasons the Communists will be forced to liquidate many anti-Communists from key managerial and technical positions in industry, and substantial industrial and economic sabotage will undoubtedly develop. Because the nation's highly industrialized economy is dependent upon the import from the West of raw materials and machinery not obtainable in eastern Europe or the USSR, Czechoslovakia will continue to trade with western Europe, although possibly on a decreased scale because of the decrease in total production.

The Communist coup will have little effect upon Czechoslovak foreign policy which has consistently followed the lead of the USSR. The coup may, however, have political repercussions in western Europe. In France, Italy, and Germany, the existing political divisions probably will be intensified because the non-Communists will be more determined to prevent Communist participation in the governments of these countries. Meanwhile, Communist morale in western Europe will be improved by the Kremlin's success in Czechoslovakia.

- 2 -

COMMUNIST MILITARY AND POLITICAL
OUTLOOK IN MANCHURIA

The Chinese National Government's military situation in Manchuria continues to grow more precarious. Present indications are that, without adequate supplies or reinforcements, the Nationalists cannot maintain their present garrisons in southern Manchuria which have been marooned for some time. Consequently, despite the recent reorganization of the Nationalist command in Manchuria, the Nationalist foothold centering around Mukden probably cannot survive for a period of more than six months without the delivery of substantial outside aid.

If Mukden falls, National Government influence in Manchuria will be destroyed and control will pass to the Communists who will then be able to move more troops to China proper. The imminent possibility of a Nationalist collapse in Manchuria has given rise to a new series of representations by National Government officials who hope to elicit prompt US aid.

Despite considerable speculation suggesting that the Communists intend to establish an independent Manchurian regime, with a separate government, such an autonomous state seems unlikely. Chinese Communist propaganda has insisted that Manchuria is an integral part of China and has represented the Communist program as a crusade for the "liberation" of China as a whole. The Communists will probably persevere in an aggressive strategy in China and will therefore seek to enlarge the area under their control rather than to make a piecemeal consolidation of their gains. The establishment of an autonomous Manchurian state would make the Communists more vulnerable to the accusation that they are puppets of the USSR; there are some indications of current Soviet interest in, and preparatory activity toward, the establishment of such a regime in Manchuria. Because of the intensely nationalistic spirit of the Chinese people, however, the Communists are most

- 3 -

TOP SECRET

anxious to protect themselves from the charge of Soviet dominance.

The Communists in China are therefore more likely, following their assumption of full control in Manchuria, to establish a political structure which will be designed to become a component part of a Communist government of China but will have an almost free hand in managing its own regional affairs. Such a setup would harmonize with the Chinese Communists' present "border region" system, a loose governmental structure which has always allowed a considerable amount of local independence and thus has overcome many regional antagonisms.

- 4 -

TOP SECRET

63. Daily Summary Excerpt, 4 March 1948, USSR: Possible Kremlin Disagreement on Tactics

4. **USSR:** **Possible Kremlin disagreement on tactics**--US Embassy Budapest reports that the Hungarian Prime Minister recently revealed the following impressions concerning possible disagreement within the Kremlin over Soviet tactics: (a) one group, allegedly favored by Stalin, desires to consolidate present Soviet gains and temporarily settle differences with the west; (b) the other group, led by Molotov, wants to press rapidly for greater expansion before US aid to Europe can be effective; and (c) the Molotov group feels that US preoccupation with the presidential election presents "a golden opportunity" for Soviet expansion and that Soviet action should be timed accordingly.

(CIA Comment: Several unsubstantiated rumors of divergent opinions within the Politburo over tactics in the "cold war" tend to support the Prime Minister's observations. CIA believes that a definitive decision by the Kremlin awaits: (a) the outcome of the Italian elections; and (b) more substantial indications of western, particularly US, determination to check further Communist expansion.)

- 2 -

64. Daily Summary Excerpt, 16 March 1948, Czechoslovaks Believe USSR Willing to Risk War

CONFIDENTIAL
TOP SECRET

GENERAL

1. <u>Czechoslovaks believe USSR willing to risk war</u>--US Ambassador Steinhardt has been told [   ]
that the Deputy Foreign Minister of the Soviet Union recently confided in Premier Gottwald the possibility that war will break out "when the weather gets better." Steinhardt's informant gained the impression that the Czechoslovak Cabinet's present view is that the Soviet Union regards the establishment of Communist-dominated governments throughout Europe before the fall of 1948 as essential and has decided to devote every effort to that end during the next few months despite the possibility of war with the western powers.

(CIA Comment: CIA does not believe that the USSR is presently prepared to risk war in the pursuit of its aims in Europe.)

Document No. 060

NO CHANGE in Class. ☐
☐ DECLASSIFIED
Class. CHANGED TO: TS S
Auth: ___, 4 Apr 77
Date: 13 MAR 1978 by: 028

- 1 -

CONFIDENTIAL
TOP SECRET

16 March 1948

MEMORANDUM FOR THE PRESIDENT

Under date of 22 December 1947, CIA reported that there was a possibility of steps being taken in Berlin by the Soviet authorities to force the other occupying powers to remove from Berlin. Delay in the formation of a separate Eastern German Government and in Soviet attempts to force the Western Powers from Berlin has probably been caused in large measure by the firm attitude of US officials in Berlin. While no further reports have been received indicating that the USSR has decided to force the Western Powers from Berlin, the recent US, UK, France, Benelux discussions in London concerning the formation of a West German State to be included in a Western European Union invite some form of Soviet response stronger than the mere protests received so far.

Soviet response will be timed to follow overt allied implementation of the London decisions, and will consist of the announcement of plans, such as a plebiscite, for an Eastern Zone "all German state", claiming to represent the whole German people. Announcement of such plans would be followed by an intensified Soviet campaign to oust the Western Powers from Berlin. The most urgent dangers are: (1) "incidents" arising from the presence in Berlin of young, undisciplined troops; (2) aggravation of the situation by such German malcontents as want an East-West war; (3) any tendency towards war hysteria or lack of firmness and patience on the part of US officials in Berlin.

s/ RHH - by hand DCI to Admiral Leahy
R. H. Hillenkoetter   3/16/48
Rear Admiral, USN
Director of Central Intelligence

Encl:
    Copy, Memo for President,
    12/22/47
Distribution:
    Orig. & 1 - President
    Director
    Asst Dir., ORE
    Central Records

SECRET

65. *(Continued)*

12 March 1948   I M-13

MEMORANDUM FOR THE DIRECTOR, CIA

FROM: THE ASSISTANT DIRECTOR, ORE

SUBJECT: PROBABLE SOVIET REACTIONS IN BERLIN TO
           WESTERN EUROPEAN UNION TALKS

Attention is invited to a Memorandum for the President from the Director of CIA, dated 22 December 1947, a copy of which is attached. Delay in the formation of a separate Eastern German Government and in Soviet attempts to force the Western Powers from Berlin has probably been caused in large measure by the firm attitude of US officials in Berlin. While no further reports have been received indicating that the USSR has decided to force the Western Powers from Berlin, the recent US, UK, France, Benelux discussions in London concerning the formation of a West German State to be included in a Western European Union invite some form of Soviet response stronger than the mere protests received so far.

Soviet response will be timed to follow overt allied implementation of the London decisions, and will consist of the announcement of plans, such as a plebiscite, for an Eastern Zone "all German State", claiming to represent the whole German people. Announcement of such plans would be followed by an intensified Soviet campaign to oust the Western Powers from Berlin. The most urgent dangers are: (1) "incidents" arising from the presence in Berlin of young, undisciplined troops; (2) aggravation of the situation by such German malcontents as want an East-West war; (3) any tendency towards war hysteria or lack of firmness and patience on the part of US officials in Berlin.

THEODORE BABBITT
Assistant Director
Reports and Estimates

Attach:
     Memo. 22 Dec. 1947

 # This was covered by memo. 16 March 1948
DCI to Pres. (ER 8404) ~~SECRET~~
in files QS/ORE

MAR 12 1948
ORE 4

181

65. *(Continued)*

22 December 1947

MEMORANDUM FOR THE PRESIDENT

The breakdown of the CFM in London may cause the USSR to undertake a program of intensified obstructionism and calculated insult in an effort to force the US and the other Western Powers to withdraw from Berlin all representatives except a small Allied Control Authority group. The implementation of such a program could create a situation of great tension which might lead to armed clashes between Soviet personnel and that of the other occupying powers.

The failure of the CFM to reach agreement on any question and the CFM's subsequent indefinite adjournment will result in an accelerated consolidation of eastern Germany. The USSR will attempt to incorporate thoroughly the economic system of its Zone into the Soviet economy and to orient the political system still more closely to the Soviet ideology. Soviet authorities will encounter difficulties in accomplishing both objectives because of the presence of US officials and troops in Berlin.

The presence there of this personnel hinders the ruthless and forcible communization of all eastern Germany, helps to sustain non-Communist opposition, and demonstrates that the US does not intend to abandon or partition the country. Berlin, of course, could hardly serve as the capital of an eastern German state, should the USSR eventually establish one, so long as the Western Powers maintain troops in the city. The Kremlin is aware of this situation.

The Kremlin is aware, also, that the present quadripartite occupation of Berlin furnishes the US with an excellent listening post and a base of operations for intelligence activities in the Eastern Zone as well as providing political refugees from Soviet areas with a convenient haven. Masters of propaganda themselves, the Soviet authorities are highly sensitive to the great propaganda value of the continued presence of US and the other Western Power forces and the guarantees they provide of relative political freedom for the residents of the city.

65. *(Continued)*

- 2 -

The USSR, consequently, cannot expect the US and the other Western Powers to evacuate the city voluntarily. The USSR, therefore, will probably use every means short of armed force to compel these powers to leave the city.

These devices may include additional obstruction to transport and travel to and within the city, "failure" of services such as electric supply, reduction of that part of the food supply which comes from the Soviet Zone, flagrant violations of Kommandatura agreements, instigation of unrest among Germans in the US sector, disregard of the elected municipal government, a deliberately intensified campaign of insult or personal injury to US personnel, and terrorization of their German employees.

The degree of danger inherent in such a campaign will depend on the accuracy with which Soviet authorities gauge US determination to remain and the state of discipline of US officials and troops. Overly enthusiastic resort to insults or personal violence by Soviet troops or Communists could well create "incidents", street fights, brawls, and other public disturbances which, in turn, might well lead to high-level repercussions of the gravest character. Only the greatest determination and tact on both sides could prevent a serious incident from deteriorating beyond control of the Berlin authorities. Even if Soviet estimates of limits to US patience are accurate, the situation could and probably would be aggravated by the activities of German malcontents, who for one reason or another, seek to bring about an open East-West conflict.

The Kremlin will probably defer its maximum effort to force Western Power evacuation of Berlin until it has fully calculated the risks and considered the problem in the light of Soviet strategy elsewhere. Nevertheless, in view of probable irresponsible action by local Soviet officials, the day-to-day developments in the immediate future will test the firmness, patience, and discipline of all US personnel in Berlin.

R. H. HILLENKOETTER
Rear Admiral, USN
Director of Central Intelligence

475157

TOP SECRET

IM-18

MEMORANDUM FOR THE PRESIDENT

The Central Intelligence Agency and the intelligence
organizations of the Departments of State, War, Navy and Air
Force agree that if the Congress passes a universal military
training act and/or a selective service act these measures,
taken singly or together, will not of themselves cause the
USSR to resort to military action within the next 60 days.

DEC. T.S.

46   **17** MAR 1948

~~CONFIDENTIAL~~   636

2. <u>Turks fear war may be imminent</u>--US Ambassador Wilson
   in Ankara reports that Secretary General Carim of the
   Turkish Foreign Office is "deeply pessimistic" over the
   international situation. Carim fears that the USSR is prepared to begin open war at any time and that the initial attack
   might be directed against Turkey. According to Wilson, Carim
   reasons that in view of the hardening attitude of the western
   democracies, the USSR will be relatively weaker a year hence
   and would therfore gain by precipitating action now. Carim
   believes that the Soviet armies would quickly over-run western Europe and the Middle East.

        (CIA Comment: CIA does not believe that the USSR
   plans a military venture in the immediate future in either
   Europe or the Middle East.)

861

- 1 -

~~CONFIDENTIAL~~ ~~TOP SECRET~~

NO CHANGE in Class. ☐
☐ DECLASSIFIED

Class.   TS   S   Ⓒ

Auth: 77

Date: **13 MAR 1978**   By: **028**

6. **GERMANY:** <u>USSR may close Eastern Zone border</u>--US Political Adviser reports from Frankfurt that
....] gendarme officials from southern and western Thuringia met on 15 March at Soviet instigation and were informed of an alert plan for which they were to prepare immediately. The plan is allegedly to be put into effect when Soviet officials move to abolish the Christian Democratic Union and the Liberal Democratic Party and arrest the parties' leaders. The gendarmes reportedly will reinforce the border police in order to prevent the escape of the political leaders into the western Zones.

(CIA Comment: Although US border detachments have not reported physical evidence of a tightening of the border, such a Soviet move may be imminent; this step might also be taken in connection with a purge of "unreliable" elements from the Social- ist Unity Party. The move probably would not foreshadow inter- ruption of US, UK, and French traffic with Berlin.)

- 3 -

69. ORE 22-48 Excerpt, 2 April 1948, Possibility of Direct Soviet Military Action During 1948

ORE 22-48

TOP SECRET

POSSIBILITY OF DIRECT SOVIET MILITARY ACTION DURING 1948

Report by a Joint Ad Hoc Committee *

THE PROBLEM

1. We have been directed to estimate the likelihood of a Soviet resort to direct military action during 1948.

DISCUSSION

2. Our conclusions are based on considerations discussed in the Enclosure.

CONCLUSIONS

3. The preponderance of available evidence and of considerations derived from the "logic of the situation" supports the conclusion that the USSR will not resort to direct military action during 1948.

4. However, in view of the combat readiness and disposition of the Soviet armed forces and the strategic advantage which the USSR might impute to the occupation of Western Europe and the Near East, the possibility must be recognized that the USSR might resort to direct military action in 1948, particularly if the Kremlin should interpret some US move, or series of moves, as indicating an intention to attack the USSR or its satellites.

---

* This estimate was prepared by a joint ad hoc committee representing CIA and the intelligence agencies of the Department of State, the Army, the Navy, and the Air Force. The date of the estimate is 30 March 1948.

1

TOP SECRET

70. Weekly Summary Excerpt, 9 April 1948, Soviet Walkout From Allied Control Council; Diminished Communist Capabilities in Italy

Both the recent Soviet walkout from the Allied Control Council (ACC) and recent Soviet interference with transportation into Berlin seem to indicate that the USSR: (1) has abandoned hope of using the ACC to hinder the present western European reconstruction program, and (2) intends to accelerate preparations for the establishment of an eastern "German state" whenever the Kremlin decides that the western powers can be successfully blamed for partitioning Germany. In this preparatory phase, the USSR may place the Soviet Zone under a "democratic" and "loyal" German administration, created from the Communist-dominated Peoples' Congress and strengthened by trained Germans from the former Moscow Free Germany Committee. Both the presence of the western powers in Berlin and the functioning of the ACC hamper the realization of the Soviet objectives and, unless allied determination remains obviously strong, further Soviet attempts to eliminate these hindrances may be expected. (A CIA Special Estimate titled "Possible Program of Future Soviet Moves in Western Germany" is now being prepared.)

- iii -

70. *(Continued)*

TOP SECRET

DIMINISHED COMMUNIST CAPABILITIES IN ITALY

The prospects have sharply diminished that the Italian Communist Party will obtain a sufficiently large plurality in the 18 April elections to ensure Communist or left-wing socialist representation in the next Italian Government. Concurrently, the Party's capabilities for successful large-scale insurrection, without active military assistance from Yugoslavia, have been considerably reduced. Unless the Communists receive substantial outside aid, the Government now appears sufficiently strong to prevent its overthrow by force and to put down large-scale rebellion. Whether the Kremlin, even under these circumstances, will direct an insurrection either before or after the elections cannot be predicted. If, as seems probable, the Communists fail to secure representation in the new government, they will then launch a new program of strikes and sabotage to wreck the recovery program and discredit the government.

The reduction in Communist capabilities for successful large-scale insurrection springs largely from four factors. In the past few months, the Italian armed services and security forces have been greatly strengthened, not only by new equipment but also by a considerably improved morale. Concurrently, the Communist para-military forces have been weakened and to some extent disrupted by government seizure of clandestine munitions dumps and caches and the interception of arms shipped in from abroad. No evidence available indicates that Yugoslav forces--the most logical source of outside assistance--are being prepared for action in Italy. Finally, and probably most important, the Italian masses appear less inclined than ever to support a Communist uprising and have become increasingly anti-Communist in their attitude.

Communist capabilities for effective revolt, in the absence of outside aid, now appear limited to localized successes, particularly in north Italy. These capabilities are based upon military potential and the party's following in labor. The Communist semi-military organization, the Apparato, consists of

- 1 -

TOP SECRET

70. *(Continued)*

approximately 100,000 ex-Partisans, armed and trained, and
about 100,000 reserves in training. The Apparato has general
headquarters at Milan and operational headquarters in cities
on the main highway between Milan and the other Communist
stronghold of Bologna. Communist munitions dumps are believed to contain extensive supplies of arms, including armored
cars, light field guns, anti-tank guns, mortars, machine guns,
and a few tanks. To increase their armaments, the Communists would attempt to seize Government arsenals and ammunition dumps, and, if unsuccessful in capturing them, would make
every effort to blow them up.

In addition to their military potential, the Communists
possess a powerful revolutionary weapon in their control of the
Italian General Confederation of Labor (CGIL), which has five
million workers in industry and various public services. Domination of the agricultural Workers' Confederation, which has
approximately two million members, gives the Communists
almost complete control of the agriculture of the important Po
Valley region; virtual Communist control of the industrial unions
would facilitate seizure by the workers of most industrial establishments. The Communists, furthermore, dominate the news-
paper printers' union and have infiltrated communications.
Public utilities, particularly gas and electric services, are Communist-dominated and could be disrupted in case of revolution.

The De Gasperi Government, however, with control of
armed forces totaling approximately 336,000 men, would probably
be able to prevent Italian Communists from taking over the central
government. Army strength is concentrated in northern Italy,
and army divisions are disposed at Udine, Treviso, Milan, Torino,
and Lucca. Supplementary to the army are the security forces of
the Ministry of the Interior: 75,000 carabinieri, a mobile reserve
corps of 16,000 civil police, 80,000 regular members of the civil
police, 36,357 finance guards, and 5,000 railway police. The
carabinieri maintain their heaviest concentrations in the north.
Critical areas, such as Bologna, have been reinforced by special

- 2 -

70. *(Continued)*

reserves of the security forces. In the event of insurrection, the Italian Navy could employ its units to protect Italian ports and could land many of its approximately 35,000 men to assist the ground forces. The bulk of the Italian fleet is based at Taranto and La Spezia. The Italian Air Force, with personnel numbering 25,000, has about 500 planes, mostly obsolescent, of which about 60 are fighters in tactical units.

- 3 -

71. Daily Summary Excerpt, 12 April 1948, Colombia: Continuation of Bogota Conference Favored

THE AMERICAS

5. **COLOMBIA:** Continuation of Bogota Conference favored-- US Embassy Bogota reports that delegation leaders are unanimously in favor of continuing the conference at Bogota, "unless the situation so worsens as to make it physically impossible."

Reports from US Consulates in Colombia indicate that the Government is still making progress toward restoring order and that uprisings outside the capital city were relatively small and soon brought under control. The Embassy adds that the mopping up of snipers continues in Bogota where damage and loss of life were very heavy.

A CIA source reports the belief current in Bogota that there is no substantiation for the government claim that the shooting was the result of a Communist plot, and that the shooting was in fact the result of a private dispute over litigation in which Gaitan was counsel. The Embassy transmits a report that the assassin was employed last October as butler in the Soviet Legation. The Colombian Government has announced that it has arrested the persons who took over a Bogota radio station and that two Russian agents and other foreigners were among those arrested.

(CIA Comment: CIA believes that the Colombian Government will make every attempt to lay the insurrection at the door of the Communists. The reported decision to sever diplomatic relations with the USSR is consistent with such a campaign. The weight of available evidence, however, points to the conclusion that the Communists did not instigate the revolt, which was a spontaneous reaction to Gaitan's assassination, but actively encouraged mob action once rioting had broken out.)

- 3 -

72. Weekly Summary Excerpt, 23 April 1948, New Soviet Attitude Toward Austrian Treaty; Prospective Communist Strategy Following the Italian Elections

NEW SOVIET ATTITUDE TOWARD AUSTRIAN TREATY

The apparent desire of the USSR for an early conclusion of an Austrian treaty has recently led to a definite change in Soviet tactics both at the London treaty discussions and in the administration of Soviet areas in Austria. Until recently, the USSR enjoyed an excellent tactical position in the London negotiations because of the reluctance of the western powers to commit themselves on the economic phases of the treaty without knowing the Soviet position on questions of Austrian security. The USSR has sacrificed this advantage by agreeing to defer the discussion of economic items in order to consider the security issues.

Although recent moves by the USSR in Vienna and in the Soviet-occupied zone of eastern Austria appear to be confused and defensive, they essentially reveal a Soviet desire to impress the Austrian Government and the western allies with the desirability of an Austrian treaty. Soviet steps to impede transportation between the western zones and Vienna, which have proved annoying even though never fully enforced, are probably intended to serve as a reminder of the capabilities of the USSR in Austria. Austrian leaders are particularly disturbed by the prospects of possible Soviet violence and forced partition of the country following a breakdown in treaty negotiations.

There can be little doubt that the USSR regards the present quadripartite occupation of Austria as unfavorable to its designs and considers that forced partition is not a desirable solution to the problem. The Kremlin would welcome a treaty which would both provide for quadripartite troop withdrawal and leave Austria unable to resist eventual absorption into the eastern bloc. Although the USSR, through an underestimation of Austria's political vitality and economic potential, might accept a settlement which would make it difficult for either the USSR or its Satellites to absorb Austria except by armed aggression, it is unlikely that the Kremlin will agree to any terms which would be likely to prejudice seriously its chances of eventual domination in Austria.

- 1 -

72. *(Continued)*

PROSPECTIVE COMMUNIST STRATEGY FOLLOWING THE ITALIAN ELECTIONS

The defeat suffered by the Communists in the Italian election has further reduced Communist capabilities for assuming power and has vastly improved the morale and confidence of the anti-Communists in both Italy and France. An increasing number of left-wing European Socialists and fellow-travellers may now abandon their Communist association. The Communists in western Europe thus are confronted with a considerable loss in political influence in addition to their already reduced capabilities for revolutionary action.

Italy and ~~Germany~~ France may consequently enjoy a brief respite while the Communists regroup their forces and revise their strategy. The USSR, however, can be expected to maintain its pressure in Germany. Moreover, it will probably continue its aggressive tactics in the Near East. In Iran, continuing Soviet pressure may eventually lead to actual intervention, professedly based on the 1921 Soviet-Iranian Treaty. The deteriorating situation in Palestine may soon present the Kremlin with an irresistible opportunity for greatly expanded covert intervention. Although the Satellites continue to exercise caution in their support of the guerrilla forces in Greece, they are capable of vastly increasing the scale of their covert aid. In Latin America, the USSR can be expected to seize upon any favorable opportunities for exploiting local unrest or violence.

For the immediate future, Communist activities in western Europe are likely to be directed toward rebuilding the popular front rather than an early or determined bid for power. A Communist drive to recover the allegiance of the non-Communist Left is indicated by these recent developments: (1) French Communist Leader Thorez on 18 April called upon Communists, Socialists, and Catholics to unite in defense of French "liberty and independence"; (2) the Cominform Journal, reversing its original position, is now professing to represent

- 3 -

72. *(Continued)*

TOP SECRET

all workers' parties, not merely the Communists; (3) the German Communists recently voiced approval of a "Middle-Class Auxiliary" of the Socialist Unity Party (SED), which might conceivably develop into the long-expected "nationalist" movement based on the Bismarckian concept of Russo-German cooperation; and (4) the Kremlin reportedly has issued a directive to the French Central Communist Committee calling for a program of non-violence in western Europe and intensified activity in Germany and the Near East.

Concurrently, Communist propagandists may intensify their efforts to contrast "peaceful" Soviet intentions with US "warmongering" and "imperialist designs." Such a drive would be designed to win the support of those western Europeans who are prepared to seek "peace at any price" and to encourage a relaxation of western, and particularly US, military preparedness. Such an intensified campaign would presumably be launched in the speeches and pronouncements which traditionally are made by leading Communists on May Day.

In any event, the Communists are not expected to relax their efforts to prevent recovery in Europe. Defeat of the recovery program remains a prime objective of Communist strategy. Strikes and industrial sabotage, conducted ostensibly on the basis of local economic issues rather than political considerations, therefore can be expected. Although Communist propaganda will continue to impugn US motives in promoting recovery, the Kremlin may henceforth moderate its attacks upon present western European governments.

In Greece, the Kremlin is also faced with a possible reduction of Communist capabilities. Differences between Greek Communists and Soviet-Satellite Communists have apparently arisen over problems concerning Soviet aims in Greece and the conduct of the civil war. Greek Communist leaders are reportedly disturbed by the failure of the Satellites to provide the guerrillas with enough aid to halt the continuing successes of the Greek Army, and the Minister of Interior in the Markos government is said to be distrustful

- 4 -

TOP SECRET

72. *(Continued)*

TOP SECRET

of the "selfish" policy of the USSR and fearful that Yugoslavia may be planning to seize Greek Macedonia. Moreover, certain Greek Communist leaders believe that the primary Soviet intention in the civil war is to wage a long campaign of economic attrition against the US and not to effect the rapid military defeat of Greece. In view of the successful operations of the Greek Army, it is apparent that the Kremlin must decide soon whether to authorize a drastic increase in aid to the guerrillas or allow their gradual defeat by the Greek Army.

Although Communist May Day demonstrations in Latin America may result in local disturbances, present indications are that the Latin American governments will be fully capable of controlling any outbreaks. In Mexico, the electrical workers have threatened to call a May Day strike. If they are joined by the petroleum workers, miners, and railway workers (all closely allied with the electrical workers by inter-union agreements), the resulting strike could cause a general paralysis of the country and threaten the stability of the Mexican Government. Sporadic violence may break out in Cuba, and possibly in a few other countries, though there are no indications at present of coordinated plans for strikes or public disturbances.

- 5 -

TOP SECRET

73. Daily Summary Excerpt, 24 April 1948, Reported Soviet Plans for Eastern German Regime

3. GERMANY: Reported Soviet plans for eastern German regime--
Headquarters of the European Command in Frankfurt believes
that if the Kremlin resorts to positive action in Germany about
1 May, the USSR will probably establish an eastern German government with the four powers remaining in Berlin but inopera-
tive as a controlling or governing element. The Headquarters
has received reports substantiating this conclusion; one such
report suggests that Soviet officials have decided to unify the
Soviet Zone on 1 May 1948 under a central government which
will be composed of prominent individuals in the Peoples' Council of the Peoples' Congress. The Headquarters expects the
USSR to give greater recognition and additional support to the
Peoples' Council as a possible replacement for existing political
parties in the Soviet Zone.

(CIA Comment: CIA believes that the USSR may utilize
"May Day" as an occasion for accelerating its efforts to establish a provisional government in the Soviet Zone, and that such
action would be accompanied or preceded by increased Soviet
pressure on the western powers in Berlin.)

- 2 -

ORE 29-48   SECRET

POSSIBLE PROGRAM OF FUTURE SOVIET MOVES IN GERMANY
SUMMARY

1. The following discussion covers a program that might be resorted to by the USSR in Germany in an effort to cause the Western Powers to leave Berlin, to consolidate the Soviet hold over Eastern Germany, and to extend Soviet influence into Western Germany. Until recently this review of possible Soviet intentions was considered purely speculative and the program one that would be attempted only after the USSR had concluded that Soviet interference with the Allied efforts in Western Germany could not be effected by legal international means or through local Communist subversion. The timing of the individual stages of the program would probably be conditioned upon the timing and success of Western Power action.

2. The recent Soviet walkout from the Allied Control Council and Soviet efforts to impede transportation to and from Berlin indicate that this program may already be under way, and, that while risk of war may be involved, the plan possibly can be effected without military violence.

3. It is believed, therefore, that recent Western Power action may have caused the USSR to decide that:

    a. hope no longer remains for interfering through quadripartite means with the production of Western Germany upon which the success of the European Recovery Program substantially depends;

    b. the Soviet Zone must be placed under permanent control of a well organized German group, loyal to the USSR, and supported by police state measures;

    c. the Peoples' Congress should be the instrument for the formation of such a provisional German Government;

    d. in order to prevent Allied interference with this process of political consolidation, the Allied Control Council should be abolished, or permanently boycotted, and the Western Powers forced out of Berlin;

    e. the new German "Government" should be acknowledged, at a propitious time, as the official administration for Eastern Germany, with propaganda pretensions to authority over all of Germany;

    f. the Soviet Army should remain as the "protector" of the new Reich pending creation of a new German Army, by agreement with this government; and

    g. in an effort to undermine the Western Power program Western Germany should be pressed, by all possible methods, to "rejoin" the Reich.

Note: The information in this report is as of 2 April 1948.
      The intelligence organizations of the Departments of State, Army, Navy, and the Air Force have concurred in this report.

1   SECRET

POSSIBLE PROGRAM OF FUTURE SOVIET MOVES IN GERMANY

1. With the conclusion of the London tripartite talks and the decision to consider Western Germany in the ERP planning, the Kremlin may have decided that little hope remains for the USSR to interfere with US/UK Zone production.

Three events: the results of the Soviet-sponsored Peoples' Congress, the abrupt departure of the Soviet delegation from the Allied Control Council (ACC) meeting of 20 March, and the subsequent Soviet efforts to impede both freight and passenger traffic between Berlin and the West indicate that at least the first steps in the outline of possible Soviet action may no longer be entirely in the realm of speculation.

2. CIA has believed and continues to believe that the USSR might encourage the Peoples' Congress to organize a future "national" administration and establish a *de facto* Government for the Eastern Zone while propagandistically claiming to speak for all the country. The Peoples' Congress partially confirmed this opinion when it convened on 17 March, advocated the early establishment of a Government to replace the ACC, and evidenced its pretensions to speak for the German people.

3. CIA has believed and continues to believe also that in preparation for the new "government", the USSR would attempt to discredit the ACC. While the abrupt termination of the Control Council meeting of 20 March has not yet been extended to a permanent Soviet withdrawal from the Council, Soviet officials have charged that the Western Powers, by unilateral action, have already made the work of the Council worthless.

4. The presence of the Western Powers in Berlin adds to the difficulty of establishing a Soviet puppet government in Eastern Germany, because of the "opposition" that operates from the sanctuary of the Western Powers' sections of the city. The USSR would consequently desire to effect a Western Power evacuation of Berlin as expeditiously as possible. The Soviet attempt to impede transport threatens to render untenable the position of a sizeable Allied group isolated over a hundred miles from the Western area, and, additionally, to cut off the industrial contribution of the US and UK sectors of Berlin from the Bizonal economic structure.

5. Should the Peoples' Congress, in fact, set up a "government" of the Soviet Zone, and lay claim to "represent" all of Germany, the Soviet Military Administration might accord it local recognition as the established German administration and give propaganda-credence to its pretensions to govern all of the Zones. The USSR and its satellites might then be expected to enter into provisional political and economic agreements directly with this "government", laying the foundation for eventual formal recognition at such time as the USSR considers it feasible to press the puppet government's claim to German sovereignty.

2

6.   A Soviet-sponsored provisional government which would, in all probability, control the Soviet sector of Berlin, might attempt by constant propaganda and possibly by direct interference in the public utilities affecting the Western sectors to obtain the withdrawal from Berlin of Western representation in the event that any still remained. The USSR could support this program with further concrete action similar to the transport block and declare the dissolution of the ACC, seeking to place the onus for its failure on the West.

7.   If, at any time, the Soviet Union decided that the new government of Eastern Germany is sufficiently loyal or adequately controlled by the USSR to be a trusted satellite, that further Soviet interference in Western Germany through quadripartite means is hopeless, and that the Western Powers are susceptible of blame for the partition of Germany, the USSR might officially recognize the Eastern German government, and by agreement continue the "protection" of the Red Army while developing a German Army and perfecting the police system.   Both the USSR and the Eastern German "state" would then launch a campaign for German unity and independence designed to win sufficient German converts in the Western Zones to reduce materially German cooperation in the West and to attempt to undermine the program of the Western Powers.

8.   Although each of these successive steps involves the risk of war in the event of miscalculation of Western resistance or of unforeseen circumstances, each move on the program could be implemented without the application of military force if adroitly made as merely a retaliatory measure necessitated by unilateral Western Power action, and if pressed only at opportune moments.

3

75. Weekly Summary Excerpt, 30 April 1948, Deadlock Over Transport Problems in Berlin

The deadlock over transport problems continues in Berlin despite a lull in sensational publicity. The USSR has not made a single real concession but has actually established complete but somewhat inefficient control over surface traffic moving in and out of Berlin, except incoming freight. Present hope for solution by negotiation is small. The USSR is now apparently preparing to tighten its grip on the city by attempting to enforce new restrictions on air traffic which would make all allied transport subject to Soviet regulation. So far, Soviet action on air transport has been limited to probing for western power weakness under the guise of a desire for increased air "safety." If the US-UK reaction to this probing shows indecision, the USSR may be expected to take strong action to compel western air traffic to submit to Soviet controls. Such action would probably include use of Soviet fighter planes to threaten and intimidate allied pilots.

- iv -

76. Daily Summary Excerpt, 7 May 1948, Germany: Soviet Attempt to Interrupt US Air Traffic

4. **GERMANY:** <u>Soviet attempt to interrupt US air traffic</u>--According to Acting US Political Adviser Chase, US officials received Soviet notification on 4 May that no flying would be permitted that night over the greater Berlin area. Chase reports that the US representative, in accordance with his instructions, informed his Soviet colleague that the US did not recognize such unilateral action. Chase adds that US airplanes from the Templehof Airdrome carried out a previously scheduled night operation, consisting of a normal training flight over the greater Berlin area.

(CIA Comment: CIA believes the Soviet action is an attempt to probe US reaction to Soviet-imposed regulations on air traffic between Berlin and the west and may be followed by more determined moves to restrict the air traffic of the western powers.)

77. Weekly Summary Excerpt, 14 May 1948, Formation of a Jewish State in Palestine; French Officials Attempting to Negotiate Settlement of French Vietnam Dispute

TRENDS IN BRIEF

<u>Formation of a Jewish state in Palestine</u> will enable the USSR to intensify its efforts to expand Soviet influence in the Near East and to perpetuate a chaotic condition there. Although the USSR and its Satellites will probably delay full recognition of the new state, they may grant it belligerent rights in the near future. In any event, the flow of men and munitions to Palestine from the Soviet bloc can be expected to increase substantially. The USSR will undoubtedly take advantage of the removal of immigration restrictions to increase the influx of trained Soviet agents from eastern and central Europe into Palestine where they have already had considerable success penetrating the Stern Gang, Irgun, and, to a lesser extent, Haganah.

- 1 -

77. *(Continued)*

French officials in Paris and Indochina are attempting to negotiate a temporary settlement of the French Vietnam dispute. High Commissioner Bollaert has been authorized to form a provisional Vietnam government headed by General Xuan, president of the Provisional Government of South Vietnam (Cochinchina). The formation of such a government may result in a transfer to France of the meetings with Bao Dai and might postpone indefinitely his return as head of a new regime. If a government, with nominal independence and geographic unity, should emerge under the reportedly ineffectual Xuan, the prospects for internal stability would still be slim because of the postponement of the settlement of problems concerning finance, customs, and diplomacy. Ho Chi Minh, who is supported by 80% of the population and who is allegedly loyal to Soviet foreign

- vi -

77. *(Continued)*

TOP SECRET

policy, probably would then assume control; much of his support
would come from elements who insist upon a propaganda campaign against French use of the European recovery program
to further French colonial policy. Because of the delicate balance
of control exercised by the Schuman Government, the French
will probably not risk a major policy decision involving liberal
concessions on the controversial colonial issue in Indochina.
A temporary Xuan government, therefore, will have little chance
of success.

TOP SECRET

78. Weekly Summary Excerpt, 18 June 1948, The Soviet Withdrawal From the Berlin Kommandatura

APPENDIX

THE SOVIET WITHDRAWAL FROM THE BERLIN KOMMANDATURA

The situation in Berlin has been further complicated by a Soviet "walkout" from the 16 June meeting of the Berlin Kommandatura in a maneuver similar to the abrupt Soviet departure from the Allied Control Commission (ACC) in March. As in the case of the ACC, further meetings are not scheduled, and the USSR may have decided to abandon completely the facade of quadripartite control of the German capital. Through this action, the Soviet Union has improved its position for obtaining the consolidation of the Soviet Zone necessary for formation of an East German state or for seeking, through "conciliation," the establishment with the western powers of more advantageous working arrangements for Germany as a whole, or for Berlin in particular. Soviet and Communist propaganda will undoubtedly claim that this latest Soviet action was forced by the six-power announcement of plans for a provisional government of western Germany. Agitation for western withdrawal from Berlin may increase, but it appears doubtful that the USSR will make a formal demand for such withdrawal.

If the USSR should proceed directly with the formation of an east German state, the withdrawal from the Kommandatura will provide Soviet propagandists with a "legal" claim for the incorporation of the Berlin Soviet sector into the eastern zone and will make possible increased pressure for the withdrawal of the western allies on the grounds that, having partitioned Germany, the western powers have no place in the Soviet Zone.

On the other hand, current Soviet tactics may be designed to create an "emergency" situation which would either force the western powers to call for renewed meetings of the ACC or permit the USSR to take such action without loss of face. Through apparent concessions on the question of quadripartite control of Germany or through the time-worn method

- 1 -

78. *(Continued)*

of obstinate obstructionism, the Soviet Union would attempt to use such meetings to delay the realization of allied plans for western Germany. In any event, the USSR will leave itself free to consolidate further its political and economic control of the Soviet Zone and will be prepared, at any time that appears opportune, to declare the formation of an east German state with pretensions to sovereignty over the entire country.

- ii -

4. YUGOSLAVIA: Challenge to Kremlin authority seen--US
   Charge Reams in Belgrade believes that Yugoslav insistence
   upon Belgrade as the site of the Danubian Conference, instead
   of some other Satellite capital as proposed by the USSR,
   represents the first direct and irrevocable challenge by a
   Satellite to the Kremlin's supreme authority. According to
   Reams, Soviet acceptance of Tito's request reflects the
   Kremlin's belief that Tito's position is strong enough to require the "traditional gradual undermining."

   (CIA Comment: CIA agrees that the Kremlin will
   not take any drastic steps immediately to "discipline" Tito.
   However, this incident has highlighted for the Kremlin the
   need for reconciling within the Satellite states the conflict
   between national interests and international Communism.
   Consequently, the USSR may either tighten its controls over
   the Satellites by expanding direct Soviet participation in
   Satellite governments or attempt to ease the "nationalist"
   opposition among Satellite Communists by making some
   economic concessions.)

80. Daily Summary Excerpt, 24 June 1948, Implications of Soviet-Satellite Conference; Germany: Soviet Solution for Berlin Problems Suggested

24 JUN 1948
720

GENERAL

1. Implications of Soviet-Satellite conference--US Embassy Warsaw believes that the current Soviet-Satellite meeting in Warsaw may have been called primarily to enable the eastern European powers to present a united answer to the London Conference on Germany. The Embassy concludes that the conference will be used as a major propaganda device to prove that the peoples of Europe overwhelmingly desire a "peaceful, democratic" solution of the German problem.

   (CIA Comment: CIA concurs with the Embassy's estimate and also considers it probable that an "Eastern Union" will be formed, avowedly to protect the USSR and its Satellites against aggression from a resurgent Germany sponsored by the West. CIA also believes that at this conference the USSR may inform the Satellites of its intention: (a) to establish a provisional government for eastern Germany to coincide with the one contemplated for western Germany; or (b) to attempt to neutralize Germany's contribution to the European recovery program by expressing a desire, possibly couched in face-saving terms, to reach agreement on Germany with the West.)

EUROPE

4. GERMANY: <u>Soviet solution for Berlin problems suggested</u>--
US Ambassador Murphy reports from Berlin that the Soviet
chief of liaison and protocol has suggested informally to the
US liaison officer that possibly an adjustment of present zonal
lines in Germany could be made in order to eliminate the friction caused by US-Soviet contact in Berlin. Murphy indicates
that this suggestion came during a general conversation, in the
course of which the Soviet officer asked whether the US was
not "skating on very thin ice" in relation to the danger of war.
The Soviet officer evaded any specific answer as to whether the
suggested "readjustment" would involve US withdrawal from
Berlin in exchange for parts of Saxony and Thuringia. Murphy
attaches significance to this suggestion because the Soviet
officer is known to be an intimate of Marshal Sokolovsky.
Murphy believes that the suggestion may indicate a Soviet
desire to bargain rather than force the present issue.

(CIA Comment: CIA believes that the conversation is
a feeler to test US determination to: (a) continue its present
policies in Europe in the face of Soviet threats; and (b) remain
in Berlin even if offered a face-saving chance to get out.)

- 2 -

81. Intelligence Memorandum 36, 24 June 1948, Probable Purpose of the Warsaw Conference

SECRET

Director, CIA   24 June 1948

Assistant Director, ORE

                                                 IM-36

Probable Purposes of the Warsaw Conference

    1. The meeting in Warsaw of Soviet Foreign Minister Molotov and the Foreign Ministers of the satellite states allegedly to discuss the effects of, and a reply to, the London Six-Power Agreement on western Germany apparently stems from the need to create an Eastern bloc into which eastern Germany could be economically, if not politically, fitted to match the western power inclusion of western Germany in the European recovery program. From the formality of the meeting; from the rank of the delegates; and from the comparative publicity attending the gathering, some declaration of importance may be expected at its conclusion. For psychological and political reasons, the intentions of the USSR warrant some "explanation" in advance to the satellites and a later public announcement of satellite approval.

    2. At present three courses of action in Germany, or a combination of the three, are open to the USSR. Before adopting any of these courses, the USSR will probably announce the formation of an Eastern bloc to defend itself against aggression from a resurgent Germany as established by the western powers. The Soviet action in Germany could be:

    a. Announcement of an intention to permit the Germans to create a provisional government for eastern Germany;

    b. An attempt to open negotiations in order to delay immediately further western action and to impede German contribution to ERP and eventually to achieve the overall unification of Germany through an accommodation with the western powers; or □

    c. Immediate establishment of a purportedly independent east German state with propaganda pretension of being the restoration of the Reich.

SEE REVERSE FOR DECLASSIFICATION ACTION

SECRET

211

81. *(Continued)*

3. The degree of consolidation now reached would permit the USSR to lay the foundations for a provisional government, in such forms as a "democratic" constitution and "free elections". While a provisional government in the Soviet Zone would not increase the economic benefits to the USSR, it would balance the scale of political developments in Germany permitting the Soviet Union to save face in any further negotiations.

4. For reasons elaborated in Special Evaluation No. 51, 12 June 1948, the USSR has been expected to attempt to enter into negotiations with the western powers in order to delay further or to prevent an appreciable western German contribution to the European recovery program. To be acceptable, such an attempt would have to be made before the USSR took final action to establish a satellite state in eastern Germany. Although Soviet behavior in Germany, particularly in Berlin, has been far from conciliatory it has not been so definitive or final as to preclude further negotiations and may even have been designed to force the western powers into discussions.

5. As was set forth in ORE 22 - 48, 28 April 1948, the USSR has been engaged in consolidating political and economic control of eastern Germany to enable the USSR to create a satellite German state at this time. But, as was also stated in Special Evaluation No. 51, the benefits to the USSR from such a course would not now be substantially greater than those resulting from the present system. The action would, moreover, preclude the possibility of partial Soviet control over western Germany and interference with the German contribution to the European recovery program.

6. Consultation with the satellite states, while not absolutely necessary under such stringent control as exercised by the USSR, would be desirable in order to obtain public satellite support for propaganda and psychological reasons. Any action resulting in the establishment of a German Government or in the unification of Germany, therefore, would warrant Soviet assurances to the satellites on matters of security, boundary or reparations claims, and on the type of German state to be evolved.

81. *(Continued)*

7. In view of these considerations, CIA believes that the USSR is using the Warsaw conference to inform the satellites of Soviet intentions:

    a. To form an "Eastern Union" against further German aggression sponsored by the western powers;

    b. To announce a program for the creation of a provisional government matching in independence, and possibly in timing, the one contemplated in the west; and

    c. To indicate a desire, possibly couched in face-saving terms, for resumption of negotiations with the western powers ostensibly to permit the unification of Germany, but actually to prevent the realization of Allied plans for western Germany.

- 3 -

SECRET

SUMMARY

The meeting in Warsaw of Soviet Foreign Minister Molotov and the foreign ministers of the satellite states to discuss the London agreements on Germany apparently stems from the desire to create an eastern bloc into which eastern Germany could be economically, if not politically, fitted to match the inclusion of western Germany in the European recovery program. Some declaration of importance may be expected at the conclusion of this meeting. Probably the formation of an "Eastern Union" to protect the USSR and its satellites against aggression from a western-sponsored resurgent Germany. Following that, the USSR may adopt one of three courses or a combination, these are: (a) announcement of an intention to permit the Germans to create a provisional government for the Soviet Zone; (b) an attempt to achieve the overall unification of Germany through an agreement with the western powers; and (c) immediate establishment of an allegedly independent east German state, purportedly a restoration of the German Reich. CIA believes that the USSR has convened the Warsaw meeting to establish the "Eastern Union" and to inform the satellites of its intention to announce a program for the creation of a provisional government in eastern Germany matching in independence, and possibly in timing, the one contemplated in the west and to express a desire, possibly couched in face-saving terms, to reach an eventual solution with the western powers to permit a unification of Germany that would be satisfactory to all interested nations.

Deputy Assistant Director

SECRET

82. Daily Summary Excerpt, 25 June 1948, Germany: French View on Berlin Crisis; Palestine: Jewish Extremists Increasingly Active

TOP SECRET

25 JUN 1948

721

EUROPE

1. **GERMANY: French view on Berlin crisis**--A high official of the French Foreign Office has expressed to US Ambassador Caffery his personal views that: (a) the western powers erred seriously when the Berlin crisis first arose by overstressing the importance of remaining in the city and announcing that they would remain at all costs; (b) Berlin is not in fact "any more quadripartite" than western Germany, in which quadripartite control has long been abandoned; and (c) in the face of aggressive Soviet action, the western powers would encounter almost insuperable difficulties in Berlin and, even if able to maintain military and governmental forces, they could not avoid a decline in prestige through remaining there.

(CIA Comment: CIA believes that even though a slight decline in prestige of the western powers would result from their remaining in Berlin in the face of Soviet aggressive action, such a loss would be far less than that they would suffer through a withdrawal. Moreover, any apparent weakening of tripartite solidarity on the Berlin situation would greatly reinforce Soviet determination to drive the western powers from the city.)

TOP SECRET

NO CHANGE in Class. ☐
☐ DECLASSIFIED
Class. CHANGED TO: TS S ©
DDA Memo, 4 Apr 77
Auth: DDA REG. 77/1763
Date: 14 MAR 1978 By: _____

TOP SECRET

CONFIDENTIAL

NEAR EAST-AFRICA

3. PALESTINE: <u>Jewish extremists increasingly active</u>--US Consulate General Jerusalem reports that during the past few days Irgun Zvai Leumi and the Stern Gang (Jewish extremist groups) have become increasingly active in Jerusalem. Both groups have, in contravention of the UN truce terms, brought reinforcements, arms, and supplies into the city and have taken over strategic areas which they are converting into fortified enclaves. The Consulate General has learned from various sources that the USSR is providing the Stern Gang with arms and money through the Satellites, particularly Poland. These sources also believe that the USSR will make every effort to increase its support as an effective means of gaining a foothold for subversive activities in Israel. The Consulate General feels that the Jewish extremists may become increasingly embarrassing to the Israeli authorities and may attempt to thwart any effort to settle in a reasonable way the present Jewish-Arab impasse.

- 2 -

TOP SECRET

CONFIDENTIAL

83. Weekly Summary Excerpt, 25 June 1948, Soviet Desire to Reopen Quadripartite Negotiations on Germany

EASTERN EUROPE

The continued Soviet desire to re-open quadripartite negotiations on the German problem has been indicated by the failure of the Warsaw Conference to produce formal plans for a provisional government of eastern Germany and the Warsaw communique calling for a further four-power attempt to unify Germany. Concurrently, intensified Soviet obstructionism in Berlin appears designed to force the western powers to agree to renewed discussions in which the USSR would undoubtedly demand that the entire German problem be reconsidered. These Soviet efforts are prompted primarily by a desire to obtain some measure of control of western Germany, particularly the Ruhr, or at least to sabotage or slow down the western program, including European recovery, rather than by any sincere desire for a just and equitable solution of the German question. The communique of the Warsaw Conference, in its appeal for German unity and renewed efforts for quadripartite agreement, provides the Kremlin with a propaganda theme which will undoubtedly attract many adherents not only in Germany but throughout western Europe and the US.

- 5 -

84. Daily Summary Excerpt, 30 June 1948, Implications of Possible Approach to West by Tito; Germany: Alleged Plans for East German Government

4. **Implications of possible approach to west by Tito**—The US Military and Naval Attaches in Belgrade, in raising the question of possible approaches by Marshal Tito for US support against the USSR, recommend the "boldest possible exploitation" of any such defection in "the keystone of the Soviet-satellite structure." The Attaches believe that in withstanding Soviet pressure Tito would have good prospect of success if given full support from the west. The Attaches, however, recommend that the US take action only through propaganda until approached by the Yugoslavs.

(CIA Comment: Although Tito may extend cautious feelers to the west, it is more probable that he will postpone any direct request for western support until the Kremlin has definitely closed all further avenues for a rapprochement. If the Kremlin denies the implied request for direct contact made in his 29 June answer to the Cominform resolution, Tito may then be forced to seek western aid against Soviet retaliation.)

- 2 -

84. *(Continued)*

EUROPE

7. GERMANY: <u>Alleged plans for east German government</u>--Well-informed but untested CIA sources report that: (a) an east German government, to be called an "All German Government," will be announced in the near future; (b) Otto Nuschke, member of the Christian Democratic Union and co-chairman of the Volksrat (People's Council), will be the Prime Minister; (c) indications are that the USSR intends to have the Volksrat emerge as a ready-made government; and (d) the co-secretary of the Volksrat is working on a draft peace treaty which must be ready for submission to the People's Congress in September.

(CIA Comment: CIA believes that the USSR has drawn up plans for an east German state which, in its provisional nature and approximate timing, will ostensibly parallel the scheduled west German government. The implementation of the Soviet plan, however, probably will be delayed until the USSR can "justify" its action by claiming that the western powers have ignored the plea for German unification in the Warsaw communique.)

85. Weekly Summary Excerpt, 2 July 1948, Berlin Blockade; Intensified Communist Activity in Italy; Yugoslavia's Defiance of the Kremlin's Authority

WESTERN EUROPE

GERMANY

The Soviet Union has further threatened the position of the western powers in Berlin by increasing existing restrictions on communications between the city and the western zones. The recent Soviet action in cutting off all rail communications and road and barge traffic represents the near-maximum curtailment of ground facilities within Soviet capabilities. On 23 June when the new embargoes were put into effect, the western sectors had food stocks adequate for a six-week minimum German ration and fuel stocks to supply light, power, and water for three weeks. The Soviet action, ostensibly taken in retaliation against the western decision to introduce the new west German currency in Berlin, has two possible objectives: either to force the western powers to negotiate on Soviet terms regarding Germany, or failing that, to force a western power withdrawal from Berlin.

The USSR does not seem ready to force a definite showdown but for the present appears more inclined to compel the western powers to negotiate locally regarding Berlin in the hope that such negotiations could be broadened to include Soviet demands on major issues such as the Ruhr. The USSR is attempting by various means to find a face-saving method within Germany of reconvening the Allied Control Council. Having abandoned its recent efforts to use the Polish mission in Germany for this purpose, Soviet officials have apparently directed the Communist-controlled Socialist Unity Party representatives on the Berlin City Assembly to propose that city officials ask that the ACC be convened. Present indications are that the Assembly will make such a request and the USSR will seize upon it as a means of reconvening the Council and possibly also the Kommandatura. Although Communist leaders in Soviet-controlled areas have probably prepared an action program designed to create a revolutionary situation in the western sectors, the USSR presumably will not direct that such a program be put

- 3 -

85. *(Continued)*

GERMANY

fully into effect until it has exhausted less drastic pressure devices and until public unrest develops.

The Soviet Commander, Marshal Sokolovsky, has attempted to reassure the Germans and the western powers that his new restrictions may only be temporary. The western powers are inclined, however, to take Sokolovsky's remarks with a large grain of salt. For the present, the German population in the western sectors continues markedly anti-Soviet and supports the strong stand taken by the western powers. Its faith has been further strengthened by determined US-UK efforts to fly in supplies and by continued evidence that the UK and French position remains firm. This German population may be expected to give loyal and effective support to the western powers, unless its will is sapped by starvation or its determination weakened by a belief that a western withdrawal is inevitable.

Soviet propaganda and policy moves in Germany during the past week have been very closely coordinated. Soviet-licensed newspapers in the Soviet sector of Berlin hammered at their "panic" theme of hunger and unemployment in the western part of the city. Propaganda both within and without Germany emphasized that the western powers were forcing a "split Germany" upon the German people. The Warsaw Conference accused the western powers of splitting Germany down the middle while Soviet-licensed papers in Berlin demanded that the western powers declare themselves ready to conclude a peace for all of Germany. Meanwhile, the USSR kept the backdoor open from the mounting Berlin impasse by carefully explaining in all propaganda releases that the Soviet restrictive actions are made necessary by technical difficulties rather than by political motives.

- 4 -

85. *(Continued)*

SECRET

ITALY

Greatly intensified Communist activity in Italy, including
a full-scale attack against the European recovery program and
a general strike scheduled for 2 July, may be expected as a
result of new instructions received from the Cominform. In
accord with these orders, Italian Communists will probably denounce the London agreement on Germany as a partitioning act
and will defend any Soviet counteraction as moves to assure
eventual unity of Germany under a "democratic" government.
The Communists may also engineer an ostensible separation
from the Left Wing Socialist Party in order to increase the
effectiveness of that group. If the Socialist Party at its current
Congress should swing from pro-Communist to a more moderate
position, the Communists might abandon the Popular Front device
and demand that pro-fusionist Socialists merge with the Communists. This would enable the Communists to pose as the only
party representing the Italian working class, and as such, claim
the right to participate in the Government.

- 5 -

EASTERN EUROPE

YUGOSLAVIA

<u>Tito's two-fold defiance of the Kremlin's authority,</u> in flatly rejecting the Cominform's criticism and in advocating a Balkan federation, has confronted the USSR with the necessity of making a decision which will have far-reaching effects upon the Soviet Union's eastern European empire and upon the Kremlin's control over Communist Parties throughout the world. Although the Kremlin undoubtedly feels the need to take some decisive action to regain prestige, it is faced with the unpleasant realization that: (1) drastic retaliation against Tito might prompt him to withdraw from the Soviet bloc; and (2) any accommodation with Tito will mean a considerable loss of face. This decision is complicated by the further realization that the Cominform's emphasis upon the "internationalist" character of Communism will probably weaken the Communist Parties of western Europe through the defection or elimination of "nationalist" elements and fellow travellers. The Kremlin's awareness of its difficult position is indicated by its treatment of this dispute as one merely involving Communist Parties and not governments. The Kremlin may, therefore, continue to handle the matter on a Party level in the hope of reaching some solution which will both be face-saving and prevent the defection of Yugoslavia from the Soviet bloc. While seeking a solution, however, the USSR can be expected to tighten its controls drastically over the other Satellites in order to prevent any emulation of Tito's example. Moreover, the USSR will eventually exert maximum pressure, short of war, to eliminate Tito and his lieutenants.

<u>Tito's continued refusal to bow to the Kremlin</u> reflects his realization that the die is cast and any precipitate retreat on his part would be tantamount to political suicide. By following his answer to the Cominform with a public announcement of a detailed Yugoslav Communist Party program and

- 8 -

YUGOSLAVIA

referring only indirectly to the Cominform resolution, Tito indicated that he still hopes to force the Kremlin to modify the Cominform decision and accept Yugoslavia as a full-fledged partner in the Soviet family rather than as a vassal of the USSR. Thus, Tito will probably extend no feelers immediately to the west, because such action would further jeopardize any chance of a favorable rapprochement with the Kremlin. Moreover, Tito's re-affirmation of the principles of Marx and Lenin and his pledge of continued co-operation with the USSR in foreign policy matters have increased the difficulty of achieving any early rapprochement with the west except in the sphere of economic relations. Meanwhile, Tito can be expected to take steps to strengthen his position internally while simultaneously supporting Soviet foreign policy, and maintaining close relations with the other Satellites. However, whenever Tito considers that rapprochement with the Kremlin becomes unlikely, he will probably extend cautious feelers for western support against the USSR.

Communist Parties in the other Satellites are too vulnerable to Soviet force to risk a break with the Kremlin and therefore will probably not in the near future emulate Tito's recent example in defying the Cominform. However, if Tito wins substantial concessions from the Kremlin or is successful in breaking away from Kremlin control, the "internationalist" Communists in the Satellites will face greater obstacles in controlling those "nationalist" Communist elements (particularly in Bulgaria and Hungary) which are reportedly already rebelling against blind obedience to the Kremlin. Tito's action confronts Bulgaria with a more difficult decision than any other eastern European nation. Bulgaria and Yugoslavia have achieved close economic and military cooperation since the end of World War II. Moreover, both

- 9 -

YUGOSLAVIA

countries are involved in conflicting claims on Greece and Macedonia. Although the possibility cannot be eliminated that Bulgarian Communist Premier Dimitrov will accept Tito's bid for a Balkan federation, it is more probable that Dimitrov will continue to hew to the Kremlin line because: (1) his rivalry with Tito for leadership in the Balkans militates against any rapprochement; (2) through his long training in Moscow and his association with the Comintern, he has grown too internationalist-minded to defy Communist Party discipline; and (3) he realizes that the USSR could retaliate -- by force, if necessary -- effectively against Bulgaria.

The recent Cominform blast against Tito and the stand-to-the-death statements of various Communist leaders against the European recovery program reveal that the expanded duties of the 1948 Cominform include the role of inter-Satellite taskmaster for the Kremlin. As a result of the dispute with Tito, the Cominform headquarters will probably be moved from Belgrade to Prague. Czechoslovak Communists have already announced that future editions of the official "Cominform Journal" will be distributed from the Czechoslovak capital. Besides its action in disciplining Tito, the Cominform apparently also laid down for all Party members a strict line to be taken concerning the European recovery program. Since the meeting, French Italian, and Trieste Communists have publicly stated that they will exert every effort to destroy the European recovery program. This is in strong contrast to public statements made by French and Italian Communist leaders prior to the Cominform meeting which were comparatively lacking in hostility.

- 10 -

SECRET

EASTERN EUROPE

YUGOSLAVIA

<u>Eventual reconciliation between Tito and the Kremlin</u>
appears to be a diminishing prospect in the face of Tito's determination to keep the initiative by emphatically publicizing his
position. Meanwhile, the USSR and the Satellites (except for
Albania) continue to maintain the fiction that the dispute is
between the Yugoslav Communist Party and the Cominform and
not between governments. The door thus is being left open for
a bilateral solution between Tito and the Soviet Union. However,
there has not yet been any indication of a Kremlin decision on
future handling of Tito. In reaching this decision, the Kremlin
must face the realization that: (1) the longer the dispute remains unresolved, the more difficult it will be to find a face-
saving formula for a rapprochement; and (2) any drastic disciplinary measures against Tito would further endanger the
solidarity of the eastern bloc and increase the possibility of
an understanding between Tito and the west. Meanwhile, the
USSR appears to be making preparations for large-scale rail
movements across Hungary. Although these reported preparations may be designed primarily to evacuate Soviet troops and
dependents from Hungary, and although Soviet armed intervention
in Yugoslavia is unlikely in the immediate future, the fact remains
that Hungary is a logical area in which to assemble Soviet troops
for an intensive war of nerves against the rebellious Tito.

<u>In taking direct action against the Yugoslav Government</u>,
Albania has become the only Satellite to make Tito's defection
a governmental as well as a party problem. Albania presumably
has taken this strong stand because the Hoxha regime: (1) fears
Soviet retaliation more than Yugoslav counteraction; (2) expects
Tito's defeat and hopes Albania will thereby gain a more favorable position in the Soviet orbit; (3) resents Yugoslav exploitation
of Albania's economy; and (4) wishes to seize this opportunity to
end a subservient relationship. Despite the belligerency of Hoxha's
attacks on Tito, Yugoslavia is not likely at present to risk the

- 6 -

SECRET

YUGOSLAVIA

consequences of an armed attack on Albania. Moreover, so long as Tito's dispute with the Cominform remains unresolved, the possibility increases that Yugoslavia's relations will also deteriorate critically with neighboring Bulgaria and Hungary. Such a development would create additional obstacles to an eventual accommodation between Tito and the Kremlin.

Yugoslav pressure against Greece and Trieste will be considerably lessened as a consequence of Tito's break with the Cominform. In Greece, Tito's recent actions have created obstacles to coordinated support of the Markos regime by Yugoslavia, Bulgaria, and Albania. Also, Tito will be reluctant to divert to Markos scarce war materiel and supplies necessary to strengthen his own position against possible Soviet retaliation. Moreover, because Albania must now rely upon the USSR for its supplies, Albania's contribution to the Markos forces can be expected gradually to decrease or at least become more spasmodic. In Trieste, Yugoslavia has lost the support of the local Communist Party which, despite its former dependence on the Yugoslav Communist Party for directives and funds, is hewing to the Cominform line. Yugoslavia has thus been denied its most effective weapon for economic and political infiltration of Trieste.

The possibility of Yugoslav economic overtures to the west will cause the Kremlin to proceed slowly and cautiously in threatening Tito with economic sanctions. Initially at least, any curtailment of Soviet-Satellite exports to Yugoslavia will be made only on strategic materials, such as munitions and oil, which would directly strengthen Yugoslavia's military potential. Already, shipments of Hungarian exports to Yugoslavia are reported to have been stopped while Rumanian oil destined for Yugoslavia has reportedly been diverted to Bulgaria. Czechoslovakia, which

- 7 -

86. *(Continued)*

YUGOSLAVIA

is currently facing economic difficulties resulting from unsatisfactory trade relations with the other Satellites, may add to the
Kremlin's problem by seizing upon the present Yugoslav situation as a pretext for increasing trade with the west, claiming
that the reduction of exports to Yugoslavia makes it necessary.
Possibly in anticipation of increased Soviet economic pressure,
Yugoslavia has recently become more accommodating in economic negotiations with Italy.

- 8 -

87. Weekly Summary Excerpt, 16 July 1948, International Communism; Establishment of Competing Regimes in Korea

EASTERN EUROPE

<u>International Communism</u> apparently is entering a "holding operation" phase, the second period of its development following World War II. During this phase, the Kremlin apparently intends to strip all Communist parties down to a hard core of fanatically faithful adherents. The first postwar phase was characterized by Communist attempts to build a broad base of popular support in all countries. Recognizing signs of diminishing returns in this program, the Kremlin is apparently willing to risk the loss of popular support in order to build a stronger core of Communist faithfuls. The disappointing Communist showing in the Italian election and the more recent defection of Yugoslav Communist leaders have undoubtedly indicated to the Kremlin that a tightening of Communist ranks was long overdue. The Cominform attack upon Tito was the signal for all Communist parties to reassess their membership. Although the popular following of local Communist parties will be reduced somewhat, the militant potentialities of the hard-core Communists, especially in Europe, will remain unaffected.

- 6 -

87. *(Continued)*

KOREA

The establishment of two competing "national" regimes in Korea now appears imminent. The National Assembly in South Korea has adopted a constitution and is scheduled to announce the formation of the Republic of Korea in early August; the US plans to recognize this regime as "the national Goverment of Korea envisaged by the General Assembly resolutions." Concurrently, the hastily reconvened North Korean People's Council, after denouncing US "unilateral" action in South Korea, has promulgated its own Soviet-model constitution and has scheduled elections on 25 August for the establishment of a Democratic Korean People's Republic in which South Korea will ostensibly be represented. The USSR undoubtedly will recognize its North Korean puppet regime as "national" in character and follow its formation with renewed pressure for the withdrawal of all occupation forces. The Soviet aim will be to deprive the US of an opportunity to establish a native security force in South Korea adequate to deal with aggression from the North Korean People's Army.

- 13 -

88. Daily Summary Excerpt, 17 July 1948, USSR: Reasons for Soviet Replies on Berlin; China: Soviet Ambassador Urges End of Civil War

~~TOP SECRET~~
~~CONFIDENTIAL~~

17 JUL 1948

739

3. **USSR:** Reasons for Soviet replies on Berlin--US Military Attache Moscow advances the following probable reasons for the strong Soviet reply to the Western Power notes concerning Berlin: (a) the Politburo reasons that the Western Powers are not prepared to fight over Berlin and no other course will be effective in maintaining the western position; (b) the Kremlin is determined to extend its control in Germany as far as practicable by all means short of war; and (c) the Soviet Union feels the need of making a show of Soviet strength for propaganda purposes following its recent political reverses.

(CIA Comment: CIA concurs with the analysis presented by the US Military Attache.)

Document No. 13
NO CHANGE in Class. ☐
☐ DECLASSIFIED
Class. CHANGED TO: TS S
Auth: DDA MEMO, 4 Apr 77
Date: 5 MAR 1978 By: 028

- 1 -

~~CONFIDENTIAL~~
~~TOP SECRET~~

88. *(Continued)*

FAR EAST

5. CHINA: <u>Soviet Ambassador urges end of civil war</u>--US
   Embassy Nanking reports that Soviet Ambassador Roshchin
   and the Chinese Minister of the Interior recently held a six-
   hour conversation concerning the civil war, during which the
   Ambassador urged that the Chinese civil war be brought to
   an end for the sake of all concerned. The Embassy expresses
   the opinion that this approach by the Soviet Ambassador
   suggests: (a) the USSR is concerned that US aid may strengthen
   the National Government; (b) the Chinese Communists are weaker
   than they appear to be; and (c) Soviet officials may have relatively
   little respect for the Chinese Communists, and that the USSR will
   continue to propose Soviet assistance as mediator in the Chinese
   civil war.

   (CIA Comment: While CIA is not in a position entirely
   to discount Embassy Nanking's explanation of the Soviet Ambassador's approach, CIA considers that the following considerations are pertinent: (a) the USSR may estimate that a continuation
   of hostilities would insure continued US aid and further extension
   of US influence over Nationalist China; (b) the USSR may reason

- 2 -

88. *(Continued)*

that once hostilities had ceased, Communist political penetration could be accelerated, especially if a coalition government should take over; and (c) the USSR recognizes that it would reap substantial propaganda benefits from a successful Soviet mediation of the civil war.

ORE 45-48   SECRET

THE CURRENT SITUATION IN CHINA

SUMMARY

The position of the present National Government is so precarious that its fall may occur at any time. It is quite likely, however, that it may survive with diminishing power for some time, but soon become only one of several regimes exercising governmental powers independently in Nationalist China. Even with the current US aid program, the present National Government has little prospect of reversing or even checking these trends of disintegration. The increasing instability in Nationalist China will facilitate the extension of Chinese Communist military and political influence.

Within Nationalist China the power and prestige of Chiang Kai-shek is steadily weakening because of the unsuccessful prosecution of the war under his leadership and his apparent unwillingness and inability to accomplish positive reforms. Opposition, both within the Kuomintang and among dissident elements, centered chiefly in Hong Kong, is gathering strength. In addition, deteriorating economic conditions are exerting a cumulative impact on the political structure of the National Government. Furthermore, the military forces of the Chinese Communists have been able to seize the tactical initiative on an increasingly large scale. Even with current US assistance, it is improbable that the Nationalist Army can successfully defend all of its present territories.

In foreign relations, questions concerning the neighboring states of Japan and the USSR are of paramount interest to China for reasons of security. Chinese opinion favors a "hard" peace settlement with Japan so as to prevent the resurgence of that country as a Great Power. It is equally important for China to maintain correct and if possible friendly relations with the USSR, for China unaided cannot match Soviet power. Implementation of US aid to China is complicated by the question of the extent of US controls and supervision, and US insistence upon accompanying economic, political, and military reforms. The USSR thus far has refrained from overt material assistance to the Chinese Communists and continues to recognize the National Government, but it is apparent, nevertheless, that Soviet sympathies lie with the Chinese Communists. Even if US aid should prove effective, this might prove to be only a temporary advantage for the National Government, since it might be offset by Soviet counter-aid to the Chinese Communists.

The prospect for the foreseeable future in China is at best an indefinite and inconclusive prolongation of the civil war, with the authority of the National Government limited to a dwindling area in Central and South China and isolated major cities in north and northeast China, and with political and economic disorder spreading throughout the country except possibly in Communist-held areas. The worst prospect is complete collapse of the National Government, and its replacement by a Chinese

Note: The information in this report is as of 11 June 1948.
      The intelligence organizations of the Departments of State, Army, Navy, and the Air Force have concurred in this report.

1   SECRET

89. *(Continued)*

Communist-controlled regime, under Soviet influence if not under Soviet control, and uncooperative toward the US if not openly hostile. The latter development would result in an extensive loss of US prestige and increased Communist influence throughout the Far East, as well as an intensification of threat to US interests in the Western Pacific area.

2

90. Weekly Summary Excerpt, 23 July 1948, Slackening Bulgarian Support for Greek Guerrillas

BULGARIA

Slackening Bulgarian support for the Greek guerrillas
is indicated by Bulgarian press treatment of the fighting in
Greece. Instead of front page reports of Markos successes,
the press has been carrying small back page paragraphs asserting that Markos is repulsing all attacks. This press treatment
lends credence to unconfirmed reports that Bulgaria ceased
shipping arms to Markos shortly after the Cominform attack
on Tito. If this development can be interpreted as an indication that the USSR has temporarily "written off" the Greek
venture, such a Soviet decision would have been prompted by:
(1) a desire to conserve Bulgarian and Albanian military strength
in case of trouble with Yugoslavia; (2) inability at this time to
reconcile conflicting nationalist interests between Greek, Bulgarian, Yugoslav, and Albanian Communists concerning the
disposition of Greek Macedonia and Thrace; and (3) the difficulty of achieving guerrilla success without direct intervention
which would increase the risk of open conflict with the US. If,
however, the guerrillas are able to prevent a decisive Greek
Army victory in the Grammos area, the Kremlin may order its
Satellites to increase their support of the Markos regime.

- 9 -

91. Daily Summary Excerpt, 27 July 1948, Control of Berlin Believed Primary Soviet Objective

~~TOP SECRET~~

27 JUL 1948

747

S - TS

GENERAL

1. <u>Control of Berlin believed primary Soviet objective</u>--US Ambassador Smith in Moscow detects no real evidence of an urgent Soviet desire to negotiate the overall German question and suggests that the USSR is at present primarily interested in liquidating Berlin as a center of western influence. Smith observes, however, that this does not imply that the USSR is abandoning its objectives in western Germany. Smith believes that the USSR might be induced temporarily to forego "the battle for Berlin" if sufficiently attracted by western power concessions on all of Germany.

(CIA Comment: CIA remains of the opinion that concessions on western Germany are the primary Soviet objectives and considers that unilateral control of Berlin is a secondary aim of the USSR.)

~~TOP SECRET~~

EASTERN EUROPE

SOVIET UNION

Recent rumors of dissension within the Politburo appear exaggerated. Although differences of opinion regarding Soviet strategy undoubtedly exist among the members of the Soviet ruling body, it is unlikely that these men, who owe their present positions to Stalin, would find it possible to engage in serious disputes so long as Stalin remains the arbiter of Soviet policy. Whatever may be their personal differences and animosities, it seems certain that the members of the Politburo continue to work together as a team and confine their rivalry to jockeying for Stalin's favor or to competing for control of the Party machinery in order to hold the best possible position at Stalin's death. Until recently Andrei Zhdanov, chief Soviet ideological spokesman, seemed to have gained the upper hand over Malenkov in a contest for control of the Communist Party apparatus. Latest indications are that Malenkov has regained his powerful post as a secretary of the Central Committee, which transmits the decisions of the Politburo to lower Party organs. Zhdanov may have to bear the responsibility for the inept handling of the Cominform denunciation of Tito. Malenkov's resurgence may be a rebuke to Zhdanov for his handling of the Yugoslav situation and could foreshadow a lessening in his influence and prestige.

- 8 -

93. Weekly Summary Excerpt, 6 August 1948, Germany: Far-Reaching Political and Economic Reorganization in the Soviet Zone

WESTERN EUROPE

GERMANY

A far-reaching political and economic reorganization now is under way in the Soviet Zone. The German Popular Front, the original Soviet-sponsored political organization, is being abandoned in favor of a group of political parties completely loyal to Communism and backed by reliable Communist police. Leaders of the Christian Democrats and Liberal Democrats, both members of the Popular Front, are being liquidated or eliminated. Members of these two parties are being herded into the National Democratic Party and the Farmers' Party, both headed by Moscow-trained German Communists. The Socialist Unity Party (SED), upon which the USSR will rely to control an eastern German Satellite state, is being reduced to a compact organization responsive to Cominform direction. The economy of the eastern zone, with its arrangements for Soviet control and exploitation, now resembles that of the Satellites. The former German Central Administration concerned with economic affairs is being subordinated to the SED-dominated German Economic Commission. Industrial combines, which are responsible to zonal authorities instead of to officials of various states in the zone, will direct nearly all industrial activities. The dominance of state-owned or controlled enterprises will spell the eventual elimination of effective competition from privately-owned business and will simplify central control of the economy. Control in the agrarian field will be effected through the politically-sponsored peasant cooperative movement, which operates to the disadvantage of the independent farmer. When these extensive reforms are completed, integration of the eastern zone economy with that of the western zones can be accomplished only with extreme difficulty.

- 3 -

94. Weekly Summary Excerpt, 3 September 1948, Soviet Union: The Death of Zhdanov

E A S T E R N E U R O P E

SOVIET UNION

Although the sudden death of Zhdanov, for whatever cause, removes a key figure from the Soviet directorate of world Communism and at least one obstacle to some form of temporary rapprochement with Tito, it will probably have only a limited effect upon over-all Soviet policy. Zhdanov directed the Cominform denunciation of Tito, and it is possible that the other members of the Politburo may feel that his death gives them an opportunity to correct an ineptly handled situation without loss of face. Although a temporary agreement with Tito is possible, the dispute appears to be based upon fundamental differences which would require a full capitulation on the part of either Tito or the Kremlin.

The loss of Zhdanov creates a serious organizational problem for the Kremlin. He was the only Politburo member with extensive experience in dealing with foreign Communist parties, and he has headed the postwar ideological purification of Soviet arts and sciences. In addition, he had exercised increasing authority in the party organization since the end of World War II. Malenkov appears to be the most likely prospect as Zhdanov's successor both in the party and in the Cominform. The re-emergence of Malenkov as a secretary of the Central Committee in mid-July may have been because of Zhdanov's deteriorating health. Malenkov lacks Zhdanov's experience and prestige among foreign Communist parties, however, and he cannot be expected to fill the breach caused by Zhdanov's death for some time to come.

Although Zhdanov undoubtedly exerted considerable influence on Soviet policy, his death will not bring about any major changes in the policies formulated by the Politburo. In any event, Molotov's position as probable successor to Stalin has been substantially strengthened by the elimination of a capable and ambitious rival.

- 5 -

95. Weekly Summary Excerpt, 10 September 1948, Poland: Recent Conflict Within the Communist Party

POLAND

Recent conflict within the Polish Communist Party, as revealed by Wladyslaw Gomulka's removal as a Polish Communist Party leader, represents another rebellion by a nationalistic faction within Satellite Communist parties against Moscow-enforced discipline when the interests of the nation are concerned. The Polish situation might have resulted in another Tito-rift except for the presence of 125,000 Soviet soldiers within Poland, the fact that Poland borders the USSR, and the fact that Poland's Communist Party was a "three-man" show. Great efforts were made within the party to patch up the differences with Gomulka and his public recantation quickly presented an unbroken front to the world. Despite his recantation and his retention as First Vice-Premier and Minister of Recovered Territories, Gomulka is not long for Polish political life.

- 6 -

96. Daily Summary Excerpt, 17 September 1948, China: Growing Nationalist Sentiment for Neutrality

49   17 SEP 1948

~~TOP SECRET~~

791

FAR EAST

2. **CHINA:** <u>Growing Nationalist sentiment for neutrality</u>--US Embassy Nanking has been informed by "a usually reliable source" that a new clique in the Nationalist Government has the objective of keeping China neutral in the event of an "inevitable" US-USSR war. The Embassy suggests that this information, combined with information that the Chinese Foreign Minister and the Soviet Ambassador have recently held several secret conferences, indicates that a Foreign Office group desires neutrality and is willing to appease the USSR considerably. The Embassy believes, however, that Chiang Kai-shek is basically pro-US in his orientation. The Embassy continues to believe that the USSR is seeking control of all of China via a Communist-Nationalist coalition.

(CIA Comment: Although current reports from Chinese sources concerning the growth of pro-Soviet sentiment in the National Government probably have a basis of truth, they may be designed primarily to exert pressure for more US aid. CIA believes that the USSR favors a Communist-Nationalist coalition in China, and will attempt to mediate in the Chinese civil war and to establish such a coalition at a time when Chiang Kai-shek has suffered major military reverses or is faced with a new political-economic crisis.)

CIA - C~

Document No. 61

NO CHANGE in Class. ☐

☒ DECLASSIFIED

Class. C.   TS   S   C

~~TOP SECRET~~

Auth: 4 Apr 77

DIA   77/1763

Date: 15 MAR 1978   By: 626

242

97. ORE 60-48 Excerpt, 28 September 1948, Threats to the Security of the United States

~~TOP SECRET~~

THREATS TO THE SECURITY OF THE UNITED STATES

SUMMARY

1. For the foreseeable future the USSR will be the only power capable of threatening the security of the United States. The Soviet regime, moreover, is essentially and implacably inimical toward the United States.

2. The power of the USSR to endanger the security of the United States is a consequence not only of Soviet strength, but also of the weakness and instability prevalent in Europe and Asia and of weaknesses in the military posture of the United States. The principal restraint on hostile Soviet action is the greater potential strength of the United States.

3. Soviet strengths and weaknesses and specific Soviet capabilities to threaten the United States and US security interests overseas are set forth within (paragraphs 2-17).

4. In general, the probable basic intentions of the Kremlin for the next decade are:

a. To avoid war with the United States, but to exploit to the utmost, within that limitation, the coercive power inherent in the preponderance of Soviet military strength in Eurasia, relying on the disinclination of the United States to resort to war.

b. To build up as rapidly as possible the war potential of the Soviet orbit, in an effort to equal and surpass, eventually, the war potential of the United States.

c. To wage political, economic, and psychological warfare against the United States and its allies, with a view to undermining their potential strength and increasing the relative strength of the USSR: in particular, to prevent or retard the recovery and coalition of Western Europe and the stabilization of the situation in the Near East and Far East.

d. To exploit every opportunity presented by the weakness and instability of neighboring states to expand the area of Soviet domination by political and subversive means.

5. Although the Kremlin is unlikely to resort deliberately to war to gain its ends within the next decade, it would do so if ever it came to consider such a course expedient, particularly if convinced that time was on the side of the United States. In this respect the situation will remain critical pending the successful accomplishment of US efforts to redress the balance of power. Moreover, there is constant danger of war through accident or miscalculation.

6. In any case, the fundamental hostility of the Soviet Government toward the United States and its formidable military power require, in common prudence, that the United States be prepared for the eventuality of war with the USSR.

Note: The intelligence organizations of the Departments of State and Army have concurred in this report. The Air Intelligence Division, Air Intelligence Directorate, Department of the Air Force has also concurred, but see comments in Enclosure A, p. 10. For a dissent by the Office of Naval Intelligence, see Enclosure B, p. 11.
The information in this report is as of 13 September 1948.

1

~~TOP SECRET~~

2 OCT 1948

804

GENERAL

1. <u>Possible Soviet reversal on Palestine</u>--US Embassy Moscow has been informed by an Arab source that Soviet Deputy Foreign Minister Zorin told him that the Soviet position concerning Palestine is now subject to review because the partition plan of 29 November 1947 is not being carried out. The implication, according to source, was that a dramatic Soviet reversal might take place if the UN General Assembly attempted any solution for Palestine other than reaffirmation of its original resolution.

   (CIA Comment: CIA does not believe that the USSR will change its support in the General Assembly from the Israelis to the Arabs. CIA believes, however, that the Soviet Union will oppose the adoption of a solution based on the US-UK supported Bernadotte proposals and will insist upon the original UN partition plan.)

- 1 -

~~TOP SECRET~~

99. Daily Summary Excerpt, 4 October 1948, France: USSR May Finance French Coal Strike

~~TOP SECRET~~

4 OCT 1948

805

EUROPE

3. **FRANCE:** <u>USSR may finance French coal strike</u>--According to US Embassy Paris, the French Interior Ministry has been authentically informed that Communist Party Leader Duclos recently told the French Communist Party: (a) the USSR

C/A-S.

Document No. *003*

-1 NO CHANGE in Class. ☐

☐ DECLASSIFIED

~~TOP SECRET~~ CHANGED TO: TS   S   Ⓔ

Auth: DDA Memo, 4 Apr 77
DDA REG. 77/1763

Date: 16 MAR 1978

~~TOP SECRET~~
~~CONFIDENTIAL~~

considers it absolutely necessary for the Communists to re-
enter the French Government; and (b) the USSR will finance
the French Communist Party in order to achieve this aim
and possibly will support the French coal strike.

the Communists hope to prolong the coal strike for two or
three weeks and thus deliver a severe blow on the eve of
winter.   the Kremlin has arranged for the
halting of shipments of coal from Poland to France during
this strike.

(CIA Comment: CIA believes that the Communist
strategy of trying to obtain a "Popular Front" Government
by inducing economic and political chaos would be materially
advanced by Soviet financial aid. It is unlikely, however,
that the Center and Right would consent to admit the Communists into such a Government, although some Socialists
might be inclined to do so in order to recoup their
labor and political losses.)

~~TOP SECRET~~

100. Daily Summary Excerpt, 9 October 1948, Germany: Preparations for Eastern German Government

49

~~TOP SECRET~~

9 OCT 1948

810

EUROPE

2. **GERMANY:** Preparations for eastern German government-- CIA has been informed by a usually reliable source that the Volksrat in Soviet Zone Germany has drawn up a constitution for an "Eastern German Republic" which is to be announced "in the near future." Source reports that Co-chairman Grotewohl of the Socialist Unity Party is considered to be a most likely minister-president of such a government.

CIA - See

(CIA Comment: CIA believes that the USSR will by November have established a German police organization through which it can at any time set up an eastern German government without any real lessening of present Soviet control. The creation of such a government would not necessarily involve a Soviet troop withdrawal. CIA believes that the German figurehead for a Soviet Zone government will be Wilhelm Pieck, not Grotewohl, and that the real Communist leader in Germany will continue to be Walter Ulbricht.)

Document No. 608
NO CHANGE in Class. ☐
☒ DECLASSIFIED
Class. CHANGED TO: TS S C
DDA Memo, 4 Apr 77
Auth: DDA REG. 77/1763.
TOP SECRET Date: 16 MAR 1978 By: 028

- 1 -

101. Daily Summary Excerpt, 11 October 1948, Possible Communist Strategy in Western Europe

~~TOP SECRET~~

GENERAL

1. <u>Possible Communist strategy in western Europe</u>--According to US Ambassador Kirk in Brussels, Belgian authorities view the Communist offensive in France and present Communist preparations for a wave of labor agitation in Belgium as parts of a general, coordinated effort to create social and political instability in western Europe. US Ambassador Caffery in Paris reports the conviction of Interior Minister Moch that "France is now the battlefield chosen by the Kremlin in an attempt to bring western Europe to its knees." The French Interior Ministry believes that chief Communist efforts in France are now centered on the railways in order to prevent the delivery of Saar coal. The Ministry is hopeful, however, that the attitude of non-Communist unions, combined with firm police action, will prevent a major stoppage.

   (CIA Comment: CIA agrees that the Communists are directing a labor offensive against western Europe as a whole. CIA considers that the major drive is being made in France because it is the most vulnerable country, economically and politically.)

CIA - See
CIA - See

Document No. 009
NO CHANGE in Class. ☐
☒ DECLASSIFIED
Class. CHANGED TO: TS   S   C
          DDA Memo, 4 Apr 77
Auth: DDA REG. 77/1763
~~TOP SECRET~~ 6 MAR 1978   By: 028

- 1 -

102. Weekly Summary Excerpt, 15 October 1948, The Communist-Inspired Strikes in France

The Communist-inspired strikes in France are designed primarily as an additional and timely weapon with which to further the Kremlin's primary goal of defeating the European recovery program. Consequently, the fate which befalls the French Communist Party as a result of the strikes is a secondary consideration to the USSR. The current Communist attack in France reflects the Soviet belief that such action, if taken before western aid restores French political and economic stability, would seriously dislocate the French economy and dissipate the beneficial effects of the European recovery program throughout western Europe. However, in choosing France as the first major battleground in its fight against European rehabilitation, the Kremlin has run the risk of precipitating De Gaulle's return to power and of possible outlawing of the Communist Party. Regardless of the outcome of the strike offensive in France, the Communists can be expected to resort to similar direct tactics in other ECA countries.

- 6 -

103. Weekly Summary Excerpt, 29 October 1948, UN: Soviet Veto on Berlin; Germany: Soviet Action in Eastern Germany

UNITED NATIONS

Soviet representative Vishinsky's moderate veto statement, made during the voting on the Security Council compromise proposal, suggests that the USSR may be interested in an eventual face-saving solution of the Berlin dispute. Vishinsky barely referred to the contention of the USSR that the UN has no jurisdiction over the Berlin controversy. The Soviet representative defended the veto largely on the grounds that the proposed ending of the blockade and the introduction of the Soviet currency in Berlin were not to be simultaneous. This implicit willingness to accept the UN as a forum for negotiation on Berlin indicates that there is still some possibility that the USSR is interested in finding a compromise solution to the dispute.

The Soviet Union may now be inclined toward conciliation because it recognizes that the Berlin blockade has failed to dissuade the western powers from proceeding with a separate organization for western Germany or to force them out of Berlin. The USSR may even recognize that the present success of the airlift, combined with the firm stand of the western powers, has: (1) raised western prestige in Germany and increased German hostility to the Soviet Union; (2) spurred western plans for rearmament and military coalition; and (3) precipitated the local problem of Berlin into a crisis of world scope, far exceeding Soviet calculations. While awaiting further developments in the UN, the USSR will also look for positive evidence that the airlift can, or cannot, overcome the Berlin winter.

- 2 -

WESTERN EUROPE

GERMANY

Soviet action in eastern Germany during the past three months indicates that the Kremlin is accelerating preparations which would permit the establishment of an eastern German government capable of assuring Soviet domination with or without the support of Soviet occupation troops. The Communist-dominated Socialist Unity Party (SED) is undergoing a purge which will ultimately replace all members of non-Communist parties and unreliable Communists now holding key positions in the SED with reliable Stalinist Communists. The cadre thus formed will become the instrument for tightening Communist control of the SED, the Volkskongress, and other Communist front organizations. In conjunction with Soviet domination of the German Economic Commission and the Administration of the Interior, the SED will contribute materially to Soviet control of eastern Germany through a Communist minority. Moreover, a disciplined SED will facilitate Soviet-Communist control of the Soviet sector of Berlin following the anticipated split in the Berlin city government after the 5 December western sector elections. In addition, eventual Soviet domination of eastern Germany is being facilitated by efforts to strengthen and reorganize the Administration of the Interior. The Administration, through the SED party structure, is now in practically full control of the zonal government down to a county level; the framework of the Administration thus is strikingly similar to the centralized police system of the Nazi regime. The Administration can now exercise most of the powers of a Ministry of the Interior in a totalitarian state, including control of public prosecutors through the criminal police. Approximately 15,000 specially trained and selected police, under the control of the Administration and quartered in barracks throughout the Soviet Zone, are being equipped

- 5 -

103. *(Continued)*

SECRET

GERMANY

with carbines and machine guns, and they may eventually be equipped with heavier weapons. In the hope of appealing to German nationalism, this new police force may be headed by Germans formerly identified with the Free German Committee.

- 6 -

SECRET

104. Weekly Summary Excerpt, 29 October 1948, Prospects for Invasion of South Korea by the North

KOREA

An armed invasion of South Korea by the North
Korean Peoples' Army is not likely until US troops have
been withdrawn from the area or before the Communists

- 14 -

253

KOREA

have attempted to "unify" Korea by some sort of coup.
Eventual armed conflict between the North and South
Korean governments appears probable, however, in the
light of such recent events as Soviet withdrawal from
North Korea, intensified improvement of North Korean
roads leading south, Peoples' Army troop movements
to areas nearer the 38th parallel and from Manchuria to
North Korea, and combined maneuvers. Communist
agents have been directed to intensify disturbances in
South Korea in November, ostensibly to facilitate an invasion early in 1949. Although this invasion may not
materialize, such disorders as the recent Yosu uprising
(in which a Communist-led constabulary unit attacked
town police and constabulary officers) would bolster a
Soviet claim before the UN that the South Korean regime
is unpopular and supported only by the police and the US
Army. Proven Communist complicity in such incidents
may react against the USSR in the UN, but Communist
efforts to initiate riots and strikes will continue in order
to pave the way for North Korean control of the entire
peninsula following the withdrawal of US forces.

- 15 -

SECRET

EASTERN EUROPE

SOVIET UNION

Premier Stalin's recent PRAVDA interview apparently indicates some shift in the Kremlin's estimate of its capabilities for achieving its immediate objectives in the Berlin dispute. The USSR probably still wants a negotiated settlement of the Berlin issue on terms which would permit ultimate Soviet control of Berlin and Communist penetration of western Germany. The Kremlin apparently believes, however, that such terms probably cannot be obtained from the western powers under present circumstances. Stalin's interview may therefore have been intended to prepare the ground, both within the Soviet Union and abroad, for further unilateral action on Germany, possibly including partition and the establishment of an east German state. The Soviet people have never been told of the real gravity of the Berlin situation and therefore need to be prepared for any step as drastic as the renunciation of "cooperation" with the western powers. As Soviet propaganda designed for foreign consumption, the Stalin interview reiterates the allegation that the western powers are responsible for present world tension and warns the West that the USSR may proceed unilaterally in Germany. The uncompromising stiffness of Stalin's remarks therefore suggests that in the absence of a facesaving compromise, the USSR is prepared to accelerate preparations for the formation of an east German state.

Soviet propaganda preparations for the annual celebration of the October Revolution sharply contrast with the extravagant preparations being heralded throughout the world at this time last year. The less than a dozen news items about the anniversary which have appeared may reflect Kremlin preoccupation with the world situation. This year's slogans which will be used to define the Communist "line" during the next twelve months represent little change from the pattern of themes emphasized last year.

- 7 -

SECRET

SECRET

FAR EAST

CHINA

The decisive battle for Central China is beginning. At least 16 Communist columns are sweeping down both sides of Hsuchou in a pincer movement which can either destroy that vital Nationalist base or, by isolating it, drive directly against Nanking. The imminent collapse of the ill-trained and dispirited Nationalist forces in the Hsuchou-Nanking area will probably mark the end of all organized Nationalist military resistance. In North China, the present inactivity probably foreshadows a forthcoming Communist attack in the extremely vulnerable Peiping-Tientsin-Kalgan area. The eclipse of the Nationalists in Manchuria is complete, following Nationalist evacuations of Yingkou and Hulutao.

The imminent bankruptcy of the Chinese National Government, presaged by the panicky refusal to accept gold yuan in Shanghai and Nanking, may soon result in the lifting of foreign exchange controls to permit free dealing in US currency and bullion. In Shanghai, the price of rice has reportedly increased 80 times over the ceiling price prevailing last week, and the refusal of farmers to ship food to these cities has heightened the critical food shortages.

The National Government, beset by unprecedented military and economic debacles, continues to exert every effort to avert political collapse on the home front. Regardless of the refusal of several Kuomintang officials to serve on the Cabinet and the suggestions of some Cabinet members that a peace be negotiated with the Communists, Chiang Kai-shek appears determined, at the moment, to continue his fight against the Communists to the bitter end. A satisfactory

- 11 -

SECRET

106. *(Continued)*

SECRET

CHINA

solution of the Cabinet crisis is unlikely, however, in view of the hopelessness of the general situation and the unwillingness of prominent Nationalist leaders to accept responsibility for forming a new Cabinet.

A tremendously increased Soviet war potential in the Far East may result eventually from Communist control of Manchuria and north China. With the Communists controlling these areas, including Shanghai, the USSR would have a "strong voice" in the operation of both the extensive harbor facilities and the transportation net in this vast area. This greatly increased transportation potential, if developed by an aggressive rehabilitation program, could permit the USSR to undertake an ambitious industrial expansion in north China and Manchuria. Such an expansion in these areas would provide the USSR with an agrarian-industrial base capable of supporting a far more formidable military force in active combat than it can presently maintain there. The creation of a major industrial complex in Manchuria would enable a large Soviet military force to live almost entirely off local production and to depend upon the limited capacity of the vulnerable trans-Siberian railroad only for highly critical items. The self-sufficiency of any Soviet military establishment in the Far East would be further augmented by the utilization of the warm water ports along the north China coast. Shanghai has extensive dry dock and repair facilities which could be rapidly converted to the production of both merchant and naval vessels.

- 12 -

SECRET

106. *(Continued)*

SOVIET-SATELLITE SUPPORT OF
CLANDESTINE AIR ACTIVITY TO PALESTINE

Allegations of direct Soviet support of the Israeli military machine were contained in public charges recently made by a former pilot of the Israeli Air Transport Command. The pilot's statement, much of which is supported by evidence already available, gives a detailed account of the organization of the Israeli Air Force and the Israeli Air Transport Command and describes the methods used in secretly flying considerable quantities of aircraft and munitions from Europe into Palestine. The pilot's specific charges of direct Soviet support, however, cannot be substantiated at this time. His testimony confirms reports that Prague has been a major center for the procurement of airplanes and munitions for shipment to Israel. Coordinated government direction of these procurement and shipment activities is clearly indicated by the number of Czechoslovak government agencies already implicated. These agencies include: (1) Czechoslovak consuls who have been instructed to issue visas for Israelis and foreign volunteers enroute to Czechoslovakia for training; (2) the Czechoslovak Air Force which has conducted the pilot training program, issued Czechoslovak uniforms to the trainees, and placed military airfields at the disposal of foreign aircraft operators engaged in arms-running to Palestine; and (3) the Czechoslovak Communist security police who have protected these various activities to insure secrecy and prevent local interference. Moreover, the Communist Party in Czechoslovakia has organized a corporation, with Israelis holding a minority interest, for the express purpose of facilitating the sale and delivery of Czechoslovak munitions to Israel.

Although there is no indication of the precise role played by the USSR in the Czechoslovak arms traffic, these activities could have been undertaken only with the approval

- 15 -

106. *(Continued)*

of the Soviet Union. The sale of arms and munitions to the Israelis certainly has served the Soviet desire to protract the conflict in the Near East. (Czechoslovakia has contracted to supply arms and munitions to Arab states as well as Israel.) At the same time, Czechoslovakia has been provided with much-needed hard currency. The same dual purpose probably inspired Yugoslavia to provide an airfield in southern Yugoslavia for clandestine air operations to Israel.

There is some evidence that Soviet and Czechoslovak enthusiasm for the support of Israel is diminishing. Israeli representatives in Prague have reported to the US Embassy that the Czechoslovak Government: (1) intends to discontinue the training of Israeli pilots and the recruitment of volunteers to serve in Israel; (2) is now exercising more rigid control over the movement of Jewish refugees through the country; and (3) is investigating the offices of the American Joint Distribution Committee which handles for Israel the distribution of Jewish DP's. [

] The USSR and Czechoslovakia may simply believe that greater caution is needed in order to forestall charges of violating UN truce obligations. On the other hand, the USSR may be convinced that the Israelis have won their fight and that Soviet purposes will be better served by a closer balance of military power between Israel and the Arab states.

- 16 -

ORE 49-48

CONFIDENTIAL

THE TREND OF SOVIET-YUGOSLAV RELATIONS

SUMMARY

Tito's defiance of the Cominform has precipitated the first major rift in the USSR's satellite empire and has struck at the very core of the Stalinist concept of Soviet expansion through world Communism; for, if the Kremlin should decide as a result of the Tito affair that local Communist parties cannot be relied upon as effective instruments for maintaining Soviet control over its Satellites, the Soviet leaders must then re-examine their present techniques. The primary results of such a re-examination will probably be (1) to purge thoroughly all Communist Party leadership of unreliable elements and (2) to take strong measures aimed at neutralizing the widespread anti-Soviet antagonism of the Eastern European peoples.

Early reconciliation between Tito and the Cominform is unlikely. Tito will be wary of a reconciliation because the present Soviet regime will never forgive his kind of heresy and will, despite any temporary rapprochement, inexorably seek his overthrow. Moreover, the Kremlin cannot afford the loss of face and denial of its infallibility which would result from admitting that Tito had been even partially right. Meanwhile, the Kremlin appears to be presently unable to institute effective disciplinary measures against Tito short of armed invasion, and Tito will seek to avoid any steps which might provoke the USSR into taking such action. Consequently, neither Stalin nor Tito will risk an immediate complete break between the two countries in the hope that developments will eventually produce some satisfactory solution of the present impasse. An accommodation between the two countries, however, will become increasingly difficult. As each state takes steps to consolidate its position, the differences between them will assume greater ideological as well as practical intensity.

Despite this gradual widening of the breach between Yugoslavia and the USSR, a Kremlin decision to use its potential to overthrow Tito by force would be motivated less by Yugoslav actions than by international developments. The possibility of direct Soviet action might increase if international tension increases the possibility of war, or the USSR deliberately launches World War III.

Note: The information herein is as of 5 November 1948.
The intelligence organizations of the Departments of State, Army, Navy, and the Air Force have concurred in this report.

1

CONFIDENTIAL

108. Weekly Summary Excerpt, 19 November 1948, The Kremlin "Peace Offensive"

THE KREMLIN "PEACE OFFENSIVE"

Despite the recently headlined Kremlin "peace offensive," continued Soviet-Communist pressures and expansion in various parts of the world indicate that any "softening" by the Soviet Union should be regarded only as a temporary tactical adjustment and not as a prelude to a sweeping revision of Soviet policy toward the west. The USSR apparently now intends to exploit the US refusal to engage in bilateral negotiations on Germany as a further example of US insincerity in the quest for world peace.

Western Europe   Soviet pressure continues unabated in western Europe. In France, the Communist-dominated General Confederation of Labor, which called the still unsettled coal strike and which is campaigning for rotation strikes in other industries, admitted publicly that groups of miners in the USSR and its Satellites were providing funds to finance idle strikers. In the western zones of Germany, the Communists are organizing youth and factory cells in preparation for increased agitation. In Austria, Soviet occupation authorities recently sought to counteract slowly improving economic conditions by demanding another allotment of locomotives and rolling stock as war booty. This action, combined with recent Soviet success in intimidating Austrian officials by arresting a number of Austrian citizens, may lead Austria to waver in its cooperation with the western powers.

Near East   The return of Soviet Ambassador Sadchikov to Tehran may presage a renewed campaign against the US arms program and US military missions in Iran. The latest incident in the Soviet "war of nerves" is the occupation by the USSR of a strip of territory claimed by Iran and located along the Soviet border east of the Caspian Sea. Soviet pressure

- 2 -

"PEACE OFFENSIVE"

will probably be restricted to demands for an oil concession in Iran and repeated charges that US military aid violates the 1921 Soviet-Iranian Treaty of Friendship.

Japan   As a part of expanding operations in the Far East, the USSR has increased its activity and interest in Japanese affairs. Molotov's recent reiteration of Kremlin interest in the early conclusion of a Japanese peace treaty may be the beginning of a propaganda campaign designed to harass US occupation authorities. In late September, the USSR again requested that "those powers most interested" be authorized by the Far Eastern Commission to exercise international controls over Japanese industry which would extend beyond those established by a formal peace treaty. The Soviet member of the Allied Council for Japan has also been sharply critical of both the Japanese Government and SCAP during the past three months. As one measure of Soviet intent in the Far East, radio transmitting facilities of several Siberian broadcasting stations beaming propaganda to Japan have been strengthened so that virtually any standard Japanese radio set can pick up the signal.

China   Advance propaganda announcements by prominent Chinese Communists suggest that the USSR is preparing the way for more active participation in Chinese affairs. In the most recent announcement, Liu Shao-chi, member of the Chinese Communist Central Committee, attempted in a radio commentary to prove that Chinese patriotism was not incompatible with "proletarian internationalism." Although the philosophical subtleties of Liu's reasoning will largely escape the rank and file of Chinese Communists, this public acknowledgment of Soviet primacy in the conduct of local Communist Party affairs probably represents the beginning of a Soviet-sponsored "educational" campaign to prepare the Chinese for a dominating role by the USSR in China.

- 3 -

109. Intelligence Memorandum 76 Excerpt, 19 November 1948, Economic Trends in the USSR

~~SECRET~~   *Excerpt*

CENTRAL INTELLIGENCE AGENCY

19 November 1948

INTELLIGENCE MEMORANDUM NO. 76

SUBJECT: Economic Trends in the USSR

The economy of the USSR has improved rapidly since 1945 but production is still slightly below the 1940 level. In terms of ruble values the Soviet Union is meeting the objectives of the fourth Five-Year Plan, but in terms of physical units of production many key industries are failing to attain their goals. Despite the recent Soviet announcement that during the first nine months of 1948 total production exceeded the average 1940 level by 14 percent, an analysis of the various industrial and agricultural components that make up this production index reveals a less favorable picture of Soviet Economic revival.

It must be emphasized that this is an over-all production figure which fails to reveal the lack of essential uniformity in production increases throughout the numerous segments of the economic complex. Some branches of industry have exceeded their norms while others have fallen short. The failure of some segments of industry to meet the plan requirements has far-reaching effects in a planned economy. Under the current Five-Year Plan, those main groups which have failed to reach 1940 production levels include: steel, transportation, agriculture, heavy construction, machine tools, and basic heavy machinery. The failure of these important branches to regain their 1940 levels presents serious difficulties to the Soviet planners and detracts from the sizeable advances over 1940 made by such industries as chemicals, petroleum, coal, aluminum, and electric power.

Further factors which should be taken into account in evaluating the general production increase are as follows:

a. A disproportionately large part of production must constantly be assigned to maintenance and repair of inefficient plants and low-quality equipment.

- 1 -

Document No. _____ **001**
NO CHANGE in Class. ☐
☒ DECLASSIFIED
Class. CHANGED TO: TS   S   C
Next Review Date: 1 Apr 77
Auth: _____
Date: 14/11/77   By: _____ **021**

~~SECRET~~

109. *(Continued)*

SECRET

b. A part of the increase in production must be attributed to the addition of industry and resources in newly acquired territory.

c. A sizeable part of additions to industrial capacity resulted from reparations, war booty, and exploitation of Satellites. To this must be added the productive and technical ability of engineers, technicians, skilled and semi-skilled labor in POW camps, and those groups brought in from occupied and acquired areas.

Economic recovery to the 1940 levels, then, is not as complete as the Soviets imply. It must be emphasized, however, that their state-controlled economy requires relatively little change in mobilization for war and has forced consumer goods production to the barest minimum both in time of war and of peace. This permits greater emphasis on capital goods production than is possible in capitalist countries and basically strengthens their economy.

In international economic relations, the Kremlin is currently intensifying its efforts to acquire specific items of industrial equipment and raw materials from the West, partially as the result of the combined Soviet-Satellite inability to make up these deficiencies within Eastern Europe. The ability of the Soviet countries to obtain those items will depend in part upon (1) the extent and effectiveness of export controls and (2) trade concessions that must be made in the interests of Western European recovery.

While economic considerations alone do not determine Soviet foreign policy, the state of the Soviet economy currently acts as a deterrent on the implementation of Soviet aggressive designs. The above analysis of Soviet economy, therefore, tends to substantiate the belief that Soviet efforts will continue to be concentrated upon (1) consolidation of control over the Eastern European Satellites and over occupied Germany and Austria; and (2) furthering of Moscow-dominated Communist expansion through the activities of native Communist parties. The current rate of improvement in the Soviet economy will not in itself warrant substantial changes in the timetable of Soviet policy implementation.

Selected fields of the Soviet economy are commented on in Enclosure A.

- 2 -

SECRET

264

110. Weekly Summary Excerpt, 26 November 1948, France: Soviet Pressure; Communist Labor

ment.   1

FRANCE

Soviet Pressure   The Soviet Union continues to exploit
French defeatism and fears of a resur-
gent Germany. Apparently convinced that France is the
weakest link in western European defensive planning, the
USSR has: (1) chosen France as the place to concentrate
Communist attacks upon the European recovery program;
(2) stepped up its propaganda campaign against western
plans for Germany and the Ruhr; (3) implied that the Spanish
Pyrenees, rather than the Rhine, would be the US "frontier"
in Europe; and (4) indirectly proposed, on a governmental
level, that France renounce the western bloc in order to
insure world peace and French security. At a time when
France's internal problems portend the fall of the Queuille
Government and the rise of De Gaulle, the Kremlin can be
expected to continue its cynical exploitation of French fears
and prejudices which has already caused many Frenchmen
of varying political convictions to consider critically the
implications of France's alignment with the west.

- 9 -

EASTERN EUROPE

Communist Labor   Soviet determination to throw the full,
world-wide resources of Communist
labor against the European recovery program is manifested
by Soviet support of the striking French coal miners. The
Communist-controlled Secretariat of the World Federation
of Trade Unions (WFTU) has called for "tangible demonstrations" in support of the French miners. Simultaneously,
the Soviet, Polish, Czechoslovak, Yugoslav, and Rumanian
labor movements have contributed 90,000,000 francs (about
$288,000). This unprecedented public aid, which actually
is insignificant in comparison to the total clandestine Soviet
support of the French strike, clearly demonstrates the all-
inclusiveness of the Soviet effort to sabotage the European
recovery program. The WFTU appeal, directed primarily
to western labor, may draw minor contributions from left-
wing labor groups in Italy, the UK, and the US. However,
the appeal will be flatly rejected by British and US national
labor organizations which support the European recovery
program and will hasten their formal withdrawal from WFTU.

111. Weekly Summary Excerpt, 3 December 1948, The Berlin Dispute; Communist Policy in China

THE BERLIN DISPUTE

Despite the Soviet Union's acceptance of the proposal by the UN neutrals to continue negotiations on the Berlin currency question, Soviet establishment of a regime for east Berlin, by completing the political and administrative division of the city, has greatly increased the obstacles to a settlement of both the Berlin dispute and the entire German question. The USSR has utilized the UN negotiations to gain time for consolidating the Soviet position in Berlin and eastern Germany. Moreover, by exerting greater pressure upon the western powers to withdraw from Berlin, the USSR has now relegated the currency question to relative insignificance in comparison to the far more explosive problem inherent in the establishment of two separate governments in Berlin.

"Rump" Government   Establishment of a Communist "rump" government in Berlin represents a Soviet attempt to counter the 5 December elections in the western sectors and to block UN interference in city affairs. This latest move has placed the Kremlin in the position of being able to make "paper" concessions to the west on four-power currency control for Berlin with the knowledge that such concessions can only be implemented through a centralized administration in the city. Thus, even if agreement on currency is reached, these recent Soviet moves will make it necessary for any future conference on the Berlin dispute to deal with the problem of city government. In such a conference, the USSR might demand a consolidation of the two separate city governments. Any resulting "compromise" government would: (1) provide the USSR with Communist representation in key positions, far out of proportion to that which could reasonably be expected in an open general election; (2) increase Communist ability to impair the functioning of the Berlin government; and (3) strengthen the Soviet potential for undermining the position of the western powers in Berlin.

- 2 -

111. *(Continued)*

Economic Consequences   The immediate effect in Berlin of the creation of a separate Communist government will be to intensify the political and economic impasse by making normal city government virtually inoperable. Following the 5 December elections in the western sectors of the city, the USSR may complete the economic split of the city by carrying out its already publicized threats to take measures which would: (1) require workers living in the Soviet sector and working in the western sectors or vice versa to change either their place of residence or their place of employment; (?) force some of the industrial and commercial enterprises in the west sectors to stop production while municipal gas lines, water mains, and sewers, now functioning as a city-wide unit, were being reconstructed to fit sector boundaries; (3) seriously impair maintenance and operation of surface transportation; (4) cut off electricity for the S-Bahn intercity trains in western sectors; (5) stop subways and elevated trains at zonal boundaries; and (6) disrupt telephone, telegraph, and postal services while they were being re-established on an east-west zonal basis.

Tightening Blockade   In addition to possible Soviet actions which would completely cut off still functioning municipal services from the western sectors of Berlin, recent re-groupings of the Brandenburg land police suggest that the USSR may throw a cordon around the western sectors of the city. Hitherto, a considerable unofficial barter of goods and a lively traffic in illicit items between the western sectors of Berlin and Soviet-occupied territory have materially relieved the needs of the western sector population. Although the Soviet noose around Berlin has been deliberately left loose because of trade advantages derived by the USSR, energetic police action could substantially reduce those important commercial operations. If this tightened blockade is imposed and effectively implemented, a material increase in the airlift will be necessary in order to maintain the present level of health and economic welfare of western sector residents.

- 3 -

111. *(Continued)*

SECRET

FAR EAST

CHINA

Communist Policy   Recent statements from authoritative
Chinese Communist sources empha-
size the strong ideological affinity existing between the
USSR and the Chinese Communist Party (CCP) and indicate

- 9 -

SECRET

111. *(Continued)*

CHINA

that Soviet leadership, especially in foreign affairs, will probably be faithfully followed by any Communist-dominated government in China. This pro-Soviet orientation has been revealed by: (1) recent Chinese Communist statements echoing the Soviet view that "the world is divided into two camps"; and (2) the CCP Central Committee endorsement in July of the Cominform condemnation of Tito. Chinese Communist propaganda has been accusing the "US State Department and US espionage organizations" of jointly plotting to "destroy the national liberation movement" in China. Thus a convenient pretext is being fabricated for possible future suppression or liquidation of those Chinese Communists unwilling to follow the Stalinist line.

- 10 -

112. Weekly Summary Excerpt, 17 December 1948, Soviet Union: Israeli Policy

SOVIET UNION

Israeli Policy   Although the Kremlin is unlikely to alter its
basic policy toward Israel before the 25 Jan-
uary Israeli elections, the recent marked change in Czechoslovakia's earlier friendly attitude toward Israel may reflect
an impending change in Soviet tactics in the Near East. Czechoslovak authorities have cancelled the Israeli military training
program and the Government has allegedly forbidden unscheduled

- 5 -

SOVIET UNION

air flights to Israel. This latter move, by curtailing clandestine arms shipments, represents an obvious financial loss to
Czechoslovakia and was probably dictated by the Soviet
Union. The USSR may estimate that the establishment of
Israel as a disruptive force in the Arab world has now been
accomplished and that further military aid to a country of
basically pro-western sympathies would ultimately prove
prejudicial to Soviet interests in the Near East. Nevertheless,
the Soviet Union, in the faint hope that Israel's pro-western
alignment may change after the 25 January Israeli elections,
has not yet altered its basic policy of politically supporting
Israel.

- 6 -

EASTERN EUROPE

SOVIET UNION

Austrian Treaty Soviet willingness to resume four-power discussions on the Austrian peace treaty may be accompanied by a more conciliatory attitude in an attempt to achieve an early settlement. Prospects have improved for a Soviet compromise on the major points of disagreement which were not resolved during the last conference. The USSR may ostensibly champion the Yugoslav people by initially supporting Yugoslav territorial claims, in order to strengthen the Soviet bargaining position with the West. Because of the Tito-Stalin rift, however, it is unlikely that the USSR will wish to break off negotiations over this issue. Moreover, the Kremlin may now consider that: (1) a rehabilitated Austria could serve as a bridge over which needed western materials and machinery could flow to the USSR; and (2) despite the calculated risk of quadripartite withdrawal, an "unoccupied" Austria may be more susceptible to Communist infiltration. These considerations may impel the USSR to adopt a more reasonable approach to the thorny question of external German assets in regard to both the lump sum to be paid by Austria to the USSR for restoration of German external assets and the amount and type of properties to be turned over to the USSR. The achievement of a reasonable compromise would also strengthen Soviet propaganda claims that the USSR is leading the world effort to further peace. Consequently, as long as the Kremlin considers it possible to reach an Austrian settlement, the USSR is unlikely to initiate strong measures which would disrupt the present quadripartite administration.

- 5 -

114. Weekly Summary Excerpt, 14 January 1949, Eastern Europe: Communist Penetration; Soviet Intentions in Germany

EASTERN EUROPE

Communist Penetration   Soviet determination to use the World Federation of Democratic Youth (WFDY) and its component national youth movements as instruments for the penetration of western European armed forces is suggested by a report that WFDY delegates recently attended a secret Paris conference held for this purpose. Although the WFDY has become an increasingly effective arm of Communist propaganda (it claims 50 million members in 60 countries), it has ostensibly left penetration work to Communist Party cadres. The Soviet delegate at the Paris Conference, however, reportedly discussed "disintegration work and the training of partisans," citing Communist activity in the French Army as an example for British and US youth groups, and calling for "conscript clubs" as the initial step in such work. Plans for such increased penetration activity are also indicated by: (1) the Kremlin's designation of an important Soviet Youth official to attend the Paris meeting; (2) an appeal by the WFDY to younger army elements; and (3) an accelerated campaign by the WFDY to bolster European and Latin American support for the Soviet drive in "defense of peace."

SOVIET UNION

Soviet Intentions   Recent Soviet and Satellite propaganda indicates that the Kremlin may now consider the early formation of an east German state to offer several advantages. Rather than attempt to cast the blame for a split Germany upon the western powers by waiting until the establishment of a west German provisional government, the USSR may now "justify" formation of an east German state which claims sovereignty over all of Germany on the grounds that current plans for a west German state are

- 6 -

114. *(Continued)*

SOVIET UNION

virtually completed. Such propaganda claims, however, would have little effect within Germany. Although actual Soviet troop withdrawals following establishment of the new state would depend upon how quickly the USSR could safely transfer authority to the German puppet regime, the USSR could easily recognize the new German state and then accede to its request for the continued presence of Soviet soldiers. The Kremlin would probably estimate that such an arrangement, if accompanied by partial withdrawal and implying later complete withdrawal, would have a propaganda appeal throughout Germany and could result in increased demands for withdrawal of the western powers. In addition to these advantages for the USSR, some measure of Soviet prestige within Germany might be salvaged and general attention would be temporarily diverted from the Berlin blockade. Moreover, the USSR could avoid at least partial responsibility for the continuation of the blockade by insisting that the Communist rump government had control over Berlin. In any event, such an action would have the effect of interjecting an allegedly legal government for all Germany into the Berlin conflict.

- 7 -

~~TOP SECRET~~

A N N E X

18 January 1949

THE SOVIET PROPAGANDA SHIFT

The reoccurrence of a Soviet propaganda "peace offensive" does not reflect a sincere desire by the Kremlin to negotiate outstanding east-west differences, except on Soviet terms. Neither does the Kremlin expect the US or the western governments to give serious consideration to the avowed Soviet desire for east-west agreement.

The Kremlin is attempting to weaken the position of the western powers and to delay positive western action by propaganda designed to: (a) create the illusion that the western powers, led by the US, are blocking an equitable solution of east-west problems; (b) ostensibly alleviate world tension in an attempt to persuade the new US Congress that current proposals for defense and foreign aid expenditures are unnecessary; (c) instill doubt and hesitation, both in the US and in western Europe, concerning the need for participation in the proposed Atlantic Pact; and (d) enable the Communist Parties in western Europe to regain some of the prestige and popular support lost during the recent months of direct action.

In making this tactical shift in its propaganda approach now, the Kremlin probably desired to take advantage of: (a) the convening of the US 81st Congress; (b) the appointment of a new US Secretary of State; (c) German dissatisfaction with, and western European misgivings over, the recent Ruhr decisions; and (d) the current discussions concerning the Atlantic Pact. Adoption of this propaganda line, however, has not committed the USSR to any specific course of action. The USSR can be expected to emphasize this approach as long as the Kremlin considers that it is contributing to the long-range Soviet program to defeat western recovery and defense efforts. On the other hand, the USSR will probably make still another tactical propaganda shift if the present approach encounters vigorous resistance.

- i -

~~TOP SECRET~~

Doc...t No. ___061___

SECRET

NO CHANGE in Class. ☐

☒ DECLASSIFIED

CENTRAL INTELLIGENCE AGENCY

Class. CHANGED TO: TS S C

DDA Memo, 4 Apr 77

Auth: DDA REG. 77/1763

Date: _____ 611

19 January 1949

INTELLIGENCE MEMORANDUM NO. 124

SUBJECT: Continuing Instability in Greece

1. Greece, although still free of Soviet-Communist domination, is in a dangerous state of war and political and economic instability despite almost two years of extensive US military and economic aid totaling approximately 750 million dollars.

2. The economic rehabilitation of Greece would be a long, difficult, and expensive task even if there were no guerrilla warfare or political instability. Extensive damage caused by World War II has been superimposed on a country having such indigenous problems as limited land resources, overpopulation, an agriculture oriented toward the production of semi-luxury products, and primitive agricultural, mining, and industrial methods as well as an archaic communications system.

3. The political situation in Greece has long been precarious, and Greek political leadership has been mediocre. Five years of prewar dictatorship stifled normal political life and prevented the development of young politicians. Moreover, the war itself and postwar excesses have led politicians to assume bitter and uncompromising positions. Selfish partisan interest, political bickering, and an unwieldy bureaucracy have deprived the Greek people of competent government and of a source of inspiration in their present struggle for survival.

4. The guerrilla war is the immediate cause of continuing Greek instability. The USSR and the satellites are seeking to dominate Greece through the instrument of the local Communist Party and its guerrilla organization. In view of Greece's 500-mile northern frontier and the mountainous terrain of the country, the satellites can easily and at little expense furnish tactical and material aid to the guerrillas in the amount necessary to perpetuate economic and political instability, counteract the psychological and economic value of US aid, and promote a progressive deterioration of the national will to resist. The Greek Army, on the other hand, has suffered from a defensive rather than offensive spirit, lack of aggressiveness, bad timing, and inadequate training for anti-guerrilla mountain warfare, together with poor leadership in the high command and political interference.

5. The US aid program has been attempting to solve this threefold problem. On the economic side, it has made some progress in rebuilding vital roads, ports, and other facilities and in stabilizing the currency and reviving trade. The guerrillas, however, have succeeded in countering

SEC̶

US aid by sabotage, terrorization of the agricultural population, and creation of an enormous refugee burden for the Greek state. Also, the guerrilla war and its attendant evils have made Greek businessmen afraid to invest their wealth in Greece. While in theory US funds, material, and technicians are sufficient for restoring the economy of Greece, successful completion of the task is prevented by the political and military factors.

6. The elections of 1946 brought to power the monarcho-rightist Populist Party dominated by Tsaldaris. US pressure has on several occasions forced the Populists to "broaden" the government by including Centrists and Liberals. While inclusion of these elements has given at least the appearance of a more liberal government, it has in fact increased dissension, confusion, and disunity. No political party or individual has presented a concrete program, and no political party or individual has so far subordinated party politics to national interests. So far the US has hesitated to interfere directly in Greek politics or to impose needed reforms; the Athens political merry-go-round continues, with the same faces appearing and reappearing, and popular confidence in the government continues to decrease.

7. British training and US military supplies and tactical advice have more than offset corresponding aid obtained by the guerrillas from the satellites. The guerrillas, however, continue to possess the advantages of terrain, mobility, short supply lines, escape routes, and refuge areas. Good leadership and high morale in the Greek Army could probably offset these advantages to the extent of enabling the army to clean up the guerrilla pockets in the Peloponnesus and southern and central Greece, and to contain the guerrillas in the frontier areas.

8. US aid to Greece has fallen far short of achieving its ultimate objective; it has, nevertheless, prevented the development of a situation far worse than that which now prevails. If assured that US aid will not be withdrawn or decreased, and provided competent leadership becomes available, the Greek people and armed forces are capable of continuing the war against the guerrillas. Psychologically, however, the Greeks-- after over eight years of war, hunger, disease, and privation-- are weary of fighting a war which many of them have come to regard more as a part of the major clash between East and West than as merely their own struggle for existence.

- 2 -

117. Weekly Summary Excerpt, 28 January 1949, Eastern Europe: Communist Dictatorships; Satellite Economy

EASTERN EUROPE

Communist Dictatorships   The Kremlin apparently feels that the Communists of Bulgaria, Rumania, and Hungary are strong enough to dispense with the fiction that these countries are democratic states. Communist leaders in the three Satellites have recently declared that the Soviet-sponsored regimes are now "dictatorships of the proletariat." Matyas Rakosi, Secretary General of the Hungarian Communist Party, has also stated that these "dictatorships" represent one type of government necessary to the transition from a capitalist to a socialist state. The frank admission that the Communist Party is the controlling power in Hungary indicates the early establishment of a National Front government, another basic type of Soviet regime which has already appeared in Bulgaria and Rumania.

Satellite Economy   The formation of the Council of Mutual Economic Assistance by the USSR at this time indicates that it is a defensive measure designed to offset the successes of the European recovery program. This Soviet-directed Council will attempt to coordinate further the economies of Poland, Hungary, Rumania, Czechoslovakia, and Bulgaria as a major step toward their eventual integration with the economy of the USSR. Although this latest Soviet move is undoubtedly part of a long-range plan, the immediate Kremlin objectives are to counterbalance the adverse effects on eastern European morale of the relatively rapid economic recovery in western Europe and to prevent the spread of nationalistic-economic heresies, such as Tito's. The Council's formation may have some propaganda value by renewing hope within the satellite countries that mutual cooperation may improve the low standard of living. The Council will result in some improvements in the Satellite economies by providing for more effective planning and more efficient distribution. Despite the fiction of economic equality, the Council's formation will inevitably result in tightened control of the eastern European economies by the Kremlin.

- 5 -

118. Daily Summary Excerpt, 4 February 1949, Moscow Meeting of Soviet-Satellite Military Leaders; Further Kremlin Overtures Predicted

4 FEB 1949

904

EUROPE

1. **USSR:** <u>Moscow meeting of Soviet-Satellite military leaders</u>-- US Embassy Moscow transmits a reliable report that high-level Czechoslovak and Polish military delegations have arrived there. The Embassy believes that an "elaboration of Soviet-Satellite military integration" may be the next step after the recent establishment of the Council of Mutual Economic Assistance. The US Military Attache in Moscow suggests that a conference of Soviet-Satellite military leaders may foreshadow the announcement of a military pact which would be analagous to the mutual aid council in the economic sphere.

S-S ARMY

(CIA Comment: CIA believes that the formation of a defense council is the Kremlin's next logical move as a countermeasure to the North Atlantic Pact. However, such a defense council would mean little more than a formalization of the existing integration of control of military forces.)

<u>Further Kremlin overtures predicted</u>--The US Military Attache in Moscow, in an analysis of Stalin's second press interview, predicts that the Kremlin will make "further overtures" in the near future. The MA believes that the Soviet and Satellite populace, and perhaps a sizable segment of world opinion, will accept the Soviet-inspired thesis that "Stalin strove for peaceful settlement and Truman refused."

(CIA Comment: CIA believes that the Kremlin will make additional propaganda overtures in an effort to obtain US agreement to enter into bilateral negotiations with the USSR.)

119. Daily Summary Excerpt, 11 February 1949, Evidence of Soviet Aid to Chinese Communists

~~50~~
~~TOP SECRET~~

11 FEB 1949

910

GENERAL

1. <u>Evidence of material Soviet aid to Chinese Communists</u>-- ~~reports~~ that he has seen "hundreds of Soviet-made trucks" in the environs of that city.

Army /s

    (CIA Comment: This eyewitness report by a reliable US observer is the first conclusive evidence that the Chinese Communists possess Soviet materiel in volume.)

~~TOP SECRET~~

120. Weekly Summary Excerpt, 11 February 1949, Soviet Military Bloc

EASTERN EUROPE

Soviet Military Bloc   Although the USSR has already established a military alliance with the Satellite states through an interlocking network of mutual assistance pacts, persistent reports emanating from eastern Europe indicate the formation of an eastern European military bloc to counter the establishment of the North Atlantic Pact. Speculation regarding such a move by the Kremlin has been intensified by the mysterious visit of Vishinsky to Czechoslovakia, as well as by the reported presence there of Gromyko, Zorin, the Polish Communists Berman and Zawadzki, and Soviet Ambassadors from the Satellites. Other reports place the Hungarian Minister of War and high-ranking Czechoslovak and Polish military officials in Moscow for planning of a similar nature. The formation of such an east European military organization would enable the USSR to exert more direct control of "unreliable" Satellite military establishments and would improve the morale of the Satellite Communist regimes which are becoming increasingly concerned over growing economic stability, political cooperation, and defensive preparations in western Europe.

- 9 -

121. Weekly Summary Excerpt, 18 February 1949, Soviet Plans for an East German State

SOVIET PLANS FOR AN EAST GERMAN STATE

Further Communist designs to integrate eastern Germany into the political and economic system of the Soviet bloc were apparent at the recent Socialist Unity Party (SED) Congress in Berlin. Speeches by Satellite delegates and Congress approval of the Oder-Neisse line as Germany's eastern boundary laid renewed stress on Communist efforts to reconcile the Satellite states to closer collaboration with the Soviet Zone and to eventual inclusion of the area in the Soviet orbit. Other action at the Congress indicates that the USSR is still attempting to insure Communist control of east Germany. By reviving advocacy of a "broad democratic front," the Communists are seeking the political support of formerly uncooperative elements. The establishment of an SED "Politburo" was designed to discipline the SED in order to make it a more effective instrument of Communist control.

The reversal of the SED stand for the incorporation of Berlin into the Soviet Zone indicates that the Communists believe the Berlin impasse will continue. In line with the Soviet theme of a "unified Germany," this tactical renunciation of Communist claims that Berlin is an integral part of the Soviet Zone may be designed to combat possible inclusion of the three western sectors of the city in a west German government. Moreover, by omitting Berlin from a future east German state, the USSR may feel that it can insure control over the new state by maintaining Soviet troops there to guard communication lines to a Soviet garrison in Berlin. Although the Congress again stressed the theme of German unity, Communist tactics at the Congress once more suggest that the USSR intends to create an east German state which will claim sovereignty over all Germany. The formation of such a state would probably be timed to counter the formation of a west German provisional government.

- 17 -

122. Daily Summary Excerpt, 24 February 1949, France: Implications of Communist Leader's Statement

50   24 FEB 1949

                                            920

EUROPE

2. FRANCE: <u>Implications of Communist leader's statement</u>--
US Embassy Paris interprets Communist Leader Thorez'
22 February statement as added evidence that the Kremlin
is demanding a return by the French Communists to a purer
form of Leninist-Stalinist doctrine and tactics, including
more aggressive class warfare. (Thorez reportedly suggested that if the Soviet Army were to invade France, the
French people would take the same attitude as the people
of Poland, Rumania, and Yugoslavia.) The Embassy further
regards the statement as: (a) proof of Kremlin determination to thwart the consolidation of western Europe even at
the risk of losing popular Communist support in France;
and (b) a signal to Communist militants to accelerate
sabotage of French efforts to strengthen national defense.

(CIA Comment: CIA agrees that Thorez' statement
indicates a further tightening of Communist discipline and
a reduction of the party to its "hard core." Moreover, even

CIA - 5

- 1 -

ment No. .044

CHANGE in Class. ☐
☐ DEC
Class.   S ⓒ

Auth:

17 MAR 1978   By: 028

122. *(Continued)*

TOP SECRET

though Thorez' declaration will apparently be detrimental
to Communist popularity in France, he may have made
it at this time in an effort to convince prospective members
of the Atlantic Pact that France would be unreliable in a
defensive alliance. CIA does not believe that widespread
strike action is probable in France in the immediate future.)

- 2 -

123. Daily Summary Excerpt, 4 March 1949, France: Government Policy on Communist "Treason"

~~CONFIDENTIAL~~ 50
~~TOP SECRET~~

MAR 1949

927

EUROPE

3. **FRANCE: Government policy on Communist "treason"**--US Embassy Paris has learned _____ that the Interior Ministry intends, in combatting the "treasonable" Communist line, to place emphasis "on what the Communist do rather than what they preach."   the Kremlin expects

C/R-

THE C.I.A. HAS NO OBJECTION
TO THE DECLASSIFICATION OF
THIS DOCUMENT.

NO. 028

Document No. 051

NO CHANGE in Class. ☐

- 1 -   ☐ DECLASS...

Class. ...   TS   S   Ⓒ

Auth: ...

~~TOP SECRET~~ Date: 1 7 MAR 1978   By: 028

Western European Communists not only to undermine European morale but also to engage in military and industrial espionage and eventually sabotage.   it may sometime be necessary for France to mobilize the men in every plant which is working for national defense.

(CIA Comment: CIA considers that the French Communist Party is likely to make plans for sabotage, especially against the armaments industry, but that the Communists are not likely to possess the capabilities for large-scale sabotage in the near future.)

- 2 -

EASTERN EUROPE

SOVIET UNION

Propaganda Offensive   Strenuous Soviet efforts to forestall the proposed Atlantic Pact are, by their very intensity, generally producing results opposite to those desired by the Kremlin. The recent speeches by Communist Leaders Thorez and Togliatti can be expected, if anything, to intensify existing support in France and Italy for the Pact. By publicly asserting that Communists in these countries would welcome invading Soviet forces, these leaders hoped to increase the fear of war and of Soviet occupation of Western Europe and also to demonstrate the unreliability of both France and Italy as prospective Pact members. This type of attack, however, tends to reinforce other factors that have been weakening Communist influence as a political force in France and Italy. Moreover, Communist leaders, by calling for a return to Communist militancy comparable to that of the late 1920's, are preparing the way for greater emphasis on sabotage and subversion.

Meanwhile, increased Soviet propaganda pressure on Scandinavia is also having little effect. The USSR may soon revive the Spitsbergen issue by asking Norway for assurances that no military bases will be built in the Spitsbergen archipelago. The Kremlin will probably claim that any defense preparations in the area would be a violation of the Spitsbergen Treaty of 1920. The Kremlin, anticipating Norwegian rejection of the Soviet-proposed non-aggression pact, is already accusing Norway of "aggression" and may use this as an excuse for demands on Finland, possibly by proposing joint Soviet-Finnish defense discussions. These prospective maneuvers

- 5 -

124. *(Continued)*

SOVIET UNION

probably would not change Norway's desire to join the Pact, and Finland's present Social Democratic Government would probably reject any such Soviet proposals. The Finnish Government may be strengthened by the inclusion of representatives of other non-Communist parties and thus be prepared to offer stronger opposition to future Soviet demands.

Merchant Shipping   The USSR is attempting more and more frequently to force the masters of foreign vessels to open safes and sealed envelopes during calls at Soviet-controlled ports. Such incidents have involved merchant ships of the US, the UK, and other western powers. The USSR probably hopes to obtain intelligence which would disclose the disposition of western merchant shipping if hostilities broke out.

- 6 -

125. Weekly Summary Excerpt, 11 March 1949, Germany: Berlin Currency; Soviet Union: Molotov-Mikoyan, Communist Militancy, Atlantic Pact; Yugoslavia: Greek Guerrillas

WESTERN EUROPE

GERMANY

Berlin Currency   Although Soviet reaction to the proposed issuance of the western "B" mark as the sole currency for the western sectors of Berlin will be swift and well-publicized, the USSR is not likely to interfere seriously or forcefully with the operation of the airlift. Soviet retaliatory action will probably take the form of further tightening of the blockade and may involve conversion of the Soviet eastern mark to a new currency. Soviet measures to curtail the movement of supplies from Soviet-controlled territory to the western sectors will increase the hardships of the western population, further impair the west sector economy, and probably require an increase in the airlift. Soviet authorities could tighten the land blockade by: (1) halting all rail traffic, including the S-bahn and streetcars; (2) cutting off water traffic on the canals; (3) stopping or sharply reducing pedestrian traffic between the western sectors and Soviet-controlled areas; (4) barring all mail service; (5) cutting west-sector long-distance phone cables, local inter-sector phone lines, and all telegraph cables; and (6) splitting completely Berlin's systems of electrical, gas, and water supply, and the sewage disposal facilities. In determining the extent to which these measures will be applied, the USSR will be restrained primarily by the economic repercussions in the Soviet zone, which would be deprived of important materials and skilled labor now being received from the western sectors of the city. If the USSR converts its present eastern mark, it will do so in order to prevent eastern marks presently held in western Berlin from flowing back into Soviet-controlled territory. Such a Soviet move would leave western sector occupation authorities with the moral obligation to redeem a very large number of relatively worthless eastern marks in order to avoid undue hardship for the German holders of this currency.

- 2 -

125. *(Continued)*

EASTERN EUROPE

SOVIET UNION

Recent Soviet reaction to western economic and defensive measures, though not yet crystallized, has thus far manifested itself chiefly by top-level changes in ministerial positions in Moscow and by an apparent shift in tactics by Communist Parties outside the Soviet Union. The implications of Molotov's and Mikoyan's shift from their ministerial posts will probably be clearer after the current session of the Soviet parliament, but no basic change in Soviet policy toward the West is expected. The USSR will continue its attacks on the Atlantic Pact, its obstructionist policy in the UN, and its attempts to gain control over all of Germany. Meanwhile, however, Communist Parties outside the USSR are apparently reverting to the active, militant policy of the 1920's.

Molotov-Mikoyan   The Kremlin decision to relieve Molotov from his position as Foreign Minister and Mikoyan as Minister of Foreign Trade, although not an indication of any fundamental change in Soviet policy, probably does reflect a Soviet reassessment of the progress of the cold war. Molotov's shift may reflect the Kremlin's belief that the problem of formal relations with the West has been reduced to secondary importance by western gains and the growing inability of the USSR to make progress on the diplomatic level. Similarly, western gains have made it more imperative for the USSR to consolidate its position in Eastern Europe and Communist China. Thus, although Molotov may have been released for the purpose of taking over Stalin's position as Premier, he, as well as Mikoyan, may have been relieved of ministerial duties in order to concentrate on the pressing political and economic problems of the Soviet sphere.

- 5 -

125. *(Continued)*

~~SECRET~~

~~SOVIET UNION~~

Communist Militancy   The apparent failure of recent Soviet
                       diplomatic and propaganda weapons
to sabotage US-European defense efforts and to gain popular
support for Communism has prompted the Kremlin to order
Communist Parties outside the Soviet Union to prepare for
militant and subversive methods in pursuit of Soviet objectives.
This announced reversion to the active militant policy employed
by the Communist Party in the late 1920's may, therefore,
signify the end of postwar tactics which were characterized
by so-called "legal" Communist operations within established
political frameworks. This shift in political tactics apparently
implies a renunciation of the popular-front technique of cooperation with non-Communist governmental factions.

Atlantic Pact   Continued Soviet efforts to defeat the purposes
                 of the Atlantic Pact are revealed by recent
Polish feelers for non-aggression pacts with the Scandinavian
countries. The Polish campaign is apparently concentrating
on the minimum goal of preventing a formal Swedish alliance
with the West. Aside from the strategic and political factors
which make Scandinavia a natural goal for Soviet hegemony,
the USSR's industrialization plans for Poland and Czechoslovakia depend upon an uninterrupted flow of imports from
Sweden. Likewise, Polish coal has long played a significant
part in Scandinavian industry, especially Sweden's. Thus,
aside from the USSR's interest in preventing closer political
and military cooperation between Sweden and the West, the
Soviet Union is desirous of maintaining uninterrupted the vital
economic lifeline from Scandinavia to the Satellites.

- 6 -

~~SECRET~~

YUGOSLAVIA

Reports of increased military activity in Bulgaria and Albania, combined with recent changes in Communist activities in northern Greece, suggest that the Kremlin is preparing a greatly intensified campaign for the overthrow of Tito. Realizing that six months of dialectical battle and relatively minor diplomatic and economic reprisals have, if anything, driven Tito further toward the western camp, the Kremlin now appears to be planning more drastic steps, which may possibly end in overt military action.

Greek Guerrillas An apparent shift in Communist activity in Greece strongly suggests that the Kremlin has decided to abandon temporarily its campaign to gain control over all of Greece and instead to attempt to exploit the Macedonian question as an additional weapon against Tito. The guerrilla radio has announced that an autonomous Macedonian state would be proclaimed in March. This new strategy is probably an attempt to gain the support of the large Slavo-Macedonian population in northern Greece. The autonomous Macedonian state envisaged by the Communists would, if established, tend to undermine the Tito regime and would thwart Tito's deep-seated ambitions for a Macedonian state under Yugoslav control. The Kremlin may also believe that it can secure such long-range benefits as an Aegean port, a land route between Bulgaria and Albania, a curtailment of Greek economic resources, and a base which could serve as a strategic threat against Greece, Yugoslavia, and Turkish Thrace. Aside from the possibilities such a plan offers for increasing the pressure against Tito, however, it is unlikely that the USSR will derive much benefit from raising the controversial Macedonian question at this time. Although

- 7 -

YUGOSLAVIA

Greek Communist leaders have, in a hedging statement,
announced their support for an independent Macedonia, the
rank and file will resent any move aimed at the dismemberment of Greece. Moreover, even with Slavo-Macedonian
reinforcements, the guerrillas would be too weak to hold
ground against the Greek Army without open intervention by
the Satellites.

Military Preparations   Meanwhile, the USSR is reportedly
                         stepping up military preparations
elsewhere. Top-ranking Satellite military leaders are reported to be meeting at Debrecen, Hungary. Although the
meeting may be designed to establish a "defensive" East
European military bloc as a counter to the Atlantic Pact,
plans for exerting greater military pressure on Yugoslavia
may also be on the agenda. Bulgaria is reportedly increasing its flow of supplies to the Greek guerrillas in eastern
Thrace. A noticeable increase in Soviet military activity
has been observed in Albania. Soviet supplies and arms are
arriving at Albanian ports, and numerous reports have been
received indicating the landing of Soviet personnel and aircraft. Moreover, increased Albanian protests of Yugoslav-
inspired border incidents, although at this stage probably
a stepping-up of the war of nerves, could be used as an
excuse for eventual armed action against Tito.

Yugoslav Reaction   The Tito regime, in the face of these
                     signs of increased Soviet pressure,
shows no sign of capitulating to the Kremlin. Finally breaking an enigmatic silence on the proposal for an autonomous
Macedonia, the Yugoslav Government has issued a denunciation, contending that the proposed campaign for an independent
Macedonia: (1) would only create confusion in the ranks of

- 8 -

YUGOSLAVIA

Greek and Macedonian guerrillas; and (2) was merely a part of the Cominform campaign against Yugoslavia. The Tito regime will exert every effort to prevent the formation of such a state and will publicly accuse Bulgaria of violating its past pledges for cooperation in handling the Macedonian question. In conclusion, there is no reason to believe that Tito will be intimidated by these Soviet measures, and any attempt short of overt military action will probably fail to dislodge him. Moreover, present Satellite armed forces are not strong enough to overcome the Yugoslav Army unless they are strongly supported by Soviet troops and materiel.

- 9 -

50

~~TOP SECRET~~

1 7 MAR 1949

938

S - S

~~S~~ - S

GENERAL

1. **Present Soviet intentions in Iran**--US Ambassador Wiley in Tehran considers that the only uncertainty about Soviet intentions in Iran is the timing of a Soviet move to return to the country. Wiley believes that the recent setbacks suffered by the Soviet Union, particularly the imminent conclusion of the Atlantic Pact, make it possible that the USSR may enter Iran in the near future.

In transmitting Ambassador Wiley's views concerning Iran to US Embassy Moscow, the Department of State has requested the Embassy's judgment on the probable effect upon the USSR of a US statement of continuing concern over the security of Greece, Turkey, and Iran, such statement to be made simultaneously with the conclusion of the Atlantic Pact. The Department points out that the UK, which had previously urged that such a declaration accompany the conclusion of the Atlantic Pact, now opposes such a statement, especially the inclusion of Iran.

(CIA Comment: The USSR is not likely to take overt action in Iran at this time, especially because such action would decisively facilitate the rapid and effective implementation of the Atlantic Pact.)

Document No. _____ 063

NO CHANGE in Class. ☐

☐ DECLASSIFIED

Class. CHANGED TO: TS S Ⓒ

Auth: DDA Memo, 4 Apr 77
DDA REG. 77/1763

Date: 17 MAR 1978 By: 028

~~TOP SECRET~~

EASTERN EUROPE

SOVIET UNION

Molotov-Mikoyan Shift   No basic change in Soviet policy toward
                          the West can be expected as a result of
recent personnel changes in the Soviet hierarchy. These changes
were probably designed to increase the efficiency of party and
state mechanisms, both politically and economically. The relatively rapid consolidation of the West, as currently exemplified
by the Atlantic Pact, is the immediate reason for the personnel
changes. The realignment of personnel simultaneously presages
intensified efforts to consolidate and strengthen the Soviet orbit
politically, economically, and militarily.

The cold war can be expected to continue undiminished in
intensity. Recent speeches by western European Communist
leaders suggest that subversion and sabotage, in addition to more
conventional tactics, eventually will play a more important role in
Soviet-Communist strategy against the West. Responsibility for
formal political and economic relations with the West has passed
from Molotov and Mikoyan to Vishinsky and Menshikov, both technical executives without policy function who can be expected to
adhere religiously to policies established by the Politburo.

The relief of Molotov, Mikoyan, and Voznesensky from
operational responsibility will leave them free to concentrate on
pressing problems of political and economic policy of the entire
Soviet orbit. Molotov, as heir apparent to the Soviet throne, would
be the logical choice to assume over-all command. Such responsibility would bring him one step closer to eventual assumption of
complete power in the event of Stalin's retirement or death.

Mikoyan and Voznesensky are the best-qualified Soviet
leaders to deal with the economic consolidation and strengthening
of the Soviet bloc. Mikoyan is apparently the leading figure in
the Soviet-inspired Council of Economic Mutual Assistance (CEMA)
which has already begun to assume the function of economic planning
for the entire Soviet bloc.

One of the first results of this Soviet realignment will
probably be shown in the handling of the case of Tito. Tito's defection, with its ramifications, is undoubtedly the most pressing internal
problem of the Soviet sphere and demands a drastic solution to prevent the further spread of nationalistic deviation.

- 5 -

N E A R   E A S T - A F R I C A

IRAN

Soviet Relations   Intensified Soviet pressure against Iran is
expected as a result of the recent serious
deterioration in relations between the two countries. Principal
factors causing this deterioration have been: (1) the suppression

- 9 -

127. *(Continued)*

IRAN

of the pro-Soviet Tudeh Party in Iran; (2) far more belligerent anti-Soviet Iranian propaganda; (3) the shipment of US arms to Iran; and (4) public reference to the possibility of Iranian participation in a Mediterranean or Near Eastern pact. The USSR probably sees in these developments a further threat to its principal immediate aims in Iran: gaining control over Iranian oil and blocking closer military ties between Iran and the West. Increased Soviet pressure will probably not take the form of overt military intervention. Instead, the USSR will probably renew its demands that Iran maintain "friendly" relations with the USSR and build up Soviet troop concentrations on the Iranian border. The Soviet Union may also attempt to incite uprisings in Azerbaijan. In order to counteract such measures, Iran will probably inform the UN Security Council of the deterioration in Soviet-Iranian relations and press for a US denial of Soviet charges that Iran is being turned into an offensive base against the USSR.

- 10 -

128. Daily Summary Excerpt, 4 April 1949, US Policy in Germany

4 APR 1949

953

EUROPE

2. GERMANY: Review of US policy in Germany requested--US Political Adviser Riddleberger in Frankfurt believes that the events of recent weeks in western Germany indicate the necessity

C/A-
C/A-

- 1 -

128. *(Continued)*

for a careful re-evaluation of US policy. According to Riddleberger, the unsatisfactory political situation in the western zones arises principally from the disunity of the western powers concerning Germany and is evidenced by mounting confusion, doubt, and disillusionment, particularly in connection with the slow formation of the west German government. Riddleberger points out that the strong desire for trade between west and east Germany, combined with a desire for political unity, produces a growing west German tendency to favor rapprochement with Communist-run east Germany. Riddleberger observes that west German responsiveness to Soviet peace and unity propaganda is much greater than it would have been some months ago.

(CIA Comment: CIA considers that the lack of agreement among the western occupying powers is the chief deterrent to progress on a west German state and that such disunity encourages German expectations of western concessions on the issue of centralization. Concerning the tendency to favor rapprochement with east Germany, CIA believes that even though west German conservative commercial circles desire eastern markets, the desire of west Germans as a whole for political unification on Soviet terms is weak. CIA does not believe that west Germans are very receptive to Soviet propaganda for "peace and unity.")

- 2 -

129. Weekly Summary Excerpt, 8 April 1949, Communist Deviation in Bulgaria

BULGARIA

Communist Deviation   The arrest of Traicho Kostov, vice premier and second most important Communist leader in Bulgaria, along with several other leaders in the Government and Party, indicates that the Kremlin has not yet been able to obtain the complete loyalty of the Satellite Communists. These arrests underscore the seriousness of the Kremlin's problem and the strength of Tito-like nationalism; they occurred in a Satellite often used by the Kremlin as an example for the other Satellites. Moreover, Kostov has generally been regarded as absolutely loyal to Moscow. The official communique describing his expulsion charged that Kostov: (1) lacked sincerity in his dealings with Soviet representatives (he apparently resisted economic exploitation of Bulgaria by the USSR); (2) disregarded Party and Government directives; (3) promoted distrust and suspicion within the Bulgarian Communist Party; and (4) opposed the Bulgarian Politburo. Apparently Kostov's cardinal sin was his effort as chairman of the Committee for Economic and Financial Questions to oppose Soviet exploitation of the Bulgarian economy. Although it is not known to what extent Kostov and those arrested with him had succeeded in forming an anti-Cominform organization, the recent denunciation by Interior Minister Yugov of the tendency of nationalist deviationists to form sects suggests that at least a loose kind of grouping was developing.

- 5 -

130. Weekly Summary Excerpt, 22 April 1949, Soviet Tactics in Germany; Satellite Communist Purges

W E S T E R N   E U R O P E

GERMANY

Soviet Tactics Soviet tactics in Germany continue to suggest that although Soviet control of all Germany undoubtedly remains the maximum objective, the Kremlin has decided that a "neutral" Germany, prevented from making a

- 3 -

130. *(Continued)*

GERMANY

firm alignment with the West, is a more feasible goal for the immediate future. The Kremlin may reason that the traditional tendency of German commerce to look eastward for markets and raw materials will bring Germany under eventual Soviet domination.

Meanwhile, rumors have been active recently that the Soviet Union will soon lift the Berlin blockade. Although there has been little or no concrete evidence to support such rumors, it must seem self-evident to the Kremlin that if the USSR is to regain the initiative and if the Soviet campaign for "German unity" is to have any appreciable success among the German people, the Berlin blockade will have to be lifted. Any such Soviet offer, if made now, would certainly be part of an over-all "peace offer" and probably would be made in such a way as to camouflage the Soviet defeat on the blockade. The current Paris "peace congress" would seem to provide an ideal setting for such a Soviet offer, but there is no evidence that Soviet strategy has changed enough to permit an offer on Germany actually acceptable to the western powers.

- 4 -

130. *(Continued)*

SATELLITE COMMUNIST PURGES

The recent purges of high-level Communist officials in Bulgaria indicate that Kremlin efforts to establish reliable Communist leadership in the Satellites are meeting with increasing difficulties. In attempting to eradicate Satellite "nationalism," the Kremlin is confronted with two almost equally unpleasant alternatives, neither of which can be wholly successful. If the USSR continues its liquidation of old-line Satellite Communists, the morale and cohesion of the local Communist parties, as well as their control over the Eastern European countries, may be jeopardized. If the Kremlin chooses the other alternative and relaxes its control over the Satellite governments and Party leaders, it runs the risk of further defections like Tito's. Neither course of action will make it any easier for Satellite Communists to perform the nearly impossible task of justifying Moscow's ruthless exploitation of Eastern European resources or increase Satellite dependability in the event of hostilities.

Since Tito's defection last summer, purges of high-level Communist personnel have occurred in Poland, Albania, guerrilla Greece, and, most recently, in Bulgaria. Meanwhile, recurring reports from practically all of the Satellites also indicate continued nationalist dissensions within the ranks of the various Communist parties. In many instances, reports regarding as yet unpurged nationalist leaders within the Satellite parties reveal that the existence of these schisms is common knowledge. The "deviationists" are usually officials connected with economic planning who can see most clearly the pattern of Moscow's ruthless exploitation of the Satellites. In the face of resurgent nationalism among the Satellites and increasing prosperity in Western Europe, the

- 18 -

130. *(Continued)*

SECRET

Kremlin cannot afford the risk of relaxing its grip over the
Communist parties in Eastern Europe. Thus, the Kremlin
will probably be forced to use even more brutal state-police
methods in retaining and consolidating its control over the
Satellites, even though such methods are not a basic cure
for nationalist deviation.

- 19 -

SECRET

306

131. Weekly Summary Excerpt, 29 April 1949, Soviet Propaganda on Gains in Far East; Soviet Union: Israeli Relations

Soviet Propaganda   In a further effort to counteract the effect of the Atlantic Pact and growing political and economic unity in Western Europe, the USSR is placing greater propaganda emphasis on Communist gains in the Far East. By stressing that the Communist victories in China will result in important changes in the world balance-of-power, the USSR hopes to: (1) convince audiences at home and in the colonial areas that Soviet power is invincible; and (2) undermine western confidence in the ability of the West to prevent further Soviet expansion. With fewer opportunities in Europe for propaganda exploitation, the USSR will probably devote its propaganda efforts more and more to the Far East and colonial areas. As part of this new emphasis, Soviet propaganda will portray the USSR as the exclusive champion of independence for the countries of southeast Asia and of industrialization of all backward areas. Simultaneously, Soviet propaganda will accuse the western powers of advocating the perpetuation of agricultural economies in Asia and will portray the Truman point-four program as a device to exploit the backward areas of the world and to keep them at the mercy of the industrial West.

- 4 -

131. *(Continued)*

EASTERN EUROPE

SOVIET UNION

Israeli Relations   Increasing Communist attacks on Zionism and the Israeli Government, although placing a strain on Israeli-Soviet relations, are unlikely to change either the Kremlin's external policy toward Israel or Israel's generally neutral position between East and West. In recent months, the Communist parties in the Soviet orbit, the US, and even in Israel have reverted to traditional Communist opposition to Zionist nationalism, and Soviet propaganda has begun to condemn the "bourgeois" nature of the new Israeli Government. The Satellite states, apparently reluctant to lose large segments of their skilled and educated citizens, have drastically reduced emigration to Israel, thereby discouraging Israeli hopes of fulfilling its immigration requirements. Within the Soviet Union, the current anti-Jewish campaign seems to have been inspired in part by the growth of pro-Zionist sentiment among Soviet Jews after Israel's emergence as an independent state. These attacks, however, rather than representing a fundamental change in Kremlin external policy toward Israel, appear to stem primarily from internal Soviet considerations. For, so long as support of Israel will serve to weaken US-UK influence in the Near East, the USSR will continue to aid Israel on a diplomatic level and in the UN. Nonetheless, because Zionism is basically incompatible with Communism and any non-Communist government is automatically suspect, the USSR feels forced to attack the present Israeli Government and to eliminate all Zionist influence within the Soviet orbit.

- 9 -

132. ORE 46-49 Excerpt, 3 May 1949, The Possibility of Direct Soviet Military Action During 1949

ORE 46-49

THE POSSIBILITY OF DIRECT SOVIET MILITARY ACTION DURING 1949
Report of a Joint Ad Hoc Committee *

THE PROBLEM

1. We have been directed to estimate the likelihood of a Soviet resort to direct military action during 1949.

DISCUSSION

2. Our conclusions are based on considerations discussed in the Enclosure.

CONCLUSIONS

3. The USSR has an overwhelming preponderance of immediately available military power on the Eurasian continent and a consequent capability of resorting to direct military action at any time. The principal deterrent to such action is the superior war-making potential of the United States.

4. There is no conclusive factual evidence of Soviet preparation for direct military aggression during 1949.

5. A deliberate Soviet resort to direct military action against the West during 1949 is improbable. Moreover, the USSR is likely to exercise some care to avoid an unintended outbreak of hostilities with the United States.

6. As part of its efforts to counteract the Atlantic Pact and US military aid program, however, the USSR will seek to intensify and exploit the universal fear of a new war. In this it will pay special attention to Scandinavia, Yugoslavia, and Iran. It is unlikely, however, to resort to even localized direct military action.

7. The fact remains that international tension has increased during 1948. It will probably increase further during 1949. In these circumstances, the danger of an unintended outbreak of hostilities through miscalculation on either side must be considered to have increased.**

---

* This estimate was prepared by a Joint Ad Hoc Committee composed of designated representatives of the CIA and of the intelligence organizations of the Departments of State, the Army, the Navy, and the Air Force. It has been concurred in by the Directors of those agencies, except as indicated in the footnote below. The date of the estimate is 21 April 1949.

** The Director of Intelligence, Department of the Army, believes that the last sentence of paragraph 7 implies a greater possibility of war in 1949 than, in fact, exists; and that it should read "In these circumstances, the small but continuing danger of an unintended outbreak of hostilities through miscalculation on either side must be considered."

1

50

~~CONFIDENTIAL~~
~~SECRET~~

981

THE C.I.A. HAS NO OBJECTION
TO THE DECLASSIFICATION OF
THIS DOCUMENT.

GENERAL   NO. 628

1. **USSR reportedly planning action against Iran**--US Ambassador Wiley transmits information, which is unconfirmed but from a good source, that the USSR plans an "important action" against Iran on 10 May. According to Wiley's information, Soviet intentions "exceed a mere frontier incident but are short of a warlike move." Wiley's informant mentioned the possibility of a movement affecting the Kurds.

   S-TS

   (CIA Comment: CIA does not believe that the USSR contemplates a military invasion of Iran at this time. The USSR, however, may plan to stir up trouble not only among the Kurds in Iran but also among those in northern Iraq and Syria. The Kremlin may also plan to use members of the former autonomous government of Iranian Azerbaijan to create disturbances. Iran would be able to cope with such disorders, unless the insurgents are provided with strong overt support from the USSR.)

~~CONFIDENTIAL SEC~~

134. Weekly Summary Excerpt, 6 May 1949, Soviet Union: German Objectives

EASTERN EUROPE

SOVIET UNION

German Objectives   Soviet agreement to lift the Berlin blockade and enter into four-power discussions on Germany does not represent any change in the Soviet objective to establish a Germany which will eventually fall under Soviet domination. It is still too early, however, to predict the sincerity of the Soviet desire to achieve an understanding with the West on Germany or the extent of the concessions the USSR would make in order to reach an agreement. The lifting of the blockade has been accompanied by a relaxation of Soviet pressure throughout the western periphery of the Soviet orbit and by an intensification of the Soviet propaganda "peace" campaign. On the other hand, May Day Communist propaganda savagely attacked the western powers, recent Communist statements have called for active preparation for militant action, and steps are still being taken toward the establishment of an East German state. Progress of the CFM alone, therefore, will demonstrate whether the USSR: (1) has agreed to enter into four-power discussions to sound out the western position and retrieve itself from the unfavorable situation created by the Berlin blockade; or (2) now considers it a sounder strategy to seek a "neutral" Germany in order to delay the final consolidation of the West German state and give the USSR some voice in all Germany.

CFM Proposals   Initial Soviet proposals at the forthcoming CFM will be designed to appeal strongly to an increasingly articulate German nationalism. After attempting to secure a commitment on postponing the West German state, the USSR will probably propose a general settlement for all Germany based on a return to four-power cooperation and the Yalta and Potsdam agreements. The Soviet terms

- 2 -

SOVIET UNION

will include the principal demands of the 1948 Warsaw
communique which advocated: (1) establishment of a centralized government for all Germany; (2) conclusion of a peace
treaty and withdrawal of occupation troops within one year;
and (3) control over Ruhr production and distribution by the
US, the USSR, the UK, and France. Depending primarily upon
the intensity of the Soviet desire to obtain the withdrawal of
US troops from Europe, the USSR may later in the negotiations
seek a ''compromise'' agreement. Such a compromise might
involve the acceptance of a federal government composed of
the East and West German zonal organizations. The USSR
would insist, however, that such a federation be established
in a manner which, in addition to not threatening Soviet political and economic control in East Germany, would provide
for sufficient Soviet influence in West Germany to offer
reasonable prospects for subsequently establishing a centralized Germany not wholly western-oriented and susceptible
to eventual Soviet domination.

East German State   Despite Soviet agreement to resume
                     discussions on Germany, the USSR is
continuing its preparations for establishing an East German
state. The executive agencies of the East German government have long been in operation, and elections for the Peoples'
Congress in mid-May will provide a pseudo-democratic legislative body capable of functioning as a parliament. In addition
to being a significant step toward the Soviet aim of eventual
economic integration of East Germany with Poland and Czechoslovakia, the recently announced East German-Polish trade
agreement (which is aimed at increasing 1949 trade between
East Germany and Poland to $152 million or doubling the
volume of goods exchanged by the two countries during 1948)
is another move toward the formalization of an East German

- 3 -

SOVIET UNION

government. The trade agreement was negotiated by the
East German authorities, thus reflecting the Soviet policy
of continuing to grant more governmental authority to the
East German economic administration, with the possible
idea of eventually making the East German regime a full
member of the Council of Economic Mutual Assistance.
These Soviet actions are designed to build up the status and
importance of the local administrative agencies in the eastern zone of Germany and can be used by the USSR both as
a lever in negotiating with the western powers at the coming
Council of Foreign Ministers and as a counter to the establishment of a West German state. In the event of an impasse in
the CFM, the USSR will have the machinery necessary for the
establishment of a Satellite regime in eastern Germany.

"Peace" Campaign   Simultaneously with the lifting of the
                    Berlin blockade, and in an apparent
effort to forestall further western consolidation, the Kremlin
is intensifying its "peace" campaign throughout the western
periphery of the Soviet orbit. The Soviet bloc has again extended feelers toward accommodation with the West; it has
at least tapered off its past intransigent attitude in numerous
cases. Soviet bloc countries have recently made concerted
attempts to expand trade with the West and seek western
financial assistance in an effort to mitigate the unfavorable
impact of western economic pressure. Hungarian officials
have shown a markedly more friendly attitude toward the US
Embassy in Hungary; Albania has granted diplomatic recognition to Italy; the Greek guerrillas have made a rather broad
peace offer ostensibly intended to lay the groundwork for
future negotiation of the Greek problem (see page 14); Soviet
pressure on Iran has apparently tapered off, and the USSR has
renewed its offer to discuss trade with that country; and Soviet

- 4 -

SOVIET UNION

pressure on Scandinavia has markedly decreased in comparison with that of the past few months. These developments may be designed to lull western suspicion at the forthcoming CFM meeting. The course of quadripartite discussions on Germany will determine whether the USSR is merely waging another campaign in its "peace offensive," or whether the Kremlin is laying the groundwork for achieving a temporary accommodation with the West.

May Day Slogans   The savagery with which the US was attacked in Moscow's May Day orders would seem to belie Soviet sincerity in re-opening discussions on Germany and in making overtures on other fronts. May Day propaganda, however, is designed for home consumption and for guidance to Communist parties throughout the world. In this context, the May Day slogans are a logical development of the Kremlin's principal psychological weapon--the peace campaign. For the faithful, the US must still be branded as the leading capitalist nation dedicated to the overthrow of the Soviet Union, while the common peace-loving masses throughout the world are pictured as sharing the Soviet desire for peace. Thus, the slogan that "the friendship between the peoples of the USSR, the US, and the UK forms the best guarantee for a lasting peace" is directed primarily toward driving a wedge between these peace-loving masses and their war-mongering governments.

- 5 -

~~50~~
~~TOP SECRET~~

20 MAY 1949

993

CIA-S

GENERAL

1. <u>Continued Soviet restrictions on Berlin</u>--US Representative Riddleberger in Berlin reports, in reviewing the present status of Soviet restrictions on transport, trade, and communications between Berlin and the western zones, that "Berlin remains today in a state of semi-blockade." According to Riddleberger, the USSR may be having "second thoughts" on lifting the blockade because the Soviet action has failed to: (a) retard progress toward the establishment of a west German government; (b) produce a "crack" in over-all western trade policy vis-a-vis the Soviet bloc; or (c) release a flow of western zone goods essential to the Soviet Zone and to the continuation of the Soviet reparations policy. Riddleberger therefore raises the possibility that the USSR may have intended to lift the blockade only enough to permit reconvening the CFM while simultaneously retaining a favorable bargaining position in the event that no over-all settlement on Germany is reached and it later becomes necessary to negotiate some provisional arrangement for Berlin. Riddleberger believes, in view of continued Soviet restrictions on Berlin trade, that the Department of State should decide whether Soviet implementation of the Jessup-Malik agreement has been sufficient to warrant the convening of the CFM.

(CIA Comment: CIA agrees that the USSR may be attempting to preserve the most favorable position possible in the event of a breakdown of the CFM negotiations. CIA further believes that the USSR will attempt at Paris to exploit certain remaining transport restrictions in bargaining on the over-all problem of German trade and its relation to western export policy. CIA believes, however, that the Kremlin's strong desire to hold the CFM meeting would impel the USSR to modify its restrictions on Berlin trade if confronted by a western refusal to convene the CFM under present conditions.)

THE C.I.A. HAS NO OBJECTION
TO THE DECLASSIFICATION OR 1
THIS DOCUMENT.

NO. **029**

~~TOP SECRET~~ ~~CONFIDENTIAL~~

Document No. **043**

NO CHANGE in Class. ☐

☐ DECLASSIFIED

Class. CHANGED TO: TS S C

Auth: ___ , 4 Apr 77

PEA ___ 77/1763

Date: 20 MAR 1978 By: **029**

FRENCH MILITARY PLANS IN INDOCHINA

French plans to shift both manpower and materiel from their forces in French-occupied Germany and North Africa for an autumn military campaign against Communist-led rebels in north Indochina materially affect the strategic interests of the US in both the Western European and Far East theatres. In addition to reducing the defense potential of Western Union by shipping arms and equipment from French-occupied western Germany, the French action may impair the prestige of the US in the Far East because the French forces will be using US-made and US-supplied arms and equipment. Moreover, the expenditure of French resources for the military operations in Indochina reduces the effectiveness of aid received under the European recovery program and delays the economic recovery of France.

The French, who have been attempting to suppress a Communist-led insurrection in Indochina since 1945, maintain that complete control of the China-Indochina border is necessary to keep the Chinese Communists from providing both men and materiel to the rebels or from evading Indochina. The French also point out that a stabilization of their position in Indochina is essential if Southeast Asia is to be made secure against the menace of Communism. As another part of their program to re-establish control throughout Indochina, the French recently signed an agreement with Bao Dai, former emperor of one of the Indochinese states, granting him authority to establish an "independent" government for Indochina within the French Union. Bao Dai will probably announce the formation of his government within the next two weeks, and the French hope that he will gain the support of the

- 15 -

136. *(Continued)*

non-Communist followers in the rebel group. The French
are convinced, however, that substantial military success
against the resistance movement is necessary to Bao Dai's
initial political success. In formulating their plans for
Indochina, both Bao Dai and the French envisage public
support from the US and military aid, which they have
already indirectly requested. US compliance with these
requests would provide the Far East Communist propagandists with another opportunity to charge that the US is
supporting reactionary colonial powers against the interests
of the Asian peoples.

- 16 -

SECRET

PROBABLE DEVELOPMENTS IN CHINA

SUMMARY

Introductory Note: The purpose of the following discussion is to present probable developments in China which will affect US interests during the next six to twelve months.

1. Communist military forces are capable during the summer months of 1949 of destroying all semblance of unity in the National Government of China; and before the year is out, the Communists will have formed a central government which will seek international recognition.

2. The US cannot reverse or significantly check this course of events, nor is there any prospect that the Soviet orientation of the Chinese Communists can be altered in the immediate future. However, during the coming months, developments in China will raise a number of problems on which the US may either take action advancing, or avoid action compromising, its interests in China and elsewhere. Chief among these are the formation of a Communist central government claiming international recognition, Communist aims regarding Taiwan and Hong Kong, the Communist need for foreign trade, and US aid to anti-Communist groups in China. In addition, US interests probably will be affected adversely by the expansion of Communist influence throughout the Far East, particularly if a Chinese Communist regime gains seats on the Far Eastern Commission and the Allied Council for Japan, and acquires China's claims regarding a future Japanese peace treaty.

3. The government to be organized by the Chinese Communists will be proclaimed as a "coalition," but actually will be a Communist dictatorship. In foreign affairs the Communists during the coming months will continue to be solidly aligned with the USSR. The new regime will honor the Sino-Soviet Treaty of 1945 and its attitude in international relations will be governed by the Moscow line. It will probably maintain an unfriendly attitude toward the US in particular and all other governments that impede the world Communist movement, as well as denounce China's existing international agreements with those governments.

4. Communist armed forces, now decisively superior to the Nationalists, will continue their program of area-by-area acquisition. They are capable of eliminating all effective military resistance in the south, southwest, and northwest by the end of 1950.

5. The Chinese Communists will probably not be faced with serious food shortages during the next year. Some progress will be made in reviving transportation and industry, and the Communists will have a relatively stable currency. The Communists' principal economic problem in the coming months will be that of acquiring petroleum, machinery, and perhaps cotton. There is little prospect of substantial Soviet aid, and domestic resources must be supplemented by these essential imports. Therefore, China's economic recovery during the next year will probably depend on active Western trade and close ties with occupied Japan.

Note: The intelligence organizations of the Departments of Army, Navy, and the Air Force have concurred in this report; for a dissent of the Intelligence Organization of the Department of State, see Enclosure A, p. 21. This report contains information available to CIA as of 2 June 1949.

SECRET

1

138. Weekly Summary Excerpt, 17 June 1949, China: Soviet Orientation

FAR EAST

CHINA

Soviet Orientation   Meanwhile, Chinese Communist statements have been entirely in accord with
orthodox Communist doctrine and the Party continues in its
unwavering acknowledgement of Soviet leadership in the
international Communist movement.   Despite this orthodoxy,
the Chinese Communists may erect a temporary facade of

- 9 -

138. *(Continued)*

CHINA

friendly cooperation with the western powers in order to
expedite trade and commerce essential to China. In fact,
China's tremendous economic needs and the inability of
the USSR to fill those needs offer the most likely prospect
at present for the development of friction between the two
nations.

- 10 -

139. **Weekly Summary Excerpt, 24 June 1949, The CFM Meeting; Eastern Europe: Purges**

THE CFM MEETING

The recent meeting of the Council of Foreign Ministers, which made substantial progress on the Austrian treaty and agreed in principle on a modus vivendi for Germany, clearly revealed that the Kremlin does not yet believe that the unification of Germany would contribute to eventual Soviet control over Germany. The Kremlin is not ready to relax its grip on Berlin and east Germany and apparently believes that ultimate Soviet objectives can best be obtained by a slight relaxation in cold war tension and continuation of the partition of Germany.

The failure of Vishinsky to build up a consistent propaganda pattern at Paris, as well as his defensive attitude and apparent improvisation, suggests that some basic change took place in the Soviet attitude not long before the meeting. The rude jolt to the USSR from the May elections in the Soviet Zone Germany and continuing difficulties in maintaining Soviet control over the Satellites may have contributed to the Soviet decision to mark time on the German question. More fundamentally, however, the USSR may have estimated that a western economic recession is now approaching more rapidly than was previously believed and consequently that the future will provide more favorable opportunities for the attainment of Soviet objectives in Germany and Western Europe.

The Kremlin probably reasons that the western powers, particularly the US, will be in a weaker position in the event of a depression to oppose the USSR because: (1) an economy-minded US would be more reluctant to give adequate support to the European recovery program and the Military Aid Program; (2) economic difficulties would weaken US-British-French solidarity; (3) Western Europe would be increasingly reluctant to maintain trade restrictions against Eastern Europe; and (4) economic distress would make western Germany more receptive to Soviet overtures. With this in mind, the USSR apparently felt it necessary to preserve the status quo while making certain that the door remained open for future negotiations through the machinery of the CFM. A more truculent Soviet attitude at Paris might have increased western determination to re-arm and impelled western legislatures to continue their financial support of the "cold war" despite economic troubles at home.

- 2 -

139. *(Continued)*

EASTERN EUROPE

By means of purging "nationalists" in the Satellite Communist parties, a more aggressive campaign against the Catholic Church, and an intensification of its attacks upon Tito, the Kremlin is continuing its attempts to consolidate its position and control in the Satellite countries. The vigor and intensity of Soviet activity in the Satellite area reflects continuing Soviet concern over the ability of the local Communist regimes to serve Soviet interests. Confronted with growing economic recovery in Western Europe in comparison with economic hardship in the Satellites, a still-defiant Yugoslavia, and a more aggressively hostile Catholic Church, the Kremlin has apparently decided to take prompt and drastic steps toward eliminating the last vestiges of opposition in its uneasy Satellites.

Party Purges   The vigorous efforts being made in Hungary and Bulgaria to eradicate "nationalist" deviationists indicate that the Kremlin has not yet solved the problem of "home-grown" Communism. In both countries, the ruling group of Moscow adherents is attacking a prominent nationalist Communist leader in order to make an example of him. Former Bulgarian economic czar Traicho Kostov and ex-Hungarian Foreign Minister Laszlo Rajk have already been expelled from the Communist Party. The Hungarian regime now seeks to destroy Rajk totally by levelling at him the sensational charge of espionage for the US, while the propaganda assault on Kostov, in which even the Cominform journal is being utilized, continues unabated. Both Kostov and Rajk had a substantial party following and had risen to power locally without direct Kremlin support. Their destruction will demoralize anti-Moscow Bulgarian and Hungarian Communists and forestall the rise of any

- 4 -

139. *(Continued)*

Communists who might consider the national interest before that of the USSR.

Anti-Catholic Drive   The Soviet Union's continuing drive against the Catholic Church is currently being focused on Czechoslovakia, where the probable imminent arrest of Archbishop Beran may follow the pattern established in the recent Mindszenty trial in Hungary. (In Poland the Communist Government is preparing cases against certain Catholic bishops for collaboration with the Nazis.) The Czechoslovak Government is publicly accusing Beran of political activity against the state and will probably arrest him soon on trumped-up charges of treason based upon evidence allegedly found in the Archbishop's personal files. Beran's arrest will immobilize the last effective anti-Communist force in Czechoslovakia. Meanwhile, Soviet determination to eradicate Catholic power and influence in the Satellites has been matched by the increasingly aggressive anti-Communist stand of the Vatican. Communist plans to establish national or Communist-manipulated churches have apparently caused the Vatican to abandon all hope of achieving a modus vivendi in the Satellites and instead to embark on a vigorous campaign to resist Communist anti-Catholic pressure. In addition to stepping up its radio propaganda designed to stiffen Catholic resistance in the Satellites, the Vatican has already meted out severe penalties of excommunication and suspension to Catholics in Hungary and Czechoslovakia who participate in the anti-Church campaign. In addition, the Church may soon issue a fundamental encyclical warning all Catholics in the Soviet orbit against cooperating with the Communists and appealing to the Christian world for aid and intervention. Despite these Vatican moves, however, the Communists retain a definite advantage in the struggle. Basing their strategy on cutting the ties

- 5 -

139. *(Continued)*

binding local Catholic churches with Rome, on separating the Church hierarchy from the parish priests and the people, and on abolishing Catholic control over education, the Communist regimes have the means and determination eventually to destroy all effective Catholic resistance in the Satellites.

Polish Changes   In tightening their grip on Poland, the pro-Moscow Communists have continued their slander campaign against the Catholic Church and are grooming Aleksander Zawadski, a faithful Moscow follower, for titular leadership in the Party. Since Gomulka was read out of the Party leadership about a year ago, Zawadski's ascent has been steady and rapid until now he appears to be the Number One prospect to serve as the Party's front man. Service with the Red army and as a political commissar in the Soviet-sponsored Polish Army corps, plus eleven years of political imprisonment, have made Zawadski a convinced and ruthless Communist and a logical Kremlin choice to head the Polish Communist Party and perhaps eventually the Polish Government.

Albanian Weakness   The Soviet "penetrationists," who have assumed direct control of the Hoxha administration in Albania, are concentrating their main efforts toward stabilizing the regime on alleviating the nation's transportation difficulties. During 1949, Soviet railway technicians helped open a railroad running between the capitol at Tirana and the principal supply port at Durazzo. Despite the presence and activities of the Soviet representatives in Albania and other Soviet efforts to maintain this weak and distant Satellite outpost, Hoxha remains pessimistic about the future of both himself and his country. His pessimism is based upon: (1) Albania's basic poverty and lack of self-sufficiency; (2) the current hostility of the people toward his pro-Soviet regime; and (3) the isolation of Albania from the rest of the Soviet bloc.

- 6 -

140. Intelligence Memorandum 202, 25 July 1949, Review of CIA Estimate ORE 60-48: Threats to the Security of the United States

#2432

CENTRAL INTELLIGENCE AGENCY

3

INTELLIGENCE MEMORANDUM NO. 202   25 July 1949

SUBJECT: Review of CIA Estimate ORE 60-48: Threats to the Security of the
United States (Published 28 September 1948).

1. The threats to US security and the possibility of direct Soviet
military action against the West have been under continuing review during the
last few years. In ORE 60-48, dated 13 September 1948, entitled "Threats
to the Security of the United States," it was estimated that within the next
decade the USSR was unlikely deliberately to resort to war to gain its end
unless it considered that it was in imminent danger of attack by the
Western Powers. In ORE 46-49, dated 21 April 1949, entitled "Possibility
of Direct Military Action during 1949," it was estimated that a deliberate
Soviet resort to military action against the West in 1949 was improbable. It
was pointed out in the latter study, however, that international tension had
increased during 1948 and that it would probably increase further during 1949.
In these circumstances it was estimated that the danger of an unintended
outbreak of hostilities through miscalculation on either side must be
considered to have increased.

2. A review of developments since publication of ORE 46-49, lends
further confirmation to the basic estimate that the USSR is unlikely

Note: This memorandum is in process of coordination with the intelligence
organizations of the Departments of State, Army, Navy, and the Air
Force.

TOP SECRET

Document No. _____
NO CHANGE in Class. ☐
☒ DECLASSIFIED
Class. CHANGED TO: TS   S
DA Memo, 4 Apr 77
Auth: DDA REG. 77/1763
Date: 16/11/77 By: 02

TOP SECRET

deliberately to resort to direct military action during the next decade and
to the specific estimate that a resort to military action during 1949 is
improbable. These developments likewise point to a substantial reduction
in the danger of an unintended outbreak of hostilities through miscalculation
on either side. The most significant may be noted as follows:

a. The USSR accepted the signing of the Atlantic Pact without the
threatening moves against Finland, Scandinavia, Yugoslavia, and Iran, which
were considered possible.

b. International tension has been substantially reduced by Soviet
initiative in proposing to lift the Berlin Blockade in consideration of a
reconvening of the Council of Foreign Ministers. The USSR has likewise indicated a desire to increase East-West trade and to continue discussions on
a Four-Power basis in further meetings of the CFM.

c. The increasing evidences of nationalist "deviationism" and
economic difficulties in the satellite states bring into sharp relief the
basic weaknesses in the position of the USSR and the need for a protracted
period of peace in order to consolidate its position within its own sphere.

d. The unexpectedly rapid rise of a strong Communist State in
China offers the USSR, on the one hand, the opportunity of quickly expanding
its influence by peaceful means in Asia and, on the other, confronts it with
the delicate problem of attempting to bring the new Communist regime into
the framework of an international dictatorship directed from Moscow. A
deliberate resort to military action to attain its objectives in Western

- 2 -

TOP SECRET

140. *(Continued)*

Europe might adversely affect these favorable prospects of attaining Soviet objectives in the Far East by peaceful means.

_c_. The development of the economic recession in the US and the dollar crisis in the UK appears to have confirmed the USSR in its belief that a general economic crisis in the capitalist world is at hand. Under these circumstances the USSR undoubtedly anticipates that US support of Western Europe will be substantially weakened, that Western unity will be disrupted by conflicting economic interests and that, as a result, opportunities will open up for the attainment of Soviet objectives without resort to military action.

3. It is concluded, therefore, that the danger of war as the result of deliberate Soviet military action or of miscalculations on the part of either side will be less during the next year or two than at any time in recent years. However, if economic conditions deteriorate, particularly in Japan or Germany, it is possible that Communist exploitation of these difficulties might create local disturbances that would increase the internal security problem of US occupation forces.

- 3 -

141. Weekly Summary Excerpt, 29 July 1949, Nationalism in the Satellites

NATIONALISM IN THE SATELLITES

Although the widespread purges of Satellite Communist parties during the past year were motivated largely by the Kremlin's desire to crush a rising "nationalistic" sentiment, there remains little likelihood that resurgent nationalism will lead any of the Satellites to emulate Tito's nationalist revolt in the near future. In this eastern European nationalism, however, the Kremlin faces an elusive opponent which grows in proportion to the Kremlin's efforts to destroy it. Many of the rank and file Satellite Party members who have adopted the economic and social theories of Communism are becoming increasingly restive under Soviet exploitation of their nations. This feeling, which is also nurtured by a long tradition of anti-Russianism, will undoubtedly have continuing though ineffective repercussions within the various Satellite Communist hierarchies as Party leaders continue to be faced with the choice of supporting their own national interests or accepting mounting exploitation by the Kremlin.

At the present time, however, Satellite "nationalism," both within and outside the Communist parties, is an undisciplined and leaderless force which the Kremlin is fully capable of controlling. Moreover, growing numbers of thoroughly loyal Kremlin followers being installed in power in the Satellites are consolidating their control of the Satellite security forces through a combination of blind loyalty, intensive espionage, and ruthless terror. Nationalist Communists who have succeeded in reaching positions of authority either have been, or are being, eliminated. The Kremlin's successful ouster, without overt repercussions, of such popular Communist leaders as Gomulka (Poland), Rajk (Hungary), and Kostov (Bulgaria) is sufficient warning to other Satellite leaders with "nationalistic" tendencies.

- 14 -

141. *(Continued)*

In Poland, where nationalism is probably as strongly ingrained in the Communists as anywhere in eastern Europe, tight Kremlin controls and the Soviet occupation troops render any "anti-nationalist" coup within the Party highly improbable at this time. The least secure sector of the Soviet power position in eastern Europe is located in isolated and tiny Albania, but even there the USSR has been making strenuous efforts to maintain an unpopular pro-Soviet group in power through repeated purges of "nationalist" elements. In Bulgaria and Hungary, effective nationalist opposition has been eliminated for the present as a result of the recent dismissal and disgrace of Bulgarian economic czar Kostov and Hungarian Foreign Minister Rajk. Czechoslovakia remains the only Satellite where the Communist Party has not been publicly purged during the last year of "nationalist" tendencies and elements.

- 15 -

142. Daily Summary Excerpt, 22 August 1949, Soviet Military Move Against Tito Held Unlikely

22 AUG 1949

1071

GENERAL

1. <u>Soviet military move against Tito held unlikely</u>--US Ambassador Kirk reports that foreign diplomatic observers in Moscow continue to discount the probability of direct Soviet action against Tito at this time despite the ominous tone of the latest Soviet note to Yugoslavia. According to Kirk, the US Embassy is in general agreement with the view of most observers that the Kremlin is counting on the liquidation of Tito as a consequence of the serious Yugoslav economic situation and a Soviet "war of nerves" accompanied by harassing measures short of hostilities.

CIA-S
CIA-S

US Embassy Belgrade reports, concerning current rumors of Soviet troop movements along the Yugoslav border, that although the Yugoslav Government is believed fully aware of such rumors, there is no evidence that new security measures are being taken.

(CIA Comment: CIA agrees that overt Soviet military action against Yugoslavia remains doubtful. CIA considers the rumors from Hungary and Rumania regarding Soviet troops movements along the Yugoslav border to be a part of the Soviet "war of nerves" rather than an indication of imminent military action by the USSR.)

- 1 -

143. Weekly Summary Excerpt, 9 September 1949, Indochina: Ho's Defiance

INDOCHINA

Ho's Defiance   Recent defiant statements by Ho Chi Minh's resistance government in Indochina have virtually eliminated the prospect of Ho's agreeing to a compromise settlement for "independence" within the framework of the French Union. The Ho regime has flatly denied that Bao Dai has won more concessions for Vietnam than were embodied in earlier agreements between Ho and the French. Moreover, the Ho regime is demanding unqualified independence for Indochina, offering no concessions to the French and demanding none. Meanwhile, Ho's relationship with the Kremlin and the Chinese Communists remains obscure. His present defiant stand was at least in part the result of his encouragement over Communist victories in China, and Ho has stated his willingness to accept military equipment from the Chinese Communists. On the other hand, Ho still maintains that neutrality between the US and the USSR is both possible and desirable, and his repudiation of the French Union is inconsistent with recent pleas by Radio Moscow for Franco-Vietnamese conciliation within the Union.

144. Weekly Summary Excerpt, 23 September 1949, Eastern Europe: Communist Deviation; Hungary: Treason Trial

EASTERN EUROPE

Communist Deviation   Within recent weeks, the dis-
integrating effect on international
Communism of Tito's defection from the Soviet orbit has
become increasingly apparent and could eventually result
in the formation of a Tito supported, anti-Stalinist Communist movement. In France, Germany, and Italy, Communists supporting Tito have defied the Party, and there
are increasing indications that groups as yet unorganized
have rallied to his support even in the Satellites. At some
future time, these dissidents who opposed Soviet Communism both before and after the Tito-Kremlin rift may
unite to form an organization which would seriously
challenge the Soviet position as the leading Communist
state and as the sole interpreter of Communist doctrine.
A necessary premise to amalgamation of these dissident
Communist groups is the need to abandon the many sharply
divergent interpretations of the Marxist-Leninist doctrine.
If a dispute on these divergent views could be postponed
temporarily, a Communist movement, not oriented toward
Moscow and without prejudice to national sovereignty, might
develop that would carry considerably more appeal and influence, especially in non-Communist countries, than Stalin-
ism. In the Satellites, the USSR has already felt it necessary
to take stringent measures against nationalist deviation. Tito
would undoubtedly sympathize with any such anti-Stalinist
defection, but he is not likely to give his overt support to it
at this time. If, however, an independent Communist movement gains momentum, he might well aspire to become its
rallying point.

- 5 -

144. *(Continued)*

HUNGARY

Treason Trial   The current trial in Budapest involving
                 ex-Minister of Interior Laszlo Rajk and
other disaffected Communists differs in one important
respect from the numerous postwar treason trials in the
Satellites. Until now, the arch-enemy, has been the
"imperialist" West. In the current trial, Tito has replaced
the West as the principal villain. Although the trial is thus
another weapon being used by the Kremlin in the war of
nerves against Yugoslavia, it is designed primarily to
unify the Party by eliminating a dangerous deviationist
group and to demonstrate to Communists throughout the
Soviet orbit the futility of defying the USSR. That the Kremlin feels it necessary to stage the trial at this time, however,
indicates both the strength of anti-Moscow feeling among
Satellite Communists and the need for continuing drastic
measures by the USSR to keep its Satellite parties in line.

- 7 -

SECRET

SOVIET UNION

Atomic Explosion   With the announcement of an atomic
                   explosion in the USSR, Soviet capabilities
for fighting the cold war have been increased. No immediate
change in Soviet policy or tactics is expected. In fact, the
improvement in the Soviet power position resulting from
possession of the atomic bomb makes it less likely that the
USSR will relax its intransigence in East-West negotiations.
Moreover, the USSR can use the new situation to advantage
as additional support for nearly all the major policy lines it
has followed since the end of World War II.

- 5 -

SECRET

145. *(Continued)*

SOVIET UNION

In its continuing efforts to check growing Western European economic and military unity, the USSR will now exploit the world-wide fear of an atomic war. In this respect, the USSR has seriously weakened the psychological advantage until now held by the US as a result of monopoly of atomic weapons, particularly since the announcement was made before the US had succeeded in building a strong political, economic, and military bulwark against Soviet expansion.

Meanwhile, the USSR may find it easier to gain support for a UN compromise between the US and Soviet positions on control of atomic energy. The Soviet stand, calling for destruction of atomic weapons before international controls are imposed, will have greater propaganda effect inasmuch as Soviet spokesmen can now assert that Soviet atomic weapons will also be destroyed. The USSR will not relax its opposition to effective international control of atomic energy but, in view of the advantages accruing to the USSR from an international convention outlawing atomic weapons, will probably increase its efforts to compromise the US atomic energy position.

Lastly, Soviet possession of the atomic weapon will greatly strengthen the current Soviet "peace offensive." It will enable Communist front organizations to point to the willingness of the USSR to destroy all atomic weapons and to stress the greater urgency for acceptance of the Soviet proposal for a five-power peace pact.

- 6 -

146. Daily Summary Excerpt, 6 October 1949, Molotov Reported Handling Soviet Internal Problems

24713　　　　　　51　　　　　　　- 6 OCT 1949

~~TOP SECRET~~　　　　　　1109

GENERAL

1. <u>Molotov reported handling Soviet internal problems</u>--　　　s - TS
According to US Ambassador Jessup at the UN, Soviet
Foreign Minister Vishinsky told British Foreign Secretary Bevin, in response to his query concerning the
health of ex-Foreign Minister Molotov, that Molotov is
now concerned solely with economic-financial problems
and the rehabilitation of the Soviet economy.

(CIA Comment: Confirmation of this report that
Stalin's right-hand man is engaged solely with internal
problems would point to an increased Soviet emphasis
upon dealing with domestic and Satellite difficulties
springing from Tito's defection and the present adverse
position of the USSR in the cold war.)

CONFIDENTIAL

147. Weekly Summary Excerpt, 7 October 1949, Germany: East Zone Government

WESTERN EUROPE

GERMANY

East Zone Government   Formation on 7 October of the
Soviet-sponsored German Demo-
cratic Republic in East Germany is a logical Soviet reaction to developments in West Germany and represents
a Soviet effort to regain the initiative in Germany. The
new regime, by claiming sovereignty over all Germany,
will enable the USSR to counter the attraction of the
Bonn Government as the focal point of German unity.
Moreover, establishment of the new regime with its
capital in Berlin may result in increased Soviet pressure
for the withdrawal of the western powers from Berlin.
In an attempt to obtain the maximum political advantages
from the East German state, the USSR will grant the
new regime the appearance of greater independence than
the West German Government through such propaganda
devices as promises of early troop withdrawal, a separate
peace treaty, and diplomatic recognition by the USSR and
the Satellites. It is unlikely, however, that the USSR will
risk early withdrawal of its troops from the Soviet Zone.
Moreover, the Kremlin is unlikely to propose seriously
a merger of the East and West governments until the
Soviet position throughout Germany is considerably
stronger.

- 2 -

148. Intelligence Memorandum 248 Excerpt, 7 November 1949, Satellite Relations With the USSR and the West

Excerpt

CENTRAL INTELLIGENCE AGENCY

7 November 1949

INTELLIGENCE MEMORANDUM NO. 248

SUBJECT: Satellite Relations with the USSR and the West

Summary.

The separation of any Cominform Satellite from the Soviet orbit is unlikely under current conditions. Circumstances comparable to those which enabled Tito successfully to challenge Soviet domination in Yugoslavia do not exist in the other Satellites. By the drastic remedial measures to which it has resorted, the Kremlin has indicated its awareness of the grave dangers to its control of Eastern Europe inherent in satellite nationalism.

The Cominform Satellites can be expected to maintain a basically antagonistic policy toward the US reflecting that of the Soviet Union. Any relaxation of satellite antagonism toward the US would be a temporary tactic motivated by opportunistic considerations.

The current shift in the Yugoslav attitude toward the US is based on motives of self-preservation before the mounting pressure from the Soviet bloc. However, the continued dependence of Yugoslavia on US support

Note: This memorandum has not been coordinated with the intelligence organizations of the Departments of State, Army, Navy, and the Air Force.

Document No. 001
NO CHANGE in Class. ☐
☒ DECLASSIFIED
Class. CHANGED TO: TS S C
Auth:
Date: 21/11/77 By: 011

148. *(Continued)*

against the Soviet Union will probably result in a gradually improved Yugoslav attitude toward the US.

Approximately 90 percent of the populations within the Satellites are hostile to the Communist regimes imposed on them. Although opposition elements in the various Satellites constitute a majority of the population, Communist measures aimed at separating them and destroying their organization and leadership, render such elements ineffective as opponents to Communist domination of Eastern Europe.

Local Communist control over the satellite peoples is exercised through the traditional Communist instruments which include the Party, security organs, and the armed forces. In addition, subsidiary political, cultural, and economic organizations are used to disseminate Communist influence.

The presence or availability of Soviet military might in the Satellites constitutes the most potent factor in maintaining the Communist regimes in power. The various Communist parties under the immediate direction and control of reliable Soviet agents, form the chief vehicles by which the sovietization of Eastern Europe is being carried out. The entire political, military, and economic life of the Satellites is being geared to the implementation of Soviet aims under a tight Kremlin control. In some instances, the Soviet Embassy itself serves as the main command channel between the Kremlin and the satellite governments; in others, trusted local Communists have direct access to Moscow.

The USSR has already attained a high degree of economic control over the Satellites. One of the major points of Soviet vulnerability, however, is the subordination of satellite economic welfare to Soviet interest. Considerable popular resentment, even in Communist circles, has resulted from the forceful transformation of the economic structure of Eastern Europe, the lowered standard of living, and the failure of the USSR to meet the industrial requirements of the Satellites. Thus far, however, Soviet political and economic control has been sufficient to prevent effective nationalist deviation from Kremlin authority. Meanwhile, the US export control program has contributed substantially to slowing the rate of economic development in the Satellites and has added to the strain in present Soviet-Satellite relations.

~ 3 ~

149. Weekly Summary Excerpt, 10 November 1949, Soviet Union: Malenkov Speech

SOVIET UNION

Malenkov Speech   In a speech more bellicose and boastful than the 1948 address, Politburo-member Malenkov keynoted the thirty-second anniversary of the Bolshevik Revolution with a repetition of the well-worn Soviet propaganda line. Although Malenkov's speech indicated that the Kremlin to a greater extent than ever before considers the US its principal enemy, there was no hint of a change in Soviet cold war tactics or of the abandonment of well-tested Soviet subversive methods for the achievement of economic and political goals. With regard to Germany, Malenkov's remarks implied a continuing Soviet desire for a unified Germany under Communist control and emphasized that such a solution was vital to the preservation of world peace. The Communist regime in China was referred to almost deferentially, much as a junior partner rather than a Satellite, and by linking India with China as a decisive factor in the East-West struggle, Malenkov also implied that China was a springboard rather than a resting point for Soviet expansion in the Far East. Malenkov's exaggerated assertions of internal economic achievements are intended to conceal the inadequacies of the current five-year plan and prepare the way for its abandonment in January 1950 in favor of a "master" plan for the entire orbit under the direction of the Council for Economic Mutual Assistance. Delivery of this important address by Malenkov clearly established him as the number three man in the Soviet hierarchy, ranking behind only Stalin and Molotov.

- 6 -

24/57

52

~~TOP SECRET~~

29 NOV 1949

1153

CIA-S

GENERAL

1. <u>Soviet attack "reported" for 1950</u>--The US Consul in Bremen transmits a report from an "old and reliable" contact residing in western Berlin that "war is expected in the spring of 1950." Source asserts that a Soviet army of 600,000 is on the new Polish border, that the USSR is operating two former German rocket bases, and that these rockets have a range of 4800 kilometers (approximately 3,000 miles). The Consul comments that "source is in touch with intimates of Minister President Grotewohl"; he further comments that the foregoing is believed to be a reliable report concerning information which the USSR is now furnishing top officials of the East German Government.

(CIA Comment: CIA estimates that such an attack by the USSR in the spring of 1950 is improbable. This report probably represents an extension of the Soviet propaganda line designed to rally East Germans behind the Soviet puppet government and to frighten those elements of the German population which are supporting the West.)

Document No. **048**

NO CHANGE in Class. ☐

☐ DECLASSIFIED

Class. CHANGED TO: TS S ©

ID1 Memo, 4 Apr 77

Auth: DDA REG 77/1863

Date: 1 5 MAR 1978 By: **023**

~~T O P SECRET~~ ~~CONFIDENTIAL~~

151. Daily Summary Excerpt, 5 December 1949, Comments on Soviet Plans Against Tito

52

~~TOP SECRET~~

5 DEC 1949

1158

GENERAL

T3/3

1. <u>Comments on Soviet plans against Tito</u>--In discussing the possibility of Soviet armed action to liquidate Tito, US Embassy Belgrade expresses the opinion that the Kremlin will not "move openly" with military forces against Tito until convinced that his liquidation is absolutely essential. The Embassy adds that if Tito's heretical influence can be weakened or if he can be "ideologically sealed off" the Kremlin may feel that the risk of resorting to arms would not be justified. The Embassy does not believe that Soviet attempts to establish Tito as a "Fascist spy" will be successful in eliminating the dangers to the Soviet system inherent in Titoism; the Embassy points out, however, that the Kremlin "might well feel otherwise."

   (CIA Comment: CIA believes that although the Kremlin continues to be fully aware of the danger of Titoism, full scale military operations against Tito would not be undertaken unless the Kremlin is convinced that the US would not intervene militarily.)

- 1 -

~~TOP SECRET~~ ~~CONFIDENTIAL~~

152. Weekly Summary Excerpt, 9 December 1949, Palestine: Soviet Policy

NEAR EAST - AFRICA

PALESTINE

Soviet Policy   In openly supporting the internationalization of Jerusalem, the USSR has once again
demonstrated its desire to gain a voice in Near Eastern
affairs and to foster dissension and unrest in the area and
has highlighted the deterioration of Soviet-Israeli relations.
The USSR probably supports internationalization, not
only for the opportunity it affords for a direct Soviet voice
in the administration of Jerusalem but in the hope that the
plan will prove unworkable and thus give rise to irridentist
agitation and political instability. Although the USSR has
abandoned its support for Israel on this issue, basic Soviet
objectives remain unchanged: namely, to reduce Anglo-
American influence, promote disunity in the Near East, and
foster political and economic instability. Thus, in pursuance
of these aims, the USSR at first supported Israel. With the
gradual strengthening of US-Israeli ties, the USSR has reduced its support and is again laying emphasis on its basic
anti-Zionist policy. Similarly, Soviet support for a separate
Arab state in Palestine is designed primarily to weaken
UK-supported Jordan and to increase fragmentation in the
Arab world.

- 10 -

52   14 DEC 1949

24770   ~~TOP SECRET~~   1166

GENERAL

1. Estimate of Soviet position in Europe--US Ambassador
   Kirk in Moscow suggests that the Kremlin's year-end
   estimate of the European scene is probably characterized
   by: (a) satisfaction in general regarding Satellite control and evolution; (b) continuing anger and concern over
   Tito, tempered by the belief that incipient Titoism is
   being effectively suppressed in the remaining Satellites;
   and (c) real hopes for eventual advances in Germany and
   Western Europe. Kirk points out that although the Kremlin
   is aware of increased western integration and the loss of
   Communist control of world labor, the Kremlin nevertheless may expect these western gains to be wiped out
   eventually by the "deepening economic crisis" and
   "contradictions" between the western powers. The
   Ambassador concludes that Moscow may again, as in
   1947, be considerably over-estimating Soviet prospects
   outside the Iron Curtain in Europe.

   (CIA Comment: CIA believes that despite the
   Kremlin's optimistic expectations for an eventual
   western economic crisis and increasing disunity
   among the western powers, the Kremlin probably
   recognizes that the USSR has suffered a temporary
   setback in Europe caused by: (a) military, economic,
   and political measures undertaken by the western
   powers; (b) the problems arising from Tito's deviations;
   and (c) reduced effectiveness of Communist parties in
   Western European nations.)

Document No. _061_

NO CHANGE in Class. ☐

☐ DECLASSIFIED

Class. CHANGED TO: TS   S   C

DDA Memo, 4 Apr 77

Auth: DDA REG. 77/1763

By: _____

Date: 15 MAR 1978

- 1 -

~~TOP SECRET~~

~~CONFIDENTIAL~~

154. Daily Summary Excerpt, 4 January 1950, Implications of Mao's Prolonged Stay in Moscow

52   4 JAN 1950

24784   T O P   S E C R E T   1180

C/A - Conf

GENERAL

1. Implications of Mao's prolonged stay in Moscow --
Commenting on the recent statement by Chinese
Communist leader Mao Tse-tung that he expected
to remain in the USSR for "several weeks," US
Embassy Moscow considers it odd that Mao would
absent himself from China for an extended period
at this critical time. The Embassy cites previous
reports of the "nationalistic" flavor of Mao's leadership and suggests that: (a) Mao's return to Peiping
is being delayed by failure to reach agreement in
negotiations with the USSR; and (b) strongly pro-
Kremlin elements in the Chinese Communist Party may
be expected to take advantage of Mao's absence to
strengthen their position at the expense of the "nationalistic" faction in the Party.

   (CIA Comment: CIA believes that Mao's return to
China may be delayed by an inability to reach agreement
on certain provisions of a revised Sino-Soviet treaty.
CIA has no evidence, however, that Mao is out of favor
with the Kremlin or that an anti-Mao coup is being
planned in China.)

Document No. ___2___
NO CHANGE in Class. ☐
☐ DECLASSIFIED
Class. CHANGED TO: TS   S   Ⓒ
DDA Memo, 4 Apr 77
Auth: DDA REG. 77/1763
Date: 1 6 MAR 1978 By: ___

CONFIDENTIAL
T O P   S E C R E T

346

155. Weekly Summary Excerpt, 13 January 1950, Far East: Soviet Relations; Korea: Troop Buildup

FAR EAST

Soviet Relations   Mao Tse-tung's protracted stay in Moscow
has aroused speculation regarding a deterioration in Sino-Soviet relations and Chinese Communist
resistance to Soviet encroachment. Although the length of
Mao's visit may be the result of difficulties in reaching agreement on a revised Sino-Soviet treaty, the treaty will probably

- 8 -

155. *(Continued)*

CHINA

be signed this month and it is unlikely that Mao is
proving dangerously intractable. Mao is a genuine
and orthodox Stalinist, is in firm control of the
Chinese Communist Party, and is recognized as its
head by all Party leaders and by the Chinese people
generally. There is no evidence that any Communist
faction is strong enough to succeed in an anti-Mao
coup or that the USSR would be so rash as to replace
Mao at this time. The Kremlin probably realizes that
for some time its position in China will be best served
by retaining the voluntary cooperation of the Chinese
Communists rather than by using open or implied
coercion.

- 9 -

155. *(Continued)*

KOREA

Troop Build Up   The continuing southward movement of
the expanding Korean People's Army
toward the thirty-eighth parallel probably constitutes a
defensive measure to offset the growing strength of the
offensively minded South Korean Army. The influx of
Chinese Communist-trained troops from Manchuria, however, will partially solve North Korea's manpower shortage
and will add materially to the combat potential of the North
Korean Army. North Korean military strength has been
further bolstered by the assignment of tanks and heavy
field guns to units in the thirty-eighth parallel zone and by
the development of North Korean air capabilities. Despite
this increase in North Korean military strength, the possibility of an invasion of South Korea is unlikely unless North
Korean forces can develop a clear-cut superiority over the
increasingly efficient South Korean Army.

- 11 -

156. Daily Summary Excerpt, 1 February 1950, Implications of Soviet Recognition of the Ho Regime in Indochina

A N N E X

1 February 1950

IMPLICATIONS OF SOVIET RECOGNITION OF THE HO REGIME IN INDOCHINA

Soviet recognition of Ho Chi Minh's "Democratic Republic of Vietnam" early this week, following similar action by the Chinese Communists, has jeopardized the already uneasy position of the French--and the French-sponsored Bao Dai regime--in Indochina. The implicit threat in the Communist diplomatic maneuvers is strengthened by the presence of Chinese Communist forces on the Indochina frontier and their ability to make substantial military supplies available to the pro-Communist Ho regime. This combination of political and military pressure may, by itself, force the French to withdraw from Indochina within a year. In the unlikely event that the Chinese Communist Government should send a major military force into Indochina for action against the French, French withdrawal could be expected within six months.

If France is driven from Indochina, the resulting emergence of an indigenous Communist-dominated regime in Vietnam, together with pressures exerted by Peiping and Moscow, would probably bring about the orientation of adjacent Thailand and Burma toward the Communist orbit. Under these circumstances, other Asian states--Malaya and Indonesia, particularly--would become highly vulnerable to the extension of Communist influence.

Meanwhile, by recognizing the Ho regime, the USSR has revealed its determination to force France completely out of Indochina and to install a Communist government. Alone, France is incapable of preventing such a development. Although Western nations are committed to support of the

- i -

156. *(Continued)*

French on the diplomatic level--the US and the UK, for example, plan shortly to extend recognition to the French-sponsored Bao Dai regime--such actions are unlikely to halt the present trend in Indochina. Prospects for obtaining additional diplomatic support for the French or Bao Dai are poor in view of the unwillingness of most Asian nations to assist what they regard as a "colonialist" puppet regime. In fact, many of these nations can interpret Soviet and Chinese recognition of Ho as concrete action in support of Asian nationalism.

In resisting the Communist advance, France can now turn for assistance only to the US, which, in the face of recent actions by the USSR and China in seizing the initiative in Southeast Asia, is now confronted with the general alternatives of either increasing its support of Bao Dai or withdrawing such support as has already been afforded. Adoption of the first alternative sets up Bao Dai as the principal anti-Communist instrument in Indochina, despite the inherent weakness of his position. Asian nations, moreover, would tend to interpret such US action as support of continued Western colonialism. The second alternative, which would result in the inevitable downfall of Bao Dai, would open the way for intensified Communist action in Southeast Asia and would render increasingly difficult the containment of Soviet influence throughout the Far East.

- ii -

157. Daily Summary Excerpt, 3 February 1950, French Views on Indochina

24810   53   3 FEB 1950

~~TOP SECRET~~   1206

GENERAL

1. <u>French views on Indochina</u>--According to US Ambassador Bruce in Paris, Parodi, Secretary of the French Foreign Office, is very "gloomy" about the implications for Indochina of recent Soviet actions. Parodi is inclined to believe that the Chinese Communists will grant strong support in equipment and technicians to the Vietnamese guerrilla leader Ho Chi Minh and that they may even launch a direct military assault against Indochina. Parodi stated that the French, in either case, could not withstand indefinitely and that his Government was planning to make inquiries concerning US intentions if such developments should materialize.

      (CIA Comment: CIA believes that the Chinese Communists can make substantial military supplies available to Ho Chi Minh but that they are unlikely to send a major military force into Indochina.)

CIA /s

~~CONFIDENTIAL~~ ~~SECRET~~

158. Weekly Summary Excerpt, 3 February 1950, UN: Soviet Walkout; Southeast Asia: Soviet Pressure

EASTERN EUROPE

Soviet Walkout   One major purpose of the Soviet UN walkout was probably to contribute to the Soviet effort to isolate China from Western influce by making it as difficult as possible for the US to reverse its China policy. The dramatic Soviet boycott of the UN, along with abuses of US officials and property in China, makes US recognition of the Peiping regime increasingly difficult in the face of opposition in the US Congress and press. The USSR is, therefore, encouraging a situation in which US recognition of the Chinese Communist regime could be widely construed and propagandized as an outright surrender to Soviet pressure. The walkout, although ostensibly designed to force the early unseating of Nationalist delegates, may actually have delayed the shift to Communist Chinese representation in the UN.

Although Chinese and Soviet recognition of Ho Chi Minh (Communist leader in Indochina) is primarily aimed at fostering revolutionary activity in Southeast Asia, this action may also be parts of the Soviet effort to minimize contacts between China and the West. Such Soviet moves which effectively postpone the establishment of US and French relations with China correspond to the general Soviet policy of discouraging Western contacts with the Soviet Satellites in Europe.

- 6 -

SECRET

SOUTHEAST ASIA

Soviet Pressure   The extension of Soviet recognition to the
United States of Indonesia and to Ho Chi
Minh (Communist leader opposing the Bao Dai Government
in Indochina) may presage greatly increased Soviet pressure
against the Western position in Southeast Asia. In Indochina,
support from the USSR and the Chinese Communists will
probably strengthen resistance to Bao Dai and may turn the
balance in favor of Ho. Moreover, the extension of Soviet
recognition to Ho will: (1) counteract the expected political
impact of Western recognition of Bao Dai; and (2) probably
increase the reluctance of neighboring countries to follow
the Western lead in recognizing Bao Dai. In Indonesia, where
political leaders are attempting to maintain a neutral position
between the US and the USSR, Soviet recognition will arouse
little suspicion that the USSR may eventually use its mission
to work with subversive groups. Near the Chinese border in
the Burmese hill state of Kengtung, Chinese "Communist"
freebooters are creating enough trouble to arouse some
apprehension in Rangoon.

- 11 -

SECRET

354

FRANCE

Indochina Policy   Although popular support at home for the
                    French Government's Indochina policy
has increased as a result of Soviet and Chinese recognition
of Ho Chi Minh, prospects for implementing the policy successfully remain poor. The level of the military effort being
maintained in Indochina is close to the maximum of French
capabilities; if the Chinese Communists provide appreciable
support to Ho Chi Minh in the form of military technicians
and equipment, France will be incapable of containing the
resistance movement without outside assistance. The French

- 3 -

159. *(Continued)*

SECRET

FRANCE

are likely, therefore, to increase their efforts to obtain British and US support, basing their claim on the growing urgency of regarding Indochina as a critical battleground in the East-West struggle.

- 4 -

SECRET

FAR EAST

Sino-Soviet Pact   By concluding an ostensibly benevolent
treaty with the Chinese Communists, the
USSR has obtained a three-year period of grace in which to
tighten its grip on Communist China. The treaty will at
once confute the "imperialists" outside China and conciliate
internal opposition to the Communist regime. By not immediately relinquishing control over Dairen, Port Arthur,
and the Manchurian railways, however, the USSR will maintain control of strategic assets in China, while continuing
to advance the process by which Soviet influence in China
becomes Soviet control. The USSR can be expected to
gradually strengthen its grip on the Chinese Communist
Party apparatus, on the armed forces, on the secret police,
and on communications and informational media. One immediate result of the treaty will be the strengthening of the
Stalinist faction of the Chinese Communist Party for action
against the rather sizeable bloc of nationalistic Chinese
Communists.

- 9 -

SECRET

161. Daily Summary Excerpt, 21 February 1950, Soviet Military Preparations in Austria; Increased Communist Pressure in Southeast Asia

24825   **53**   ~~TOP SECRET~~
                                                                                        ~ ~ FEB 1950

                                                                                             1221

GENERAL

1. Reported Soviet military preparations in Austria--US   S-TS
   Ambassador Johnson in Rio de Janeiro reports that the
   Brazilian Minister in Vienna has been informed by
   Austrian Foreign Minister Gruber that he is "absolutely
   sure" the Soviet command in Vienna began about twenty
   days ago military preparations which indicate the USSR
   is planning large-scale military action. In support of
   his conviction, Gruber stated that: (a) new strategic
   points in Austria have been occupied by considerable
   Soviet forces; (b) large quantities of modern materiel
   and equipment are continuously arriving at Soviet garrisons; and (c) Soviet lines of communication are being
   carefully protected by new contingents of selected troops.
   Gruber also assured the Brazilian Minister that he is expecting momentarily a Soviet "surprise" in Europe, not
   excluding the possibility of the opening of hostilities in
   some sector.

       (CIA Comment: CIA has no reliable information
   justifying the belief that the USSR is planning large-scale
   military action in Europe in the immediate future. CIA
   believes, however, that the preponderance of Soviet military strength in Europe and stringent security measures
   in the Soviet sphere provide the USSR with the capabilities
   for initiating military operations with little or no advance
   information becoming available to the Western Powers.)

2. Increased Communist pressure in Southeast Asia predicted--   C/A-S
   US Ambassador Kirk in Moscow suggests that the recently
   concluded Sino-Soviet Treaty prepares the way for these two
   principal partners in World Communism to assume in the
   near future "militant initiative in Southeast Asia to a maximum degree short of open war." The Ambassador believes

- 1 -

~~TOP SECRET~~   ~~CONFIDENTIAL~~

161. *(Continued)*

TOP SECRET

that Stalin and Mao probably estimate that Communist
expansion in Southeast Asia in the near future is both
militarily and politically feasible. Kirk considers Burma
and Indochina to be the prime targets in Southeast Asia
because their inclusion in the Communist sphere would
advance Communist forces toward the goal of world domination and because these countries, plus Thailand, would provide China with a solution to its food problem.

(CIA Comment: CIA concurs in the above estimate
of Soviet intent in Southeast Asia.)

- 2 -

CONFIDENTIAL
TOP SECRET

359

162. Weekly Summary Excerpt, 24 February 1950, China: Treaty With USSR

FAR EAST

CHINA

TREATY WITH USSR

Secret Protocols The recently announced treaty between China and the USSR was almost certainly accompanied by secret protocols designed to provide for a stronger Soviet position in the Chinese military organization, in strategic segments of the Chinese economy, and in China's border regions. It is not likely that protracted negotiations would have been necessary to reach agreement on the published text of the treaty.

Military Agreements Unpublished military agreements probably provide for: (1) Soviet assistance to the Chinese Communist ground and naval forces and their embryonic air force; (2) Soviet access to Chinese naval and air bases; (3) the "joint" development of such bases using Soviet equipment and technicians; (4) the exchange of military and technical personnel; and (5) the dispatch of a Soviet military mission to China. The USSR will probably give special attention to the development of the Chinese Communist air arm, which it will be in a position to dominate from the outset; to Chinese Communist service schools; and to the selection of reliable Chinese Stalinists as political and intelligence officers.

Economic Terms In the economic field, the USSR has probably obtained secret rights to maintain its preferred position in Manchuria, establish Soviet trading firms, assign Soviet advisers and technicians to strategic segments of the Chinese economy, extend Soviet air privileges in the border regions and to China proper, and

- 12 -

162. *(Continued)*

CHINA

engage in preclusive buying of strategic minerals. One economic pact may deal specifically with Sinkiang; an arrangement for the joint development of that province, together with provision for Soviet advisers with the provincial government, would make it unnecessary for the USSR to seek territorial concessions in Sinkiang at this time.

Possible Friction   Meanwhile, friction will probably develop between China and the USSR over implementation of the published $300 million credit agreement. As in the case of similar Soviet credits to the European Satellites, the USSR may use the agreement as a lever to extract concessions from the Chinese. The USSR will not only tend to overrate the value of Soviet goods but may insist on deducting from the credit any costs of technical advisory assistance, on receiving credit for the return of equipment originally obtained in the dismantling of Manchurian industrial installations, and on charging exorbitant transportation costs.

- 13 -

163. Weekly Summary Excerpt, 17 March 1950, Indochina: Ho's Orientation; Current Soviet Tactics in Germany

FAR EAST

INDOCHINA

Ho's Orientation   Although Moscow-trained Ho Chi Minh has never been proven to be either a Tito-like nationalist or a Moscow-dominated Communist, recent developments may indicate his sub-servience to the Kremlin. Broadcasts from the Ho-controlled radio in Indochina have reportedly attacked Tito and failed to mention the diplomatic recognition extended by the Yugoslav Government to the Ho regime. French authorities have also reported that Ho is on his way to Peiping and Moscow to sign treaties of alliance with Mao Tse Tung and Stalin. Ho's brief flirtation with Yugoslavia regarding recongition may have been the result of a mistake by his Bangkok representative, who made the initial approach to Tito along with a general invitation to all nations.

- 16 -

163. *(Continued)*

CURRENT SOVIET TACTICS IN GERMANY

Current Soviet tactics in Germany reflect both the Kremlin's growing optimism regarding its improved world power position and its increased confidence in gaining eventual control over all of Germany on Soviet terms. These tactics are characterized by an uncompromising designation of the East German regime as the sole focal point of German unity and by Soviet insistence upon political progress toward the establishment of a Peoples Democracy in East Germany. This Soviet attitude is evident in: (1) the demand for absolute acceptance of the National Front policy of German unity through friendship with the USSR; (2) consistent reiteration by East German political officials that the Oder-Neisse boundary is permanent, and their acceptance of the recent Polish decision to evict the German minority; and (3) the purge of the bourgeois parties in East Germany. The USSR is unlikely to change its present tactics as long as the Kremlin does not foresee participation of West Germany in an effective political and military Western bloc.

The USSR is unlikely to conclude a separate peace treaty with the East German Government (GDR) in the near future unless the Western Powers sign a separate peace agreement with West Germany. The USSR could, however, take action short of a formal peace treaty, such as a declared termination of the state of war. Any advantages accruing to the USSR from a separate peace treaty at this time would be limited to propaganda and the enhancement of the prestige of the National Front and the GDR. Moreover, the conclusion by the USSR of a separate treaty with East Germany would weaken the Soviet claim,

- 13 -

163. *(Continued)*

based on the Yalta and Potsdam agreements, to a voice in West Germany and the Ruhr. The Kremlin may also be reluctant to conclude a separate peace treaty in the belief that it would lead to the alignment of West Germany with a Western political and military bloc.

Continuation of present Soviet tactics in Germany will lead to further political consolidation in East Germany resulting, for all practical purposes, in a one-party system by the time of the scheduled October 1950 elections. At the same time, continued efforts will be made to expand and strengthen the East German internal security force. The USSR is unlikely to undertake actual troop withdrawal or rectification of the Oder-Neisse line, in order to enhance Soviet-Communist appeal in Germany. The current Soviet attitude toward the German problem, combined with continued harassing actions in Berlin, also reduces the likelihood of an early Soviet offer to reopen Four Power negotiations on Germany. The city of Berlin will remain a "special situation" for the USSR and will probably be subjected to increased economic and political pressure in the near future.

- 14 -

164. Weekly Summary Excerpt, 31 March 1950, China: Military Plans

FAR EAST

CHINA

Military Plans   Despite repeated reports that the
                  Chinese Communists are preparing
for a large military campaign aimed at gaining control
over all of Southeast Asia, it is unlikely that such a
campaign will be launched in the near future. The
primary objective of the Communists in China for 1950
continues to be the complete elimination of all Nationalist
resistance and the extension of Communist control over
all territories formerly held by the Nationalists. Present
international Communist strategy, formulated and announced
by the USSR and endorsed by the Chinese Communist Party,
does not envisage the employment of the regular armed
forces of a Communist nation for large-scale operations as
a means of gaining control over non-Communist nations.
Moreover, a military adventure by the Chinese Communists
into Southeast Asia would contribute little to an early solution of the economic difficulties which derive at least in
part from the Nationalist blockade and air attacks. Despite
reported Communist dissension over such matters as the
degree of subservience to the USSR, policy toward the West
and methods to alleviate peasant unrest, there is no conclusive evidence of disagreement concerning the necessity
for early occupation of Taiwan and Hainan and the elimination
of the Nationalist Navy and Air Force.

- 11 -

165. ORE 91-49 Excerpt, 6 April 1950, Estimate of the Effects of the Soviet Possession of the Atomic Bomb Upon the Security of the United States and Upon the Probabilities of Direct Soviet Military Action

FOREWORD

The subject matter of the present estimate has been under consideration since October 1949. At the outset, representatives of all the agencies concerned agreed that, as a basis for estimating the effects of the Soviet possession of the atomic bomb upon the probability of direct Soviet military action, it was essential to re-examine carefully the problem of over-all Soviet objectives and intentions. The examination of this problem, as well as of the related problems of the effects of the Soviet atomic bomb upon the probability of war and upon the security of the US, revealed wide differences in attitude and opinion among the intelligence agencies. The examination of these problems also brought to light many operational and policy questions of far-reaching importance that will require some time to resolve and which are in large part beyond the cognizance of the intelligence agencies.

A CIA draft was submitted to the IAC agencies on 10 February 1950. From the comments made by the IAC agencies on this draft it was apparent that no early agreement could be reached. In view of the time already elapsed and the broader significance of many of the issues that emerged during the study,

CIA considered that it was more important to publish this paper at this time than to attempt the time-consuming, if not impossible, task of obtaining agreement. It considered, furthermore, that it would be more useful to publish a straightforward point of view, accompanied by contrary opinions, than to present a watered-down version.

Insofar as was possible in good conscience, the 10 February CIA draft has been modified in consideration of the comments received from the IAC agencies, particularly to clarify passages regarding which agency comment revealed evident misunderstanding. This revised estimate is now presented with the final comments of the IAC agencies thereon.

The Director of Intelligence, Atomic Energy Commission, has concurred in this estimate. The several dissents of the intelligence organizations of the Departments of State, the Army, the Navy, and the Air Force are to be found in Appendixes A, B, C, and D respectively (pp. 29-36). It should be noted that these dissents are on various grounds and that the several departmental agencies disagree among themselves as well as with CIA.

This paper is to be considered as an interim report. The subject is under continuing urgent consideration in an effort to obtain the greatest possible resolution of these differences, and a subsequent report will be published when this has been accomplished.

1

TOP SECRET

ESTIMATE OF THE EFFECTS OF THE SOVIET POSSESSION OF THE ATOMIC BOMB UPON THE SECURITY OF THE UNITED STATES AND UPON THE PROBABILITIES OF DIRECT SOVIET MILITARY ACTION

I. Statement of the Problem.

To estimate the effects of the Soviet possession of the atomic bomb upon the security of the United States and upon the probabilities of direct Soviet military action.

II. Discussion.

1. Soviet atomic capabilities (see Enclosure A).

2. Estimate of basic Soviet intentions and objectives, particularly with respect to the use of military force (see Enclosure B).

3. Effects of the possession of the atomic bomb upon the USSR and its policy (see Enclosure C).

4. Effects outside the USSR of Soviet atomic capabilities (see Enclosure D).

III. Summary and Conclusions.

1. *Soviet Atomic Capabilities.*

a. It is estimated tentatively that the USSR will probably have a stockpile of 100 atomic bombs, approximately as destructive as the Nagasaki bomb, some time during 1953.

b. On even less certain grounds it is estimated that the USSR will probably have a stockpile of 200 bombs some time between mid-1954 and the end of 1955.

c. The USSR either has or can easily produce enough TU-4's (B-29's) and trained crews willing and able to attempt the delivery against all key US targets any number of atomic bombs the USSR can produce.

d. Preliminary and highly tentative US estimates indicate that an atomic attack of approximately 200 bombs delivered on pre-scribed targets might prove decisive in knocking the US out of a war. There is at present no reliable estimate of the size of the stockpile required to insure the delivery of 200 bombs on the prescribed targets. (For more detailed analysis, see Enclosure A.)

2. *Soviet Intentions and Objectives in Relation to the Probabilities of War.*

Before attempting to estimate the effect of the Soviet possession of the atomic bomb upon the probabilities of war, we believe it timely to re-examine basic Soviet objectives in the world situation, as the Kremlin conceives it, and to estimate the means which the Kremlin deems appropriate for their accomplishment, with particular reference to the use of military force. Our conclusions, as they apply to the probabilities of war, apart from any consideration of the atomic bomb, are given below:

a. The basic objective of Soviet foreign policy is clearly the attainment of a Communist world under Soviet domination. In pursuit of this objective, the USSR regards the US as its major opponent and will wage against it a relentless, unceasing struggle in which any weapon or tactic is admissible which promises *success in terms of over-all Soviet objectives.* Nothing in the subsequent analysis, therefore, should be interpreted to imply that Soviet leaders would not resort to military action at any time they considered it *advantageous* to do so. The purpose of this analysis is objectively to estimate the methods which Soviet leaders are likely to consider advantageous in terms of their over-all objectives and the circumstances under which they might consider

Note: For the position of the other intelligence agencies with respect to this paper, see "Foreword" on preceding page.

TOP SECRET

165. *(Continued)*

a resort to military action either advantageous or necessary.

b. There would appear to be no firm basis for an assumption that the USSR presently *intends* deliberately to use military force to attain a Communist world or further to expand Soviet territory *if this involves war with a potentially stronger US.* An analysis of the Stalinist concepts which motivate Soviet leaders, as opposed to an interpretation of their motives and actions in the light of Western concepts, suggests strongly that the preferred objective of Soviet policy is to achieve a Soviet-dominated Communist world through revolutionary * rather than military means. Analysis of Soviet foreign policy likewise indicates that Soviet statesmen are following Stalinist doctrines and tactics in conducting Soviet international relations in the interest of the world revolution.

c. Soviet leaders, however, are thoroughly aware of the fact that they are pursuing their revolutionary objectives within the context of a traditional world power conflict. They are responsive in this context to the expansionist aims and the security requirements of the preceding imperial Russian regime. Their estimate of the objectives and behavior of the Western Powers, however, probably is still determined primarily by the Stalinist concept of a capitalist-imperialist world ruled by military force which will eventually be used against the Soviet Union. To ensure the protection of the base of the revolutionary movement in the USSR, therefore, they must maintain invincible military strength and use diplomacy to improve the strategic position of the USSR in relation to the world power situation as well as to further their revolutionary objectives. At the same time they recognize fully the value of the threat of Soviet military power as an adjunct to their revolutionary program.

d. The presently active Soviet threat to US security, therefore, while including the ever-present danger inherent in Soviet military power, appears to be a Soviet intention and determination to hasten, by every means short

of war, the economic and political disintegration of the non-Communist world which Soviet leaders firmly believe will inevitably come about according to the Marxist concept of the laws of historical development. In view of the magnitude of the economic, political, and social problems facing the non-Communist world today, it is unlikely that Soviet leaders will lose confidence in the validity of this Marxist concept until the non-Communist world has *demonstrated over a considerable period of time* that it can reverse the trends of the last forty years and re-establish a stable and self-confident international economic, political, and social order. The first line of US defense in this context, therefore, is the restoration of international stability and the maintenance of a sound internal structure.

e. In terms of this approach to their objectives, the role presently assigned by Soviet leaders to Soviet military power appears to be: (1) defense in the world power situation, accompanied by preparations for the eventuality of war; (2) intimidation in support of their revolutionary program; and (3) where consistent with their objectives, local use against military and economic forces already weakened by Communist subversion but not in aggression that would automatically involve war with the US. Even if the USSR should gain military superiority (i.e., in overall military potential) over the US and its allies, it is estimated that so long as it deems the opportunity to exist it will still prefer to seek its objectives by exploiting measures short of an all-out attack.

f. Although the USSR may hope and intend to pursue its objectives by measures short of war, at least until it has military superiority over the US and its allies, there is nevertheless a continuing danger of war, based upon the following considerations:

(1) The strength of Soviet military forces in being and the aggressive Soviet revolutionary program require that the US maintain a strong military and strategic posture. Were it not for the likelihood of US intervention, the USSR, when the situation was ripe, would probably use its military forces in actual intervention, progressively to support the ac-

---

* The term "revolutionary" is used to connote all means short of all-out war involving the US.

cession to power of Communist parties in the states directly beyond its area of control. Correspondingly, internal resistance to the rise of Communism in these areas would weaken without the support of a strong US.

(2) The USSR, with its doctrinaire concepts of capitalist behavior and its hyper-sensitiveness over security, may interpret, as potentially aggressive, future steps which the US and the other Western Powers might take to improve their defensive position against the threat inherent in Soviet military power. Similarly, continuing Soviet successes in the "cold war," accompanied by an increasing emphasis on US and Western military preparations, could well create a situation in which the USSR would estimate that the Western Powers were determined to prevent the future spread of Communism by military action against the USSR. It is always possible, therefore, that the USSR would initiate a war if it should estimate that a Western attack was impending.

(3) The basic Soviet concept of hostility (the "cold war") as the normal relationship between the Soviet Union and the non-Communist states, operating as it does against a background of a power conflict in which each side is armed and suspicious of the aims of the other, creates a situation in which miscalculations or diplomatic impasses might result in war. Furthermore, as the Soviet military potential increases relative to that of the US and its allies, the USSR will probably be willing to take greater risks than before in its exploitation of diplomatic opportunities or revolutionary situations.

(4) If, after gaining military superiority (i.e., in over-all military potential) over the US and its allies, Soviet leaders should lose confidence in the Marxist concept of the inevitable disintegration of the capitalist world and hence in their ability ultimately to attain their objectives by means short of war, the temptation to resort to military action against the US and its allies might well prove irresistible. *This conclusion should be qualified in the light of the possibilities inherent in atomic warfare, as discussed in the following section.* (For more detailed analysis, see Enclosure B.)

3. *Effects of the Soviet Possession of the Atomic Bomb upon the Probabilities of War.*

It is not yet possible to estimate with any precision the effects of the Soviet possession of the atomic bomb upon the probability of war. The implications of atomic warfare—either military or psychological—have not yet been fully appraised. In particular we have as yet no clear indications concerning the place of atomic warfare in Soviet military concepts or concerning the effect of US retaliatory capabilities upon any Soviet consideration of a deliberate and unprovoked atomic attack upon the US.

The capabilities of atomic warfare, however, clearly inject a new factor into an appraisal of Soviet intentions which requires the most careful evaluation and which, in any event, has vital implications for US defense planning. Although, in general, it appears unlikely that the possession of the atomic bomb will alter the basic considerations—as outlined above—which underlie Soviet policy, a Soviet capability for effective direct attack upon the continental US must be considered to increase the danger that the USSR might resort to military action to attain its objectives.

The military services have estimated that the destructive effect of atomic attack *actually delivered upon selected targets* in the US would be as follows:

(a) 10-50 bombs.

1. Would seriously hamper war mobilization and delay overseas shipments of US forces and material.

2. Would delay or reduce materially the scale of the US atomic retaliation.

(b) 50-125 bombs.

1. Would intensify the effects of (a)-1, above, and prevent the *immediate* launching of an atomic offensive against the USSR.

(c) Up to 200 bombs.

1. Reduce the US capability for an atomic offensive, possibly to a critical degree, and create conditions that might destroy the US capabilities for offensive war.

Atomic attack, therefore, introduces the *possibility* that the USSR under (a) and (b)

165. *(Continued)*

above could seriously cripple the US and under (c) might well knock the US out of the war.

If, therefore, the USSR should estimate that it had the capability of making a crippling attack upon the US that would eliminate the US margin of over-all military superiority, the danger that war might develop either from a Soviet estimate that a Western attack was imminent, or from miscalculations or impasses in the normal diplomatic maneuvering within the context of the world power conflict, would be increased.

Similarly, a Soviet estimate that it could deliver a *decisive* attack that would quickly knock the US out of the war would increase the possibility of a decision deliberately to resort to military action to eliminate the major obstacle to a Communist world. Such a decision, under these circumstances, might conceivably be made prior to a Soviet conviction that the USSR could not ultimately attain its objectives by means short of war. It could certainly be made prior to the attainment of superiority in over-all military potential as compared with the US and its allies.

There is no present means, however, of determining with any accuracy whether the USSR is likely to estimate that it has the capabilities to accomplish the results indicated above. In fact, no realistic US estimate has yet been made of Soviet capabilities to deliver atomic bombs on targets in the US, *taking into account Soviet operational factors and US defensive capabilities.* In terms of general Soviet objectives and the methods to which the USSR appears to be committed in attaining them, it would appear that Soviet leaders would require a high degree of certainty before deliberately undertaking the risk involved in a direct atomic attack in the face of the substantial US retaliatory capabilities. The following conditions would probably be essential to any such decision:

(a) Virtual certainty of attaining surprise (only in this way could the indicated results be achieved).

(b) Virtual certainty that effective US retaliation could be prevented. (Although the US may appear more vulnerable to atomic attack than the USSR, in terms of large concentrations of population and industry, the *Soviet regime* itself is probably peculiarly vulnerable to atomic attack. As a dictatorship, all elements of Soviet control are centered in Moscow. Initiative throughout the lower echelons and the provincial officialdom is nonexistent. The destruction of the control center, many of the leaders, and the means of communication might therefore lead to complete disintegration and revolution.)

(c) A more effective means of delivery than the TU-4 (B-29). (If there are doubts about the ability of the B-36 to deliver the atom bomb against the USSR, how much greater the doubts that the Soviet B-29 could deliver it successfully against an effective and alert US defense.)

The greatest danger that the Soviet atomic capability would lead to overt Soviet military action would appear, therefore, to derive from a Soviet estimate that it could launch a successful surprise attack that would seriously cripple or virtually eliminate US retaliatory capabilities. The likelihood that the USSR will reach such an estimate will vary inversely in relation to the effectiveness and alertness of the US defenses against such an attack, and to possible measures taken to make US retaliatory bases and equipment immune to attack.

In terms of the above analysis, present US estimates of destructive effects (given above) of varying numbers of atomic bombs actually delivered on selected targets in the US, combined with US estimates of the Soviet atomic bomb production schedule, can furnish only the roughest guide as to the timetable of theoretical Soviet capabilities.

On this tentative basis it is estimated that beginning shortly after 1 January 1951 the USSR will begin to build up a theoretical capability for launching a progressively crippling attack upon the US.

On the same basis, it is estimated that at some indeterminate time after mid-1954 the USSR will have the theoretical capability of delivering 200 atomic bombs on targets in the US which might well constitute a "decisive" attack, i.e., with respect to the ability of the US to wage offensive warfare.

It appears imperative from the foregoing that an effort be made to determine Soviet

165. *(Continued)*

capabilities on the most realistic basis, that is, in terms of Soviet operational factors and US defensive capabilities. For if it is determined that an atomic attack could knock the US out of a war, the implication would be that the atomic bomb is, after all, an "absolute weapon." Such a conclusion would have vast implications for US foreign policy and for the composition of the entire US military establishment.

4. Possible Soviet Courses of Action with Respect to Its Atomic Capabilities—Short of Direct Attack.

The precise effects of the Soviet atomic capabilities upon the security of the US will depend in part upon how the USSR chooses to use them. Consideration must be given to several alternative courses of action that are available to the USSR, and to the fact that we have no information on the Soviet evaluation of atomic warfare in terms of the effects upon the USSR of US atomic capabilities.

a. Possession of the atomic bomb has not yet produced any apparent change in Soviet policy or tactics, and probably will not do so at least through 1950. The USSR has merely integrated the "bomb" into its general propaganda and its "peace offensive." It will probably in any event continue to stir up mass opinion in the West against rearmament and against the use of atomic weapons in the event of war. In this way it may hope to create sufficient public pressure on the Western governments to neutralize the US bomb.

b. It would appear that on balance the destruction of existing stockpiles of atomic bombs and the barring of further production would be militarily advantageous to the USSR, except with respect to the possibility of a direct Soviet attack upon the continental US. Soviet considerations of security and national sovereignty probably preclude the possibility of an agreement for the control of atomic energy production that would meet the current requirements of the Western Powers, but the USSR may renew pressure for an international agreement to outlaw the use of the atomic bomb in warfare.

c. While the outlawing of the use of the bomb might be militarily advantageous to the USSR, in terms of operations in Europe or Asia, the USSR may estimate that the political and psychological advantages of retaining the threat of atomic warfare outweigh the military advantages of excluding it. When the USSR acquires what it considers an operational stockpile of bombs, its capabilities for employing threats and intimidation through diplomatic channels in an effort to detach individual states from the Western bloc will be considerably increased. With the exception of the UK, the US, and possibly Japan, however, this increased capability will not result from apprehension on the part of these states that they will be directly attacked with atomic bombs, but rather from the increased Soviet military capabilities vis-a-vis the US and from general apprehension concerning the effects of an atomic war. The USSR could not expect that the threat of direct atomic attack would carry particular weight against those states which estimated that a Soviet attack would bring the US into a war and that under those circumstances their territories would not be of sufficient strategic importance to justify the use against them of the limited Soviet supply of atomic bombs.

(For more detailed analysis, see Enclosure C.)

5. Effects of Soviet Possession of the Atomic Bomb upon the Security of the US.

a. Assuming the continued stockpiling of bombs by the USSR and the US, Soviet atomic capabilities have the following military implications for the security of the US in the event of war.

(1) The continental US will be for the first time liable to devastating attack. This has vital implications for the mobilization of the US war potential.

(2) The Soviet atomic capability would appear to make it imperative not only that US defenses against atomic attack, particularly the requirements for air defense, be greatly strengthened, but that steps be taken to make US retaliatory bases and equipment, in part at least, *invulnerable* to surprise attack. These measures are clearly essential to the

165. *(Continued)*

preservation of US retaliatory capabilities which in turn would contribute the greatest deterrent to a Soviet attack.

(3) If it is accepted, on the basis of a *realistic estimate*, that an atomic attack could knock the US out of a war, the implication would appear to be that the atomic bomb is after all an "absolute weapon." The acceptance of this implication would in turn have vital implications with regard to the composition of the entire US military establishment.

(4) The Soviet military potential is increased.

(5) The loss of the US monopoly of the atomic bomb has reduced the effectiveness both militarily and psychologically of the US commitment to defend the UK and Western Europe.

(6) The US has lost its capability of making a decisive atomic attack upon the war-making potential of the USSR without danger of retaliation in kind.

(7) Soviet possession of the atomic bomb would seriously affect US capabilities for air operations from the UK or other advanced bases and for amphibious operations against the European continent or other areas within range of Soviet attack.

(8) Soviet atomic retaliatory capabilities raise the question as to whether it is militarily desirable for the US to base its strategic plans upon the use of the atomic bomb except in retaliation against a Soviet attack. (In view of the preponderance of its conventional military forces and the damage it would sustain from a US atomic attack, the USSR might consider it advantageous not to use the bomb first and hope thereby to forestall the US use of the bomb.)

(9) If the use of the atomic bomb were eliminated, US strategic concepts for the conduct of a war with the USSR would have to be drastically revised.

(10) Should an international agreement be reached to outlaw the use of the atomic bomb the USSR would be in a better strategic position than the US. We can probably assume that the USSR would not hesitate to violate the agreement in the event of war if it considered it advantageous to do so, while the US

would abide by the agreement. Under these circumstances the USSR would have the option of using the bomb or not, according to its strategic plans, and thereby acquire the initiative. If neither side used the bomb, the US would lose its capabilities for immediate effective attack upon the Soviet military potential, and the USSR's relative capabilities would be increased through the preponderance of its conventional military strength.

b. The political and psychological effects on US security of a continuing Soviet atomic capability are estimated as follows:

(1) The possession of the bomb and the resultant increase in Soviet military power will increase somewhat the effectiveness of Soviet subversive activities and propaganda in the "cold war."

(2) Through 1950 at least, Soviet possession of the bomb will not cause any change in the present alignment of the principal nations, or in the support of current US programs to counter Soviet aggression. It will probably result, however, in demands from Western Europe for larger amounts of US equipment and for further US commitments for the active defense of Western Europe.

(3) The UK, because of its extreme vulnerability to atomic attack, may become somewhat cautious about joining with the US in any actions which the UK estimated might provoke the USSR into using armed force against the Western Powers. It will continue through 1950 at least, however, to base its foreign policy on a close US-UK strategic and economic relationship.

(4) The longer-range effects of Soviet atomic capabilities upon the political alignment of the non-Communist states will depend in the first instance upon the extent and soundness of European economic and military recovery and upon the policy and strength of the US. If present efforts to restore the economic and military strength of Western Europe fall short of their goals, there will develop a strong, though not necessarily decisive, movement for accommodation or neutrality. If at the same time, there should be indications of a serious weakening in US

165. *(Continued)*

strength or in US commitments to resist Soviet aggression, the movement for accommodation or neutrality would probably become decisive.

Assuming that US support of its NAT allies and Japan remains firm and that the economic and military recovery of Europe is accomplished on a firm and stable basis, there will be a strong probability that the non-Soviet states, including the UK and Japan, will remain firm in their alignments with the US if the Soviet Union should threaten atomic warfare when it has attained an operational stockpile of bombs, or if a deterioration in relations between the USSR and the Western Powers suggested that an atomic war was imminent. In the latter circumstances, the UK would be strongly influenced by its appraisal of the issues at stake; it would not be inclined to follow the US unless it considered these issues vital to its security.

In the final analysis, however, the future public appraisal of the significance of the atomic bomb will probably be the determining factor on the will to resist. It is impossible at this time to predict with any assurance what this appraisal will be. In general, three alternative trends appear possible in the interim.

a. Increasing fear of the effects of an atomic struggle may have produced in all countries, but particularly in the UK, US, and Japan, an irresistible, organized popular demand for renewed efforts to bring about an agreement between the US and the USSR for at least the prohibition of the use of atomic weapons. If, under these circumstances, this objective were not attained, it must be considered possible that the UK and Japan, because of their extreme vulnerability, could be detached from the US camp and that the US public might force an accommodation with the USSR.

b. The concept may become generally accepted that the threat of mutual retaliation will preclude the use of the bomb by either side. Under these circumstances the effect of Soviet atomic capabilities would be negligible.

c. The present public attitude of indifference or relative unconcern may continue; or a strong determination to resist, regardless of consequences, may develop. Under either of these circumstances, the countries concerned would probably stand firm in their alignment with the US.

(For more detailed analysis, see Enclosure D.)

APPENDIX A

DISSENT BY THE INTELLIGENCE ORGANIZATION, DEPARTMENT OF STATE

The Intelligence Organization of the Department of State dissents from the subject paper.

The subject paper indicates that, except under extreme—and apparently unlikely—circumstances, the USSR will not deliberately employ military force in its struggle against the US.

We do not possess evidence which suggests that the USSR is now planning to launch a military attack on the US. Neither do we possess evidence, or have reason to believe, that at any given date the USSR will with certainty decide to launch a military assault on the US.

We do not consider, however, that *lack* of evidence of a Soviet intention to use military force on the US can be taken as *evidence* of the *absence* of such a Soviet intention.

The subject paper states that "the burden of proof" of a Soviet intention to resort to world military conquest "lies on those who would assert" that this is the Soviet intention.

We believe that this statement reflects a fundamental misunderstanding of the problem which faces us at the present time. It is accepted by all intelligence agencies of the government that the Soviet Union's basic objective is to establish a Communist world under Soviet domination. It is also accepted that Soviet leaders will employ any methods and tactics which in their mind offer promise of success.

Prior to the Soviet development of an atomic weapon it was generally agreed that an early Soviet military attack on the West was unlikely, if not precluded, because of the preponderance of strength which its economic potential and its atomic monopoly gave the West. With Soviet possession of an atomic weapon this particular assumption obviously is subject to reconsideration.

In the interest of the national security, therefore, we are faced with the necessity of answering the question: Is there evidence on the basis of which it can be assumed that Soviet leaders will not resort to military action against the US now that they possess an atomic weapon?

The subject paper recognizes many aspects of the crucially important potential of the A-bomb in expanding Soviet capabilities, but it fails to bring into focus the problem of whether or not this development will have a decisive effect on Soviet policy and intentions. While it recognizes numerous conditioning factors, it takes the position that the USSR is still unlikely to employ military force in its struggle with the West. This position is based upon arguments to the effect that a) Communist ideology rigidly prescribes reliance upon the international Communist apparatus rather than upon employment of Soviet armed forces for the attainment of a Communist world dominated by the USSR, and b) Russian imperial history reveals that Russian expansionism has traditionally been cautious and has not been pursued at the risk of a military clash with a "major" power.

Considering the import to US defense and foreign policy of an assurance that the USSR is not likely to resort to military action, we consider these arguments undependable.

The first argument is in direct contradiction to earlier assertion in the CIA paper that the USSR in pursuit of its objective "will wage a relentless, unceasing struggle [against the US] in which any weapon or tactic is admissible which promises success in terms of overall Soviet objectives" and that nothing in the paper "should be interpreted to imply that Soviet leaders would not resort to military action at any time they considered it advantageous to do so." Furthermore, this emphasis upon revolutionary policy not only rests upon a doubtful interpretation of the extremely complex question of the role of the USSR as the "first socialist state" in effecting

29

165. *(Continued)*

world revolution, but also assumes a rigidity in tactics—in the means to be employed in reaching a fixed objective—comparable to the firmness with which that objective itself is held, an assumption which is demonstrably false.

The second argument, that a resort to military action by the USSR is precluded by the fact that Russia since time immemorial has been cautious in its foreign policy, is based upon a misreading of the actual historical facts. Russian history is characterized by neither recklessness nor caution in foreign affairs, but a mixture of recklessness and caution, depending upon the circumstances existing at a given time and on the make-up of the rulers in power. Russian rulers can no more be generally dubbed "cautious" than can the rulers of Prussia. Moreover, it is questionable that the pattern of Russian history under the Tsars is in itself a safe guide by which to predict the actions of Soviet leaders.

The danger of accepting these arguments as a basis for assuming the line of action which Soviet leaders will follow is illustrated by the subject paper itself. At a time when all evidence indicates increasingly militant activity on the part of the USSR in virtually all areas of the world, the paper asserts that "[the existing] situation is one in which both Russian tradition and Communist doctrine counsel patience and restraint, and it appears that the USSR is prepared to accept the *status quo* for the time being. The USSR can afford to be patient, being firmly convinced that time is on its side, that the conflicting interests of the capitalist powers will prevent any truly dangerous development, and that the eventual economic collapse of the capitalist world will present new revolutionary opportunities."

The Intelligence Organization of the Department of State has reached the following conclusions as to Soviet intentions regarding the deliberate use of military force in the Soviet struggle against the non-Communist world.

1. There is at present no evidence which indicates a Soviet determination at any given time to employ military force against the non-Communist world.

2. The Soviet Union is, however, engaged in what is considers to be a life-and-death struggle with the non-Communist world. In this struggle Soviet leaders can be expected to employ any weapon or tactic which promises success.

3. The only sound test by which to judge Soviet intentions to resort to military action is, therefore, the pragmatic test of whether or not such action would, at a given moment, appear *advantageous* to the Soviet Union.

4. Prior to Soviet development of an atomic weapon, all evidence indicated that the preponderance of strength enjoyed by the US in consequence of its over-all economic superiority and its atomic monopoly made unlikely a Soviet estimate that it would be to the advantage of the USSR to resort to military action.

5. Soviet development of an atomic weapon may have decisively changed this situation, particularly if surprise employment of the weapon could sharply reduce retaliatory action or make it impossible.

The subject report does not effectively deal with this possibility of a change. We feel that the report confuses the issues on Soviet motives and leaves unclear the new balance of factors which will probably determine the Soviet estimate of the advantage the USSR could gain through a deliberate employment of military forces.

TOP SECRET

APPENDIX B

DISSENT BY THE ASSISTANT CHIEF OF STAFF, G-2, DEPARTMENT OF THE ARMY

1. The Assistant Chief of Staff, G-2, dissents with the subject paper. It is recommended that this paper be withdrawn and JIC 502 be substituted therefor as a basis for resolving differences in attitude and opinion. The differences of opinion are considered to be so divergent that it is impractical to consider resolving them on the basis of the present paper.

2. This dissent is based on the following:

a. The threat of Soviet aggression is minimized to the point where dissemination of the paper and its use for planning purposes could seriously affect the security of the United States. A major portion of the paper is devoted to developing the thesis that it is unjustifiable to assume that the U.S.S.R. definitely intends to resort to military aggression involving the United States. This portion of the paper is unrealistic and not germane to the problem.

The conclusions as they apply to the probabilities of war are developed apart from any consideration of the atomic bomb (p. 3, III, 2, last sentence) in spite of the fact that the statement of the problem (p. 3, I) requires such consideration.

b. The second major difference of opinion is the manner in which the subject matter contained in the enclosure is presented. Refinements of logic and multiplicity of alternatives make the paper extremely difficult to understand. As a study, it fails to reach clear-cut conclusions.

TOP SECRET

31

165. *(Continued)*

APPENDIX C

DISSENT BY THE OFFICE OF NAVAL INTELLIGENCE

1. The Office of Naval Intelligence dissents from ORE 91-49.

2. The discussion (enclosures A through D) is generally in accordance with ONI's views, but it is not considered that the Summary and Conclusions are properly drawn from the enclosures. The following comments are therefore directed primarily toward the Summary and Conclusions:

(a) There is no integrated analysis of what the effects of Soviet possession of atomic weapons will be. Instead, there is an examination based on several mutually exclusive hypotheses. From these hypotheses one may choose estimates which range from no change in Soviet policy to basic and alarming changes in that policy.

(b) It is noted that one argument in ORE 91-49 rests on extremely hypothetical speculations as to "what might happen" if the Soviet leaders abandoned their Marxist view of the eventual collapse of capitalism and imperialism. There is at present no indication that the Soviets are losing confidence in their Marxist philosophy and, furthermore, there is no basis on which to predict what their policies might be should they abandon that philosophy.

(c) The hypothesis that a major war may result from miscalculation is considered, in the light of recent events, to be unrealistic. If either the U.S. or the USSR should let an incident or diplomatic impasse develop into a war, it is considered that such a war, as well as the incident or the impasse, would result from a plan, not from a blunder.

(d) In many instances ORE 91-49 exceeds the bounds of intelligence and draws inferences and conclusions of an operational and planning nature.

TOP SECRET

APPENDIX D

DISSENT BY THE DIRECTOR OF INTELLIGENCE, UNITED STATES AIR FORCE

1. The following comment concentrates on the one point which the D/I, USAF, considers of such overriding importance as to make the CIA estimate, ORE 91-49, dangerous as an intelligence basis for national policy.

2. The Director of Intelligence, USAF, believes the primary reason why the Kremlin has not resorted to military action against the United States to date is the fact that the Kremlin has believed, and still continues to believe, it is operating from an inferior power position. ORE 91-49, therefore, failed to point out the full and true character of the Soviet threat. Unless the full and true character of this threat is pointed out, Soviet total relative power may be permitted to grow to the point where the U.S. can no longer cope with it successfully.

3. Subject paper states that (a) the USSR regards the U.S. as its main opponent; (b) it will wage against the U.S. a relentless, unceasing struggle in which any weapon or tactic is admissible; and (c) that nothing in the paper should be construed as implying that "the Soviet leaders would not resort to military action at any time they considered it *advantageous* to do so." While these statements, in the opinion of the D/I are correct as far as they go, the rest of the subject paper actually weakens and contradicts this original position.

4. The paper completely misses the inter-relationship between war and revolution. It does not realize, as the Soviets do, that a great power such as the U.S. cannot be overthrown by revolution alone but that revolution can be the result only of a preceding war. It therefore overlooks the fact that Soviet policy aims above all at preparing for the show-down war against the United States. Therefore the first line of U.S. defense is not, as the paper suggests, the "restoration of international stability and the maintenance of a sound internal structure" but is to recognize that we are at war right now, and that an all-out national effort designed to maintain permanent military and political superiority over the Soviet Union, is required.

5. The paper begs the issue under discussion when it states that there appears "to be no firm basis for an assumption that the USSR presently intends deliberately to use military force . . . if this involves war with a potentially stronger U.S." Actually, there is a very firm basis for the assumption that they would do no such thing, simply because an aggressor has never resorted to war if he were sure that he would lose. The problem at issue is (a) whether the acquisition of an atomic capability has provided the Soviet Union for the first time in history with a clear-cut capability that would enable them to win the war against the U.S.; and (b) whether, under conditions of atomic warfare, the lack of instantly available American military power vitiates the importance of the great American war *potential*. Another no less important problem would be to determine how the Soviets will integrate the atomic bomb into their traditional strategy and tactics. To this problem ORE 91-49 does not address itself.

6. The D/I, USAF, sets forth the following for the record:

a. Communist thinking, from Marx to Stalin, clearly recognizes the inter-relationship between war and revolution, and, specifically, the fact that no major revolution is feasible without war.

b. The Soviets are clearly on record that (1) they consider the Soviet Union as an operational base and (2) they consider the Red Army as the main weapon of the proletariat. The Soviets know that they have never expanded beyond their frontiers without the use of military means, i.e., all the territories taken by them were taken by the Red Army or a satellite force (Tito, Mao).

TOP SECRET

35

165. *(Continued)*

c. In "Problems of Leninism", Stalin stated clearly that capitalism can be overthrown only by violence, and ultimately only by war. Actually the theory that capitalism will fall of its own weight has never been Stalin's idea, and there is much evidence that he has opposed this concept as ideological "deviationism".

d. The Soviets made a major contribution to the outbreak of World War II. They did nothing to prevent that war, and everything to make it a reality.

e. There are numerous recent statements by Soviet authorities to the effect that World War I produced Communism in Russia; that World War II produced Communism in Eastern Europe and China; and that World War III will see the victory of Communism throughout the world.

f. There is ample reason to believe that the Kremlin regards its growing atomic capability to be the major force which will eventually place them in position to liquidate the center of hard-core opposition—the United States—utilizing all means at their disposal, including military action.

SECRET

COMMUNISM IN SOUTHEAST ASIA

The Chinese Communist regime in Peiping is already taking active measures to support the "national liberation" movements throughout Southeast Asia. Moral and material aid is being furnished in varying degrees and in general the Chinese Communists are strengthening their ties with local Communist movements and are gradually welding the Overseas Chinese communities into useful instruments of Chinese Communist policy. The degree of Communist penetration and current trends in Chinese Communist relations with the several Southeast Asian states are summarized below.

Indochina   Although the Ho regime has been receiving some support from the Chinese Communists in the form of arms deliveries and the free movement of resistance troops back and forth across the China border, there is no firm evidence that the Chinese Communists are moving their own troops across the border or planning to do so in the near future. Politically, the Chinese Communists and the Ho regime have accorded each other de jure recognition, but have not as yet exchanged diplomatic missions or concluded any form of treaty or agreement. Steps may soon be taken (or may already be in process) to formalize these relations; when this occurs, Chinese Communist support for the Ho forces will probably increase.

Thailand   Thailand has not recognized the Peiping regime and has shown, of late, a rather firm disposition to resist Communist psychological pressure. The Peiping regime does not appear especially interested in establishing diplomatic relations with Thailand, even though such a move could facilitate the acquisition of Thai rice. Within Thailand,

- 5 -

SECRET

166. *(Continued)*

as elsewhere in Southeast Asia, the Overseas Chinese community continues to be a special target of Chinese Communist propaganda and organizational activity. Communist agents are proceeding with a program of infiltration, not only of the Chinese community, but also of trade unions, youth groups, and other organizations which can be exploited to the disadvantage and embarrassment of the Thai Government. If Thailand should receive US military aid or participate in a non-Communist association of Asiatic states, the Chinese Communists would increase their pressure on Thailand through propaganda, and possibly through the stimulation of internal disturbances.

Malaya   There is evidence that the Chinese Communists have been infiltrating agents into Malaya to support the terrorist movement and to gain influence in trade unions and other organizations. The Malayan Chinese, who make up nearly half the total population of the Malayan peninsula, are responding favorably to Chinese Communist efforts to win support and sympathy for Peiping, and the morale of the terrorists appears to have risen somewhat as a result of the growing prestige and aggressiveness of the Chinese Communists. Chinese Communist support for the "liberation" movement in Malaya, however, is complicated by the fact that the terrorist organization is composed almost exclusively of Chinese and is opposed as much by the native Malayans as by the British, with the result that Communist propaganda in favor of Malayan nationalism has a rather hollow sound. The campaign to win the Chinese half of the population to the Communist cause will continue in vigorous fashion and will succeed in proportion as the Peiping regime can solve its internal problems and maintain the prestige of a dynamic political movement. There is, however, no early prospect that the Chinese Communists will recognize the terrorists as the "government" of the Malayan peninsula.

- 6 -

166. *(Continued)*

Burma   Burma recognized the Chinese Communist
regime on 17 December 1949, but the establishment of diplomatic relations between the two governments has not yet been accomplished. As a result of the
establishment of a "purified" Burmese Communist regime
at Prome, the Peiping regime may stall on the formalization
of its relations with Burma in the hope that the Prome regime
survives and flourishes. Peiping may then recognize that
regime as the "government" of Burma, and ignore the
Rangoon authorities altogether.

Indonesia   Although the USI on 4 April 1950 received a
communication from Peiping expressing the
Chinese Communists' willingness to establish diplomatic relations with the new republic, and Premier Hatta expressed
agreement to such a step, the Chinese Communists have made
no further moves in this direction, nor have they given any
publicity to the matter. Despite internal instability, the USI
does not appear to be vulnerable in any important degree to
armed Communist activity, nor could armed groups receive
significant assistance from the Asiatic mainland. Communist
strategy for the USI appears to turn on the establishment of
diplomatic relations with Jakarta and the eventual staffing
of Soviet and Chinese Communist missions there, from which
organizational and propaganda work will be carried on among
both the Overseas Chinese and native Communist and leftist
movements. The USI will delay the actual exchange of diplomatic missions with both the USSR and the Peiping regime as
long as possible because of a keen awareness among many USI
officials of the dangers of allowing Communist officials from
abroad to establish direct contact with local dissident elements.

- 7 -

166. *(Continued)*

SECRET

The Philippines   The Philippine Government has not re-
                     cognized the Chinese Communist regime
and has given no indication that it will do so in the near future.
The Philippine response to the establishment of a Communist
state on the Chinese mainland has been mainly one of fear that
the Overseas Chinese in the Philippines would align themselves
with the Chinese Communists and become a menacing fifth
column within the islands. The Quirino regime has taken steps
to restrict Chinese immigration sharply and to deport Chinese
who are under suspicion for illegal entry or subversive activities. There are some indications that the civil liberties of
the Chinese community may be seriously abridged, a development which would draw the full wrath of the Chinese Communist
propaganda machine. While conclusive evidence of direct
Chinese Communist support for the local Huk rebellion in
the Philippines is lacking, it is almost certain that some
liaison exists.

- 8 -

SECRET

167. Weekly Summary Excerpt, 21 April 1950, China: Party Purge

FAR EAST

CHINA

Party Purge   Friction between the Stalinist leadership and anti-Stalinist factions in the middle echelons of the Chinese Communist Party may soon lead to a public purge of selected anti-Stalinist Party figures. There is no reliable evidence, however, that the purge will extend to the Politburo or to the major Chinese Communist military commanders.

Party Chairman Mao Tse-tung has not wavered in his Stalinist orientation and his leadership does not appear to be challenged either by such firm Stalinists as the Party's number two man, Liu Shao-chi, or such allegedly lukewarm Stalinists as Chou En-lai. Even if a dispute should arise in the Politburo, it would probably be resolved, as in the past, without violence.

Within the Party's military hierarchy, it is not known whether any of the major field commanders are in fact anti-Stalinist. These military leaders, owing to the size and importance of their various commands, are still in a strong position in relation to the non-military Party leadership, and the Peiping regime will probably proceed with caution in efforts to restrict and reduce their authority further. None of the military leaders seems a likely candidate for purging at least until the completion of military operations against the Nationalists, which should see them safely through 1950. Beyond that time, Peiping will presumably be reluctant to take action against any one of the military leaders until assured of the fidelity or neutrality of all the rest, and until convinced that political indoctrination has made the troops loyal primarily to Peiping rather than to their old commanders.

- 10 -

168. Weekly Summary Excerpt, 28 April 1950, The Soviet Offensive

THE SOVIET OFFENSIVE

Since the beginning of 1950, the USSR has gradually stepped up and expanded its diplomatic, political, and economic offensive against the West and the cold war has now reached another peak of aggressiveness and militancy.

Soviet objectives have not changed and the tactics now being used differ only in intensity and scope from those employed since the end of World War II. Although the USSR has improved its power position by announcing its possession of atomic secrets, increasing its military and industrial strength, consolidating its control of Eastern Europe, and making spectacular gains in the Far East, there is no indication that the USSR is yet willing to initiate armed conflict with the West. The strengthened Soviet power position, however, does permit the Soviet Union to apply greater pressures than it has in the past and on more fronts simultaneously.

As in the past, the present Soviet offensive is characterized by violence, subversion, unfounded accusations, and defiant, belligerent propaganda. Each time since the end of World War II that the Soviet Union has unleashed an intensive campaign of this kind, its effect has been to spur the Western Powers to greater defensive efforts.

Despite the results of these campaigns in the past, Communist doctrine and the very nature of the Soviet system tend to commit the Soviet leaders to achieve their ends through aggressive, militant means. Violence and subversion are an integral part of the Communist revolutionary technique and are naturally accompanied by a vigorous diplomatic offensive. Moreover, Soviet leaders consider it necessary to maintain the morale of

- 2 -

Communists at home and abroad by demonstrating the power of the Soviet Union. Closely allied with this need, the Kremlin may feel that only by attacking and vilifying the West can it justify the rigid controls it maintains on the Soviet and Satellite people and prepare them psychologically for war. It seems likely, therefore, that the Soviet Union will continue its tactics of aggressive arrogance for some time, the intensity of the effort growing in proportion to increases in Soviet strength and concentrating on those issues and areas where Western strength is weakest.

Baltic Plane   The current Soviet offensive reached its peak of militancy with the recent aircraft incident in the Baltic. In addition to attempting to prove to the world that the Soviet Union can be neither imposed upon nor intimidated, the USSR has sought to emphasize the military significance of the flight, thus playing upon popular war fears and lending weight to peace appeals. Moreover, in decorating the Soviet pilots who presumably participated, Moscow was, in effect, pointing with pride to the ability of Soviet defensive aviation to protect the homeland from US strategic air power. Finally, the plane incident has been used to convince the Soviet and Satellite peoples that Western aggression is not merely a figment of Kremlin imagination.

Other Aspects   Soviet self-assurance is apparent in other East-West issues. Soviet defiance of the UN continues. Western missions are being subjected to increased insult and intimidation throughout the Soviet orbit. The tone of Soviet propaganda is growing steadily more provocative, and Communist parties outside the Soviet orbit show a mounting militancy. Concurrently with these aggressive moves, Moscow is probing the defenses of the opposition on a number of fronts. It is testing the degree of Western determination to remain in Berlin; it is agitating, through diplomacy and propaganda, the questions of Trieste and the Turkish Straits; and its support of the Communist movements of Asia is becoming more open and more direct.

- 3 -

169. Weekly Summary Excerpt, 5 May 1950, China: Military Plans

FAR EAST

CHINA

Military Plans Although the capture of Hainan has placed the Chinese Communist Army in a position to invade Southeast Asia, there are no concrete indications that the Communists are ready to depart from previous international Communist strategy or to run the risk of precipitating general hostilities by taking such a step at this time. Moreover, the Communist troops available for such an invasion probably will be needed for more immediate and pressing problems confronting the Peiping regime. Many of the troops involved in the Hainan invasion will be occupied for some time in consolidating Communist control over that island; other troops in South China will be needed to strengthen Communist control over the many wide areas which remain in the hands of local authorities, brigands, or organized thieving bands. Moreover, a considerable number of Chinese troops probably will be employed to establish a strategic reserve for the coming invasion of Nationalist-held Taiwan. The Communists have already stated that they are planning to utilize a force of one million men for the invasion of this last Nationalist stronghold. There is also the possibility that the Chinese Communists may wish to augment their forces along the Hong Kong border in preparation for increasing their pressure against the British crown colony. Although the Communist conquest of Hainan probably will not result in organized military invasion of any Southeast Asian areas, the Chinese Communists, in addition to supplying advisers and technical personnel to the various Communist-led resistance groups in Southeast Asia and the Philippines, will be in a position to facilitate the shipment of material aid to these same areas.

- 12 -

24913

~~T.O.P. SECRET~~

6 JUN 1950

1309

GENERAL

1. <u>Possible Kremlin conference on Southeast Asia</u>--US Embassy Bangkok expresses the opinion that the imminent departure for Moscow of the Soviet Minister and the former Charge, following the recent departure of other Soviet officials, may indicate that an important consultation or planning conference on Southeast Asia will soon take place in Moscow. According to the Embassy, the British representatives in Bangkok concur in the view that the USSR may be calling an urgent meeting in order to decide upon immediate steps to prevent or counter the strengthening of Southeast Asia by the Western Powers.

   (CIA Comment: The recall of Soviet representatives from Bangkok, combined with the recall for consultations of top diplomatic personnel from all the Soviet diplomatic posts (except China) in Eastern Asia, indicates that the Kremlin is probably reviewing its over-all policy for the Far East. The additional presence in Moscow of the Soviet Ambassador to the US, a Far Eastern expert familiar with US thinking, is further evidence that the USSR is formulating new tactics designed to counter Western attempts to strengthen anti-Communist efforts in the Far East, especially in Southeast Asia.)

- 1 -

~~TOP SECRET~~

171. Weekly Summary Excerpt, 9 June 1950, Soviet Union: New SEA Policy

SOVIET UNION

New SEA Policy   The recall to Moscow of leading Soviet diplo-
                  mats from Far Eastern posts and from the
US indicates that the Kremlin may be reviewing its entire Far
Eastern policy in order to plan for more aggressive action to
counter Western anti-Communist efforts in the Far East, especially in Southeast Asia. Such a conference of Soviet representatives from Japan, India, Thailand, and possibly North
Korea, together with the recall of the Soviet Ambassador to
the US, who is a Far Eastern expert, emphasizes the importance
of the area to the USSR at this time.

In Japan, the Kremlin might decide to shift from "legitimate" activities to concentrate on a subversive program as the
most effective means of obstructing Western progress in Japan.
The issuance of a second Soviet note demanding trial of Hirohito
and the intensification of Communist activity in the face of a
proposal to outlaw the Party indicate that the USSR is willing to
risk having the Japanese Communist Party driven underground.

- 7 -

172. ORE 18-50 Excerpt, 19 June 1950, Current Capabilities of the Northern Korean Regime

CURRENT CAPABILITIES OF THE NORTHERN KOREAN REGIME

ESTIMATE OF CURRENT CAPABILITIES

The "Democratic People's Republic" of northern Korea is a firmly controlled Soviet Satellite that exercises no independent initiative and depends entirely on the support of the USSR for existence. At the present time there is no serious internal threat to the regime's stability, and, barring an outbreak of general hostilities, the Communists will continue to make progress toward their ultimate domestic goals. The Communist regime in northern Korea suffers from a shortage of skilled administrative personnel and from weaknesses in its economy and its official Party organizations. There is widespread, although passive, popular discontent with the Communist government. Despite these weaknesses, however, the regime has, with Soviet assistance, clearly demonstrated an ability to continue its control and development of northern Korea along predetermined political, economic, and social lines.

The northern Korean regime is also capable, in pursuit of its major external aim of extending control over southern Korea, of continuing and increasing its support of the present program of propaganda, infiltration, sabotage, subversion, and guerrilla operations against southern Korea. This program will not be sufficient in itself, however, to cause a collapse of the southern Korean regime and the extension of Communist control over the south so long as US economic and military aid to southern Korea is not substantially reduced or seriously dissipated.

At the same time the capability of the northern Korean armed forces for both short- and long-term overt military operations is being further developed. Although the northern and southern forces are nearly equal in terms of combat effectives, training, and leadership,

the northern Koreans possess a superiority in armor, heavy artillery, and aircraft. Thus, northern Korea's armed forces, even as presently constituted and supported, have a capability for attaining limited objectives in short-term military operations against southern Korea, including the capture of Seoul.

Northern Korea's capability for long-term military operations is dependent upon increased logistical support from the USSR. If the foreign supporters of each faction were called upon for increased assistance, there is no reason to believe that Soviet support would be withheld and considerations of proximity and availability of such assistance would greatly favor the northern Korean regime. Soviet assistance to northern Korea, however, probably would not be in the form of direct participation of regular Soviet or Chinese Communist military units except as a last resort. The USSR would be restrained from using its troops by the fear of general war; and its suspected desire to restrict and control Chinese influence in northern Korea would militate against sanctioning the use of regular Chinese Communist units in Korea.

Despite the apparent military superiority of northern over southern Korea, it is not certain that the northern regime, lacking the active participation of Soviet and Chinese Communist military units, would be able to gain effective control over all of southern Korea. The key factors which would hinder Communist attempts to extend effective control under these circumstances are: (1) the anti-Communist attitude of the southern Koreans; (2) a continuing will to resist on the part of southern troops; (3) the Communist regime's lack of popular support; and (4) the regime's lack of trained administrators and technicians.

Note: The intelligence organizations of the Departments of State, Army, Navy, and the Air Force have concurred in this report. It contains information available to CIA as of 15 May 1950.

~~T O P S E C R E T~~ ~~CONFIDENTIAL~~

26 JUN 1950

24930

54

1326

GENERAL

s/TS

1. <u>Embassy Moscow's views on Korean conflict</u>--US Embassy
   Moscow, in assessing the implications of the present Korean
   conflict, expresses the opinion that the North Korean offensive against the Republic of Korea constitutes a clear-cut
   Soviet challenge to the United States which should be answered
   firmly and swiftly because it constitutes a direct threat to US
   leadership of the free world against Soviet-Communist imperialism. The Embassy points out that the defeat of the
   Republic of Korea would have grave and unfavorable repercussions for the US position in Japan, Southeast Asia, and in
   other areas as well, and expresses the view that the US is
   obligated to make clear to the world without delay that the
   US is prepared to assist the Republic of Korea maintain its
   independence by all means at US disposal, including military
   assistance and vigorous action in the UN Security Council. The
   Embassy believes that any delay on the part of the US "could
   suggest" to the USSR the possibility of precipitating with
   impunity immediate action against Indochina and other points
   along the boundary of the Soviet sphere. The Embassy also
   believes that the USSR probably calculated that the US will
   be inclined to accept "neutralization" of the Korean civil war
   which would lead to eventual victory by North Korea, thus expanding the Soviet empire without the use of Soviet military
   forces. The Embassy reiterates its belief that the USSR is not
   yet ready to risk full-scale war with the West, and comments
   that the present Korean situation thus offers the US an opportunity to show firmness and determination and, at the same time,
   to unmask important Soviet weaknesses to the eyes of the world
   and particularly in Asia, where popular ideas of Soviet power
   have been grossly exaggerated as a result of recent Soviet
   political and propaganda successes.

Document No. _73_

NO CHANGE in Class. ☐
☐ DECLASSIFIED
Class. CHANGED TO: TS   S   C
         DDA Memo, 4 Apr. 77
Auth: DDA REG. 77/1763
Date: 29 MAR 1978   By: ___

- 1 -

~~T O P S E C R E T~~ ~~CONFIDENTIAL~~

173. *(Continued)*

(CIA Comment: CIA concurs in general with Embassy
Moscow's estimate of Soviet intent in precipitating civil war
in Korea, and further agrees that successful aggression in
Korea will encourage the USSR to launch similar ventures elsewhere in the Far East. In sponsoring the aggression in Korea,
the Kremlin probably calculated that no firm or effective
countermeasures would be taken by the West. However, the
Kremlin is not willing to undertake a global war at this time,
and firm and effective countermeasures by the West would
probably lead the Kremlin to permit a settlement to be negotiated between the North and South Koreans. If the venture in Korea
is successful, the Kremlin will fully exploit the "western failure"
in Korea in an effort to undermine the western position throughout
the world. Effective action by the UN to control the Korean situation is possible only through military sanctions involving the immediate conclusion of "interim agreements" providing for armed
contingents from member nations to enforce the UN cease fire
order.)

- 2 -

174. Daily Summary Excerpt, 27 June 1950, Soviet Troop Movement Toward Yugoslavia Reported

50/5

3. Soviet troop movement against Yugoslavia reported--
A [ ]source[ ] transmits reports from fairly
reliable informants that a considerable number of troops
are being moved through Rumania toward Bulgaria and
Yugoslavia. According to source, seven military trains
composed of fifteen to twenty cars which are completely
blacked-out are transporting tanks, artillery, and munitions
to the south.

    (CIA Comment: CIA believes that a buildup of
Soviet military equipment and strategic transport facilities
in the Balkans has been under way for some time. There
is little evidence, however, that Soviet military personnel
in the Balkans have been increased sufficiently to enable
the USSR to undertake military action in the area at this
time.)

- 2 -

175. Daily Summary Excerpt, 28 June 1950, No Soviet Military Preparations in Germany and Austria

4. <u>No Soviet military preparations in Germany and Austria</u>--
General Handy, Commander in Chief of US Forces in
Europe, reports that there are no indications of aggressive Communist military action in Germany. Handy states
that the bulk of the Soviet occupation armies seem to be
engaged in normal maneuvers and that the German Democratic Republic has manifested no warlike intentions.

     General Keyes, Commander of US forces in Austria,
reports that there are no indications of a change in the
present situation in Austria at this time.

     (CIA Comment: No evidence is available indicating
Soviet preparations for military operations in the West
European theater, but Soviet military capabilities in Europe
make it possible for the USSR to take aggressive action with
a minimum of preparation or advance notice.)

ARMY/S
ARMY/S

- 2 -

176. Weekly Summary Excerpt, 30 June 1950, The Korean Situation

THE KOREAN SITUATION

The Soviet-inspired invasion of South Korea and the prompt and vigorous US reaction have overnight changed the complexion of the cold war and will lead to the development of new and critical problems for the US in nearly every quarter of the globe. It is not believed that the USSR desires a global war at this time. It is probable, however, that a concerted attempt will be made to make the US effort in Korea as difficult and costly as possible. (The USSR has sizeable forces of Chinese Communist troops at its disposal for this purpose.) The implications to the US of defeat in Korea would be far-reaching. It would become nearly impossible to develop effective anti-Communist resistance in Southeast Asia, and progress toward building a strong Atlantic community would be seriously threatened. A US victory in Korea would also pose serious problems for the US.

Increased Demands   The adoption of a vigorous stand by the US against Communist expansion has, in general, been favorably received throughout the non-Soviet world. The adoption of this stand, however, implies that any failure by the US to take similarly prompt and effective action to stop any further aggressive moves may have even more serious repercussions to US and Western prestige than would have resulted from failure to come to the aid of South Korea. The Korean invasion has increased fears that the USSR will take aggressive action in other "soft spots" on the Soviet periphery, thus tending to create in these areas greater demands for US military and economic aid. The areas most immediately affected are Southeast Asia (particularly Indochina), Iran, Yugoslavia, Greece, and Germany.

- 2 -

53148

~~SECRET~~

CENTRAL INTELLIGENCE AGENCY

~~CONFIDENTIAL~~ 30 June 1950

12

INTELLIGENCE MEMORANDUM NO. 301

SUBJECT: Estimate of Soviet Intentions and Capabilities for Military Aggression.

Although the USSR is considered to be unwilling to undertake a global conflict with the West at this time, the Soviet-inspired attack on Korea and the US reaction make it critical to examine Soviet intentions with respect to exploiting other areas bordering the Soviet-dominated sphere along the general lines being followed in Korea.

Within the limitation of aggressive actions short of global war, the Kremlin has available to it three general lines of action: (1) the encouragement of guerrilla activities and creation of local disturbances; (2) the incitement of rebellions, local uprisings which could lead to autonomous movements splitting off parts of presently non-Communist areas; and (3) the use of a Soviet-controlled regime to attack and capture control of an adjacent nation or area. Prospects for a Soviet decision to launch a new Korean-type venture or to institute general harrassing measures along the Soviet-dominated border line must be measured in terms of developments in the situation in Korea. If the USSR is successful in picking-off Korea and if Soviet leaders do not become convinced that the new US policy prompted by the Korean incident requires immediate action to overrun all vulnerable areas before they can be sufficiently strengthened, then the Kremlin will probably call for a quiet period. If the Korean venture backfires on the Kremlin, then the minimum reaction will probably be instigation of all possible pressure tactics to divert world and internal Soviet attention from the Korean failure. Finally, if, as is more probable, hostilities in Korea are prolonged, the USSR might use Chinese Communist troops in Korea or possibly elsewhere in Asia, to engage the West in exorbitantly costly Far Eastern operations without directly involving Soviet forces. The likelihood of the Kremlin undertaking another Korean-type venture or aggression by some other short-of-war techniques in other peripheral areas will depend largely on local Soviet-Communist capabilities, and prospects for local resistance as well as UN and US reaction.

Note: This memorandum has not been coordinated with the intelligence organizations of the Departments of State, Army, Navy, and the Air Force.

7/10/50—DCI authorized addtl dissem by ORE to Dept of State

Document No.

NO CHANGE IN Class.

DECLASSIFIED

CLASS. CHANGED TO: TS S C

~~SECRET~~

Auth: DDA

Date:

~~CONFIDENTIAL~~

DOCUMENT NO. 1

NO CHANGE IN CLASS. ☐
☐ DECLASSIFIED
CLASS. CHANGED TO: TS S (C)
NEXT REVIEW DATE:
AUTH: HR 70-2
DATE: 30 Jan 80   REVIEWER: 006514

177. *(Continued)*

In Korea, the USSR is determined to continue the present attack and Chinese Communist forces may participate to whatever extent is necessary. Such Communist Chinese participation may be overt, under the pretext of North Korean "invitation" or the Chinese Communist troops may be advertised as "volunteers." In any event, the Soviet objective in Korea will be to make the situation as costly to the US, and as damaging to US prestige, as possible.

The Kremlin may welcome the resulting involvement of the US with the Peiping regime. The USSR may seek to encourage the gradual extension of such US involvement by precipitating incidents in Southeast Asia and elsewhere which will draw the US into costly, difficult, and embarrassing situations.

The USSR will continue to furnish substantial supplies and equipment, including air and naval craft, to the North Koreans, and perhaps later to its other Asiatic puppets. The USSR may also contribute to the North Koreans by supplying "volunteers," in aviation, technical, and advisory capacities.

1. **Vulnerable Areas.**

The main areas vulnerable to Soviet-Communist aggression short of employment of Soviet military forces are, in order of probability: Iran, Yugoslavia, Indochina (Southeast Asia), Turkey, Greece, Germany, and Austria. Other vulnerable points are Formosa and Hong Kong.

A. **Iran.**

The USSR has sufficient troops on the Soviet-Iranian border to take over Iran without warning. The pro-Soviet Tudeh Party and other subversive elements both within and outside Iran are capable of creating serious disturbances, but the Iranian armed forces are believed able to cope with such a development. Nevertheless, the Kremlin might use these disorders, particularly in the northern areas, to invoke the 1921 Irano-Soviet Treaty and, under the pretext that Soviet security was endangered, launch an invasion of Iran. The frequency with which the USSR implies that it may have to invoke the treaty and the almost constant troop movements and Soviet feints in the border area make it impossible to detect accurately when this activity may presage an actual invasion.

- 2 -

B. <u>Yugoslavia</u>

There is no evidence available to indicate that there are sufficient Soviet-Satellite forces present in the Balkans to launch a full-scale military attack on Yugoslavia with any prospect of success. Immediate and forceful Western reaction to the Soviet-directed invasion of Southern Korea has greatly increased the likelihood that an attack on Yugoslavia would evoke at least an equally strong Western reaction with a greater risk of general war, which the Kremlin considers undesireable at this time.

The USSR, however, will probably push its efforts to overthrow the Tito Government by all means short of open aggression. Widespread peasant and labor disaffection in Yugoslavia as well as virulent regional antagonisms afford the Kremlin considerable potentialities for the creation of internal disorder and/or guerrilla incursions. Yugoslav popular sentiment against Communism and the USSR is so strong as to suggest that the Cominform will attempt to camouflage much of its activities against the regime under the guise of existing anti-Communist currents. The strength and reliability of the Yugoslav security forces, however, are estimated to be adequate to control any probable increase in such activities in the near future. Meanwhile, the widespread training of guerrillas in adjacent Satellites points to an increase in border activity and incidents.

177. *(Continued)*

~~SECRET~~
~~CONFIDENTIAL~~

C. The Far East

In any Soviet aggression in the Far East, the Chinese Communist forces will be the primary instrument of the Kremlin. The Peiping regime now has a total of some two million experienced combat troops, and an estimated one and one-half million of these troops can be committed to action in mainland Asia and against the island of Taiwan. Taiwan is the Chinese Communists' sole remaining major military objective in the conquest of China, and even before the recent US policy statement regarding Taiwan, Peiping estimated that one million troops might be necessary for the capture of the island. The present US defense of Taiwan makes it unlikely that the Communists will attempt an invasion at this time.

Soviet aggression in Southeast Asia will probably for the most part be confined to an increase in present support of local Communist guerrilla activities. Stepping up guerrilla warfare in Indochina, the Philippines, Malaya, and Burma will necessitate a substantial increase in materiel and assistance, which would have to be provided primarily by China. The Chinese Communists, however, might also contribute experienced troops, probably camouflaged as nationals of the country concerned, to support Southeast Asian Communists.

In addition to continuing the present guerrilla warfare, Communists will probably encourage increased labor unrest and sabotage in Malaya (including Singapore), Burma, Thailand, the Philippines, and Indonesia.

The principal deterrents to Chinese Communists military action in Southeast Asia against Indochina and Burma are the risk of provoking global war and the anti-Chinese feeling widely prevalent in the area and the relatively severe logistical problem. In the special case of Hong Kong, an additional deterrent is the presence of UK troops. The Chinese Communists are capable of taking the island of Macao at will.

~~CONFIDENTIAL~~

- 4 -

~~SECRET~~

~~CONFIDENTIAL~~

D. <u>Turkey</u>

The USSR can obtain control of Turkey only by direct military action. There is no subversive element in Turkey strong enough to bring about revolution or civil war; there is no group of Turks outside the country which the Kremlin could successfully exploit for the invasion of Turkey in the Korean pattern; the Turkish Government and people are determined to resist any act of aggression. Reports of troop movements in the Balkans and of projected maneuvers in the Black Sea, the recent departure of the Soviet Ambassador and other Soviet and Satellite diplomats from Turkey, together with sharply increased Bulgarian radio and press fulminations against Turkey indicate the possibility of a Bulgarian invasion of Turkish Thrace. Sooner or later, however, Soviet troops would have to be dispatched to assist the Bulgarians, and the Kremlin, realizing that a Soviet attack on Turkey would probably precipitate a global war, is considered to be unwilling to embark on such a course at this time.

~~CONFIDENTIAL~~

- 5 -

177. *(Continued)*

E. Greece.

Soviet-inspired aggression against Greece, direct or indirect, does not appear imminent. Even in the improbable event that the Soviet bloc is willing to risk the near-certainty of global war by directly attacking a country so closely tied to the US, a military offensive against Greece would probably come only as part of (or following) an attack on the strategically more important target of Yugoslavia. A more likely development would be a renewal of the guerrilla campaign, which might seriously burden Greece next fall or winter, when the Greek Army's demobilization is scheduled to be completed and when as many as 20,000 combat-fit guerrilla reserves may be available in the satellite states. At present, however, a new guerrilla campaign would have only limited direct effects on Greek internal security, because guerrilla reserves are low and Greek Army preparedness is at a relatively high level.

- 6 -

177. *(Continued)*

F. Germany and Austria

In both Germany and Austria, the USSR is able to take short-of-war measures which could cause a dispersal of US efforts and contribute heavily to the Soviet "war of nerves." Local border clashes between East and West German police forces will probably take place. These would have a nuisance value, but would not directly involve either Soviet or US forces. Strong provocative action can be expected in Berlin both by Soviet troops and by German paramilitary formations in the form of interference with public utilities and with East-West communications. Such interference with communications would tie up substantial numbers of US aircraft and require a high degree of US concentration on the Berlin situation. In addition, Soviet action in Berlin in the light of the current tense situation would sufficiently alarm the West Berlin population to cause serious unrest and produce adverse effects on the already unstable economy of the Western sectors of the city.

Minor steps by the Soviet occupation forces in Austria to interfere with the Western position in Vienna are probable primarily for their diversionary value and their contribution to the Soviet war of nerves. The USSR is unlikely to take action against public utilities and communications, which would reach the proportions of a blockade of Vienna, because such a blockade would result in a partion of Austria, which the Kremlin does not desire at this time.

- 7 -

178. Daily Summary Excerpt, 6 July 1950, Views of Hong Kong Residents on Korean Problem

57

24938

~~TOP SECRET~~

~~CONFIDENTIAL~~

8 JUL 1950

1334

2. <u>Views of Hong Kong residents on Korean problem</u>--US Consul General Rankin in Hong Kong reports that the initial hearty approval among Hong Kong residents of US and UN action regarding Korea is now being followed by sober realization that the conflict may spread. Rankin adds that local Chinese feel that the Chinese Communists probably will not attack the US 7th Fleet guarding Formosa but that Communist forces will be used in North Korea if the fighting goes against the North Koreans. The Consul General comments that another possible Chinese Communist action could be against Burma, which Hong Kong Chinese consider to be a push-over for the three Communist divisions now on the Sino-Burma border. Rankin also expresses the opinion that a direct attack on the Crown Colony by the Chinese Communists cannot be ruled out since there are nearly 100,000 Communist troops massing in the Canton area with only half of them scheduled to move north.

CIA-S

- 1 -

004

~~CONFIDENTIAL~~

~~TOP SECRET~~

235038/1

178. *(Continued)*

(CIA Comment: The Chinese Communist forces are fully capable of launching military operations against Taiwan, Korea, Hong Kong, and Southeast Asia simultaneously but they are not likely to undertake such aggressive action unless specifically directed to do so by the Kremlin. The USSR, which is currently maintaining an official aloofness from the Korean situation and which is considered to be reluctant to undertake a global conflict at this time, is not likely to encourage military ventures by the Chinese Communists outside their borders where Western military forces would be encountered until the outcome of the present conflict in Korea becomes more apparent. The Chinese Communists, however, are capable of rendering Hong Kong virtually untenable to the UK through a program of economic boycott, sabotage, and strikes which could be initiated at any time.)

- 2 -

24939   57   7 JUL 1950

T O ~~CONFIDENTIAL~~ R E T   1335

KOREA

1. <u>Invaders' momentum undiminished</u>--US troop actions have failed to date in slowing the momentum of the North Korean attack and the weight of the invaders' offensive indicates that their immediate objective is the speedy defeat of all defending forces in South Korea. The tactical skill and resourcefulness of the attacking forces is probably the result of intensive and thorough training, plus the presence of Korean combat veterans who served with the Chinese Communist Manchurian armies and a considerable number of Soviet military advisers. In addition, the North Korean forces probably contain many Korean combat veterans who served with Soviet forces in major combat operations, such as, the defense of Stalingrad. Latest information indicates that 150 South Korean Assemblymen were able to escape from Seoul and report to their Government. The missing 60 Assemblymen, who apparently remained in Seoul voluntarily, include virtually all the middle-of-the-roaders. This group offers the invaders their best opportunity to set up a "legitimate" facade for any provisional government in the occupied areas.

ments

- 1 -

Document No. _005_
NO CHANGE in Class. ☐
☐ DECLASSIFIED
Class. CHANGED TO: TS   S Ⓒ
     DDA Memo, 4 Apr 77
Auth: DDA REG. 77/1763
Date: 3 0 MAR 1978 By: _023_

235038/1

180. Weekly Summary Excerpt, 7 July 1950, The Korean Situation: Soviet Intentions and Capabilities

THE KOREAN SITUATION

Soviet Intentions and Capabilities

Two weeks after the beginning of hostilities in Korea, the world was still waiting for some firm indication of Soviet intentions regarding not only Korea but other countries on the Soviet periphery. It became clear, however, that the North Koreans were not to be intimidated by US involvement in the fighting and that the all-out effort to overrun South Korea would continue unabated. As long as the North Korean advance continues, the USSR can remain aloof; the crucial moment will come when and if the battle turns in favor of US and South Korean forces. At that time, the USSR must decide whether to permit a North Korean defeat or to take whatever steps are necessary to prolong the action.

Soviet Intentions   At the moment, the Soviet and Communist propaganda line offers no clue regarding Soviet intentions. Soviet propagandists would have no difficulty in using the present line as a basis either for withdrawal from South Korea or for prolongation of hostilities, even including armed action in other areas. The key to the fateful Soviet decision will be the extent to which the USSR desires to risk instigating global war. All evidence available leads to the conclusion that the USSR is not ready for war. Nevertheless, the USSR has substantial capabilities, without directly involving Soviet troops, for prolonging the fighting in Korea, as well as for initiating hostilities elsewhere. Thus, although the USSR would prefer to confine the conflict to Korea, a reversal there might impel the USSR to take greater risks of starting a global war either by committing substantial Chinese Communist forces in Korea or by sanctioning aggressive actions by Satellite forces in other areas

- 2 -

180. *(Continued)*

of the world. The decisiveness of the US reaction to the Korean invasion will thus cause the Kremlin to move cautiously, but the danger still exists that the USSR, as it did two weeks ago, will again miscalculate the Western reaction to any future moves it may feel are necessary.

The Far East   The Korean invasion has had its most immediate and compelling impact on the Far East, particularly as it has affected international Communist intentions to speed the expansion of Communism throughout the area through the instrumentality of the Peiping regime. Pending clarification of the Soviet position, the Peiping regime has not yet committed itself and, as far as Korea is concerned, will probably not take any action at least as long as North Korean forces continue to advance. Meanwhile, Chinese Communist troop strength and dispositions would permit military aggression in a number of places with little or no warning, and the Peiping regime can be expected to give strong support to guerrilla activities and subversion throughout Southeast Asia.

Military Potential   The Korean invasion has produced a deluge of reports of Chinese Communist troop movements indicating a Chinese intent to support the North Korean invasion. Most of these reports, however, have emanated from Chinese Nationalist sources and are merely propaganda for US consumption. Actually, the Communists are apparently still strengthening their forces opposite Taiwan, and possibly Hong Kong, and no significant changes have occurred in troop dispositions along Southeast Asian frontiers. Reported movements of large troop formations from South and Central China toward the Northeast are largely discounted. Communist troops already in North China and Manchuria are sufficient to provide substantial support to the North Koreans and of these approximately 40-50,000

- 3 -

180. *(Continued)*

are of Korean nationality. Despite these reported troop movements and Chinese Communist capability to launch simultaneous and successful military actions in Korea, Hong Kong, Macao, and Indochina, no immediate action is expected. With regard to Taiwan, the US committment to defend the island has almost certainly delayed the invasion timetable if only because it will make occupation of the is-land too costly an operation for the Peiping regime to under-take without outside assistance.

Non-military Action   Meanwhile, the Chinese Communist regime will continue and probably increase its efforts short of military aggression to further the spread of Communism throughout Southeast Asia. Political sup-port and military supplies will be granted Ho Chi Minh's forces in Indochina, efforts will be made to strengthen the insurgent movement in Malaya, and the tempo of organizational activity among labor and political groups will be stepped up. In this campaign, efforts by the Peiping regime to use the nine million Overseas Chinese will be impeded by its recent loss of popu-larity at home and a growing anticipation in Overseas Chinese communities that the spread of Communism may be reversed as a result of US action in Korea. An intensification of Peiping's efforts to gain control of the Overseas Chinese may well lead to a split which, while reducing the exploitability of the Overseas Chinese as instruments for extending Chinese Communist influence, may also result in the adoption of more militant tactics by the pro-Communist faction. An immediately explosive situation in South-east Asia, however, derives from the presence in northern Burma of approximately 2,000 Chinese Nationalist troops. The Peiping regime has demanded their internment, the Burmese Government is ap-parently incapable of doing so, and the Chinese Communists thus have a legal "excuse" for carrying out local or major military operations in Burma.

- 4 -

~~SECRET~~

CENTRAL INTELLIGENCE AGENCY

INTELLIGENCE MEMORANDUM NO. 302

63

8 July 1950

SUBJECT: Consequences of the Korean Incident

I. <u>Soviet Purposes in Launching the Northern Korean Attack.</u>

A. Apart from immediate strategic advantages, the basic Soviet objectives in launching the Northern Korean attack probably were to: (1) test the strength of US commitments implicit in the policy of containment of Communist expansion; and (2) gain political advantages for the further expansion of Communism in both Asia and Europe by undermining the confidence of non-Communist states in the value of US support.

B. The Soviet estimate of the reaction to the North Korean attack was probably that: (1) UN action would be slow and cumbersome; (2) the US would not intervene with its own forces; (3) South Korea would therefore collapse promptly, presenting the UN with a fait accompli; (4) the episode would therefore be completely localized; and (5) the fighting could be portrayed as US-instigated South Korean aggression and the North Korean victory as a victory of Asiatic nationalism against Western colonialism.

II. <u>Probable Developments from the Korean Incident.</u>

There are at present four major alternative courses of action open to the USSR. They are not mutually exclusive courses of action. In particular, it is estimated that the USSR is very likely to try to prolong the fighting in Korea(alternative "B" below) for the short run and then within a few weeks or months, if conditions appear favorable to Soviet leaders, shift to the more aggressive course of creating similar incidents elsewhere (alternative"C" below). The alternatives are examined not in order of probability, but in order of increasing risk of global war and increasing expenditure of effort on the part of the USSR:

<u>Alternative A.</u>   The USSR may localize the Korean fighting, permitting US forces to drive the North Koreans back to the 38th Parallel and refrain from creating similar incidents elsewhere. In the meantime, the USSR would remain uncommitted in Korea and would develop the propaganda themes of US aggression and imperialistic interference in domestic affairs of an Asiatic nation.

Note: This memorandum has not been coordinated with the intelligence organizations of the Departments of State, Army, Navy, and the Air Force.

Document No. 001
NO CHANGE in Class. ☐
☒ DECLASSIFIED
Class. CHANGED TO: TS S C
EDA Memo, 4 Apr 77
Auth: DDA REG. 77/1763
Date: 5/1/78 By: 023

F-51

SECRET

1. This alternative is the most cautious course for the USSR to take. Its adoption would indicate complete surprise at the US reaction to the Korean incident and would suggest strongly that the USSR was unwilling to run even a minimum risk of provoking a global conflict involving the US and the USSR.

2. US prestige and political influence would be substantially augmented, particularly with Western European allies and other nations aligned with the US.

3. Soviet prestige and influence would be damaged, but there would be compensations in the form of secondary political gains that would accrue as a result of:
   (a) promoting the "peace campaign" and portraying the US as military aggressor;
   (b) exploiting the theme of Asian nationalism versus Western imperialism;
   (c) maintaining the North Korean and Chinese Communist threat to South Korea as an embarrassment to development of a constructive US or UN policy in Korea.

4. This alternative course of action is unlikely; Soviet advantages would be secondary, comparatively long-range, and intangible, while Soviet disadvantages would be immediate.

Alternative B. The USSR may localize the Korean fighting, still refrain from creating similar incidents elsewhere, but in order to prolong US involvement in Korea, give increasing material aid to the North Koreans, perhaps employing Chinese Communist troops, either covertly or overtly. The USSR would remain uncommitted in Korea and would develop the propaganda themes of US aggression and imperialistic interference in domestic affairs of an Asiatic nation.

1. This alternative is a moderately cautious course for the USSR to take. The USSR would probably consider that its adoption would involve only a slight risk of provoking a global conflict involving the US and the USSR.

2. US prestige would be seriously damaged if the USSR succeeded in prolonging the incident in this way. Western European allies and other nations aligned with the US would question the immediate military value of US commitments even though expecting them to be honored.

3. Soviet prestige would be augmented if the fighting in Korea were prolonged without an open Soviet commitment.

-2-

SECRET

181. *(Continued)*

4. The USSR would obtain appreciable secondary, comparatively long-range gains in political influence as a result of promoting the "peace campaign" and portraying US as imperialistic Western aggressor in Asia, unless successfully countered by a US "Truth" campaign.

5. Deep involvement of US military forces in Korea would seriously limit US capabilities to support similar commitments elsewhere. Moreover, the Western European allies of the US would feel dangerously exposed for some time (even if the US began a partial mobiliazation for war).

6. The USSR probably will adopt this alternative course of action at least for the short run, since there would be few Soviet disadvantages or risks and the Soviet gains would be appreciable.

7. This alternative will appear especially attractive to the USSR because at any time, if conditions appeared favorable to Soviet leaders, the USSR could shift to the more ambitious program (alternative "C", immediately below), in which alternative "B" would merely be a first phase.

Alternative C. The USSR, while attempting to prolong the fighting in Korea as in alternative "B", may also attempt to disperse and perhaps overstrain US military forces-in-readiness by creating a series of incidents similar to the Korean affair. Without directly and openly involving Soviet forces, such incidents could be created in Formosa, Indochina, Burma, Iran, Yugoslavia, and Greece. The effects of such incidents could be aggravated by renewed pressure on Berlin and, possibly, Vienna.

1. This alternative would be a comparatively aggressive course for the USSR to take. Its adoption would indicate willingness to run an appreciable risk of provoking a global conflict because of the possible US reaction. The USSR could easily turn to this alternative at any time, but it is not likely to turn to it until the USSR has fully analyzed the implications of the US commitment in Korea.

2. Having employed its armed forces in support of its commitment in Korea, the US will have to honor similar commitments or lose most of the advantages of the policy of supporting the Korean commitment.

3. The US does not have the military forces-in-readiness to honor its commitments with US military forces and equipment in many areas other than Korea (perhaps none) without a substantial increase in US military forces and industrial productivity in the military field, bringing about what would amount to at least a partial (as distinguished from a general) mobilization for war.

- 3 -

181. *(Continued)*

4. Deep involvement of US military forces in the Far East or Near East would leave Western Europe even more dangerously exposed than at present.

5. At some point further Korean-style incidents (requiring the commitment of US forces to stabilize the situation) presumably would force the US to adopt one of the following alternatives:

(a) revise the policy of general containment by limiting US commitments and by planning to combat Soviet aggression only at those selected points where existing US military strength would permit;

(b) begin partial military and industrial mobilization in an attempt to enable the US to combat any further Soviet-sponsored aggression anywhere in the world; or

(c) begin total mobilization to enable the US to threaten to meet any Soviet or Soviet-sponsored aggression with war against the USSR.

6. The USSR probably will adopt alternative "C" sooner or later if Soviet leaders do not estimate the risk of global war involved to be substantial or are prepared for a global war if it develops.

7. If Soviet development of this alternative course of action leads to a general US mobilization, it appears at this time that the USSR probably would in that event continue limited aggressions, accompanied by the customary "peace" propaganda, discounting actual US initiation of a general war and perhaps estimating that the political and economic strains of mobilization would weaken or discredit the US and its foreign policy. The USSR, however, may:

(a) desist from further aggression of the Korean type, fearing a global war and taking mobilization as an indication of greater risk than Soviet leaders had anticipated in choosing this course of action; or

(b) expecting US-initiated global war, attempt to seize the initiative by immediately attacking the US (in effect turning to alternative "D", below).

Alternative D. The USSR may consider US intervention in Korea either as the prelude of an inevitable global war or as justification for beginning a global war for which it is prepared—in either case immediately attacking the US and its allies.

-4-

181. *(Continued)*

1. Nothing in the Korean situation as yet indicates that the USSR would deliberately decide to employ Soviet forces in direct military action precipitating global war. Such a decision is unlikely if, as now seems probable, Soviet leaders believe that:

(a) there are continuing opportunities to expand Soviet influence by the comparatively cheap and safe means of Soviet-controlled Communist revolutionary activity (including propaganda, sabotage, subversion, guerrilla warfare, and organized military action by local Communist troops—as in Korea), which can be supported by Soviet diplomacy and the mere threat of Soviet military strength-in-readiness; and

(b) there is substantial risk involved for the USSR in the global war that almost certainly would ensue from direct military action by Soviet forces.

2. The USSR would appear to have little reason to be pessimistic about gains by methods short of global war, particularly by adopting the courses of action described in Alternatives "B" and "C" above.

3. The USSR is unlikely to choose the alternative of deliberately provoking global war at this time in view of: (a) the general superiority of the US and its allies in total power-potential; and (b) the fact that the present Soviet atomic capability is insufficient to neutralize US atomic retaliatory capabilities and to offset the generally superior power-potential of the US and its allies by interfering with the US military and industrial mobilization.

III. Effects of a Failure of US Forces to Hold South Korea.

A. The immediate consequences of a failure to hold South Korea would be a damaging blow to US prestige with loss in political influence greater than the loss that would have been incurred if the US had not undertaken to support its moral commitment in South Korea.

B. The US would be confronted with a choice between two undesirable alternatives: (1) accepting the loss of US prestige; or (2) attempting to regain as much prestige as possible by committing substantial US military resources in a difficult and costly invasion of an area which is not of primary strategic importance to the over-all US military position. In either case US foreign policy and military capabilities would be discredited at home and abroad.

C. If US forces were expelled from Korea, the USSR would probably adopt alternative "C" as described above (Section II). It might be tempted, however, to postpone further aggressive action elsewhere until it had determined whether, as a result of the loss of world confidence in the effectiveness of US aid, other areas might not be brought within its sphere of influence through intimidation alone.

~~TOP SECRET~~
~~CONFIDENTIAL~~

#32391

CENTRAL INTELLIGENCE AGENCY

86

INTELLIGENCE MEMORANDUM NO. 304   10 July 1950

SUBJECT: Effects of a Voluntary Withdrawal of US Forces from Korea.

Reference: IM 302, 8 July 1950, "Consequences of the Korean
Incident."

CONCLUSIONS

Voluntary withdrawal of US forces from Korea would be a calamity,
seriously handicapping efforts to maintain US alliances and build political
influence among the nations on whose strength and energetic cooperation
the policy of containment of Soviet-Communist expansion depends. It would
discredit US foreign policy and undermine confidence in US military
capabilities. Voluntary withdrawal would be more damaging than a failure
to send US troops to Korea in the first place or than a failure of US
forces to hold Korea. Not only would US commitments be shown to be unreliable when put to a severe test, but also considerable doubt would be
cast on the ability of the US to back up its commitments with military
force.

DISCUSSION

1. US withdrawal from intervention in Korea on behalf of the UN,
especially since UN action resulted mainly from US initiative, would disillusion all nations heretofore hopeful that US leadership within the
framework of the UN could preserve world peace. As a voluntary act of the
US, a withdrawal would damage US standing in UN affairs and would undermine the effectiveness of the UN as a device for mobilizing Western resistance to Soviet-Communist aggression.

2. The Western European allies and other nations closely aligned
with the US would lose confidence in the military value of US commitments
to assist them against armed aggression. This lack of confidence would
militate against energetic measures to oppose the expansion of Soviet-
Communism through the NATO and MDAP programs. Although some slight credit

Note: This memorandum has not been coordinated with the intelligence
organizations of the Departments of State, Army, Navy, and the
Air Force.

DOCUMENT NO.
NO CHANGE IN CLASS. ☐
☐ DECLASSIFIED
CLASS. CHANGED TO: TS S © 1990
NEXT REVIEW DATE:
AUTH: HR 70-2
DATE: 3 Jan 90 REVIEWER: 006514

VOID

023

~~TOP SECRET~~ CONFIDENTIAL

182. *(Continued)*

still might accrue to the US for initially attempting to honor its commitment in South Korea, most of the nations allied or aligned with the US are more concerned about US ability to counter threats of Soviet aggression than about US intentions to do so.

3. Pro-US governments, particularly in areas where the USSR could initiate limited military aggressions without openly using Soviet forces, would suffer serious losses of prestige. In some cases they might lose political control of the country or feel compelled to seek an accommodation with the USSR (for example, Indochina, Iran).

4. Whether or not US forces withdraw from Korea, the USSR has the capability of creating a series of incidents generally similar to the Korean affair, each one threatening either to bankrupt the US policy of containing Soviet expansion or to disperse and overstrain US military forces-in-readiness. Without directly and openly involving Soviet forces, such incidents could be created in Formosa, Indochina, Burma, Iran, Yugoslavia, Greece, and Turkey. The USSR will proceed with limited aggressions similar to the Korean incident if it does not estimate the risk of global war to be substantial or is prepared for a global war if it develops. Voluntary US withdrawal from Korea probably would encourage rather than discourage Soviet initiation of limited wars in other areas.

5. Upon withdrawal from Korea or certainly after another Korean-style incident, the US presumably would be forced to adopt one of the three following alternatives:

    (a) Drastically revise the policy of general containment by reducing or limiting US commitments and by planning to combat Soviet-inspired aggression only at selected points where existing military strength would be adequate for the task;

    (b) Begin partial military and industrial mobilization in an attempt to enable the US to combat any further Soviet-inspired aggression anywhere in the world; or,

    (c) Begin total mobilization to enable the US to threaten to meet any Soviet or Soviet-sponsored aggression with war against the USSR.

6. If the US, under the pressure of Soviet-sponsored aggressions, did not drastically revise the policy of general containment but began mobilization on a fairly large scale, it would be politically and

182. *(Continued)*

~~CONFIDENTIAL~~

psychologically more advantageous for the US to mobilize in support of US and UN intervention in Korea rather than to mobilize after a voluntary withdrawal from Korea.

 (a) US mobilization after a voluntary withdrawal of US forces from Korea would do little to reduce the disillusion and defeatism that would spread in the Western world as a consequence of the withdrawal itself. While this disillusion and defeatism might not be fatal, it would seriously handicap military, political, and economic efforts to strengthen the North Atlantic community.

 (b) If the US should withdraw its forces from Korea and then begin partial mobilization, Soviet leaders would be more likely to anticipate war aimed directly at the USSR than if the mobilization were begun in support of the UN intervention in Korea. It is possible that the USSR, if it should anticipate global war, would try to seize the initiative by attacking the US.

- 3 -

183. Daily Summary Excerpt, 12 July 1950, Possible Assault on Taiwan

57

24943 ~~TOP CONFIDENTIAL~~ 1339

1 JUL 1950

2. <u>Possible Assault on Taiwan</u>--US Embassy Saigon transmits a US Army report that the Chinese Communist Government is planning an attack on Taiwan "around 15 July" and that the attack may coincide with an uprising on the island. As supporting evidence the report points to: (1) recent troop movements and concentrations in East China; (2) preparations of Chinese mainland airfields and the arrival of aircraft and personnel needed for airborne operations; (3) recent declarations regarding Taiwan by Chinese Foreign Minister Chou En-lai; (4) a reported journey to Moscow by Mao Tse-tung on 4 July; (5) a recent Nationalist purge on Taiwan which source believes will strengthen opposition to Chiang Kai-shek; and (6) the extent of the US involvement in Korea, which source

CIA/S

- 1 -

~~CONFIDENTIAL~~
~~TOP SECRET~~

183. *(Continued)*

T O P   S E C R E T

feels increases prospects for the success of an early
attack on Taiwan.

    (CIA Comment: CIA has no information regarding
a second Moscow trip by Mao nor is there any available
evidence supporting the report that Communist China has
selected 15 July to invade Taiwan. However, an analysis
of recent Chinese Communist troop movements, propaganda
and press comment indicates that the Peiping regime may
now be capable of launching an assault against Taiwan.)

- 2 -

CONFIDENTIAL

184. Weekly Summary Excerpt, 14 July 1950, Communist China's Role

COMMUNIST CHINA'S ROLE

As it becomes more apparent that the fighting in Korea will be prolonged, the military capabilities of the Chinese Communists, as well as Soviet intentions regarding the use of these capabilities, provide the principal key to the outcome of the fighting in Korea and to whether the fighting will spread to other areas of the Far East. Before the US action in Korea, the Chinese Communists were believed capable of launching, individually or simultaneously, successful military action against Korea, Hong Kong and Macao, or Indochina; a Chinese Communist invasion of Taiwan, though costly, was also considered within Communist capabilities. Events since then, however, have affected Chinese Communist capabilities for action in the three key areas of Korea, Taiwan, and Indochina, and have raised new political and strategic problems regarding the use of Chinese Communist military forces in these areas.

Aid to Korea   The USSR will be confronted with a difficult problem if forced to decide whether to permit a North Korean defeat or to use Chinese Communist troops to win or prolong the struggle indefinitely. Although a North Korean defeat would have obvious disadvantages, the commitment of Chinese Communist forces would not necessarily prevent such a defeat and a defeat under these circumstances would be far more disastrous, not only because it would be a greater blow to Soviet prestige throughout the world, but because it would seriously threaten Soviet control over the Chinese Communist regime. Even a victory in Korea through the use of Chinese Communist troops would have its disadvantages for the Kremlin. The presence of Chinese Communist troops in Korea would complicate if not jeopardize Soviet direction of Korean affairs; Chinese Communist prestige, as opposed to that of the USSR, would be enhanced; and Peiping might be tempted as a result of success in Korea

- 9 -

184. *(Continued)*

SECRET

to challenge Soviet leadership in Asia. In addition to these purely internal difficulties, the use of Chinese Communist forces in Korea would increase the risk of global war, not only because of possible UN or US reaction but because the USSR itself would be under greater compulsion to assure a victory in Korea, possibly by committing Soviet troops.

Taiwan Invasion   The principal problems confronting the Kremlin in deciding whether to permit an invasion of Taiwan are the nature and extent of US reaction and the risk of global war precipitated because of the spread of Communist military aggression. Several factors may lead to a decision to launch an assault on Taiwan before the typhoon season in late August. Recent evidence indicates that Chinese Communist forces are poised for the invasion and available land, sea and air forces may now be capable of launching a successful assault. If a sizeable beachhead is established, the resultant panic in Nationalist ranks might well induce desertions and snowballing defections sufficient to cause a virtual collapse of organized Nationalist resistance. The Peiping regime is already publicly committed to the Taiwan operation and the operation would not divert forces which might be needed in Korea. In addition, the USSR may reason that US support of Taiwan would gain less international support than the defense of South Korea and that the invasion should be undertaken before the US can reinforce its "neutralization" forces in the Formosa Strait. Despite these favorable considerations the fact remains that an invasion of Taiwan would be an immensely costly operation with the resulting political and strategic advantages balanced by the increased risk of precipitating a global war which it is believed the USSR does not presently desire.

- 10 -

SECRET

184. *(Continued)*

Support for Indochina   Indochina offers the Chinese Communists their greatest opportunity
for expanding Communist influence in Asia with the minimum
military or political risks. From a military viewpoint, the
Indochina conflict has been a stalemate. Despite considerable
successes, the French have been unable fully to capitalize on
their superiority in equipment and manpower because of the
essentially guerrilla nature of the fighting and the terrain
which prevents large-scale operations. Given equipment and
supplies similar to that of the French, the forces of Ho Chi-
Minh could shift the course of the present inconclusive warfare
in their favor. The Chinese Communists have the capabilities
to supply the material needed by Ho Chi-Minh and may be expected to step up such assistance in the immediate future.

- 11 -

SECRET

POSSIBILITY OF SOVIET AGGRESSION AGAINST IRAN

27 July 1950

Conclusion

Unless the Soviet Union definitely modifies what appears to have been its previous policy of abstaining from open military action by Soviet forces, it seems probable that the USSR will not attack Iran but will intensify its efforts to build up subversive forces within Iran and to weaken the country by means of propaganda, border activities, and diplomatic pressure. (NOTE: The basic question of general Soviet intentions with respect to the open military action is not discussed here.)

Discussion

1. Recent reports of increased activity along the Iranian border have obscured the fact that, for almost four years, Soviet forces have been in a position to overrun Iran without warning. In view of the advantages that would have accrued to the USSR from the acquisition of Iran and of the means at its disposal for cloaking aggressive action in a semblance of legality, it seems reasonable to assume that the USSR has been reluctant to employ its own troops in direct aggression. Although in attacking Iran, the USSR could make initially effective use of Iranians-in-exile, Soviet Azerbaijanis, and disaffected elements within Iran, Soviet troops would also have to be used--a condition that does not apply in other sensitive areas such as Formosa, Southeast Asia, and the Balkans.

2. Soviet domination of Iran would give the USSR important advantages:

   a. The extension of the Soviet frontiers to Iraq and Pakistan would facilitate penetration of the Near East and the Indian subcontinent.

SECRET

185. *(Continued)*

b. The USSR would also be in a more favorable position for extending its control over these areas in the event of global war.

c. The USSR would have access to Iran's great oil resources.

d. The US would be denied an important potential base of operations against the USSR. Conversely, the USSR would obtain buffer territory between its vital Baku oil fields and the bases from which Baku might be attacked.

3. If the USSR were to decide upon an invasion of Iran, it would have open to it several courses which would, either singly or in combination, have the effect of cloaking its action with a semblance of legality. It could:

a. Set out to "liberate" Iranian Azerbaijan with a "volunteer" army of Iranians-in-exile and Soviet Azerbaijanis. Clashes between the invaders and the Iranian armed forces would provoke the USSR to send in troops allegedly to restore order. The Soviet forces could overrun northern Iran in a few days and the entire country shortly thereafter.

b. Create provocative border incidents and instigate disturbances in northern Iran through the use of such elements as Soviet agents, dissident Kurdish factions, or Tudeh Party members. Claiming that such disorders jeopardized Soviet security, the USSR would send in troops to restore order as in para. a. above.

c. Invade Iran with Soviet troops under the pretext that, in violation of the 1921 Irano-Soviet Treaty of Friendship, US activities in Iran were making that country a base for attack on the USSR by a third power. Recent Soviet notes have made this allegation and have requested Iran to rectify the situation. The treaty provides that if Iran is unable to comply with such a request, the USSR may intervene.

- 2 -

423

185. *(Continued)*

4. Past Soviet attempts to subjugate Iran through subversion and intimidation achieved little success, and the present government is firmly committed to a policy of withstanding Soviet threats and pressures and of maintaining a pro-US alignment. If, however, Iran loses confidence in the ability of the US to fulfill its commitments or comes to believe that the US has little interest in the preservation of Iranian independence, the Iranian Government may feel compelled to seek an accord with the USSR or at least to attempt a course of neutrality. In either case, the USSR would be in a greatly improved position for taking over the country without the use of force.

- 3 -

SECRET

SOVIET/SATELLITE INTENTIONS

As the USSR and its Satellites continued to talk loudly of "peace" and the warlike intentions of the Western "imperialists," there was no slackening of reports that the USSR itself was preparing to initiate further aggressive moves around the Soviet perimeter. Although possessing the capability to move militarily in a number of places with little advance warning, with the possible exception of continued preparations for an attack on Taiwan, the USSR has not yet given any firm indication of its intention to expand the Korean conflict and increase the risk of global warfare involving the Soviet Union. Meanwhile, Soviet diplomatic activity was aimed primarily at South Asia and the Soviet Far East.

Korean Support   Although there has been no evidence of troop movements from Manchuria into northern Korea since the outbreak of hostilities, North Korean forces may soon be reinforced by Korean veterans of the Chinese Communist Army. Within the next three weeks, North Korean forces will probably have made the maximum advance possible with the troops currently available in Korea. If the USSR desires a quick victory before UN forces are further reinforced, it will have to call upon additional experienced troops for use in Korea. Although the North Koreans may have committed practically all their available organized and trained units merely to achieve a quick victory regardless of the risk, it seems more probable that the Northern Command has been assured of reinforcements. Such reinforcements would at the minimum consist of the 40-50,000 Koreans believed to be available in Manchuria and would be used to replace the heavy casualties resulting from the rapid North Korean advance, to cover the exposed flanks and rear, and, if necessary, to provide momentum for the final push against reinforced UN troops. The USSR could use these "Korean"

- 2 -

SECRET

186. *(Continued)*

reinforcements with little danger of political repercussions. There is at present no indication, however, as to whether the USSR will risk the political disadvantages involved in committing non-Korean reinforcements should such a step become necessary.

Taiwan Assault   The considerable increase in troop movements in South and Southeast China during the past two months indicates the probable concentration of Chinese Communist troops in assembly areas from which they could be rapidly moved to embarkation points for an assault on Taiwan. Further reports have suggested both accelerated purchase and movement to the Fukien coastal area of small boats and junks and the concentration of operational supplies, notably aviation gasoline. There are no indications that the US pronouncement of 27 June 1950 has caused the Chinese Communists to abandon these preparations. Barring effective opposition by US naval units, Chinese Communist forces are capable of securing an initial lodgment of 75,000 fully equipped troops on Taiwan and within two or three weeks of establishing control over the entire island. An early assault may well be launched. Communist China is committed to the annexation of Taiwan and so long as Taiwan remains in Nationalist hands Peiping loses some political prestige. Although such considerations do not in themselves require an early invasion attempt, for military reasons the Communists must attempt an invasion before the US strengthens its defensive screen of the island. In addition, a successful assault on Taiwan would: (1) demonstrate world Communist power; (2) strengthen the Soviet and Chinese strategic position in the Far East; and (3) promote lack of confidence in US commitments and undermine non-Communist opposition to Soviet aggression. Although an invasion of Taiwan, by enlarging the area of conflict between Communist and US forces, would increase the risk of global

- 3 -

186. *(Continued)*

war involving the USSR, such an invasion would probably encounter much less international opposition than would Chinese Communist military operations against Korea, Hong Kong, or Southeast Asia. Moreover, in view of the fact that the Kremlin has permitted North Korean forces to become directly involved with US forces, it may be willing to permit the Chinese Communists to become similarly involved, thereby creating a further drain on US resources.

- 4 -

SOVIET RETURN TO THE UN

By returning to the UN, the USSR is seeking to re-establish maximum diplomatic and propaganda maneuverability and perhaps to lay the groundwork for a negotiated settlement in Korea if the turn of events there convinces the Kremlin of the need for such a settlement. The Soviet Union may also hope to gain support in Asia by attacking the highly vulnerable US position on Taiwan.

The Soviet boycott was proving more and more disadvantageous to the USSR. Purely aside from failing to accomplish its avowed purpose--seating the Chinese Communist representative--the boycott denied the USSR the use of the UN either as a medium through which it could obstruct world action in support of South Korea or as a sounding board for Soviet propaganda. Moreover, the Kremlin probably reasoned that by boycotting the UN it was contributing both to the potentialities of the UN to marshal non-Communist world opinion and to the growing determination of the Western world to mobilize against Soviet aggression.

The vitriolic and obstructionist attitude of the USSR in the first three days following its return to the SC does not preclude a later Soviet effort to negotiate a settlement in Korea. By initially concentrating on the Chinese representation issue and procedural maneuvers, the USSR is attempting to confuse the questions of Korea and China as well as to save face by demonstrating that it has not abandoned the issue which precipitated the boycott and is therefore not returning to the UN out of weakness. Moreover, the USSR is under no immediate compulsion to seek a settlement of the Korean issue while UN forces are still suffering reverses in Korea. For the present, therefore, the Kremlin can be

- 2 -

ET

187. *(Continued)*

expected to make every effort to prevent the UN from focussing its attention exclusively on North Korean aggression. In such an effort, the USSR will concentrate its attacks where it considers the US to be most vulnerable--namely, the question of Chinese representation in the UN and the US stand regarding Formosa.

In the longer run, however, the USSR probably believes that it must offer some form of negotiated settlement in Korea if it is to counter the effect the Korean war has had in stimulating Western military preparations and to protect its position in North Korea. While North Korean successes continue, any Soviet peace offer would probably not go beyond proposals for the withdrawal of UN military forces and the holding of all-Korean elections possibly with some nominal international supervision. The USSR would exploit some such formula to portray the Soviet Union as a disinterested party concerned only with the restoration and maintenance of peace. It would also be designed to capitalize on North Korean victories by attempting a negotiated settlement on favorable terms before an eventual UN counter-offensive might carry across the 38th Parallel and culminate in the unification of Korea under UN auspices. Even if mediation on terms acceptable to the USSR is not feasible, the Soviet Union can seek to achieve more limited objectives by attempting to shift the blame for continued hostilities to the US and to block any UN-approved move to cross the 38th Parallel.

- 3 -

FAR EASTERN STRUGGLE

Soviet Moves   The latest propaganda and diplomatic moves by the USSR and Communist China involving the Far East are further tactical developments in the continuing Soviet offensive in the United Nations. Chinese Communist charges before the UN of US aggression against Taiwan and accusations that the US has violated Chinese Communist territory fall into the now familiar pattern of the Soviet campaign to picture the US as the aggressor in Korea and other areas of the Far East, to divide the Western Powers on the controversial questions of Taiwan and Chinese representation in the UN, and to confuse UN discussion of the Korean situation.

These latest moves offer few definite clues regarding future Soviet and Chinese Communist moves in the Far East and could be designed to pave the way for a number of widely varying Soviet actions. For example, charges that the US has violated Chinese territory in themselves are inconclusive: they may be designed merely to maintain the initiative in the SC and to promote Western fears of Chinese Communist intervention in Korea in an attempt to improve the Soviet bargaining position in any negotiations for a Korean solution. On the other hand, these accusations may actually be the propaganda build-up for Chinese Communist military aggression in Korea or elsewhere. Similarly, airing the Taiwan issue in the SC does not rule out an invasion of Taiwan, inasmuch as branding the US as the aggressor might later serve as justification for an attack. Turning the issue over to the UN, however, could serve as an excuse for the present failure to fulfill the pledge to "liberate" Taiwan. Finally, both moves may be further preparations for a later Soviet attempt to trade a North Korean withdrawal to the 38th Parallel for some concessions on Taiwan and seating the Chinese Communists in the UN.

- 4 -

189. Weekly Summary Excerpt, 8 September 1950, North Korean Reserves

North Korean Reserves   The numerous reports of a readily
available strategic manpower re-
serve in Manchuria composed of Korean veterans (who had
served with Chinese Communist forces in the Manchurian
campaign of 1946-48) tend to be discounted by the non-appear-
ance of such troops in the combat area. It is logical to assume
that if such a reserve had been in existence on 25 June, it
would have been committed shortly after UN forces had been
committed and when its use might have proved decisive. Moreover, since mid-July the North Korean Army has been using
recruits with as little as two weeks' training. In addition, even
if not immediately available in concentration areas on 27 June, there
has been ample time since that date to organize and equip any.
Korean veterans in Manchuria who would have been far more

- 7 -

189. *(Continued)*

TOP SECRET

useful in combat than the inexperienced reinforcements being used. Thus, it is likely that the North Koreans will have to depend for further replacements on: (1) non-veteran Koreans recruited in Manchuria and that part of Korea now in Communist hands; (2) untrained Chinese Communist or Soviet manpower resources; or (3) Chinese Communist or Soviet military units, if it is decided to commit such forces in order either to defend the 38th parallel or to drive UN forces out of Korea.

- 8 -

TOP SECRET

190. Intelligence Memorandum 324, 8 September 1950, Probability of Direct Chinese Communist Intervention in Korea

29

CENTRAL INTELLIGENCE AGENCY

INTELLIGENCE MEMORANDUM NO. 324   8 September 1950

SUBJECT: Probability of Direct Chinese Communist Intervention in
             Korea

PROBLEM: To assess the probability of an open Commitment of
             Chinese Communist armed forces in Korea.

SCOPE: The commitment of both regular and local Chinese Com-
             munist ground forces, and the use of the Chinese Com-
             munist Air Force in support of the North Korean
             invaders are considered.

ASSUMPTIONS: (1) Limited covert Chinese Communist assistance to the
             North Korean invaders, including the provision of
             individual soldiers, is assumed to be in progress at
             present.
             (2) The provision of overt assistance by the Chinese
             Communists would require approval by the USSR and such
             approval would indicate that the USSR is prepared to
             accept an increased risk of precipitating general
             hostilities.

1. Conclusions.

    Although there is no direct evidence to indicate whether or not
the Chinese Communists will intervene in North Korea, it is evident
that the Chinese Communists or the USSR must supply trained and
equipped combat replacements if the North Korean invasion is to
achieve complete control over South Korea before the end of the year.

    Reports of an increasing Chinese Communist build-up of military
strength in Manchuria, coupled with the known potential in that area,
make it clear that intervention in Korea is well within immediate
Chinese Communist capabilities. Moreover, recent Chinese Communist
accusations regarding US "aggression" and "violation of the
Manchurian border" may be stage-setting for an imminent overt move.

Note: This memorandum has not been coordinated with the intelligence
       organizations of the Departments of State, Army, Navy, and the
       Air Force.

       The memorandum was prepared in accord with the request of the
       Director of Intelligence, Headquarters, United States Air
       Force.

SECRET

In view of the momentous repercussions from such an overt action, however, it appears more probable that the Chinese Communist participation in the Korean conflict will be more indirect, although significant, and will be limited to integrating into the North Korean forces "Manchurian volunteers," perhaps including air units as well as ground troops.

2. Present Status of North Korean Forces.

The decision whether or not to commit Chinese Communist forces will depend in part on the availability of Korean manpower, both in Manchuria and that part of Korea now in Communist hands. Current estimates by the Department of the Army state that 40,000 trained Korean veterans who had served with the Chinese Communists in the Manchurian campaigns of 1946 to 1948 remain in Manchuria and there constitute a strategic North Korean reserve. It is noteworthy, however, that (1) since 1 August North Koreans have been using combat replacements with as little as two week's training; and (2) the North Koreans would logically have committed all available organized Korean units soon after UN forces had been committed because at that time the impact of 40,000 trained troops probably would have been decisive.

The foregoing considerations indicate either that any Korean reserve in Manchuria was so dispersed that it did not constitute an effective reserve or that this reserve never in fact existed. Moreover, the possibility that Korean reserves in Manchuria have now been collected and reorganized and that some are now enroute to the combat area tends to be discounted by the fact that the time elapsed since 25 June should have permitted the organization and commitment of the majority of this reserve which would have been far superior in quality to those virtually untrained North Korean troops that have actually been utilized in the fighting. On balance, therefore, it appears highly probable that if a Communist victory in Korea is to be achieved by the end of the year the North Korean forces must now rely on either Soviet or Chinese Communist resources for decisive augmentation.

3. Chinese Communist Capabilities for Intervention.

The Chinese Communists have approximately four million men under arms, including regulars, Military District troops, and provincial forces. Following the fall of Manchuria there were approximately 565,000 Military District troops in Manchuria (including 165,100 ex-Nationalists), and possibly 100,000 to 125,000 of these MD troops have now been integrated into the regular army and organized as combat forces. These units, as well as the remaining MD troops, probably are Soviet-equipped. In addition, reports during the past three months have indicated a considerable increase in regular troop strength in Manchuria. It is estimated that the major elements

- 2 -

SECRET

190. *(Continued)*

of Lin Piao's 4th Field Army—totalling perhaps 100,000 combat veterans—are now in Manchuria and are probably located along or adjacent to the Korean border, in position for rapid commitment in Korea.

Approximately 210,000 Communist regulars under Nieh Jung-chen's command are presently deployed in the North China area. Some of these troops have been reported enroute to Manchuria.

The Chinese Communists are believed to possess an air force totalling 200 to 250 operational combat aircraft, some units of which are reportedly deployed in Manchuria.

4. Indications of Chinese Communist Intention to Intervene.

  a. Propaganda.

    Numerous Chinese Communist propaganda attacks on the US during recent weeks, charging the US with "intervention" and "aggression" in Taiwan, have been climaxed by two new protests to the UN claiming US air attacks in violation of the Manchuria-Korea border. It is possible that these charges, besides serving a useful propaganda function, may be aimed at providing an excuse for Chinese Communist intervention in Korea.

  b. Military Activity.

    Since the fall of Hainan in April 1950, reliable reports have indicated that elements of Lin Piao's 4th Field Army were being moved northward from the Canton area.[1] Major elements of the 4th Field Army are now believed to be either in or enroute to Manchuria. Other reports indicate that military construction is in progress near Antung and along the Yalu River. Strengthening of Manchurian border defenses might either be a logical security development in view of the Korean conflict or a prelude to the offensive employment of forces in the area.

    Reports of increased activity at Antung on the Manchuria-Korea border include the reported arrival of Chinese Communist aircraft.[2] Antung has also been reported as the main base of the

---

1. Reports of preparation for this move were received as early as February 1950, well in advance of the assault on Hainan by LIN's forces. Although these preparations may have been part of announced CCF plans for demobilization, it appears more likely that these elements were Korean troops of Lin Piao's army being released to the North Korean Army.

2. The three airfields in the Antung area could handle a total of 300 aircraft.

- 3 -

190. *(Continued)*

North Korean Air Force, where that depleted force can seek refuge from UN air attacks. Numerous reports of recent North Korean activity, including revetment construction at airfields south of the 38th Parallel have been received. These construction reports could indicate the imminent forward movement of air reinforcements for the North Koreans. Although some of this anticipated air support might be provided by the as yet untested Chinese Communist Air Force, there is no firm evidence to support such a contention.

5. <u>Factors Militating Against Chinese Communist Intervention.</u>

The commitment of Chinese Communist armed forces in Korea would clearly transform the Korean conflict from an ostensibly "internal" dispute to an international struggle. The decision to commit Chinese Communist troops to the Korean conflict would significantly affect the Soviet position in China as well as in Korea, and Soviet influence over both Peiping and Pyongyang might be jeopardized. Other factors which might tend to deter Chinese Communist intervention in the Korean war, but which would be of minor consequence in so momentous a decision, are: (1) Chinese national and military pride might cause friction if Chinese troops were placed under Soviet or Korean command; and (2) Chinese Communist intervention would probably eliminate all prospects for China's admission to the United Nations.

- 4 -

191. Weekly Summary Excerpt, 15 September 1950, Soviet/Communist Activity

SOVIET/COMMUNIST ACTIVITY

Communist China and Korea

Military Assistance   Numerous reports of Chinese Communist troop movements in Manchuria, coupled with Peiping's recent charges of US aggression and violations of Chinese territory, have increased speculation concerning both Chinese Communist intervention in Korea and disagreement between the USSR and China on matters of military policy. It is being argued that victory in Korea can only be achieved by using Chinese Communist (or Soviet) forces, that the USSR desires to weaken the US by involving it in a protracted struggle with China, and that the Chinese Communists are blaming the USSR for initiating the Korean venture and thus postponing the invasion of Taiwan. Despite the apparent logic of this reasoning, there is no evidence indicating a Chinese-Soviet disagreement, and cogent political and military considerations make it unlikely that Chinese Communist forces will be directly and openly committed in Korea.

Global War   The commitment of Chinese Communist forces in Korea, by enlarging the scope of the conflict, would substantially increase the risk of general war. Soviet actions since the Korean fighting began indicate that the USSR still not only wishes to avoid global war but believes it can make substantial gains in Asia by continuing its strategy of relying on indigenous "liberation" forces assisted, but not to the point of overt intervention, by neighboring Communist regimes.

Political Difficulties   Purely aside from these considerations, and even if the USSR were willing to assume a greater risk of general war, commitment of Chinese Communist forces in Korea would entail serious political difficulties for both the USSR and the Peiping regime. It would tend

- 9 -

T̶O̶P̶ ̶S̶E̶C̶R̶E̶T̶

to strain rather than solidify the Chinese-Soviet alliance, partly because in the event of the conflict spreading to China, the Peiping regime would expect substantial aid beyond mere material assistance from the USSR, aid which the USSR would be reluctant to grant for fear of itself becoming involved in the conflict. The Soviet Union consequently might face serious political problems in retaining control over Peiping and Pyongyang, and prospects for Communist China's admission to the UN would be virtually eliminated.

Indirect Aid   The decision to provide indirect assistance, such as the commitment of Manchurian "volunteer" units, would present some difficulties. Moreover, victory might not be assured by the maximum scale of such indirect assistance. If large numbers of non-Korean manpower were necessary, they probably could not be supplied without being recognizable as direct Chinese Communist intervention, thus inviting retaliation against China by UN forces, as would direct involvement.

Interim Considerations   Although decisive Chinese Communist intervention, either direct or indirect, is thus unlikely, both the USSR and the Peiping regime will continue their attempts to exploit Western fears of this eventuality. Charges of US border violations and aggression not only fit into the "peace" propaganda campaign but are designed by increasing Western fear of Chinese Communist military action to obtain Western political concessions for the Peiping regime as well as to create an atmosphere for obtaining a favorable settlement in Korea.

- - - - - -

- 10 -

192. Weekly Summary Excerpt, 22 September 1950, Korean Developments

KOREAN DEVELOPMENTS

The UN landing at Inchon, by rapidly changing the outlook of the campaign in South Korea, brings appreciably nearer the time when North Korea, as well as the USSR, must implement crucial political and military decisions regarding the ultimate fate of North Korea. With presently available forces, the North Koreans will be unable to hold South Korea; a choice of the four broad alternative courses of action available to the enemy, therefore, depends in the last analysis on the extent to which the USSR is willing to write off North Korean field forces or perhaps North Korea as a whole. These courses of action are: (1) North Korean military action aimed primarily at defending North Korea from invasion by UN forces, possibly combined with North Korean peace proposals; (2) commitment of Chinese Communist or Soviet troops north of the 38th Parallel; (3) an attempt by the USSR itself to settle the conflict diplomatically; or (4) efforts by some third party, perhaps under Soviet influence, to mediate the conflict.

Military Prospects   Successful consolidation of the UN beachhead at Inchon and Seoul would effectively interdict the main route of supply for the estimated 120-130,000 North Korean troops engaged in southeastern Korea. Unless UN forces can be expelled from the Seoul area, organized resistance in the south cannot last long. It is estimated, however, that with the exception of 15-20,000 relatively ineffective security troops, all North Korean combat units have already been committed to the fighting in the southeast. Moreover, it is not believed that Korean reserves now being trained could undertake action against the Inchon beachhead soon enough to prevent the retreat, with heavy losses, of North Korean troops from the southeast. Militarily, then, the most probable course

- 2 -

192. *(Continued)*

of action by North Korean forces, and the one offering the
best chance of success, would be the commitment of North
Korean reserves to a defensive role and a simultaneous withdrawal of as many combat units as possible over secondary
lines of communication from the southeast to defensive positions along the 38th Parallel.

Soviet Plans   Given this probable military development,
the USSR must soon: (1) refrain from intervening and rely on the North Korean forces to prevent their
own military defeat by UN forces; (2) employ Chinese Communist or Soviet troops in North Korea; or (3) attempt to
achieve a diplomatic settlement. The disadvantages to the
Soviet Union of the two latter alternatives make the first the
most likely Soviet course of action.

Both the commitment of non-Korean military units
and a diplomatic solution negotiated by the Soviet Union
itself would force the USSR to disavow its previous stand
regarding the Korean question. Since the invasion began,
the USSR has made every effort to localize the conflict and
to disassociate itself completely from the North Korean action
as well as from the UN action. Military action at this time
would clearly undermine this position, and even further weaken
the current Soviet peace offensive, while Soviet diplomatic
action would force the USSR to accept the legality of UN action.
The USSR might, however, encourage the North Koreans or
some third party to seek a settlement. In either event, the
North Korean position would probably be so weak as to leave
the terms of settlement largely in the hands of the UN.

Global War   Soviet unwillingness to substantially increase
the risk of global war and the Soviet appreciation
that the employment of Soviet or Chinese Communist troops
in Korea would represent such a risk are even more compelling

- 3 -

reasons for the USSR to refrain from military intervention, even at the expense of a Communist military defeat in North Korea. Faced with the prospect of UN air and naval harassment of lines of communication in North Korea, the USSR would probably not employ its troops or those of Communist China without providing them with substantial air cover. Inevitable conflict with UN aircraft might lead to a situation which the USSR might consider itself unable to control short of precipitating general war. Even if the USSR issued prior warning of such a move, it could not be assured that UN air forces would refrain from such attacks. Moreover, Soviet or Chinese Communist aid to the North Koreans would leave Chinese and Manchurian supply routes, and possibly industrial installations, open to air attack. The USSR would probably avoid risking damage to this segment of the Communist Far Eastern potential unless it intended to initiate general war in the immediate future.

Diplomatic Action   Any Soviet offer of a negotiated settlement, in addition to requiring the USSR to abandon its position of refusing to accept the legality of the UN's position in Korea, would place the USSR in a very disadvantageous position. Such an offer would have to go beyond a pious call for a "peaceful settlement"; in view of the changed military situation, the USSR no longer has any trump cards. Its bargaining position is so weak that prospects for a settlement favorable to the USSR are extremely limited. The USSR might attempt to improve its bargaining position by threatening to reoccupy North Korea; such a threat, however, would entail the strong risk of being forced to carry it through. An unfavorable settlement in which the USSR had participated or which had been preceded by a military bluff would be more damaging to Soviet prestige than the consequences of a continuation of the present hands-off

- 4 -

~~TOP SECRET~~

policy. The Kremlin, therefore, is more likely to seek to thwart UN efforts through its usual tactics of obstructionism in the UN, coupled with guerrilla warfare, subversion, sabotage, and propaganda within Korea. Although the North Koreans either themselves or through a third party would also be at a disadvantage in seeking a diplomatic solution, if military developments make such an attempt advisable, neither they nor the USSR will be restrained by those considerations of prestige which would deter such action by the USSR alone.

- 5 -

TOP SECRET

193. Daily Summary Excerpt, 30 September 1950, Possible Chinese Intervention in Korea

43020 T ~~CONFIDENTIAL~~ ~~SECRET~~ 82 14.

FAR EAST

2. <u>Possible Chinese Communist Intervention in Korea</u>.--US
Ambassador Kirk has received reports from his [   ] c/A/s
and [   ] colleagues in Moscow that Chinese Communist
leaders in Peiping favor Chinese military intervention in
the Korean war if UN forces cross the 38th Parallel. According to Kirk's information, reports concerning the existence of this sentiment among Chinese Communists have come
from the [   ] charge and the [   ] ambassador in Peiping.
The [   ] representative is reported to have told his government that a Chinese Communist decision on intervention has

Document No. _078_

NO CHANGE in Class. ☐   - 1 -

☐ DECLASSIFIED

Class. CHANGED TO: TS   S (c)

DDA Memo, 4 Apr 77

Auth: DDA REG. 77/1763

Date: 3 0 MAR 1978 By: _DK3_

~~CONFIDENTIAL~~

~~CONFIDENTIAL~~

193. *(Continued)*

crystallized since mid-September and is based on the conviction
that the entering of US forces into North Korea would indicate
a basic US aim to carry the war to Manchuria and China in
order to return Chiang Kai-shek to power in China. In commenting on this information, Kirk says he finds it difficult
to accept these reports as authoritative analyses of Chinese
Communist plans. He takes the line that the logical moment
for Communist armed intervention came when the UN forces
were desperately defending a small area in southern Korea and
when the influx of an overwhelming number of Chinese ground
forces would have proved a decisive factor. He warns that
prudence is indicated in this situation but expresses his view
that the Chinese Communists, through press propaganda and
through personal contacts with foreign diplomatic personnel,
have taken a strong line since the Inchon landing in the hope
of bluffing the UN on the 38th Parallel issue.

- 2 -

194. Daily Summary Excerpt, 3 October 1950, Possible Chinese Communist Intervention in Korea

GENERAL

Possible Chinese Communist intervention in Korea--US
Embassy London transmits a report from the UK Foreign
Office that Chinese Communist Foreign Minister Chou En-
lai called in Indian Ambassador Panikkar in Peiping on
3 October and informed him that if UN armed forces crossed
the 38th Parallel, China would send troops across the frontier
to participate in the defense of North Korea. Chou En-lai reportedly added that this action would not be taken if only South
Korean forces crossed the Parallel.

(CIA Comment: The Chinese Communists have long
had the capability for military intervention in Korea on a
scale sufficient to materially affect the course of events in
Korea, and they now are supporting Soviet efforts to intimidate and divide the US and its UN allies over the issue of
crossing the 38th Parallel. CIA estimates, however, that the
Chinese Communists would not consider it in their interests
to intervene openly in Korea if, as now seems likely, they
anticipate that war with the UN nations would result.

The "reliability and accuracy" of the source of this
report are open to question. It is also entirely possible that
he is being used by the Chinese Communists to plant this
information in an effort to influence US and UK policy.)

- 1 -

195. Weekly Summary Excerpt, 6 October 1950, Korea and Soviet Policy; Chinese Communist Problems

KOREA AND SOVIET POLICY

Over-all Soviet Policy The loss of North Korea and the defeat of the North Korean Communist regime are not likely to produce any immediate or drastic Soviet reaction. The Kremlin will probably view the Korean failure as a temporary setback to its long-range expansionist plans, but not one so damaging to the over-all Soviet position at home or abroad as to require an immediate change in the tactics it has been pursuing since the end of World War II. In the immediate post-Korea period, the Kremlin will be most concerned with the effect the Korean invasion has had in: (1) uniting the non-Communist world against Communist aggression and stimulating Western rearmament; (2) revealing to the Satellites and Communist Parties Soviet fallibility and failure to rescue one of its Satellites; (3) weakening Communist promises of early success for Communist-led colonial liberation movements; and (4) demonstrating that Soviet power and influence in Asia will not go unchallenged by the West. The USSR will probably be reluctant to attempt another Korean-type venture in the near future, fearing either failure and thus even greater disadvantages than grew out of the Korean invasion, or the necessity to use Soviet troops to achieve success, thus increasing the risk of general war. The USSR will therefore attempt to minimize the UN victory while continuing and intensifying its support for subversive and guerrilla operations by local Communists, especially in Indochina, and the current "peace" propaganda campaign will be pressed with renewed vigor.

Korean Settlement Meanwhile, in Korea itself, the possibility continues to diminish that the USSR or the Chinese Communists will intervene militarily to prevent the UN occupation of North Korea. Soviet propaganda and diplomatic

- 5 -

195. *(Continued)*

activity of recent weeks suggest that the USSR has, temporarily at least, written off Korea. Continued Chinese Communist threats (made through the Indian Ambassador at
Peiping) to intervene if US troops cross the 38th Parallel
are believed to be primarily a last-ditch attempt to intimidate the US from taking such a step. In the interim,
the USSR will use its rapidly diminishing opportunities for
obstructing UN action in Korea, but probably will make no
serious effort to reach agreement with the Western Powers.
Realizing that military developments have destroyed any
favorable bargaining position which either the USSR or North
Korea once possessed, the Kremlin will probably not counten-
ance a North Korean peace bid and instead will attempt to make
the UN victory as costly as possible.

- 6 -

CHINESE COMMUNIST PROBLEMS

Foreign Policy   Foreign Minister Chou En-lai's recent
lengthy review of Communist China's for-
eign policy contains no new assertions or accusations and
none of the guarded threats is sufficiently strong to indicate
any major change in Peiping's foreign policy. The statement
that US "intervention" in China will be repelled is an idle
one, as the promise to liberate Taiwan specified no time
limit; and the intention to liberate Tibet, preferably through
negotiation, but if necessary by force of arms, has been expressed before. The Foreign Minister's remarks regarding
diplomatic relations with Western countries, relations with
the USSR, and the hostile attitude of the US have been uttered
many times in the past. Those parts of Chou's speech which
have been interpreted as indicating a Chinese Communist
intent to occupy North Korea or invade Indochina are in fact
estimated to indicate less drastic actions. The statement
that the Korean Communists can "obtain final victory"
through "persistent, long-term resistance" probably implies
extensive Chinese support of North Korean guerrillas and
sanctuary for North Korean leaders. However, the intimation
that Communist China is now prepared to rush to its neighbor's
assistance was probably an attempt to bluff the UN into not
crossing the 38th Parallel, rather than a forewarning of
Chinese intervention. Finally, Chou's remarks on the UN
suggested Peiping's interest in participating in any UN settlement of the Korean question.

- 8 -

196. Daily Summary Excerpt, 9 October 1950, Chinese Communist Intervention in Korea Discounted

GENERAL

1. <u>Chinese Communists intervention in Korea discounted--</u>   S/S
   US Ambassador Murphy in Brussels has been informed by
   a high official of the Belgian Foreign Office that the Belgian
   Government, which has many contacts in China, has no information "of a disturbing nature" regarding the possibility
   of direct military intervention in Korea by the Chinese Communists. The official expressed the opinion that the recent
   statements of Chou En-lai, Chinese Foreign Minister, should
   be closely examined because the Chinese were evidently prepared to make equivocal statements to please the Russians,
   without, however, making a definite commitment to act openly
   in Korea. The Belgian official also pointed out that present
   Chinese obligations were great and their supply and economic
   situation very difficult.

   (CIA Comment: Communist China has carefully refrained from making a public commitment to aid North Korea
   by direct intervention. Public and private threats by Communist
   China officials to intervene directly in North Korea have probably been designed primarily to deter UN forces from going
   beyond the 38th Parallel.)

- 1 -

197. ORE 58-50 Excerpt, 12 October 1950, Critical Situations in the Far East

CRITICAL SITUATIONS IN THE FAR EAST

A. Threat of Full Chinese Communist Intervention in Korea

I. **Statement of the Problem.**

1. To estimate the threat of full-scale Chinese Communist intervention in Korea.

II. **Capabilities.**

2. The Chinese Communist ground forces, currently lacking requisite air and naval support, are capable of intervening effectively, but not necessarily decisively, in the Korean conflict.

III. **Factors Bearing on Intent.**

3. *Indications of Intentions.* Despite statements by Chou En-lai, troop movements to Manchuria, and propaganda charges of atrocities and border violations, there are no convincing indications of an actual Chinese Communist intention to resort to full-scale intervention in Korea.

4. *Factors Favoring Chinese Communist Intervention.*

a. Intervention, if resulting in defeat of UN forces, would: (1) constitute a major gain in prestige for Communist China, confirming it as the premier Asiatic power; (2) constitute a major gain for World Communism with concomitant increase in Communist China's stature in the Sino-Soviet axis; (3) result in the elimination of the possibility of a common frontier with a Western-type democracy; and (4) permit the retention of sources of Manchurian electric power along the Yalu River.

b. Intervention, even if not resulting in a decisive defeat of UN forces, would: (1) enable the Chinese Communists to utilize foreign war as an explanation for failure to carry out previously announced economic reforms; (2) be consistent with and furnish strong impetus to anti-Western trends in Asia; and (3) justify a claim for maximum Soviet military and/or economic aid to China.

c. Intervention, with or without assurance of final victory, might serve the cause of World Communism, particularly the cause of the Soviet Union, in that it would involve the Western bloc in a costly and possibly inconclusive war in the Far East.

d. The Communist cause generally and the Sino-Soviet bloc particularly face the prospect of a major setback in the struggle with the non-Communist world if UN forces are permitted to achieve complete victory in Korea.

5. *Factors Opposing Chinese Communist Intervention.*

a. The Chinese Communists undoubtedly fear the consequences of war with the US. Their domestic problems are of such magnitude that the regime's entire domestic program and economy would be jeopardized by the strains and the material damage which would be sustained in war with the US. Anti-Communist forces would be encouraged and the regime's very existence would be endangered.

b. Intervention would minimize the possibility of Chinese membership in the UN and of a seat on the Security Council.

c. Open intervention would be extremely costly unless protected by powerful Soviet air cover and naval support. Such Soviet aid might not be forthcoming because it would constitute Soviet intervention.

d. Acceptance of major Soviet aid would make Peiping more dependent on Soviet help and increase Soviet control in Manchuria to a point probably unwelcome to the Chinese Communists.

e. If unsuccessful, Chinese intervention would lay Peiping open to Chinese resentment on the grounds that China would be acting as a Soviet catspaw.

f. From a military standpoint the most favorable time for intervention in Korea has passed.

g. Continued covert aid would offer most of the advantages of overt intervention, while

3

450

4   TOP SECRET

avoiding its risks and disadvantages. Covert aid would enable the Chinese Communists to:

    (1) Avoid further antagonizing of the UN and reduce risk of war with the US;

    (2) Promote the China-led Asiatic peoples' "revolutionary struggle," while ostensibly supporting peace;

    (3) Maintain freedom of action for later choice between abandonment of aid or continuing such covert aid as might be appropriate to Chinese Communist needs in Korea;

    (4) Satisfy the "aid Korea" demand in Communist circles in China and Asia generally, without risking war with the US.

IV. Probability of Chinese Communist Action.

6. While full-scale Chinese Communist intervention in Korea must be regarded as a continuing possibility, a consideration of all known factors leads to the conclusion that barring a Soviet decision for global war, such action is not probable in 1950. During this period, intervention will probably be confined to continued covert assistance to the North Koreans.

TOP SECRET

TOP SECRET

KOREAN SITUATION

Military Tactics   Despite the UN peace ultimatum, the
North Koreans have reiterated their
determination to continue resistance throughout Korea for
as long as possible. Although the North Koreans will continue to receive substantial material assistance from the
USSR and Communist China, they will be forced to rely
largely on their own manpower resources, except in the
unlikely event of direct Chinese Communist or Soviet intervention. Some Korean units may still be transferred from
Chinese armies to North Korea and Peiping may send a
few Chinese troops across the Yalu River to protect its
bridges and the hydroelectric plant at Suiho. The principal
Chinese Communist contribution, however, probably will
consist of military and other supplies, bases for reorganiz-
ing and re-equipping North Korean troops, and sanctuary
for North Korean leaders charged with directing long-term
guerrilla resistance. The North Koreans, meanwhile, probably now have at their disposal approximately 15 major units
of division size or less, comprising approximately 140,000
men. Only 40,000 of these have seen combat in the south,
the remainder being hastily trained conscripts with little
combat efficiency. The entire force, while capable of stiff
defensive action at key points, is estimated to lack the
strength or experience to continue prolonged organized
resistance.

- 5 -

TOP SECRET

199. ORE 29-50 Excerpt, 13 October 1950, Consequences to the US of Communist Domination of Mainland Southeast Asia

SECRET

CONSEQUENCES TO THE US OF COMMUNIST DOMINATION OF MAINLAND SOUTHEAST ASIA[1]

SUMMARY AND CONCLUSIONS

Communist domination of mainland Southeast Asia would not be critical[2] to US security interests but would have serious immediate and direct consequences. The gravest of such consequences would be a spreading of doubt and fear among other threatened non-Communist countries as to the ability of the US to back up its proclaimed intention to halt Communist expansion everywhere. Unless offset by positive additions to the security of non-Communist countries in other sensitive areas of the world, the psychological effect of the loss of mainland Southeast Asia would not only strengthen Communist propaganda that the advance of Communism is inexorable but would encourage countries vulnerable to Soviet pressure to adopt "neutral" attitudes in the cold war, or possibly even lead them to an accommodation with Communism.

Domination of the Southeast Asian mainland would increase the threat to such Western outposts in the Pacific as the island chain extending from Japan to Australia and New Zealand. The extension of Communist control, via Burma, to the borders of India and Pakistan would augment the slowly developing Communist threat to the Indian subcontinent. The fall of the Southeast Asian mainland would increase the feeling of insecurity already present in Japan as a result

of Communist successes in China and would further underline the apparent economic advantages to the Japanese of association with a Communist-dominated Asian sphere.

The countries of mainland Southeast Asia produce such materials on the US strategic list as rubber, tin, shellac, kapok, and teak in substantial volume. Although access to these countries is not considered to be "absolutely essential in an emergency" by the National Security Resources Board, US access to this area is considered "desirable." Unlimited Soviet access to the strategic materials of mainland Southeast Asia would probably be "desirable" for the USSR but would not be "absolutely essential in an emergency" and therefore denial of the resources of the area to the Soviet Union would not be essential to the US strategic position. Communist control over the rice surpluses of the Southeast Asian mainland would, however, provide the USSR with considerable bargaining power in its relations with other countries of the Far East.

Loss of the area would indirectly affect US security interests through its important economic consequences for countries aligned with the US. Loss of Malaya would deprive the UK of its greatest net dollar earner. An immediate consequence of the loss of Indochina might be a strengthening of the defense of Western Europe since French expenditures for men and materiel in Indochina would be available to fulfill other commitments. Exclusion of Japan from trade with Southeast Asia would seriously frustrate Japanese prospects for economic recovery.

Communist domination of mainland Southeast Asia would place unfriendly forces astride the most direct and best-developed sea and air

---

[1] Assumption: (a) that major US policies in the Far East will be implemented substantially as now conceived; and (b) that Communist control of Southeast Asia will result in denial of the area to US and pro-Western nations.

[2] By "would not be critical to US security interests" is meant that the loss of the area to Communist domination would not have a decisively adverse effect on the capabilities of the US to win a global war.

Note: The Office of Naval Intelligence has concurred in this estimate; for dissents of the intelligence organizations of the Departments of State, Army, and the Air Force, see Enclosures A, B, and C, respectively. The estimate contains information available to CIA as of 15 September 1950.

SECRET

1

2   S E C R E T

routes between the Western Pacific and India and the Near East. The denial to the US of intermediate routes in mainland Southeast Asia would be significant because communications between the US and India and the Near East would be essential in a global war. In the event of such a war, the development of Soviet submarine and air bases in mainland Southeast Asia probably would compel the detour of US and allied shipping and air transportation in the Southeast Asia region via considerably longer alternate routes to the south. This extension of friendly lines of communication would hamper US strategic movements in this region and tend to isolate the major non-Communist bases in the Far East — the offshore island chain and Australia — from existing bases in East Africa and the Near and Middle East, as well as from potential bases on the Indian sub-continent.

Besides disrupting established lines of communication in the area, the denial of actual military facilities in mainland Southeast Asia — in particular, the loss of the major naval operating bases at Singapore — would compel the utilization of less desirable peripheral bases. Soviet exploitation of the naval and air bases in mainland Southeast Asia probably would be limited by the difficulties of logistic support but would, nevertheless, increase the threat to existing lines of communication.

The loss of any portion of mainland Southeast Asia would increase possibilities for the extension of Communist control over the remainder. The fall of Indochina would provide the Communists with a staging area in addition to China for military operations against the rest of mainland Southeast Asia, and this threat might well inspire accommodation in both Thailand and Burma. Assuming Thailand's loss, the already considerable difficulty faced by the British in maintaining security in Malaya would be greatly aggravated. Assuming Burma's internal collapse, unfavorable trends in India would be accelerated. If Burma were overcome by external aggression, however, a stiffening of the attitude of the Government of India toward International Communism could be anticipated.

SECRET

200. Daily Summary Excerpt, 16 October 1950, Possible Chinese Communist Intervention in Korea

66

48037^T ~~OP SECRET~~

16 OCT 1950
1420

FAR EAST

<u>Possible Chinese Communist intervention in Korea</u>--According to US Embassy Hague, [

] four divisions of unidentified troops, presumed to be Chinese, have crossed the Manchurian border into North Korea.

(CIA Comment: There have been numerous reports during recent weeks regarding four Chinese Communist units (variously identified as Armies and Divisions) which are alleged to have crossed into Korea from Manchuria, and the Netherlands Charge's report may be a repetition of these earlier claims. CIA continues to believe that the Chinese Communists, while continuing to assist the North Koreans, probably will not intervene openly in the present fighting in Korea.)

- 1 -

~~TOP SECRET~~

201. Daily Summary Excerpt, 20 October 1950, Chinese Communist Intervention in Korea

48041 ~~TOP CONFIDENTIAL~~ 66

20 OCT 1950

1424

GENERAL

Chinese Communist intervention in Korea--The US Military Liaison Officer in Hong Kong transmits a report that the Peiping regime has decided to take military action in North Korea. (The report is attributed to a representative of the
[

]）

According to source, 400,000 Chinese Communist troops had been moved to the Korean border and alerted to cross on the night of 18 October or "two days later."

(CIA Comment: For some time the Chinese Communists have possessed the capability for direct military intervention in the Korean conflict. CIA believes, however, that the optimum time for such action has passed. The USSR and China are not considered at this time to be willing to assume the increased risk of precipitating a third World War which would result from direct Chinese Communist intervention in Korea.)

- 1 -

Document No. 17
PO DIT TT 1: Class. ☐
☐ ☐)
CI. ... TS S (C
R... 4 77
Auth: ....)
~~TOP SECRET~~ Date 2 4 MAR 1978 BY: /3.

456

48050   66   ~~TOP SECRET~~   28 OCT 1950

1431

GENERAL

Reports on Chinese involvement in Korea--According to a
[ ] source in Hong Kong, it was decided in early October
at a conference in Peiping attended by Chinese, Soviet and
North Korean leaders that if UN troops crossed the 38th
Parallel and North Korean forces were unable to hold them,
the main part of the North Korean forces would be withdrawn
to Manchuria for future use while the balance would carry on
guerrilla warfare in Korea. Meanwhile, another[ ] source
in Hong Kong has learned that the Chinese Communists and
the USSR regard the Korean war as virtually ended and are
not planning a counteroffensive. Source added that the bulk
of the Chinese Communist units had been withdrawn from
Korea, leaving only skeleton forces in order to create the
impression that a large number of Chinese Communist forces
were still present, thus deceiving US intelligence so that the
maximum number of US troops would be committed in Korea
for the longest possible time.

(CIA Comment: CIA concurs in general with these indications of over-all Soviet and Chinese Communist intentions
regarding Korea. The presence of independent organized
Chinese Communist units in Korea has not yet been confirmed;
the above reports concerning skeleton Chinese forces, however,
are consistent with fragmentary field reports thus far received
on Chinese Communist participation in the Korean fighting.

Document No. 24   - 1 -
NO CHANGE in Class. ☐
☐ DECLASSIFIED
Class. CHANGED TO: TS   S   ⓒ
     DDA Memo, 4 Apr 77
Auth: DDA REG. 77/1763
Date: 24 MAR 1978   By: 123

~~TOP SECRET~~

235031

203. Daily Summary Excerpt, 30 October 1950, POW Reports of Chinese Communist Forces in North Korea

48051   66

1432

GENERAL

1. <u>POW reports of Chinese Communist forces in North Korea</u>-- The Commanding General of the US Eighth Army in Korea reports that the ten Chinese Communist prisoners of war captured as of 30 October have claimed during interrogations that the 119th and 120th divisions of the Chinese Communist 40th Army and the 117th division of the 39th Army are now in Korea.

    (CIA Comment: Although there are major units of Chinese Communist forces along the Manchurian-Korean border, the presence of Chinese Communist units in Korea has not been confirmed. CIA continues to believe that direct Chinese Communist intervention in Korea is unlikely at this time. However, there is a strong possibility that the Peiping regime may move troops across the border in an effort to establish a "cordon sanitaire" around the Suiho hydroelectric plant and other strategic border installations essential to the Manchurian economy. There is also the possibility that these Chinese were sent into North Korea to plant reports of Chinese Communist forces in North Korea in the hope of slowing the UN advance, and thereby providing time for North Korean forces to reorganize. Ordinarily, privates in the Chinese army do not possess the detailed order-of-battle information which these POW's passed on to US field interrogators.)

- 1 -

204. Daily Summary Excerpt, 31 October 1950, Chinese Communist Troops in Korea

48052   66   31 OCT 1950

~~TOP SECRET~~   1433

GENERAL

1. Chinese Communist troops in Korea--US Embassy Seoul   CIA S
transmits the estimate of US Eighth Army headquarters
that, although information is still "sketchy" and confirmation is lacking, two regiments of Chinese Communist troops
may be engaged in the Eighth Army sector. Eighth Army
headquarters has not yet definitely established whether these
Chinese Communist troops are fighting as independent units
or are "sandwiched" among North Korean forces. A later
field report states that POW's captured north of Hamhung
identified their unit as the Chinese Communist 124th Division.
The POW's, who were wearing new cold-weather uniforms,
spoke in the Peiping and North Manchurian dialects and said
that their unit had entered Korea on or about 16 October.

(CIA Comment: There probably are small numbers
of Chinese Communist troops currently operating in Korea,
but CIA does not believe that the appearance of these Chinese
Communist soldiers indicates that the Chinese Communists
intend to intervene directly or openly in the Korean war.)

- 1 -

~~TOP SECRET~~

3. CHINA: "Intervention" in Korea--US Consul General Wilkinson in Hong Kong transmits a report [   ] that during an August conference of top Sino-Soviet leaders, the decision was made for Communist China to "participate in the Korean war." [   ] the formal decision was made on 24 October at a meeting presided over by Chinese Premier Mao Tse-tung. [   ] also claims that twenty Chinese Communist armies are now in Manchuria (the strength of a Chinese Communist army ranges from 20-30,000); included in these twenty armies are eight armies of the Fourth Field Army as well as elements of the other three Field Armies of the Chinese Communist forces.

CIA/S
CIA/S
CIA/S
CIA/S
CIA/SO/S

Reports from US representatives in London and Rangoon and from [   ] sources in Taiwan indicate considerable troop movement from China proper into south Manchuria during October. According to these reports, Mukden is under martial law and a state of war emergency exists with air raid precautions and other defense preparations under way. Factories in Mukden and Antung are being dismantled and moved north. Twenty jet fighters of unknown nationality have appeared over Mukden. The city is said to be in a state of panic, with many Communist officials and residents moving north. "Large numbers" of Russian troops, both in and out of uniform, have arrived, as well as materiel, including self-propelled guns and naval mines. The UK Consul in Mukden has told the British Foreign Office that he has been ordered to leave by 3 November, ostensibly because he objected to preparation of Chinese Communist defense installations in the UK consular compound.

(CIA Comment: Major units of the Chinese Communist Fourth Field Army have been moving to Manchuria for several months. Although elements of the other three Field Armies could be moving north, there is no confirmation that units of these

- 2 -

205. *(Continued)*

Field Armies are in Manchuria. There is no confirmation
that a high-level Sino-Soviet conference decided that Communist China should intervene in Korea, but it is quite possible
that the Peiping regime decided to increase its support and
assistance to the North Koreans. Such a decision could logically
lead to large-scale defensive preparations by the Chinese Communists in anticipation of possible UN retaliation for this increased
military assistance. On the basis of available evidence, CIA continues to believe that Chinese Communist participation in the
Korean conflict will be limited to defense of the Manchurian
border and that open large-scale intervention by Communist
China is not likely.)

- 3 -

206. Weekly Summary Excerpt, 3 November 1950, Chinese Communist Plans: Korean Intervention

CHINESE COMMUNIST PLANS

Korean Intervention   Fresh, newly-equipped North Korean troops have appeared in the Korean fighting, and it has been clearly established that Chinese Communist troop units are also opposing UN forces. Present field estimates are that between 15,000 and 20,000 Chinese Communist troops organized in task force units are operating in North Korea while the parent units remain in Manchuria. Finally, current reports of Soviet-type jet aircraft in the Antung-Sinuiju area indicate that the USSR may be providing at least logistic air support for the defense of the Manchurian border.

These indications of increased Chinese Communist support and assistance to North Korean forces point to a decision to establish a "cordon sanitaire" south of the Yalu River. Although the possibility cannot be excluded that the Chinese Communists, under Soviet direction, are committing themselves to a full-scale intervention in Korea, their main objectives appear to be to guarantee the security of the Manchurian border and insure the continued flow of electric power from the vital Suiho hydroelectric system to the industries of Manchuria. The Suiho hydroelectric system is of vital importance to Manchuria, and Peiping's apprehension may have been increased by the recent statement of a South Korean general that allocation of power to Manchuria would be cut off. The reported evacuation of industrial machinery and civilian personnel from Mukden and intensification of air-raid precautions in that city appear to indicate that Peiping anticipates possible UN retaliatory action against Communist China for Peiping's activities in Korea.

207. Weekly Summary Excerpt, 10 November 1950, The Korean Situation: Chinese Intentions

THE KOREAN SITUATION

Chinese Intentions   Although the Chinese Communists, in intervening in Korea, have accepted a grave risk of US-UN retaliation and general war, the limited extent of their intervention to date may indicate that their objective is merely to halt the advance of UN forces in Korea and to keep a Communist regime in being on Korean soil. In so doing, the Chinese Communists would: (1) avert the psychological and political consequences of a disastrous outcome of the Korean venture; (2) keep UN forces away from the actual frontiers of China and the USSR; (3) retain an area in Korea as a base of Communist military and guerrilla operations; (4) prolong indefinitely the containment of UN, especially US, forces in Korea; (5) control the distribution of hydroelectric power generated in North Korea and retain other economic benefits; and (6) create the possibility of a favorable political solution in Korea.

The Chinese Communists, however, still retain full freedom of action. If successful in destroying the effective strength of UN forces in North Korea, they would pursue their advantage as far as possible. In any case, they would probably ignore an ultimatum requiring their withdrawal, and, if Chinese territory were to be attacked, they would probably enter Korea in full force. With forces available in Manchuria, the Chinese Communists are capable of committing more troops in an attempt to prevent a UN victory in northern Korea. A possible development of the present situation, therefore, is that the opposing sides will build up their combat power in successive increments to checkmate the other until forces of major magnitude are involved. At any point in this development, the danger is present that the situation may get out of control and lead to a general war.

-- 2 --

208. Daily Summary Excerpt, 17 November 1950, Chinese Communist Intentions at the UN, in North Korea

46068   69   17 NOV 1950
                 T~~OP~~ ~~SECRET~~   1447
                 ~~CONFIDENTIAL~~

GENERAL

1. Chinese Communist intentions at the UN--Indian Am-   c/A/s
   bassador Panikkar in Peiping has informed his govern-   c/A/s
   ment that the Chinese Communist Government is anxious
   to secure a peaceful settlement of the Korean issue, but
   only on the condition that Communist China participates
   in such a settlement. Panikkar adds that the impression
   in Peiping is that the Chinese Communist representatives
   due soon at the UN will be agreeable to settling the Korean
   question through discussions outside the Security Council.
   Panikkar believes the Chinese representatives may also be
   willing to discuss informally with representatives of the
   US and other powers issues of a general character. In passing
   this report to US Ambassador Henderson in New Delhi, Secretary General Bajpai of the Indian Ministry of External Affairs
   said he was withholding comment because he had lost confidence in Panikkar. Bajpai explained that he did not want
   to give the impression that the Indian Government was trying
   to bring pressure on the US to come to an understanding with
   Peiping.

   According to the US delegation to the UN, the Swedish
   representative to Moscow (now visiting New York) is inclined to
   think that the Chinese military moves were of a flexible nature,
   designed for probing and for limited purposes generally. The
   Swedish representative feels the Kremlin is not now prepared to
   allow present activities to develop into a general war.

2. Communist China's intentions in North Korea---The [   ] c/A/s
   Ambassador in Peiping has informed his government that: c/A/s
   (a) the Chinese Communist movements toward Korea are on a
   large scale; and (b) Peiping publicity points to fear and alarm c/A/c

Document No. 40
CHANGE in C...
...
...
2-3 MAR 1979

- 1 -

T~~OP SECRET~~
~~CONFIDENTIAL~~

464

concerning possible invasion. The Swedish Ambassador expressed the opinion that the lull in the Korean fighting is due partly to the strength of UN forces, but mainly to Chinese Communist feeling that power plants and reservoirs are reasonably protected.

The [   ] Charge in Peiping has expressed the opinion that Chinese Communist intervention in Korea was motivated chiefly by fear of US aggression, especially against Manchuria, and that the long-term aim of the Peiping regime is to establish a "really independent" Korean state which would not be a threat to China. The Charge feels that the short-term aim of Communist China is to protect the frontier by the creation of a border zone free of UN troops, and he believes the Chinese actually wish to avoid hostilities with UN troops provided UN forces remain outside a 50-mile zone south of the Manchurian border.

The [   ] Embassy in Peiping has expressed the view that the Chinese Communists are ready to go "to any length" to aid the North Koreans and that they are fostering mass hysteria based on alleged US intentions to invade Manchuria. The [   ] Ambassador believes the Peiping regime is convinced that: (a) the fighting in Korea will spread to Manchuria and that the USSR will aid the Chinese Communists if Manchuria is invaded; (b) the Soviet Air Force is superior to the USAF and the US cannot spare additional ground forces for Korea; and (c) a "US-dominated" Korea will constitute a threat to China.

[

                                                    ]

- 2 -

CONFIDENTIAL ~~TOP SECRET~~

     (CIA Comment: Except for the Indian Ambassador, the diplomatic community in Peiping has extremely limited contacts with Communist officials. These reports, except for troop movements and similar activities, represent personal opinions. CIA believes the Chinese Communist regime is primarily concerned with possible UN retaliatory action rather than an unprovoked US military attack. Moreover, Peiping has not yet committed itself to go "to any length" to salvage the Korean Communist regime, and maximum Chinese Communist intervention may not be necessary to achieve Peiping's objectives in Korea. CIA is convinced that, for the immediate future, Chinese Communist operations in Korea will probably continue to be defensive in nature. However, Peiping's present strategy in Korea may envisage the steady replacement of North Korean losses until the UN no longer regards the unification of all Korea as practicable.)

- 3 -

~~TOP SECRET~~